ATLAS
of

PAST
TIMES

ATLAS
of
PAST
TIMES

John Haywood

Grange
BOOKS

CONTENTS

Academic consultant
Dr. Paul Garwood
University of Oxford, UK

Project editor Susan Kennedy
Cartographic manager Richard Watts
Art editor & designer Ayala Kingsley

Editors Lauren Bourque, Peter Lewis
Cartographic editor Tim Williams
Picture researcher Ayala Kingsley
Picture management Claire Turner
Production director Clive Sparling
Proofreader Lynne Wycherley
Indexer Ann Barrett

Planned and produced by
Andromeda Oxford Limited
Kimber House
1 Kimber Road
Abingdon
Oxfordshire, OX14 1SG
UK

www.andromeda.co.uk

Published by Grange Books
an imprint of Grange Books Plc
The Grange
1–6 Kingsnorth Industrial Estate
Hoo, Nr. Rochester, Kent
ME3 9ND
www. Grangebooks.co.uk

This edition published 2003

ISBN 1-84013-643-X

Printed in Hong Kong by
Paramount Inc.

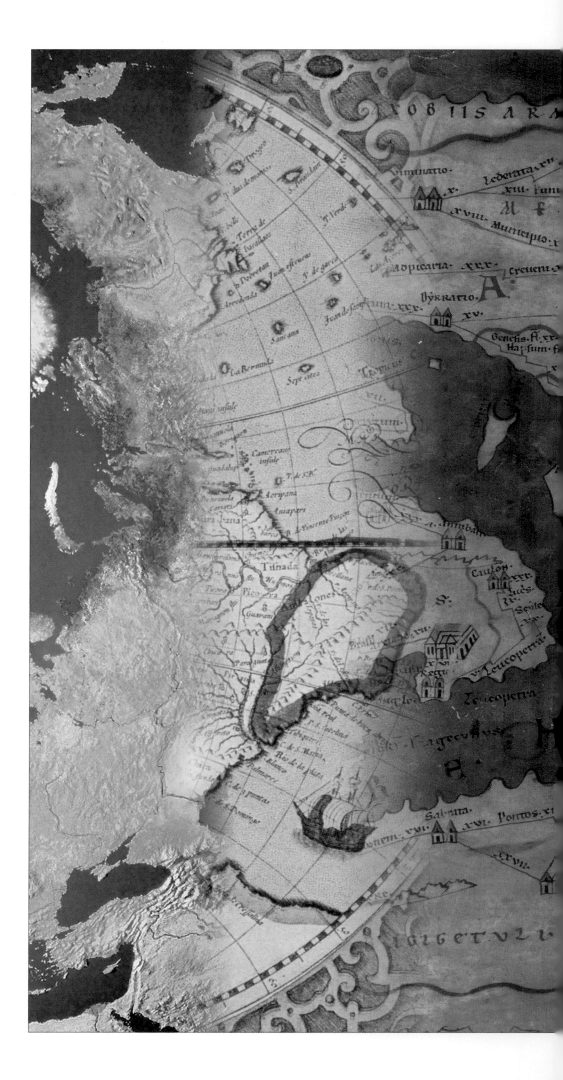

USING THIS ATLAS

This four part volume charts the global story of humans from prehistoric times to the present day. Three different types of map are used in the *Atlas of Past Times*. Here are some hints on how to study the information that appears on them.

WORLD MAPS show what the world was like at a particular moment in human history. They will tell you where there were organized states and civilizations, where people lived mostly as farmers or pastoral nomads, and where they were predominantly hunter–gatherers. By following these maps through all four volumes of the Atlas you can see how human society has evolved over time and trace the rise and fall of political empires. Black circled numbers on the world maps will help you locate references on the Timeline below.

REGIONAL MAPS show the history of a particular region of the world over an extended period of time (indicated in the top right corner of the page). To help you locate historic places, modern countries and borders are shown in light gray. Hill shading is included on some of the maps to indicate the physical landscape.

SUPPLEMENTARY MAPS add to the information in the regional maps by illustrating a particular theme or event.

The world and regional maps have been given grid references (numbers running vertically down the page, letters running horizontally across it). If you want to see if a particular place is shown on a map, the index will give you the page number and grid reference (eg. 37 4D) to help you locate it.

STANDARD MAP INFORMATION

World maps

PERSIA	civilization, state, or empire
Dutch Guiana	chiefdom, dependency, or territory
Khoisan herders	tribe, people, or cultural group

Regional maps

FRANCE	state or empire
Henan	dependency, territory, or province
Goths	tribe, people, or chiefdom
ANATOLIA	geographical region
LATVIA	modern country
—— · ——	border of modern country
✗	battle
•	site, settlement, or town

THE ANCIENT WORLD

An enormous span of human history is covered in this section, which begins more than 4 million years ago in Africa and ends at the start of the Christian era in the Middle East and Europe. During most of this time, change was incredibly slow. Our earliest human ancestors probably lived, like modern chimpanzees and baboons, in family groups. They ate plant foods and scavenged flesh from animal carcasses using simple stone tools that did not alter in the way they were made for more than a million years. Gradually humans developed larger brains and by about 100,000 years ago had evolved into the modern human species of Homo sapiens. By the end of the Ice Age, about 11,000 years ago, they had spread to almost every part of the globe. They had learned to use fire, build shelters, and hunt and kill animals with spears and other weapons, but these developments had evolved slowly, over hundreds of thousands of years.

As the climate warmed, the pace of change accelerated. Some wild foods became scarce, so people in many parts of the world began to plant wild grasses and tubers and to keep animals for meat, milk, or wool. With astonishing speed—in a little over 3,000 years—farming became established wherever soil and climatic conditions were favorable and there was a range of native plants and animals suitable for domestication.

The adoption of agriculture transformed the way human societies were organized. Crop farmers settled down to live in villages close to the fields they worked. People learned to make pottery and work metals such as copper and bronze. As distinctions in rank and wealth developed, chiefdoms emerged in many parts of the world.

The first civilizations developed in regions of great fertility, such as the Nile valley in Egypt or the Yellow River basin in China, where surplus food could be grown to feed such people as priests or craftsmen, who were not immediately involved in farming. Societies became more complex, trade helped build up wealth, and cities developed. The first writing systems were invented and people began to write down their histories and their religious myths and beliefs, giving rise to the first literature.

Wealthy, well-organized states employed great armies to coerce their less advanced neighbors. By the end of the 1st century BC, a succession of empires and states had emerged and declined in the Near and Far East, around the Mediterranean, and in parts of Central and South America.

Left Ceremonial vessel from Crete, c.1600 BC.

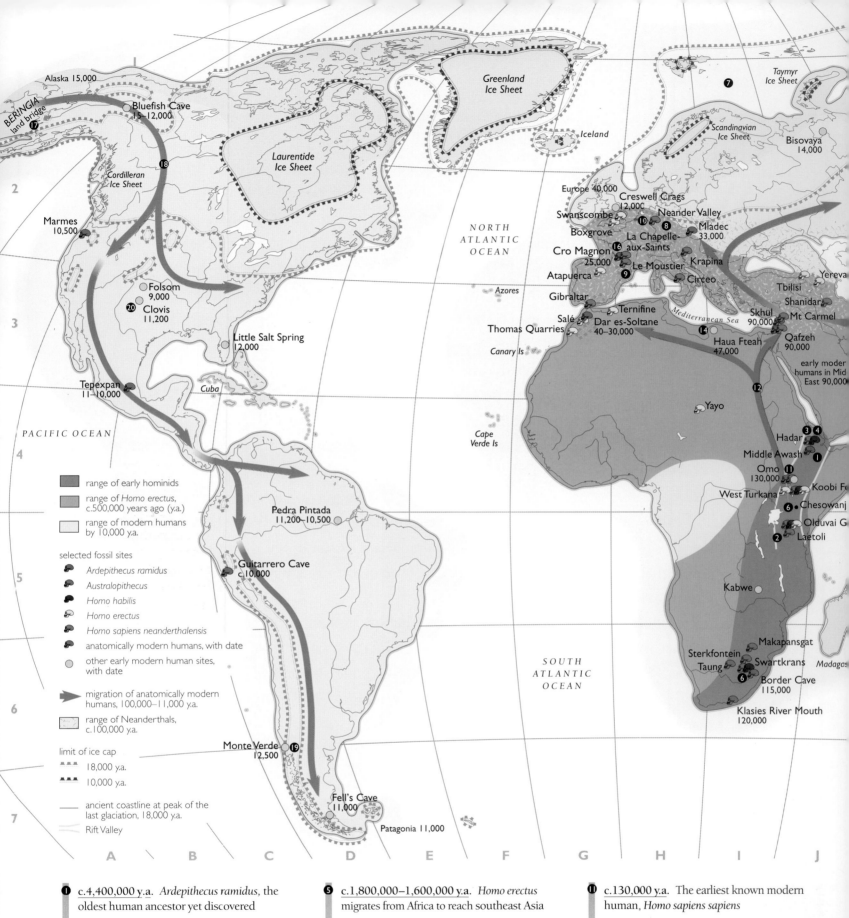

range of early hominids

range of *Homo erectus*, c.500,000 years ago (y.a.)

range of modern humans by 10,000 y.a.

selected fossil sites

🦴 *Ardepithecus ramidus*

🦴 *Australopithecus*

🦴 *Homo habilis*

🦴 *Homo erectus*

🦴 *Homo sapiens neanderthalensis*

🦴 anatomically modern humans, with date

⚪ other early modern human sites, with date

➤ migration of anatomically modern humans, 100,000–11,000 y.a.

▨ range of Neanderthals, c.100,000 y.a.

limit of ice cap

⛰⛰⛰ 18,000 y.a.

⛰⛰⛰ 10,000 y.a.

—— ancient coastline at peak of the last glaciation, 18,000 y.a.

〜〜 Rift Valley

Map labels:

Alaska 15,000
BERINGIA land bridge
Bluefish Cave 15–12,000
Cordilleran Ice Sheet
Laurentide Ice Sheet
Greenland Ice Sheet
Iceland
Taymyr Ice Sheet
Scandinavian Ice Sheet
Bisovaya 14,000
Marmes 10,500
NORTH ATLANTIC OCEAN
Europe 40,000
Creswell Crags 12,000
Swanscombe
Neander Valley
Boxgrove
Mladec 33,000
La Chapelle-aux-Saints
Cro Magnon 25,000
Le Moustier
Krapina
Atapuerca
Circeo
Yereva
Folsom 9,000
Clovis 11,200
Tbilisi
Shanidar
Gibraltar
Ternifine
Skhūl 90,000
Mt Carmel
Little Salt Spring 12,000
Azores
Salé
Dar es-Soltane 40–30,000
Mediterranean Sea
Qafzeh 90,000
PACIFIC OCEAN
Thomas Quarries
Haua Fteah 47,000
early modern humans in Mid East 90,000
Tepexpan 11–10,000
Cuba
Canary Is
Yayo
Hadar
Middle Awash
Cape Verde Is
Omo 130,000
Koobi F
West Turkana
Chesowanj
Pedra Pintada 11,200–10,500
Olduvai G
Laetoli
Guitarrero Cave c.10,000
Kabwe
Makapansgat
Sterkfontein
Swartkrans
Taung
Madagas
SOUTH ATLANTIC OCEAN
Border Cave 115,000
Monte Verde 12,500
Klasies River Mouth 120,000
Fell's Cave 11,000
Patagonia 11,000

Timeline (bottom):

❶ c.4,400,000 y.a. *Ardepithecus ramidus*, the oldest human ancestor yet discovered

❷ c.3,600,000 y.a. A family of early hominids walking on two legs leave footprints in wet mud at Laetoli, Tanzania

❸ c.3,500,000 y.a. The most complete *Australopithecus afarensis* (known to her discoverers as "Lucy")

❹ c.2,400,00 y.a. Oldest known tools are in use at Hadar, Ethiopia

❺ c.1,800,000–1,600,000 y.a. *Homo erectus* migrates from Africa to reach southeast Asia

❻ c.1,600,000 y.a. First known use of fire at Chesowanja and Swartkrans in Africa

❼ c.1,000,000 y.a. Ice Age begins

❽ c.400,000 y.a. Wood tools in use in Germany

❾ c.300,000 y.a. A site at Terra Amata, France, may be evidence of the first human structure

❿ c.150,000 y.a. Neanderthals evolve in Europe

⓫ c.130,000 y.a. The earliest known modern human, *Homo sapiens sapiens*

⓬ c.100,000 y.a. Modern humans begin to migrate out of Africa

⓭ c.60,000–40,000 y.a. Australia and New Guinea reached by island-hopping sea voyages

⓮ c.47,000 y.a. Bone flute found at Haua Fteah, North Africa, is first known musical instrument

⓯ c.40,000 y.a. Australian rock carvings and cave paintings are first examples of human art

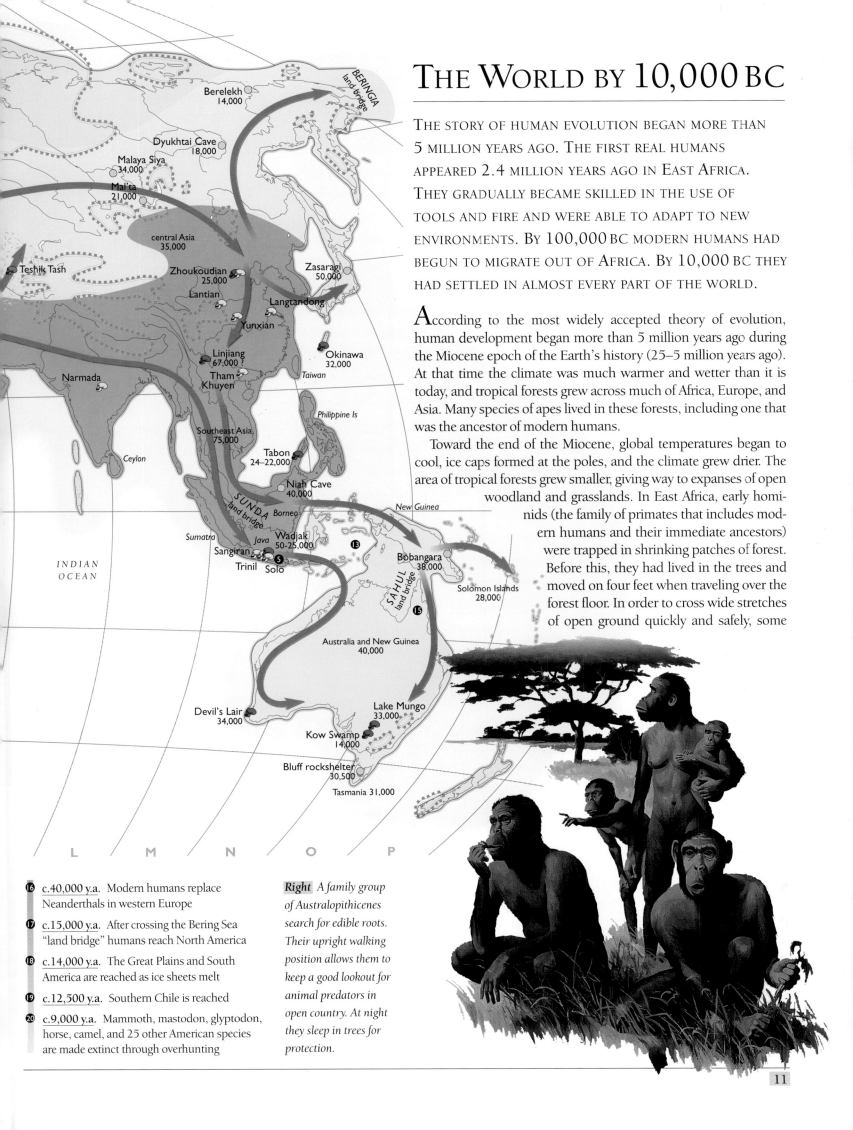

THE WORLD BY 10,000 BC

THE STORY OF HUMAN EVOLUTION BEGAN MORE THAN
5 MILLION YEARS AGO. THE FIRST REAL HUMANS
APPEARED 2.4 MILLION YEARS AGO IN EAST AFRICA.
THEY GRADUALLY BECAME SKILLED IN THE USE OF
TOOLS AND FIRE AND WERE ABLE TO ADAPT TO NEW
ENVIRONMENTS. BY 100,000 BC MODERN HUMANS HAD
BEGUN TO MIGRATE OUT OF AFRICA. BY 10,000 BC THEY
HAD SETTLED IN ALMOST EVERY PART OF THE WORLD.

According to the most widely accepted theory of evolution,
human development began more than 5 million years ago during
the Miocene epoch of the Earth's history (25–5 million years ago).
At that time the climate was much warmer and wetter than it is
today, and tropical forests grew across much of Africa, Europe, and
Asia. Many species of apes lived in these forests, including one that
was the ancestor of modern humans.

Toward the end of the Miocene, global temperatures began to
cool, ice caps formed at the poles, and the climate grew drier. The
area of tropical forests grew smaller, giving way to expanses of open
woodland and grasslands. In East Africa, early homi-
nids (the family of primates that includes modern humans and their immediate ancestors)
were trapped in shrinking patches of forest.
Before this, they had lived in the trees and
moved on four feet when traveling over the
forest floor. In order to cross wide stretches
of open ground quickly and safely, some

Berelekh 14,000
Dyukhtai Cave 18,000
Malaya Siya 34,000
Mal'ta 21,000
BERINGIA land bridge
Teshik Tash
central Asia 35,000
Zhoukoudian 25,000
Lantian
Langtandong
Yunxian
Zasaragi 50,000
Linjiang 67,000 ?
Tham Khuyen
Okinawa 32,000
Narmada
Taiwan
Ceylon
Southeast Asia 75,000
Philippine Is
Tabon 24–22,000
Niah Cave 40,000
SUNDA land bridge
Borneo
New Guinea
Sumatra
Java
Wadjak 50–25,000
Sangiran
Trinil   Solo
⑤
⑬
INDIAN OCEAN
Bobangara 38,000
SAHUL land bridge
Solomon Islands 28,000
⑮
Australia and New Guinea 40,000
Devil's Lair 34,000
Lake Mungo 33,000
Kow Swamp 14,000
Bluff rockshelter 30,500
Tasmania 31,000

L   M   N   O   P

⑯ c.40,000 y.a. Modern humans replace
Neanderthals in western Europe

⑰ c.15,000 y.a. After crossing the Bering Sea
"land bridge" humans reach North America

⑱ c.14,000 y.a. The Great Plains and South
America are reached as ice sheets melt

⑲ c.12,500 y.a. Southern Chile is reached

⑳ c.9,000 y.a. Mammoth, mastodon, glyptodon,
horse, camel, and 25 other American species
are made extinct through overhunting

Right A family group
of Australopithicenes
search for edible roots.
Their upright walking
position allows them to
keep a good lookout for
animal predators in
open country. At night
they sleep in trees for
protection.

hominids began walking on two feet, like modern humans.

These changes took place over millions of years. Fossil remains of bones provide us with evidence of our earliest ancestors. The oldest yet found, known by the scientific name of *Ardipithecus ramidus*, lived around 4.4 million years ago. They probably still inhabited the forests, living in the tree canopy as chimpanzees do, and it is unknown if they walked on two legs. A later species of hominid, *Australopithecus afarensis*, which appeared around 3.5 million years ago, was certainly able to do so.

By 3 million years ago this species had evolved into two types: "robusts" had massive teeth and jaws; "graciles," from whom modern humans are descended, had smaller teeth and jaws. Their brains were about the same size as a chimpanzee's (one-third the size of a modern human's). Like chimpanzees, they used stones and sticks as rudimentary tools. They lived on plant foods and also on the meat that they scavenged from dead animals.

THE FIRST HUMANS

The first human species evolved from the graciles around 2.4 million years ago. Its brain was about half the size of a modern human's. It has been given the name of *Homo habilis*. This simply means "handyman," because it made simple stone tools made by striking rocks together until they shattered into sharp flakes which could be used for cutting. They did not use their tools to hunt with, but to cut the meat from animals that had died naturally or been killed by predators such as lions and saber-toothed cats.

After hundreds of thousands of years *Homo habilis* gave way to a new species called *Homo erectus* ("upright man"). They were taller than modern humans, but in other respects were much like ourselves, though their brains were still much smaller. They were the first humans to live outside Africa. Between 1.8 and 1.6 million years ago they probably spread throughout tropical Asia, and after learning to use fire were also able to live in cooler areas of China and Europe. As well as giving warmth, fire was used to harden the ends of wooden tools, for cooking meat, and for protection.

Right The Rift Valley in East Africa is sometimes called the "cradle of humankind." It is the most important site for early human fossils in the world. Millions of years ago, when sudden floods occurred, soils were washed down the steep cliff sides of the valley. They covered over the bones of recently dead animals, including early humans, so preserving them from being eaten by carnivores or broken down by the weather. The Olduvai Gorge in particular has yielded unrivaled fossil evidence of our human ancestors.

Above and right Handaxes were made by carefully flaking stone or flint pebbles. These were made around 70,000 years ago, and might have been used to cut up the carcasses of animals as big as elephants.

THE ICE AGE

By now, the Earth was entering a period of climatic change, the Ice Age. In spite of its name, the climate was not cold all the time; there were frequent warm intervals, "interglacial periods," separating the cold, dry "glacial periods." The change between the two could be rapid, and animals and plants had to be able to adapt quickly—for example, by growing thicker fur or smaller leaves to prevent moisture loss—or go extinct. The way that

About 500,000 years ago *Homo erectus* began to evolve in different ways in Europe and Africa. In Europe, a species known as the Neanderthals developed. Their robust bodies and bulbous noses helped them survive the cold conditions by reducing heat loss. *Homo sapiens sapiens* ("wise man"), the first human species to resemble modern people in all anatomical respects, emerged in Africa some 130,000 years ago. As modern human populations increased, small bands slowly colonized neighboring areas, and by 100,000 years ago had migrated from Africa to the Middle East. Over the next 90,000 years their descendants spread out across most of the world. Sea levels were then much lower than today because so much of the Earth's water was frozen within glaciers and ice sheets. This allowed humans to travel easily on foot across areas of land that are now separated from each other by stretches of sea.

By 75,000 years ago modern humans had penetrated China and southeast Asia. Soon after their arrival they appear to have forced *Homo erectus* into extinction, probably because they were more skillful and resourceful hunters. Between 60,000 and 40,000 years ago they learned how to make boats or rafts and sailed to Australia and New Guinea, then a voyage of only 40 miles (64 kilometers) at its narrowest. Because of the colder climate, *Homo sapiens* was slow to migrate into Europe and central Asia. When they finally did so, around 40,000 years ago, they slowly replaced the Neanderthals already living there.

The Americas were the last continents to be reached by modern humans. By 15,000 years ago bands of hunters had penetrated as far as Alaska across a land bridge from Siberia. Great ice sheets blocked their way, making further progress impossible. When these began to melt 14,000–12,000 years ago, the Paleoindians (ancestors of the Native Americans) were able to reach the Great Plains of North America. These vast grasslands swarmed with herds of grazing animals, many species of which they hunted to extinction. The Paleoindians moved on into South America to reach Patagonia around 11,000 years ago. By this time only Antarctica and a few oceanic islands were without human inhabitants.

Homo erectus responded to these inhospitable conditions was by developing a bigger brain. This meant that greater intelligence could be applied to solving problems. By 1 million years ago the brain of *Homo erectus* was already three-quarters the size of a modern human's.

Homo erectus was a skillful toolmaker. Wooden throwing spears were used to hunt and kill wild animals, and stone handaxes to butcher them. They cleaned the skins of their prey with stone "scrapers," perhaps for clothing. They may have built simple shelters and lived in small family groups, traveling from place to place. At certain times of the year they moved their camps near to waterholes to hunt the wild animals that came there to drink, and foraged for edible plant foods such as fruits, nuts, and roots, knowing where and at what season they would be most abundant. Information of this kind would be passed on from generation to generation. The hunting–gathering way of life, as it is called, remained the way all humans lived until farming began. A few people, such as the Inuit of the Canadian Arctic and the San of the Kalahari Desert in Africa, still live like this today.

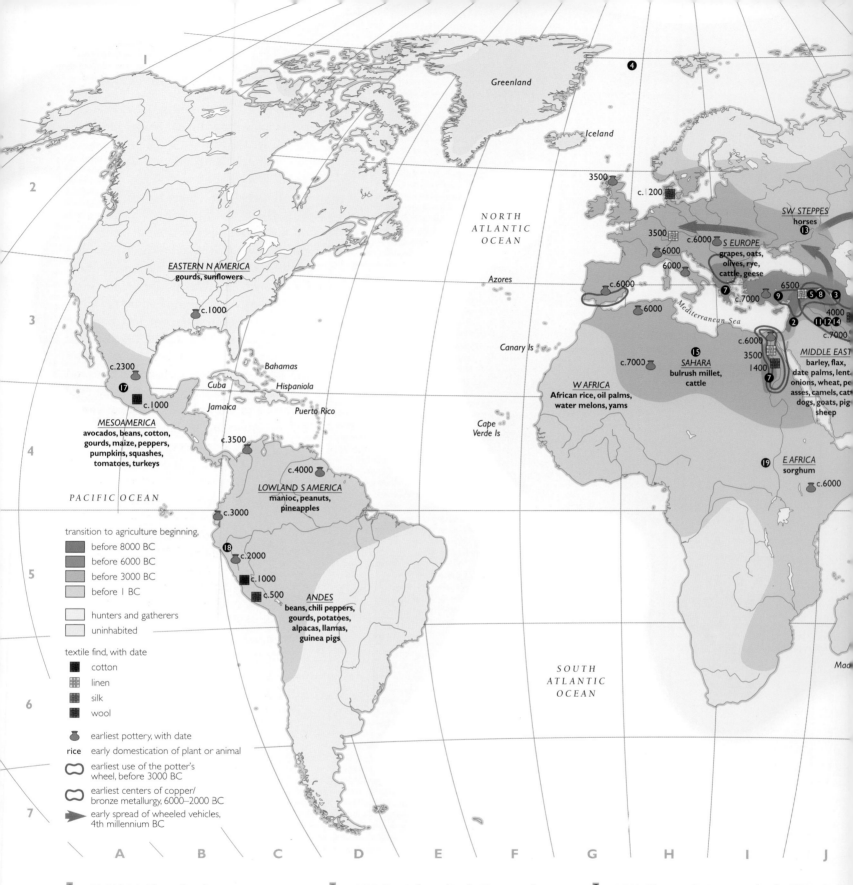

transition to agriculture beginning,
- before 8000 BC
- before 6000 BC
- before 3000 BC
- before 1 BC

- hunters and gatherers
- uninhabited

textile find, with date
- cotton
- linen
- silk
- wool

🝏 earliest pottery, with date

rice early domestication of plant or animal

⬭ earliest use of the potter's wheel, before 3000 BC

⬭ earliest centers of copper/ bronze metallurgy, 6000–2000 BC

➤ early spread of wheeled vehicles, 4th millennium BC

Map labels

GREENLAND

ICELAND

NORTH ATLANTIC OCEAN

Azores

Canary Is

Cape Verde Is

EASTERN N AMERICA
gourds, sunflowers
c.1000

c.2300
c.1000

MESOAMERICA
avocados, beans, cotton, gourds, maize, peppers, pumpkins, squashes, tomatoes, turkeys

Bahamas
Cuba
Hispaniola
Jamaica
Puerto Rico

c.3500

LOWLAND S AMERICA
manioc, peanuts, pineapples
c.4000

c.3000

c.2000

c.1000

c.500

ANDES
beans, chili peppers, gourds, potatoes, alpacas, llamas, guinea pigs

PACIFIC OCEAN

SOUTH ATLANTIC OCEAN

3500
c.1200
SW STEPPES
horses
3500
6000
6000
S EUROPE
grapes, oats, olives, rye, cattle, geese
c.6000
c.6000
6500
c.7000
6000
4000
c.7000
Mediterranean Sea
c.6000
SAHARA
bulrush millet, cattle
3500
1400
MIDDLE EAST
barley, flax, date palms, lent... onions, wheat, pe... asses, camels, catt... dogs, goats, pig... sheep
c.7000
W AFRICA
African rice, oil palms, water melons, yams
E AFRICA
sorghum
c.6000

Timeline

❶ c.11,000 BC The earliest known pots are made in Japan

❷ c.10,000 Hunter–gatherers in Syria and Israel harvest wild cereals with stone sickles

❸ c.9000 Wild sheep are domesticated by hunters in the Zagros mountains

❹ c.8000 End of the Ice Age

❺ c.8000–7700 Following the domestication of wheat and barley, the first farming villages develop in the Fertile Crescent

❻ c.6500 Rice is farmed in the Yangtze valley

❼ c.6500 Wheat, barley, sheep, and cattle farming spread to Egypt and Europe

❽ c.6500 Wild cattle are domesticated in the Middle East

❾ c.6200 The smelting of copper at Chatal Huyuk, Turkey, is the first known example of metalworking

❿ c.5500 Cotton is domesticated in the northern mountains of Pakistan

⓫ c.5000 The use of irrigation makes farming possible on the dry Mesopotamian plains

⓬ c.4500 The plow, sail, and potter's wheel come into use in Mesopotamia

⓭ c.4000 Horses are domesticated for meat and milk in southern Russia

⓮ c.3800 Bronzeworking develops in the Middle East

⓯ c.3500 Overgrazing by herds of cattle may have helped to turn the Sahara into a desert

THE WORLD BY 2000 BC

As the global climate began to warm up at the end of the Ice Age, human populations rose sharply in many parts of the world. Hunter–gatherers were forced to grow their own food as natural supplies became scarcer. Where the environment was suitable, farming began in several different places between 11,000 and 8,000 years ago. It is perhaps the most important event in human history, leading to new skills and technologies.

During the Ice Age, vast areas of the Earth were covered with grasslands grazed by huge herds of animals such as bison and reindeer. However, as it began to come to an end between 12,000 and 10,000 years ago, the climate became warmer and wetter, and the forests started to spread. Herds of large animals became scarcer, and in many places people were forced to find new sources of food, hunting small game such as deer or wild sheep, catching birds and fish, and gathering shellfish and edible plants. To ensure a reliable food supply, some people began deliberately to plant wild grasses and tubers. Others managed herds of wild animals by keeping some in pens until they were needed for food.

The next stage in the story of farming was the domestication of particular plants and animals. This was done by planting or breeding only those specimens that would produce the biggest fruits or seeds, or the best meat. Among the earliest food plants to be domesticated were the grain-bearing

Map labels

CENTRAL ASIA
camels, yaks

CHINA
millet, soybeans, rice, silkworms

INDIA
cotton, zebus

SE ASIA
rice, taros, waterchestnuts, chickens, pigs, water buffalo

SE ASIAN ARCHIPELAGO
bananas, breadfruit, coconuts

NEW GUINEA
sugar cane, sweet potatoes

Taiwan

Philippine Is

Ceylon

Borneo

Celebes

New Guinea

Sumatra

Java

Timor

INDIAN OCEAN

c.6000
c.1000
c.8000
c.7000
c.2500
c.2000
11000
c.5000
c.5000
6000
5000
2700

K L M N O P

16 **c.3000** Silkworms are domesticated in China and the first silk cloth is made

17 **c.2700** Corn is domesticated in Mexico, leading to farming settlement

18 **c.2000** Potatoes are domesticated as a staple foodcrop in the mountains of Peru

19 **c.1500** Cattle herding is introduced on the grasslands of sub-Saharan Africa

20 **c.1200–800** Pastoral farmers on the Eurasian steppes learn to ride horseback

Right Cattle herders are depicted on this rock painting from Tassili N'Ajjer in the Sahara. It dates from c.2000 BC, when the region was still largely grassland and could support both cereal farming and herding.

cereals: wheat, barley, oats, sorghum, millet, rice, and corn. Their seeds were easy to store, usually in underground pits, until the time came for planting the next year. They are still the main food source for most of the world's people today. Herd animals like cattle, sheep, goats, pigs, camels, and horses proved the most suitable for domestication. As well as meat, they provided milk, wool, and transportation.

CRADLES OF AGRICULTURE

Farming began in a number of different places around the world, at different times, and independently of each other, between 11,000 and 8,000 years ago. Some of the earliest farmers lived in the area of the Middle East called the Fertile Crescent. This region of good soil stretches through modern Israel, Lebanon, Syria, and Iraq. The Natufian people of Syria and Israel began to grow wild wheat and barley around 10,000 BC. Around the same time, people in the Zagros mountains of Iraq, farther to the east, began to domesticate wild sheep. One reason why farming developed so early in the Middle East was that it had a rich supply of native plants that were suitable for domestication, including wild wheats, barley, pulses, and nut trees. From about 8000 BC farming villages grew up right across the Fertile Crescent. From this center, cereal farming later spread through the rest of the Middle East, Egypt, parts of sub-Saharan Africa (where native grains were domesticated), Pakistan, and Europe.

In east Asia millet and rice farming was taking place in the Yellow and Yangtze river valleys of China at least 8,000 years ago. Southeast Asia and New Guinea saw the early domestication of several tropical food crops such as taro, sugar cane, bananas, and sweet potatoes. In Mexico and South America a large range of edible plants were domesticated, including corn, beans, peppers, squashes, and potatoes. Guinea pigs, alpacas, and llamas were used for food, wool, and transportation. Several regions of the world, in particular North America, southern Africa, and Australia, had few or no native plants and animals that could be easily domesticated. Farming became important in these places only after domestic animals and crops had been introduced from other parts of the world.

FARMING & TECHNOLOGY

Farming led to new discoveries and inventions. Hunter–gatherers were nomads, so everything they owned had to be carried with them from camp to camp. Farmers, on the other hand, lived more settled lives in villages, and could keep and store more possessions. They needed more tools than before, and new implements were developed for specific purposes: polished stone axes to cut down the forests to clear fields; hoes and digging sticks to make the soil ready for planting; stone sickles to harvest crops.

New technologies arose from the need to store and prepare food. Grindstones were used to make flour from harvested grains. People began to make clay pots to store food and for cooking. The earliest known pottery comes from Japan, around 11,000 BC. It was invented independently in the Middle East around 3,000 years later. As the potters grew more skillful they learned to build ovens for baking the clay. Later, the same ovens were used to smelt and cast metals from natural ores—copper and gold first, then bronze and iron. Metal produced better cutting tools, knives, and swords.

Left A wheatfield today in Galilee, Israel. Around 12,000 years ago this area was inhabited by the Natufian people, who supported themselves by hunting gazelle and harvesting grains from wild wheat and barley. They stored these in underground pits to be used in the winter when other food was scarce. With this abundance of food always available, the Natufians began to live in settled villages. In time, they started to plant the wild cereals close to their villages so that they did not have to spend so much time traveling to find food. So the transition to farming was made.

Right Preparing food was a laborious task in early farming societies. This figurine of a woman grinding wheat comes from Egypt. Analysis of skeletal remains shows that arthritis was a common disease by age 30.

Worked metal articles were worn as jewelry, emphasizing personal wealth and status. Wheels were also developed as an aid to pottery making. Only later (around 4000 BC) was it realized that they could also be attached to carts and used to move objects. Animal skins and plant fibers had long been used for shelter, clothing, and to make baskets; now spinning and weaving developed to turn cotton, flax, and wool into cloth. This could be used to make many things, including sails for sailing ships.

There were a number of technological developments that improved the efficiency of farming. The storage and channeling of river and flood waters to irrigate fields made it possible to cultivate crops in arid regions such as the Mesopotamian floodplain, the Indus valley, and South America. When the plow came into use in central and western Europe around 3000 BC, it became easier to cultivate the region's heavy soil.

In the Eurasian steppes and sub-Saharan Africa, where there were few opportunities for crop cultivation, nomadic pastoralists managed large herds of horses, cattle, and sheep by moving them to new grazing lands once the old ones were exhausted. Around 1000 BC, Eurasian herders learned the skill of horseback riding. This made it possible for them to cover much larger distances than before.

FARMING & HEALTH

The fossil remains of hunter–gatherers show that they were taller than people are today: food supplies were plentiful and they were well nourished. This was not true of early farmers. Every few years, crops failed because of bad weather, pest invasion, or disease. During times of scarcity, malnutrition was widespread. This stunted the growth of children, and as a result early farmers were shorter than modern people. Now that they were living close to animals all the time, farmers caught many animal diseases. For example, tuberculosis, a big killer before the discovery of antibiotics in the 20th century, was originally a disease of cattle. Farmers also had to work very much harder than their hunter–gatherer ancestors and they began to develop diseases of the joints, such as arthritis.

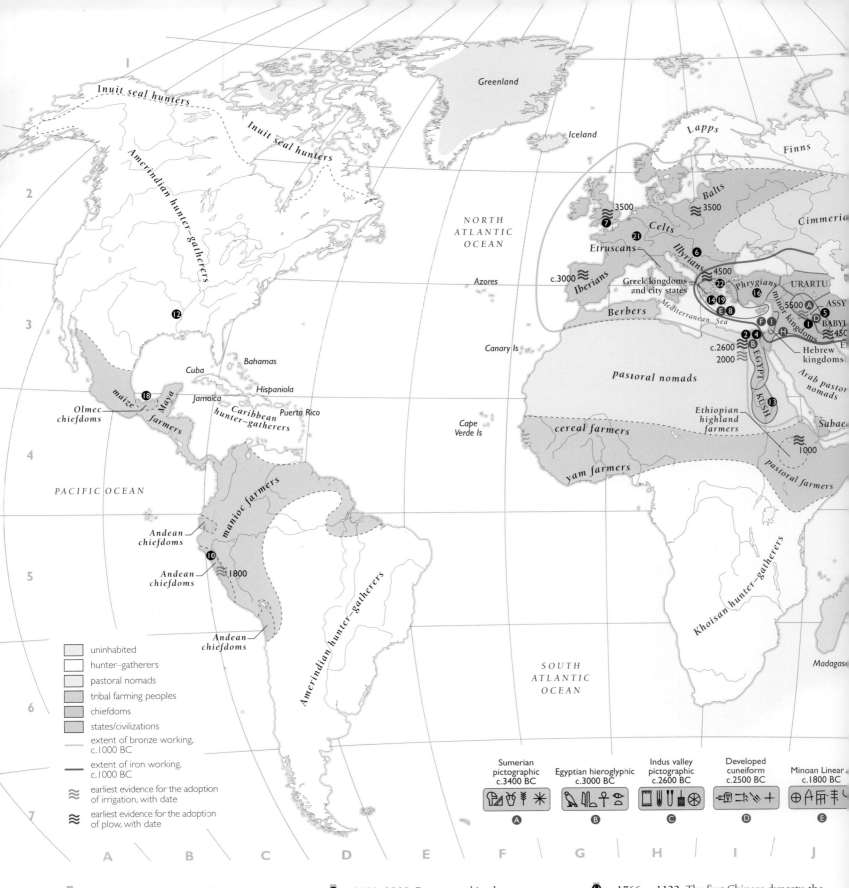

Inuit seal hunters

Inuit seal hunters

Greenland

Iceland

Lapps

Finns

Amerindian hunter–gatherers

NORTH ATLANTIC OCEAN

Azores

Canary Is

Cape Verde Is

3500

3500

Balts

Cimmeria

Celts

Etruscans

Illyrians

Phrygians

URARTU

ASSY

BABYL

Iberians

c.3000

Greek kingdoms and city states

4500

5500

450

c.2600

2000

Hebrew kingdoms

Arab pastor nomads

Berbers

Mediterranean Sea

EGYPT

KUSH

Sabae

Olmec chiefdoms

maize

Maya

Bahamas

Cuba

Jamaica

Hispaniola

Puerto Rico

farmers

Caribbean hunter–gatherers

pastoral nomads

Ethiopian highland farmers

1000

cereal farmers

manioc farmers

yam farmers

pastoral farmers

Andean chiefdoms

Andean chiefdoms

1800

PACIFIC OCEAN

Amerindian hunter–gatherers

Khoisan hunter–gatherers

SOUTH ATLANTIC OCEAN

Madagascar

Andean chiefdoms

uninhabited

hunter–gatherers

pastoral nomads

tribal farming peoples

chiefdoms

states/civilizations

extent of bronze working, c.1000 BC

extent of iron working, c.1000 BC

≈ earliest evidence for the adoption of irrigation, with date

≈ earliest evidence for the adoption of plow, with date

Sumerian pictographic c.3400 BC

Egyptian hieroglyphic c.3000 BC

Indus valley pictographic c.2600 BC

Developed cuneiform c.2500 BC

Minoan Linear A c.1800 BC

Ⓐ Ⓑ Ⓒ Ⓓ Ⓔ

❶ **c.3400** The first cities develop in Sumer (southern Iraq). At about this time a simple form of picture writing comes into use

❷ **c.3000** In Egypt, writing with hieroglyphs develops and a unified kingdom is formed

❸ **c.2600–1800** An urban-based civilization rises and falls in the Indus valley

❹ **c.2550** The Great Pyramid is built

❺ **2334–2279** Sargon of Akkad brings all of Mesopotamia under his rule

❻ **c.2500–2300** Bronze-working becomes established in central and southeast Europe

❼ **c.2000** The main stage of the great stone circle at Stonehenge, southern Britain, is completed

❽ **c.2000–1600** The first European civilization, the Minoan, flourishes on Crete

❾ **c.1900** The first bronzes in China are made at Erlitou, which becomes a center of the craft

❿ **c.1800** Large U-shaped ceremonial centers are built on the coast of Peru

⓫ **c.1766–c.1122** The first Chinese dynasty, the Shang, flourishes. The first cities are built

⓬ **c.1730–c.1350** In North America, hunter–gatherers build a series of complex earthworks at Poverty Point, Louisiana

⓭ **c.1700** The kingdom of Kush, the first African state outside Egypt, comes into being in Nubia under Egyptian influence

⓮ **c.1600–1200** The Mycenaean civilization flourishes in southern Greece

Map labels:

Inuit

Siberian hunter-gatherers

pastoral nomads

pastoral farmers
(ancestral Turko-Mongol)

Jomon hunter-gatherers

9 11 20
G ≈ 3000
ZHOU
c.3000 ≈ Wu

Iranians

Tibetans

2600
2500

15 Vedic Aryan kingdoms
C
3

Thais

Burmese

rice farmers
(ancestral Vietnamese)

300 ≈

Taiwan

Dravidians

Ceylon

Philippine Is

Austronesians

Celebes

Sumatra

Borneo

New Guinea

Java

Papuans

Timor

INDIAN
OCEAN

Lapita culture
(ancestral Polynesian)
17

Australian Aboriginal
hunter-gatherers

Tasmanian
hunter-gatherers

roto-Canaanite
c.1600 BC
F

Chinese pictographic
c.1300 BC
G

Aramaic
c.1000 BC
H

Phoenician
c.1000 BC
I

L   M   N   O   P

THE WORLD BY 1000 BC

WHEN FARMERS GREW MORE FOOD THAN THEY NEEDED, THEY USED THE SURPLUS AS WEALTH. AS A RESULT, DIFFERENCES OF RANK DEVELOPED BETWEEN PEOPLE AND SOCIETY GRADUALLY BECAME MORE COMPLEX. BY 1000 BC MORE THAN HALF THE WORLD'S POPULATION LIVED BY FARMING. IN SOME WELL-FAVORED PLACES, THE WORLD'S FIRST CIVILIZATIONS HAD EMERGED AND THE FIRST WRITING SYSTEMS COME INTO USE.

One consequence of the shift from hunting and gathering to farming was that human society began to change. Hunter–gatherers lived in small family groups. Most had to travel large distances to find enough food to survive—it has been estimated that an area of 10 square miles (26 sq km) of forest would yield enough food to support just one hunter–gatherer. Farmed by simple techniques, the same area of land could support 800 people. Without the need to travel to find food, people began to live in settled villages. As population figures rose, small family groups developed into larger tribes of about 1,000 people. The leaders of the tribe would meet to take collective decisions and settle disputes, but there were very few distinctions of wealth and status between individuals.

Below This massive stone head from Mexico depicts an Olmec chief or king. Early rulers had statues made of themselves to impress and intimidate their subjects, just as some dictators do in the modern world.

15 c.1500 Cattle-herding Aryans migrate from central Asia into northern India and begin to settle the Ganges plain

16 c.1500 Iron-working develops among the Hittites in Anatolia (Turkey)

17 c.1500–1200 The Polynesian islands (Fiji, Tonga, Samoa) are settled by people of the Lapita pottery-making culture from Melanesia

18 c.1200 The Olmecs build elaborate ceremonial centers in Mexico

19 c.1200–1180 The Sea Peoples bring an end to the Mycenaean civilization in Greece. They invade Anatolia and the Middle East, and are defeated by the Egyptians

20 c.1122 The Zhou dynasty overthrows the Shang dynasty in China

21 c.1100 The construction of hilltop forts begins in western Europe

22 c.1000 Iron-working technology spreads to southern Europe from the Middle East

CHIEFDOMS

In some parts of the world, such as New Guinea and the Amazon basin, tribal societies like this have survived into the modern world. However, in areas where the the conditions were especially favorable for agriculture, some farmers would have been able to produce more food than they and their families needed to survive. They would have used the surplus to barter for other goods or exert power over their neighbors. Through this process, distinct inequalities of wealth and power gradually grew up between individual members of the tribe, leading to the development of chiefdoms—ranked societies of around 5,000 or more people.

Anthropologists, who study the way people live, are able to surmise how these chiefdoms were organized by looking at similar groups that have survived into the modern age; for example, in the Pacific islands. They were probably divided into extended family groups called clans. Each clan had its own hereditary leaders, and some clans had more prestige than others. The leader of the most important clan was the ruler of the chiefdom, while the leading men of the clans formed a ruling elite, or aristocracy. From the excavation of graves, archeologists can tell that differences in rank often continued after death, as some people were buried surrounded by precious objects, while others received no special treatment.

Social changes of this kind were greatest where technological improvements such as irrigation or the plow increased farming efficiency so that larger surpluses of food were produced each year. The chief and other leaders controlled the economic activity of the whole community. They did not need to work: junior members of the clan were required to give them food in exchange for leadership and protection, an early form of taxation. As the chief and other clan leaders demanded fine weapons and jewelry to show off their wealth, a small class of craftsmen developed in most chiefdoms.

The chief often had a sacred role in religious rituals and there would probably be a permanent ceremonial center, or temple, which served as a focal point for the chiefdom, with or without associated residential quarters and craft workshops. Although chiefs exploited their people, they were also responsible for organizing large building works that benefited everyone, such as the large stone monuments (megaliths) and defensive hilltop forts of western Europe or the irrigation channels of Peru.

Left *The inner circle of standing stones at Stonehenge in southern England is one of the greatest monuments of prehistoric Europe. This ancient sacred site was built in several stages over hundreds of years, but the stone circle itself was completed around 2000 BC. Without the aid of wheeled vehicles or cranes, a labor force of many hundreds of people would have been used to bring the stones to the site and set them in place. They are believed to have been dragged there on sledges, some over very great distances. Only a very powerful chief could have organized such an undertaking.*

THE FIRST CIVILIZATIONS

In the period c.3500–1500 BC, in several parts of the world, chiefdoms developed independently into larger, more complex civilizations, based on cities. Their populations amounted to tens of thousands, and most were ruled by kings. The king had too many subjects to rely on family or clan loyalties alone to give him authority, and his power was often based on religion. The Egyptian kings, for example, claimed that they were living gods, while the early rulers of China ruled with the support and approval of the gods. The king might also strengthen his authority by issuing laws for everyone to obey, as certain Mesopotamian rulers did.

Civilizations developed where there were rich natural resources for farming. The earliest grew up on the fertile flood plains of

Right Seals from the Indus valley marked with an unknown script. Seals like this, used by many ancient civilizations, were pressed into wet clay and used as a form of identification tag on containers, so they probably show the name of the owner. The finely carved animals may also have been a personal symbol.

great rivers: between the Tigris and Euphrates rivers in Mesopotamia (around 3400 BC); in the Nile valley in Egypt (3000 BC); in the Indus valley of Pakistan (2600 BC); and in the Yellow River basin region of China (1700 BC). In all these places, annual flood waters supported intensive farming and ensured that good harvests were had nearly every year.

Farmers brought their food surpluses as taxes to the city where they were stored in temples or palace complexes and then reissued to the people of the city who were not directly engaged in farming: bakers, potters, weavers, metalworkers, leatherworkers, and builders. As the wealth and power of the civilization increased, more classes of job were needed—soldiers to keep control and conquer new territory, traders and merchants to travel abroad and add to the city's prosperity, bureaucrats (often priests) to administer public affairs.

WRITING

By 1000 BC the major world civilizations had independently developed writing as an aid to administration. The earliest known examples of writing are accounts of goods. Found on clay tables from the city of Uruk in Mesopotamia, they date from 3300 BC. Later on, individual rulers recorded their achievements in writing on stone monuments, and the myths and stories that were central to a civilization's religious beliefs came to be written down.

Early writing systems used simple pictures as signs (pictographs). Later they developed into more complex phonetic scripts. Both systems are still used in different parts of the world today. In Mesopotamia, scribes made the pictographs by pressing a sharpened reed onto wet clay tablets, which then dried. This form of writing is called cuneiform. The Egyptians wrote on an early type of paper made from the papyrus reeds that grew beside the Nile. In China, most early writing was done on animal bones. Historians are able to decipher many, but not all, of these early scripts. Written records tell us much about past civilizations that archeology cannot do, but they still do not give us a complete picture.

ANCIENT MESOPOTAMIA

THE WORLD'S FIRST CIVILIZATION DEVELOPED IN MESOPOTAMIA MORE THAN 5,000 YEARS AGO. FOR OVER 2,000 YEARS IT WAS THE HOME OF THE WORLD'S MOST POWERFUL AND ADVANCED STATES. THE MESO-POTAMIAN CIVILIZATION HAD A STRONG INFLUENCE ON ITS NEIGHBORS IN THE MIDDLE EAST, EGYPT, AND THE INDUS VALLEY, BUT IT WAS IN DECLINE BY 500 BC AND WAS EXTINCT BY THE START OF THE CHRISTIAN ERA.

The name Mesopotamia, meaning the "land between the rivers," refers to the floodplain that lies between the Tigris and Euphrates rivers (modern Iraq). When these rivers flooded, they spread silt over the land, so creating layers of fertile soil. But very little rain falls in this region, and the land was parched and useless for farming until people learned how to irrigate it by digging canals to carry water from the rivers to their fields. This happened around 5500 BC. They were now able to cultivate the rich soils of the plains to get a reliable harvest almost every year. The invention of the wooden plow about a thousand years later, which broke up the soil prior to the seeds being sown, increased crop yields even further. The population grew, and by 4300 BC hundreds of large villages and small towns had developed in the region.

Aside from its fertile soil, Mesopotamia lacked natural resources. Wood, stone, and metal ores for every purpose from building to jewelry had to be imported from neighboring regions in exchange for surplus food and craft items such as pottery. Trade was controlled by rich and powerful rulers who organized communal projects such as the construction of irrigation canals and flood defenses. These were particularly important as floods could cause serious damage to crops and houses. They were thought to be sent by angry gods—the Biblical story of Noah's Flood has its origins in the early myths of Mesopotamia.

Left These statuettes of a man and woman praying may be actual portraits. Such figures were often placed in Sumerian temples as signs of devotion. The Sumerians worshiped hundreds of gods, and each city had its own guardian deity.

THE FIRST CITY STATES

By 3100 BC dozens of cities with populations of up to 10,000 people had emerged in Sumer, the southern part of Mesopotamia. They were independent states, each ruled by a king. Most of the inhabitants were farmers who worked in the countryside by day and returned to the city at night. The surplus crops they raised were taken to temples in the city, from where they were distributed as food rations to people not engaged in farming—those who performed specialized tasks like metalworkers, potters, builders, merchants, soldiers, and priests. Sumerian cities came to be dominated by their huge temple complexes, which acted as great storehouses for the whole community.

Early Sumerian cities were very different to modern cities. Because money had not yet come into use there were no markets. People received food, clothing, and other items as payment for work, or bartered with one another. A small number of rich people lived in palaces, but most lived in tiny houses that lacked water or sanitation. Buildings were constructions of sun-baked mud-bricks: stone was little used, except

Map labels: BULGARIA · Troy · Gordion · Aegean Sea · TURKEY · coppe · LUKKA · TAURUS · Rhodes · Mediterranean Sea · alabaster, diorite, gold · EGYPT · Memphis · EGYPT · Nile · Thebes

Map legend:
- known empire of Sargon of Agade, c.2279
- Babylonian empire under Hammurabi, c.1750
- Hittite empire, c.1322
- Assyrian empire, c.680–627
- earliest cities, c. 3400–2000
- later cities, c.2000–500
- trade route
- tin commodity

0 300 km
0 200 mi

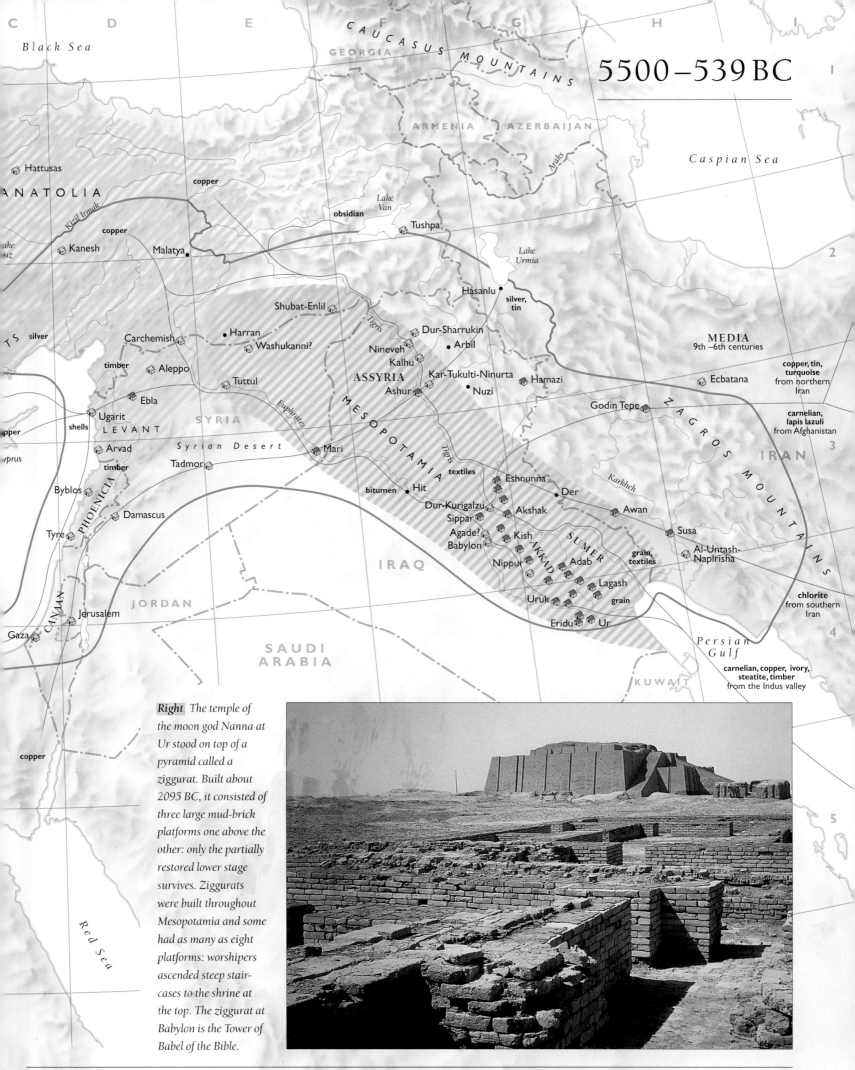

Black Sea

C D E F G H I

CAUCASUS MOUNTAINS

GEORGIA

ARMENIA AZERBAIJAN

Caspian Sea

Hattusas

ANATOLIA

copper

Kızıl Irmak

copper

Kanesh

Malatya

Lake
...uz

silver

TS

obsidian

Lake
Van

Tushpa

Hasanlu

silver,
tin

MEDIA
9th –6th centuries

copper, tin,
turquoise
from northern
Iran

Shubat-Enlil

Harran

Carchemish

Washukanni?

Dur-Sharrukin

Nineveh

Arbil

Tigris

Kalhu

ASSYRIA

Kar-Tukulti-Ninurta

Hamazi

Ecbatana

timber

Aleppo

Tuttul

Ashur

Nuzi

Godin Tepe

ZAGROS

carnelian,
lapis lazuli
from Afghanistan

Ebla

SYRIA

Euphrates

MESOPOTAMIA

IRAN

Ugarit

shells

LEVANT

Syrian Desert

Mari

Tigris

MOUNTAINS

...per

...prus

Arvad

Tadmor

timber

textiles

Eshnunna

Karkheh

Byblos

PHOENICIA

Damascus

bitumen

Hit

Der

Awan

Susa

Dur-Kurigalzu

Akshak

Tyre

Sippar

Al-Untash-
Napirisha

Agade?

Kish

SUMER

chlorite
from southern
Iran

Babylon

AKKAD

CANAAN

Nippur

Adab

grain,
textiles

Jerusalem

JORDAN

Lagash

IRAQ

Uruk

grain

Gaza

Eridu

Ur

Persian
Gulf

SAUDI
ARABIA

copper

KUWAIT

carnelian, copper, ivory,
steatite, timber
from the Indus valley

Red Sea

Right The temple of
the moon god Nanna at
Ur stood on top of a
pyramid called a
ziggurat. Built about
2095 BC, it consisted of
three large mud-brick
platforms one above the
other: only the partially
restored lower stage
survives. Ziggurats
were built throughout
Mesopotamia and some
had as many as eight
platforms: worshipers
ascended steep stair-
cases to the shrine at
the top. The ziggurat at
Babylon is the Tower of
Babel of the Bible.

for sculpture, because of its scarcity. Sometimes lions came into the cities at night and prowled around on rooftops.

By around 3400 BC the Sumerians had invented a simple form of writing to record business transactions. Cuneiform writing, made by marking wet clay with a pointed reed (see page 21), slowly grew more complex over the next several hundred years. It was eventually employed for many different purposes—to record law codes and historical chronicles, send letters, and write down religious and literary texts. Because thousands of clay tablets have survived, historians have been able to piece together a remarkably full picture of the way life was led in Mesopotamian times.

During the Early Dynastic period (2900–2334 BC), disputes were common between the Sumerian city states, and most built

THE ROYAL HUNT

In Mesopotamia, as in other ancient societies, hunting was a sport enjoyed by kings and men of high status. They would acquire prestige, and the approval of the gods, by displaying strength and courage in the hunting field, and it was a good training for war. The Assyrian kings were particularly addicted to the sport and decorated their palaces with scenes of their hunting prowess. Lions, then found in Mesopotamia, were considered especially worthy of being hunted by kings. Royal hunts were carefully managed. Wild animals were captured to be released in game parks for the king to pursue and kill from a light chariot.

Right *King Ashurbanipal dispatches a lion.*

sturdy walls for protection. Warfare grew more sophisticated: sculptures of the time depict warriors riding into battle in four-wheeled carts pulled by donkeys.

Around 2334 BC, Sargon, king of the city of Agade, managed to conquer all the city states of Mesopotamia and to extend his power northward as far as the Mediterranean coast. By uniting so many different peoples and cultures in a single state, he can be claimed to have created the first known empire in history. It did not long survive him, however, as rivalries once again sprang up between city states. For a time Ur, in the south, was successful, but Sumer was now in terminal decline. Power passed to the north, first to the cities of Ashur (Assyria) and Mari, then to Babylon.

HAMMURABI

Babylon reached its fullest heights in the reign of Hammurabi (1792–1750 BC). He is most famous for drawing up a list of laws, which he had inscribed on a large stone pillar, or stela. It is one of the oldest surviving legal records in the world and shows that women and children were considered to be the property of their husbands and fathers. Punishments were severe, with death or mutilation inflicted for even minor offenses.

Left *A wall panel from Nebuchadnezzar II's palace.*

TIMETABLE

c.5500
Farming develops on the floodplain of southern Mesopotamia

c.4500
The plow, wheel, and sail are in use

c.3400
The first cities grow up in Sumer

c.3300
Writing on clay tablets begins

2334
Sargon, king of Agade, establishes the world's first empire

2100
The first ziggurats are built

1813–1781
Assyria emerges as a powerful state under its king Shamshi-Adad

1792–1750
Babylon rises to power under Hammurabi

1595
Babylon is sacked by the Hittites

c.1500
Ironworking develops in the Middle East

911–627
Assyria is again the dominant power

626–612
Babylon takes over the Assyrian empire

539
Fall of the Babylonian empire to Cyrus the Great of Persia

THE ASSYRIAN EMPIRE

In 1595 BC the Hittites, who lived in the mountains of central Anatolia, where they were the first people to use iron, invaded and sacked Babylon. Soon after, Mesopotamia entered a dark age lasting 600 years. Recovery began in around 1000 BC in the Assyrian cities of Ashur and Nineveh, and by the 8th century the Assyrian empire was the dominant power in the Middle East.

Assyrian society appears to have been extremely militaristic. Even its art was concerned mostly with war. Royal palaces were adorned with carved reliefs showing scenes of battle and defeated enemies being executed, tortured, or taken into slavery. For a time Assyria even ruled Egypt, but it had dangerously overextended its power. Rebellions broke out and after the death of the tyrant Ashurbanipal (669–627 BC), the empire was seized by the Babylonians.

THE END OF BABYLON

Nebuchadnezzar II (r.604–562) was the most famous of the last kings of Babylon. He put down rebellions throughout the empire and dealt ruthlessly with his enemies: he was responsible for deporting the Jews to Babylon (see page 32). But he spent lavishly on wars and on rebuilding Babylon in imperial style (the Hanging Gardens of Babylon date from this time), and left the empire divided and impoverished.

In 539 BC Babylon fell easily to the armies of the Persian king Cyrus the Great (c.559–530). From his kingdom on the Persian Gulf, Cyrus had already conquered the vast kingdom of the Medes to the north and overrun Anatolia. He now ruled an empire stretching from the Mediterranean to Central Asia, the largest the world had yet seen. After centuries of overcultivation, Mesopotamia's soil was losing its fertility. Its neighbors overtook it in wealth and population, and under foreign rule its civilization gradually faded into oblivion.

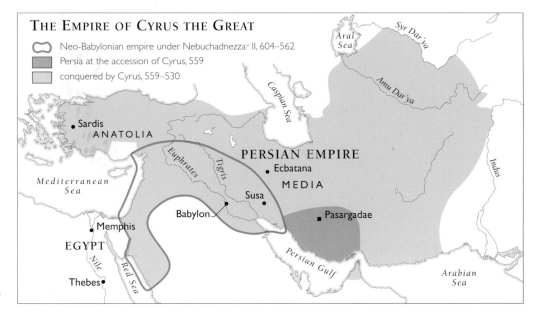

THE EMPIRE OF CYRUS THE GREAT

- Neo-Babylonian empire under Nebuchadnezzar II, 604–562
- Persia at the accession of Cyrus, 559
- conquered by Cyrus, 559–530

ANCIENT EGYPT

THE CIVILIZATION OF ANCIENT EGYPT DEPENDED COMPLETELY ON THE RIVER NILE. PREDICTABLE ANNUAL FLOODS BROUGHT THE ASSURANCE OF RICH HARVESTS YEAR AFTER YEAR, AND THE RIVER WAS THE KINGDOM'S MAIN HIGHWAY FROM NORTH TO SOUTH. TO WEST AND EAST THE DESERT PROTECTED EGYPT FROM INVASION AND WAS THE SOURCE OF BUILDING STONE AND PRECIOUS METALS. EGYPTIAN ART AND SCULPTURE VARIED LITTLE IN STYLE FOR MORE THAN 3,000 YEARS, REFLECTING THE COUNTRY'S POLITICAL AND CULTURAL STABILITY UNDER THE RULE OF THE PHARAOHS.

textiles, olive oil,
wine, pottery, timber
from Crete and Greece

to Cyrenaica

The valley of the Nile is 500 miles (800 kilometers) long, measured from the First Cataract, the rapids that marked Ancient Egypt's southern border, to the Mediterranean Sea. Until it broadens out into the delta, the valley is never more than a few miles wide. Sometimes it narrows to as little as a few hundred yards. On either side is desert. But despite the lack of rain, the Nile valley was one of the most favorable places for farming in the ancient world.

The river Nile rises far to the south of Egypt, in the East African highlands. Heavy rains falling here in early summer swell the river, and late in the summer the Egyptian Nile overflows its banks. When the floods retreat in the fall they leave the fields moist and covered with fresh silt. The Egyptians did not need to build flood defenses, or complex canals to irrigate their fields. They planted their seeds each autumn in the damp fertile soil left by the floods, and the crops grew through the warm Egyptian winter and were ready for harvesting in the spring, before the next flood. Only if the Nile failed to flood, as sometimes happened, did the people of Egypt go hungry.

EARLY CIVILIZATION

Farming began in the Nile valley after 6000 BC. The climate of North Africa was wetter then than it is today, and farming was even possible in the Sahara, then an area of grassland dotted with large lakes. Around 4000 BC, however, the climate became much drier and the Sahara turned to desert. Some farmers became nomadic herders, while others migrated into the Nile valley, which was soon densely populated.

A little while before 3000 BC a kingdom emerged in southern, or Upper, Egypt. The ancient Egyptian system of writing, using a form of pictographs known as hieroglyphs (see page 18), had come into use by this time. Traditionally the first king of Egypt is Narmer, who is said to have won a victory over Lower Egypt, uniting the two halves of the country. He established a royal capital at Memphis, strategically placed between the two. In the reigns of the kings that came after him, Egypt developed a strong system of government. The power of the king derived from the belief that he was the son of the sun god Ra and thought to be immortal.

From surviving records, historians have been able to compile detailed lists of the dynasties of kings who ruled Egypt, with approximate dates of their reigns. These stretch from 2920 to 30 BC, with only a few gaps. Historians divide the history of Egypt into distinct periods. The Early Dynastic period (2920–2649 BC) was followed by the Old Kingdom (2649–2134 BC), when the power of the monarchy increased and Egyptian influence extended southward up the Nile into the region then known as Nubia. Then came a troubled period when Egypt was divided between rival dynasties, (the First Intermediate Period, 2134–2040 BC). It was unified once again during the Middle Kingdom (2040–c.1640 BC).

THE PYRAMID BUILDERS

The most famous monuments of ancient Egypt, the pyramids, were built by the rulers of the Old and Middle Kingdoms as magnificent royal tombs. Their flared shape represented the downward slanting rays of the sun, along which the deceased king would ascend to heaven. These massive stone structures took many years to build and were completed before a king's death. When he died, his body was mummified: natural chemicals were used to preserve it artificially, and it was wrapped in bandages. Amulets (charms) were inserted between each layer of wrapping, and the mummy was placed inside one or more coffins. This

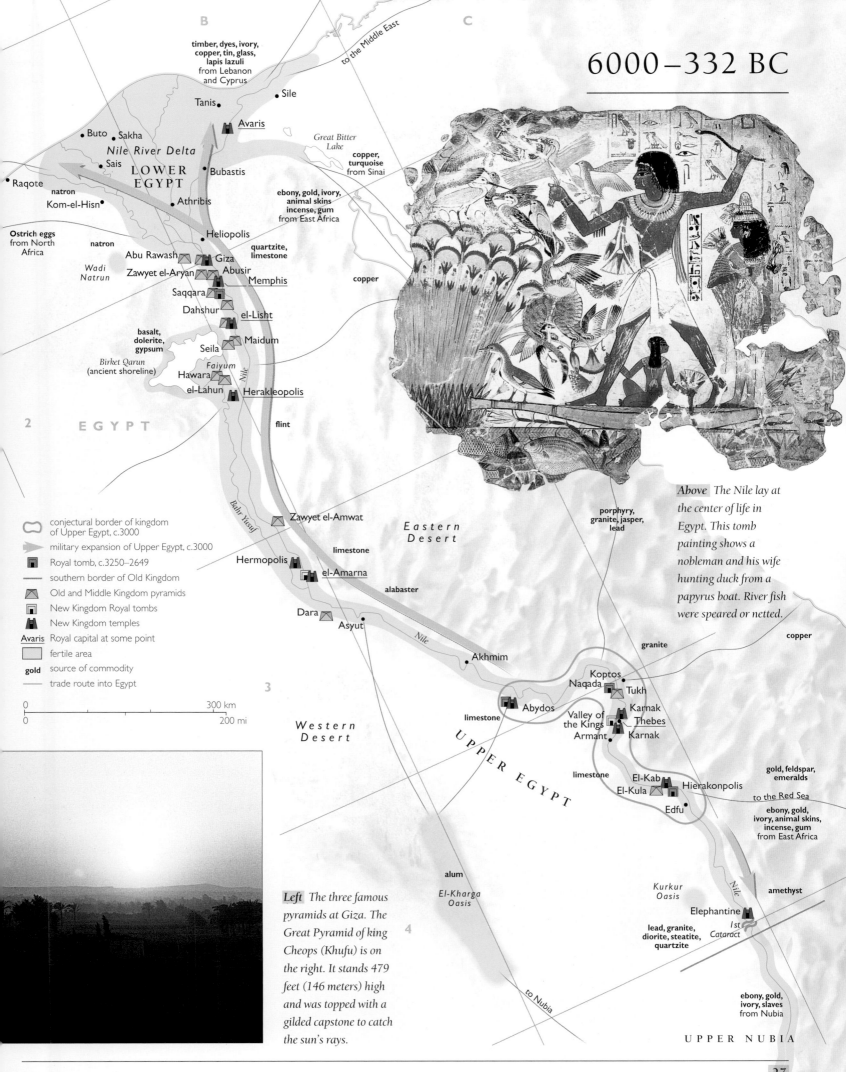

6000–332 BC

timber, dyes, ivory,
copper, tin, glass,
lapis lazuli
from Lebanon
and Cyprus

Sile

Tanis

Avaris

Buto • Sakha

• Raqote

Nile River Delta

Sais

**LOWER
EGYPT**

Kom-el-Hisn

natron

Athribis

Bubastis

*Great Bitter
Lake*

copper,
turquoise
from Sinai

ebony, gold, ivory,
animal skins
incense, gum
from East Africa

Heliopolis

copper

Ostrich eggs
from North
Africa

natron

quartzite,
limestone

Abu Rawash

Giza

*Wadi
Natrun*

Zawyet el-Aryan

Abusir

Memphis

Saqqara

Dahshur

el-Lisht

basalt,
dolerite,
gypsum

Seila

Maidum

*Birket Qarun
(ancient shoreline)*

Faiyum

Hawara

Nile

el-Lahun

Herakleopolis

flint

E G Y P T

2

Legend

- conjectural border of kingdom of Upper Egypt, c.3000
- military expansion of Upper Egypt, c.3000
- Royal tomb, c.3250–2649
- southern border of Old Kingdom
- Old and Middle Kingdom pyramids
- New Kingdom Royal tombs
- New Kingdom temples
- <u>Avaris</u> Royal capital at some point
- fertile area
- **gold** source of commodity
- trade route into Egypt

0 — 300 km
0 — 200 mi

3

Zawyet el-Amwat

*Eastern
Desert*

porphyry,
granite, jasper,
lead

limestone

Hermopolis

el-Amarna

alabaster

Dara

Asyut

Nile

Above *The Nile lay at
the center of life in
Egypt. This tomb
painting shows a
nobleman and his wife
hunting duck from a
papyrus boat. River fish
were speared or netted.*

copper

Akhmim

granite

Koptos

Naqada

Tukh

*Western
Desert*

limestone

Abydos

Valley of
the Kings

Karnak

Thebes

Karnak

Armant

U P P E R   E G Y P T

limestone

El-Kab

El-Kula

Hierakonpolis

gold, feldspar,
emeralds

to the Red Sea

Edfu

ebony, gold,
ivory, animal skins,
incense, gum
from East Africa

4

alum

*El-Kharga
Oasis*

*Kurkur
Oasis*

amethyst

Nile

Left *The three famous
pyramids at Giza. The
Great Pyramid of king
Cheops (Khufu) is on
the right. It stands 479
feet (146 meters) high
and was topped with a
gilded capstone to catch
the sun's rays.*

Elephantine

*1st
Cataract*

lead, granite,
diorite, steatite,
quartzite

to Nubia

ebony, gold,
ivory, slaves
from Nubia

U P P E R   N U B I A

to the Middle East

B

C

ensured that the king's body continued as a home for his soul. It was solemnly interred in the burial chamber, right at the center of the pyramid. The walls were inscribed with sacred texts and spells, and the chamber was furnished with luxurious possessions for the king to use in the afterlife. After the king's funeral, the entrance passage to the chamber was sealed with stones to protect it from robbers.

Contrary to popular belief, the pyramids were not built by slaves but by skilled craftsmen, helped by peasant farmers during the flood season, when no work could be done in the fields. No one knows exactly how the thousands of heavy stone blocks used to construct the pyramids were lifted into place. Pyramids were very expensive, and none were built after the end of the Middle Kingdom. Later Egyptian kings preferred to show off their wealth and power by building temples, which they endowed with monumental sculptures and carvings.

DEATH & THE AFTERLIFE

The Egyptians called their version of paradise "the field of reeds," a place just like the Nile valley where all the good things of life grew in abundance. Entry to this world was controlled by Osiris, the god of crops and annual rebirth. He was also the judge of souls—only those who had lived good lives could enter the afterlife. The journey to the underworld was a hazardous one. Spells were performed to make sure the deceased would pass safely through its trials. Funeral rites were highly elaborate—by the time of the New Kingdom, the procedure for embalming the body took 70 days. The most important ritual was "opening the mouth," when priests returned the soul to the mummy by touching it with sacred instruments and rubbing its face with milk.

Men of wealth and substance began to build their tombs as soon as they reached maturity. The chambered tomb would be their eternal home in the afterlife, so they furnished it lavishly with food, drink, rich furniture, jewelry, and all the other luxuries they would need. Provision was made for their wives as well. The walls were decorated with scenes of everyday life such as harvesting crops, hunting by the Nile, feasting, and making offerings to the gods. These would magically come alive after death. Models of their cattle and other possessions were placed in the tomb, together with small magical dolls, known as "shabti," who would act as servants and do manual work.

Right *Priests open the mouth of a mummy.*

INVASION & REVIVAL

Around 1640 BC the Middle Kingdom collapsed and was followed by a period of division known as the Second Intermediate Period (1640–1532 BC). Lower Egypt was conquered by the Hyksos, invaders who probably came from the area of Palestine. At this time Egypt was less developed than its Middle Eastern neighbors. The Hyksos introduced tools and weapons made of bronze, horses, wheeled vehicles (including war chariots), and other innovations. By the time the Hyksos were expelled, at the start of the New Kingdom (1532–1070 BC), Egypt had caught up.

There followed a period of prosperity and expansion when ancient Egypt reached the peak of its power. The New Kingdom rulers were empire builders who extended their authority across the Sinai desert into the Middle East and southward down the Nile far into Nubia, a source of slaves and gold. They exchanged diplomatic letters with their fellow rulers in Mesopotamia, and exercised power over small local states in Palestine. They made Thebes their capital and were buried in underground tombs in an isolated valley on the west side of the

Left *The New Kingdom pharaohs had huge statues made of themselves, carved from granite.*

c.6000
Farming begins in the Nile valley

c.3300–3100
The first towns develop. The hieroglyphic script is invented

c.3000
Upper and Lower Egypt are united into a single kingdom

c.2630
The first pyramid is built for king Djoser at Saqqara

2649–2134 OLD KINGDOM

2575–2465
During the 4th Dynasty, royal power increases dramatically

2134–2040
First Intermediate Period
Egypt is divided into two kingdoms

2040–1640 MIDDLE KINGDOM

2040
Mentuhotpe II reunites Egypt

1640–1532
Second Intermediate Period
The Hyksos occupy Lower Egypt

1532–1070 NEW KINGDOM

1504–1492
The Egyptian empire is at its fullest extent under Tuthmosis I

1285
Ramses II claims a victory at Qadesh against the Hittites but loses the war

1070–712
Third Intermediate Period
Egyptian power is in decline

924
Shoshenq I invades Israel and Judah

c.828–712
Egypt is divided into five kingdoms

712–332 LATE PERIOD

712
Egypt is ruled by Nubian kings

671
The Assyrians conquer Egypt

525
The Persians conquer Egypt

332
Egypt falls to Alexander the Great

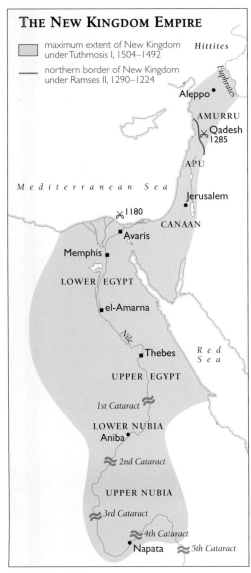

THE NEW KINGDOM EMPIRE

▢ maximum extent of New Kingdom under Tuthmosis I, 1504–1492   *Hittites*

— northern border of New Kingdom under Ramses II, 1290–1224

Euphrates

Aleppo •

AMURRU

✕ Qadesh
1285

APU

Mediterranean Sea

Jerusalem •

✕ 1180

CANAAN

■ Avaris

Memphis ■

LOWER EGYPT

■ el-Amarna

Nile

■ Thebes   *Red Sea*

UPPER EGYPT

1st Cataract ≈

LOWER NUBIA
Aniba •

≈ *2nd Cataract*

UPPER NUBIA

≈ *3rd Cataract*

≈ *4th Cataract*
Napata •   ≈ *5th Cataract*

Nile, known as the Valley of the Kings. They began to call themselves "pharaohs." The title, meaning "Great Palace," symbolized their place at the center of government.

The New Kingdom reached its fullest extent under Tuthmosis I (1504–1492 BC), who took Egyptian power as far as the river Euphrates in Syria. These possessions were later lost, though Ramses II (1290–1224 BC) attempted to restore them. His lack of success did not deter him from building numerous temples and erecting huge statues of himself. The boy-king Tutankhamen (1333–1323 BC) exercised little power during his lifetime but is famous for the rich treasures discovered in his tomb in the Valley of the Kings, excavated in the 1920s.

THE DECLINE OF EGYPT

Though an Egyptian navy succeeded in driving off an attempted invasion by the Sea Peoples in 1180 BC (see page 41), Egyptian power collapsed at the end of the New Kingdom. Some pharaohs even had trouble in paying for their tombs. There was a temporary revival of power under Shoshenq I (945–924 BC) but not enough to stave off Egypt's eventual defeat. It was conquered in turn by Nubians, Assyrians, and Persians before falling to the army of Alexander the Great in 332 BC (see page 46).

LANDS OF THE BIBLE

THE ISRAELITES, THE ANCESTORS OF THE JEWISH PEOPLE, PROBABLY
SETTLED IN CANAAN, THE AREA OF THE MIDDLE EAST THAT FORMS THE
LANDS OF THE BIBLE, IN THE 12TH CENTURY BC. THOUGH NOT AS POWER-
FUL AS MESOPOTAMIA AND EGYPT, THE ANCIENT KINGDOM OF ISRAEL HAD
LASTING IMPORTANCE IN WORLD HISTORY. UNLIKE THEIR NEIGHBORS, THE
ISRAELITES HAD ONLY ONE GOD, YAHWEH. THEIR RELIGION WAS TO HAVE
GREAT INFLUENCE ON BOTH
CHRISTIANITY AND ISLAM.

The history and founding myths of the Jewish people are recorded in the Bible. This places their origins in Mesopotamia and describes their early wanderings through the Fertile Crescent. According to the Bible narrative, the Israelites, as they are called at this period, endured a long period of captivity in Egypt but were led from there by Moses through the Sinai desert and into the "promised land" of Canaan. Under their war leader, Joshua, they conquered most of the native Canaanite peoples. One famous story recounts that the walls of Jericho tumbled to the ground when Joshua ordered his men to blow their trumpets.

The Israelites settled in tribal units, ruled by chieftains called "judges." They were opposed by the Philistines, a warlike people who lived near Gaza in the southern coastal plain, and decided to resist them by coming together under one leader. They chose Saul (c.1020–1006 BC) as their king. Saul's successor David (1006–965 BC) defeated the Philistines and other neighboring states such as Moab and Edom. These became vassal, or subject, states of Israel. The last Canaanite stronghold to be captured was Jerusalem, which became David's capital.

We cannot be certain how accurate the Biblical account is, but there is supporting archeological evidence for the story of the conquest of Canaan and the foundation of Saul's kingdom. David's military successes may have owed something to the fact that Egypt and Mesopotamia had problems of their own at this time and were unable to stop him.

David was succeeded as king by his son Solomon (965–928 BC). Solomon's reign was peaceful and he was able to concentrate on lavish building projects. The most important was a temple in Jerusalem to house the sacred Ark of the Covenant—the holy laws given to Moses on Mount Sinai by Yahweh. But the cost of Solomon's buildings was enormous and this made him unpopular with his people, many of whom were forced against their will to work on their construction. He was blamed for giving land to the Phoenician city of Tyre, to the north of Israel, in exchange for craftsmen and building supplies. He was also said to participate in the worship of other gods as well as Yahweh.

Above *Images of calfs and bulls like this one from Phoenicia were widely worshiped in the Middle East. The Israelites in the desert made a golden calf but were punished for it.*

Below *The valley of Jezreel was a major route from north to east and the scene of many battles. In the dry season it was ideal terrain for the deployment of war chariots.*

DISUNITY & DIVISION

After Solomon's death the northern tribes of Israel complained about their treatment to his successor Rehoboam (928–911 BC). When he refused to listen, a rebellion broke

Aleppo

Euphrates

Ugarit

Syrian   Desert

ASSYRIA

Hamath

Orontes

ARAM

Arvad

SYRIA

*Mediterranean
Sea*

Tadmor
(Palmyra)

Cyprus

LEVANT

Byblos

LEBANON

ARAM-ZOBAH

Sidon

Damascus

Tyre

PHOENICIA

Dan

ARAM-DAMASCUS

Hazor

Acco

*Sea of Galilee
(Sea of Chinnereth)*

Megiddo

Beth-shean

Jordan

Samaria

Joppa

KINGDOM OF
ISRAEL

AMMON

Baalath

Beth-horon

Gezer

Jericho

Rabbah

Jerusalem

Gaza

Hebron

MOAB
independent of
Israel, 843 BC

Dead Sea

ISRAEL

KINGDOM
OF JUDAH

Tamar

JORDAN

PHILISTIA

anis

Succoth

EGYPT

EGYPT

EDOM
independent of
Judah, 843 BC

Ezion-geber

SINAI

*Red
Sea*

*Red
Sea*

Mt Sinai

Legend

→ probable route taken by Hebrews from Egypt into Canaan
▨ probable extent of kingdom of Saul, c.1006
▨ Canaanite enclaves conquered by David
◻ border of kingdom of David and Solomon, 1006–928
⬙ major building project by Solomon
▦ greatest extent of kingdom of Israel
▢ greatest extent of kingdom of Judah
— border of kingdoms of Israel and Judah in 843
▨ kingdom of Egypt, 924
▨ Assyrian empire, 722

campaigns in Israel and Judah
→ Pharaoh Shoshenq I, 924
→ Sennacherib (king of Assyria), 701

0 _____ 150 km
0 _____ 100 mi

THE DEAD SEA SCROLLS

*T*he discovery of the Dead Sea Scrolls in
1947 was one of the most remarkable
archeological events of all time. A young
goatherd looking for a lost animal on a
mountainside at Qumrun near the Dead
Sea stumbled upon a cave full of pottery
jars. These turned out to contain a quan-
tity of ancient scrolls, wrapped in linen.
Among them was the earliest known copy
of the Book of Isaiah. The scrolls had been
hidden in the cave by members of an aus-
tere Jewish sect around AD 68, probably
to save them from destruction by the
Romans. Scholars previously knew nothing of this sect, but study of the scrolls
revealed that its members had deliberately
isolated themselves in the desert at some
time in the previous century to avoid persecution; there they waited for God to
destroy their enemies. The scrolls are
important as religious texts and for the
light they throw on the Jewish world just
before and during the time of Christ.

Above *One of the hidden scrolls. The dry air of
the cave preserved it for more than 2,000 years.*

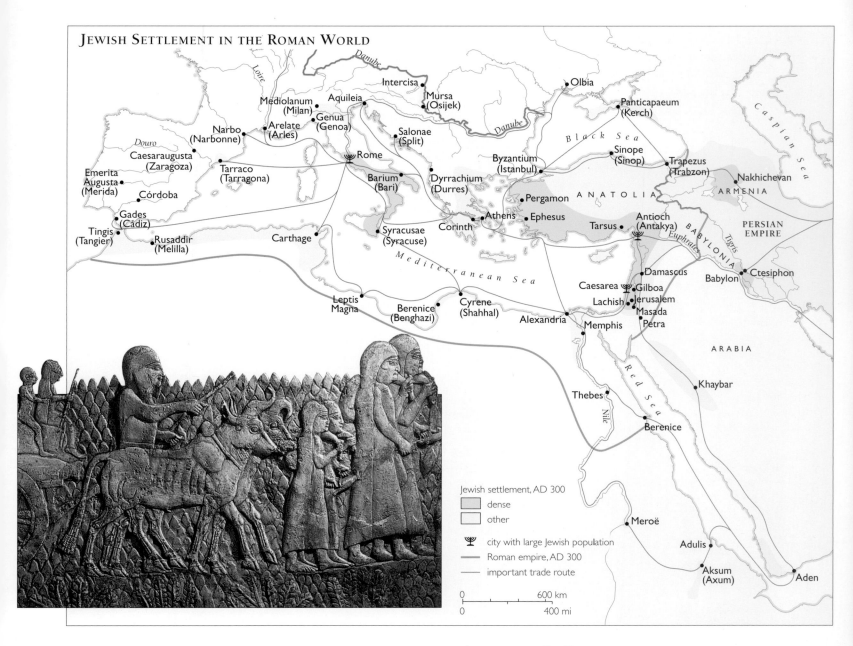

Jewish settlement, AD 300

☐ dense

☐ other

♆ city with large Jewish population

— Roman empire, AD 300

— important trade route

0   600 km

0   400 mi

Above *The first recorded deportation of Jews from their homeland took place at the hands of the Assyrian king Sennacherib who invaded Judah in 701 BC. This carved relief from the Assyrian palace of Nineveh shows Jews being marched out of the city of Lachish.*

out. As a result, the kingdom split into two parts—Israel in the north and Judah in the south, each ruled by its own king.

It was a dangerous time for the Israelites to have fallen out. The pharaoh Shoshenq had brought about a temporary revival in the declining fortunes of Egypt (see page 29). In 924 BC he invaded Judah and Israel and destroyed many cities, compelling the Israelites to pay tribute. However, they continued to quarrel with each other. The vassal states of Moab and Edom seized the opportunity to rebel successfully against their rule. The Bible also tells us that the kingdoms were further weakened by religious disputes. For example, king Ahab of Israel (873–852 BC) is said to have tried to introduce the worship of Baal, a Phoenician god. Religious leaders, known as prophets, such as Elijah and Elisha, warned against the dangers of heresy and internal division.

ASSYRIA & BABYLON

During the 9th and 8th centuries BC the main threat to the Israelite kingdoms came from Assyria, now the strongest power in the Middle East. Israel and Judah were both forced to become vassal states. Rebellions occasionally took place, but were fiercely put down, and large numbers of captives deported to Assyria.

Assyrian power collapsed in 612 BC and was immediately followed by Babylonian rule (see page 25). In 597 BC a rebellion in Judah was ruthlessly put down by the Babylonian king Nebuchadnezzar II. Jerusalem was sacked, the temple of Solomon destroyed, and its treasures plundered. Thousands of Jews (as the Israelites were now known) were deported to Babylon.

During their years of exile, the Jews were comforted and supported by their religion.

Right *The fortress of Masada, built at the tip of a steep outcrop of rock, was the site of a heroic last stand of Jewish rebels against Roman rule. When the Romans stormed the fortress after a three-year siege, the last handful of defenders killed themselves rather than surrender.*

It helped them to maintain their identity as a people while living in a foreign land. It was at this time that most of the books of the Old Testament of the Bible were written down in their present form.

THE JEWISH DIASPORA

King Cyrus of Persia destroyed the Babylonian empire in 539 BC and allowed the Jews to return home (see page 25), though many chose to stay in Babylon. The Jewish kingdoms were ruled first by Persia, then by Alexander the Great and his successors (see page 46). A Jewish rebellion against imposed Greek customs led to the creation of the independent kingdom of Judea in 142 BC, but this was short-lived. In 63 BC it became part of the Roman empire.

By now the Jews were divided into many different sects. The teachings of one Jewish leader, Jesus Christ (c.6 BC–AD 30), gave rise to a new religion, Christianity. Other Jewish sects such as the Zealots stirred up violent rebellions against Roman rule, but these were always severely dealt with. The Zealots were finally defeated with the fall of the fortress of Masada in AD 73. After this uprising the Romans destroyed the temple in Jerusalem and carried its treasures in triumph through Rome.

After each defeat more Jews were forced into exile. By AD 300 few Jews were left in their homeland, but were scattered across the Middle East and all around the Mediterranean Sea. They settled along important trade routes and in busy trading ports.

The spread of Jews around the world is known as the Diaspora. It continued until modern times because Jews were frequently forced to flee persecution in the countries where they had settled, often at the hands of Christians who accused them of murdering Christ. The Jews remained without an independent homeland until the foundation of the state of Israel in 1948.

TIMETABLE

c.1290–1100
The Israelites flee from Egypt and settle in Canaan

c.1020
Saul becomes the first king of Israel

c.1006
Saul is killed fighting against the Philistines at Gilboa

c.1000
David (r.c.1006–965) captures Jerusalem

c.950
Solomon (r.965–928) builds the temple of Jerusalem

c.928
Kingdom separates into Israel and Judah

c.850
The prophets Elijah and Elisha warn against pagan influences

721
The Assyrians conquer Israel

701
The Assyrians conquer Judah

587
The Jews are deported to Babylon by Nebuchadnezzar

587–539
The key books of the Old Testament are written during the Babylonian exile

539
Babylon falls to Cyrus of Persia who allows the Jews to return home

332–1
The Bible Lands become part of the Greek world after Alexander the Great conquers the Middle East

142
The Jewish kingdom of Judea is founded

63
Judea comes under Roman rule

6 BC
Birth of Jesus Christ

AD 70–73
Thousand of Jews are enslaved and exiled after the Romans put down the Zealot uprising at Masada

PREHISTORIC EUROPE

MODERN HUMANS HAVE INHABITED EUROPE FOR 40,000 YEARS. FOR MOST OF THIS TIME THEY LIVED BY HUNTING AND GATHERING. ABOUT 8,000 YEARS AGO, FARMING BEGAN IN SOUTHEASTERN EUROPE AND SPREAD ALMOST EVERYWHERE DURING THE NEXT 3,000 YEARS. THE INTRODUCTION OF METAL-WORKING LED TO THE DEVELOPMENT OF MORE COMPLEX WARRIOR SOCIETIES, AND TO THE EMERGENCE OF THE FIRST EUROPEAN CIVILIZATIONS.

When the first bands of modern humans moved into Europe from the Middle East 40,000 years ago, a large part of the northern continent, covered by vast ice sheets, was uninhabitable. They survived in areas of tundra and grassland by hunting herds of grazing animals such as reindeer. Where they could, they found shelter in caves, or else made themselves hide tents or huts of mammoth bones. About 10,000 years ago the European ice sheets began to retreat and humans gradually spread northward. Europe was now covered in dense forests, which made hunting more difficult. People came to depend more on plant foods, fish, and small mammals.

Farming entered southern Europe about 8,500 years ago. Groups of people living in Greece and the Balkans began to grow cereals and beans, and to raise sheep, goats, and cattle. Some crops, for example emmer wheat and barley, were almost certainly introduced to southern Europe from the Middle East, but the cultivation of others may have developed independently.

During the next 3,500 years farming spread gradually into the rest of Europe, first into southern France and Spain, and then northward to reach the British Isles and Scandinavia by about 4000 BC. In the extreme north of Europe reindeer herding did not replace the hunting and gathering way of life until well into the Christian era.

EARLY FARMERS

Early farming communities were generally small, consisting of between 40 and 60 people. Houses were usually wooden structures, so have left few material remains. In many parts of western Europe, however, the first farmers built tunnel-like tombs of large stones, known as megaliths, which they

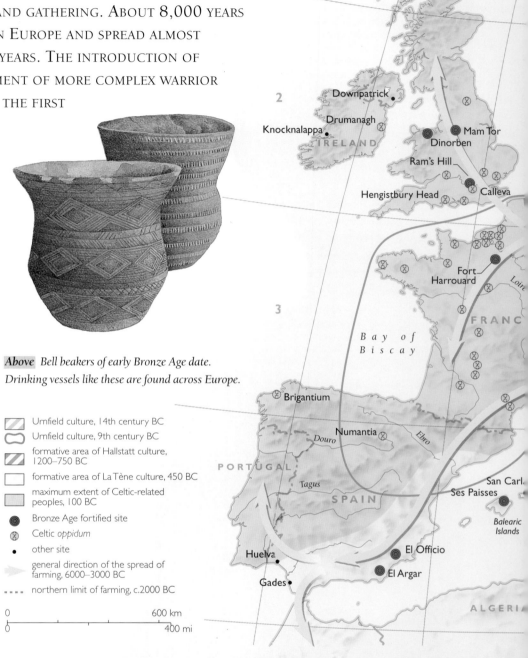

Above *Bell beakers of early Bronze Age date. Drinking vessels like these are found across Europe.*

Urnfield culture, 14th century BC
Urnfield culture, 9th century BC
formative area of Hallstatt culture, 1200–750 BC
formative area of La Tène culture, 450 BC
maximum extent of Celtic-related peoples, 100 BC
Bronze Age fortified site
Celtic *oppidum*
other site
general direction of the spread of farming, 6000–3000 BC
northern limit of farming, c.2000 BC

0   600 km
0   400 mi

THE DISCOVERY OF THE ICE MAN

When, in 1991, a party of hikers in the Ötztaler Alps came upon a body of a man emerging from a glacier, they supposed it to be that of a mountaineer who had died in a fall. But laboratory testing showed the well-preserved frozen body to be far older. He soon gained the popular name of the Ice Man. Radiocarbon dating confirmed that he had lived around 3350–3300 BC.

Right The 5,000-year-old frozen body.

The Ice Man was probably a shepherd or hunter. His ribs had been recently broken, and he may have died of cold and soon after been buried in snow. He appears to have been wearing furs and a cape made of woven reeds, and was carrying many items, including a longbow, 14 arrows, a flint knife, and a small copper ax. Before this exciting discovery, archeologists had not believed metal to be in use in this part of Europe for another several hundred years.

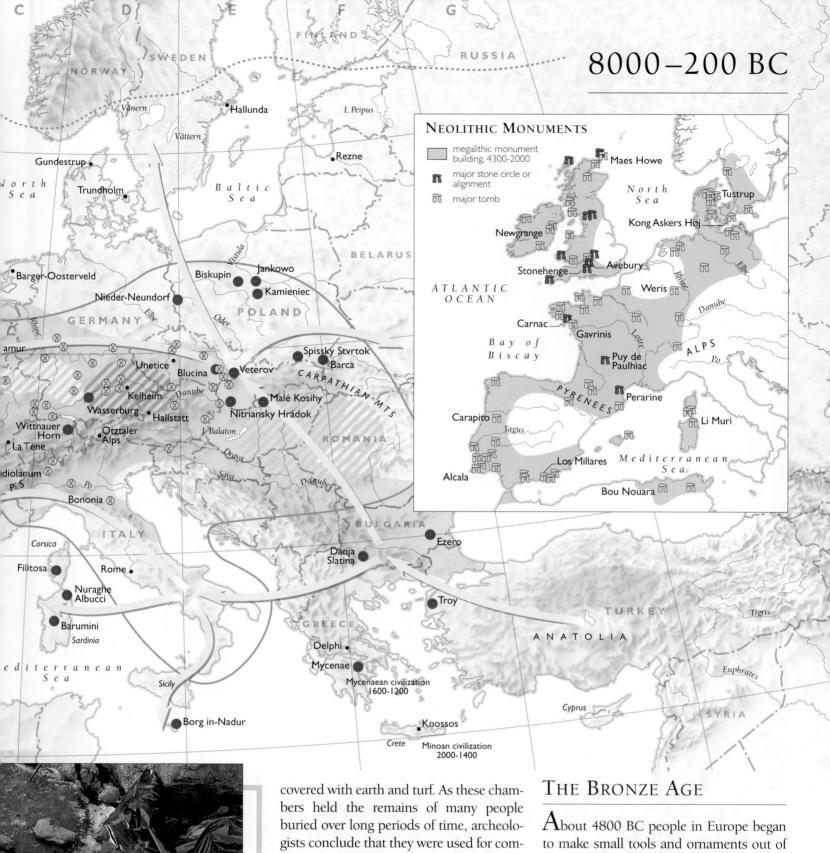

NEOLITHIC MONUMENTS

megalithic monument building, 4300–2000

major stone circle or alignment

major tomb

Map labels: Maes Howe · Tustrup · Kong Askers Hoj · Newgrange · Avebury · Stonehenge · Weris · Carnac · Gavrinis · Puy de Paulhiac · Perarine · Li Muri · Carapito · Los Millares · Alcala · Bou Nouara

Region labels: North Sea · ATLANTIC OCEAN · Bay of Biscay · ALPS · PYRENEES · Mediterranean Sea · Rhine · Loire · Danube · Elbe · Po · Tagus

Main map labels: NORWAY · SWEDEN · FINLAND · RUSSIA · Hallunda · L. Peipus · Rezne · Vänern · Vättern · Gundestrup · North Sea · Trundholm · Baltic Sea · BELARUS · Barger-Oosterveld · Biskupin · Jankowo · Kamieniec · Nieder-Neundorf · GERMANY · POLAND · Vistula · Oder · Elbe · Rhine · Spissky Stvrtok · Barca · amur · Unetice · Blucina · Veterov · CARPATHIAN MTS · Kelheim · Danube · Malé Kosihy · Wasserburg · Hallstatt · Nitriansky Hrádok · Wittnauer Horn · Otztaler Alps · L. Balaton · ROMANIA · La Tène · Drava · P S · diolanum · Sava · Danube · Po · Bononia · ITALY · BULGARIA · Ezero · Corsica · Danja Slatina · Filitosa · Rome · Troy · TURKEY · Tigris · Nuraghe Albucci · GREECE · ANATOLIA · Barumini · Sardinia · Delphi · Mediterranean Sea · Mycenae · Euphrates · Sicily · Mycenaean civilization 1600–1200 · Cyprus · SYRIA · Borg in-Nadur · Knossos · Crete · Minoan civilization 2000–1400

covered with earth and turf. As these chambers held the remains of many people buried over long periods of time, archeologists conclude that they were used for communal burials, and that there were few differences in wealth or status. Later people living in some parts of northwestern Europe began to build large stone circles and alignments known as henges (see insert map above). Their purpose is unclear, though it is probable that they had a ritual and astronomical function. Only a powerful chief would have had the resources to organize the building of an enormous structure like Stonehenge (see pages 20–21).

THE BRONZE AGE

About 4800 BC people in Europe began to make small tools and ornaments out of copper and gold. Once again, this development started in the Balkans. Metal-working also appears to have emerged independently in southern Spain about 1,500 years later.

Early metal objects were valued for their appearance, but were of little practical use as they were very soft. The next stage was to mix small amounts of arsenic or tin with copper. This produced a hard alloy called bronze, which could be used to fashion hard-edged cutting tools. Bronze-working is

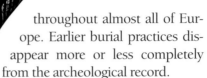

believed to have spread to southeast Europe from the Middle East around 2300 BC. As a result, metal tools began to replace stone ones in everyday use.

Craftsmen working in bronze and gold were highly skilled at making fine weapons, vessels for eating and drinking, and jewelry for personal adornment. The metal ores needed to manufacture bronze are found in only a few areas, so exchange became more important. Powerful warrior-led chiefdoms were formed. The building of thousands of hillforts throughout Europe suggests that wars occurred frequently between rival chiefdoms in the Late Bronze Age.

The growth in exchange resulted in greater contact between different groups of people in Europe. Cultural ideas spread rapidly from community to community through the mountain passes and along the rivers of central and western Europe. For example, the earliest archeological evidence of the Urnfield Culture—the custom of cremating the bodies of the dead and burying their ashes in pottery urns in huge cemeteries called urnfields—is found in Hungary around 1350 BC. Over the next 400 years it spread

throughout almost all of Europe. Earlier burial practices disappear more or less completely from the archeological record.

Trade was responsible for the rise of the first European civilization, the Minoan, which emerged on the island of Crete in the eastern Mediterranean around 2000 BC (see page 38). Its influence extended to neighboring islands in the Aegean and as far as Egypt. A little later, the warlike Mycenaean civilization arose on the Greek mainland (see page 40). Both had vanished by 1200 BC.

IRON AGE EUROPE

The introduction of iron-working into Europe between 1000 and 750 BC brought far-reaching changes. Iron tools and weapons were harder, and cheaper to make, than bronze ones, and iron ore was much more common than copper and tin ores. The early Iron Age witnessed a revival of economic life in Greece and around the Aegean Sea. Partly through the influence of Greek and Phoenician merchants and settlers, civilizations also began to emerge in Italy and southern Spain. One of the most significant was that of the Etruscans, whose city states in northern Italy were well developed (see page 50).

Above This Celtic object is known as a torc. Made of silver, it was worn around the neck, probably to denote rank.

Left An Iron Age hilltop fort in Wales. Such forts were common in Bronze and Iron Age Europe. Some would have served as tribal capitals lived in by the chief and clan leaders, others as refuges for the farmers of the surrounding country in time of war.

Right A large Iron Age
cemetery was excavated
at Hallstatt, Austria, in
the 19th century. This
painting, made at
the time, shows
some of the
graves.

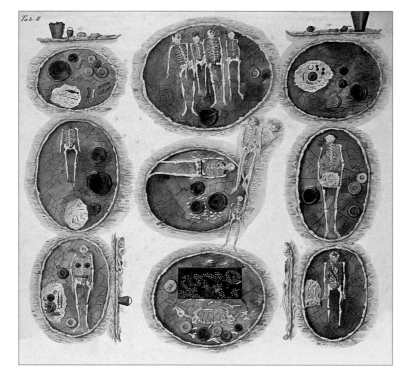

Dominating Central and western Europe were a group of peoples known as Celts to the ancient Greeks and as Gauls to the Romans. They originated in an area of the northern Alps and started expanding out of their heartland sometime after 700 BC. Objects decorated in the Hallstatt art-style (named after an Iron Age cemetery in Austria where it was first identified) have been found across western Europe and into Britain, giving evidence of widespread cultural exchange. Around 450 BC the La Tène art-style developed, which made use of lively animal motifs and intricate geometrical patterns.

From the 5th century BC onward warrior bands of Celts began to invade southern Europe, including Greece and Italy. Much of our information about the Celts comes from the works of Greek and Roman writers, who regarded them as barbarians. They describe them as being given to beer drinking, boasting, and collecting the severed heads of their enemies. Celtic chiefdoms were dominated by warrior elites. Some of their tribal centers, which the Romans referred to as *oppida*, were the size of small towns, with several thousand inhabitants.

Priests, known as druids, were important people in Celtic society. They had many gods, often associated with a particular site such as a sacred spring or tree. Weapons and precious objects were often thrown into bogs and rivers, probably as a form of sacrifice. Human sacrifices were also made.

THE END OF THE CELTS

The Celtic peoples were trapped between two expanding powers. Those living west of the river Rhine and south of the river Danube were overcome by the Romans as they expanded their empire into northern Europe between 225 BC and AD 79. At about the same time, groups of German-speaking people moved into the area east of the Rhine and north of the Danube, extinguishing the Celtic tribes living there. They remain unconquered only in Ireland and the far north of Britain.

Left A Celtic god from the Gundestrup cauldron, 2nd century BC, found in a bog in Denmark.

TIMETABLE

c.8000 BC
The Ice Age comes to an end

c.6500
The farming of cereals, cattle, and sheep begins in southeastern Europe

c.4500
Copper mining and smelting begin in the Balkans

c.3300
The Iceman is entombed in ice after dying on a hunting expedition. His body is discovered over 5,000 years later

c.4500
Farming spreads to areas of heavy soil with the introduction of the plow

c.4300
The first megalithic tombs are built in Brittany, northwest France

c.3500–2400
Europe's earliest stone temple is built at Tarxien, Malta

c.3000
Construction of Stonehenge begins. The major stone circle is completed c.2000

c.2300–1500
Bronze-working is established in Europe

c.2000
The Minoan palace civilization develops on Crete

c.2000
There is widespread European trade in amber and metals

c.1350–800
Spread of the Urnfield culture

c.750–450
The Hallstatt culture spreads through central and western Europe

c.700
Iron is now in widespread use throughout Europe

c.390
The Gauls (Celts) sack Rome

58–51
The Roman general Julius Caesar conquers the Celts of Gaul (France)

43 AD
The Roman conquest of Britain begins

THE MINOANS & MYCENAEANS

THE FIRST EUROPEAN CIVILIZATION, THE MINOAN, AROSE ON THE ISLAND OF CRETE IN THE AEGEAN SEA AROUND 2000 BC. ABOUT 400 YEARS LATER THE MYCENAEAN CIVILIZATION DEVELOPED ON THE NEARBY GREEK MAINLAND. THE MYCENAEANS CONQUERED THE MINOANS BUT WERE THEMSELVES OVERRUN BY INVADERS AROUND 1200 BC. MEMORIES OF BOTH BRONZE AGE CIVILIZATIONS WERE RETAINED IN LATER GREEK LEGENDS. ARCHEOLOGISTS HAVE SINCE DISCOVERED PHYSICAL EVIDENCE OF THEIR EXISTENCE.

Left A wall-painting of boxing boys. It was found in a Minoan house at Akrotiri more than 3,000 years after being buried under volcanic ash and lava. The Minoans appear to have enjoyed all kinds of athletic competition, including bull-leaping.

The Minoan civilization derives its name from Minos, a legendary king of Crete who was said by the later Greeks to have dominated the Aegean Sea with a great navy. Although Crete is a rocky, mountainous island with little fertile land, it owed its early success to farming. On patches of good land in the valleys wheat was grown to feed the island's inhabitants. Vines and olives, native to the region, grew abundantly on the rough hillsides, and the surplus wine and olive oil was traded overseas for valuable products, such as copper, not found in Crete. The Minoans kept flocks of sheep on the high mountain pastures and made the wool into fine cloth, which was exported to Egypt. They also made beautiful painted pottery that was sold abroad.

By 2000 BC Crete had become prosperous. Archeologists have excavated the sites of four great palaces at Knossos, Phaistos, Mallia, and Khania. Each of these palaces was probably the capital of a small kingdom. Vast storehouses in the palaces were filled with grain, jars of wine and oil, and other produce, paid by the farmers as taxes to the king. Food was distributed by palace officials to all those not involved in farming, such as craftworkers, scribes, and traders.

The Minoans were skillful sailors and their ships carried luxury goods all around the Mediterranean. They founded trading colonies on neighboring islands, and even had a trading post in Egypt. We do not know what language the Minoans spoke, but clay tablets found in the palaces are clearly marked with writing. They were probably lists of stores but no one has yet been able to decipher the script, which is known to scholars as Linear A.

FIRE & DESTRUCTION

Around 1700 BC all the palaces on Crete were destroyed by fire. They were later rebuilt, but only one of them—the palace of Knossos—regained its original splendor. A likely explanation is that a war broke out between the kingdoms for control of the island. Knossos was the winner and its king became sole ruler of Crete. The other palaces were reduced in rank, probably becoming local centers of government.

Not much later a still greater disaster occurred. In 1626 BC a massive volcanic eruption blew apart the nearby island of Thera. The Minoan city of Akrotiri on the island was completely buried in lava and ash. It was only found again when archeologists began to dig beneath the layers of ash in the 1960s. They discovered houses complete with well-preserved wall paintings. The scenes on them show that the Minoans were fascinated by the natural world, especially the sea. Similar paintings have been found at Knossos, including one depicting athletes leaping over a bull's horns. This may have been part of a religious ritual. We know that there was a dark side to Minoan civilization, as excavations at Knossos have shown that the Minoans sacrificed children to their gods.

The eruption caused severe damage to the palaces on Crete. This was later repaired

Left The palace at Knossos was discovered at the beginning of the 20th century by the British archeologist, Arthur Evans, who partially restored it. It was the largest of the Minoan palaces, with a maze of multi-storied buildings laid out around a central courtyard. The fine royal apartments were elaborately decorated.

MINOAN CRETE

	Minoan civilization, c.1600
	great Minoan palace
	lesser Minoan palace

YUGOSLAVIA

BULGARIA

FORMER YUGOSLAV
REPUBLIC OF
MACEDONIA

ALBANIA

Danube

Morava

Olt

Strymon

Aliakmon

Vardar

Pinios

Lake
Ohrid

Lake
Prespa

Vijose

Crete

Khania

Stavromeno · Tylissos · **Knossos** · Mallia

Monastiraki

Arkhanes · Pseira · Palaikastro

Hagia Triadha · Gortyn · Gournia · Kato Zakro

Phaistos · Myrtos · Hierapytna

Corfu

Cephalonia

Zante

PINDOS MOUNTAINS

GREECE

Iolcus

Orchomenus · Gla

Kastri · Thebes

Dyme

PELOPONNESE

Mycenae · Koraku

Argos · Dendra

Peristeria · Tiryns

Elliniko

Menelaion

Pylos

Sea Peoples

Thasos

Samothrace

Imbros

Lemnos

Troy

Northern
Sporades

Scyros

Euboea

Aegean Sea

Lesbos

Chios

Andros

Cea

Hagia Irni

Samos

Icaria

Miletus

Paros

Cos · Serraglia

Astipalaia

Jalysus

Sea Peoples

Phylakopi

Melos

Thera

Akrotiri

Cythera

Khania

Crete

Knossos

Rhodes

Carpathos

TURKEY

ARZAWA

Gediz

Menderes

to Cyprus, Egypt and
the Middle East

Athens

Mediterranean Sea

	Minoan influence, c.1600
	area affected by ash falls from the eruption of Thera, 1626
	Mycenaean civilization, c.1300
	Mycenaean town, with palace
Troy	fortified settlement
	site damaged or destroyed by "Sea Peoples", c.1200
	major migration, c.1200

0   200 km
0   150 mi

A   5   B   C   D   E

and Minoan civilization continued for a little while longer. It came to an end around 1450 BC when invaders conquered the island and took over the palace at Knossos.

THE MYCENAEANS

The new rulers of Crete copied the art of writing from the Minoans but used their own script (Linear B). Scholars have been able to decipher this script and found it to be an early form of Greek. From this, and from other evidence such as their burial customs, archeologists believe that the invaders were Mycenaeans, a people who migrated into the Greek mainland from the Balkans around 2000 BC. By 1600 BC they had established several fortified cities there. Their name is derived from Mycenae, one of these strongholds in southeast Greece.

Spectacular goods—ornaments of gold, silver, and electrum (a gold and silver alloy), jewelry, and bronze weapons—have been found in several deep graves at Mycenae. They date from between 1650 and 1550 BC and suggest that it was already ruled by kings: such valuable possessions would have accompanied royal burials. Archeologists judge the Mycenaeans to have been a wealthy and warlike people. Their main weapons were spears, swords, and daggers,

and they wore clumsy bronze armor and helmets covered with the teeth of wild boars. They rode to war on horse-drawn chariots, though they fought on foot.

Mycenae was only one—though perhaps the most important—of several small independent kingdoms in Greece. Like the Minoans, their rulers lived in palaces. They were smaller than those on Crete and were strongly defended with walls of huge stone blocks, so large

OVERSEAS TRADE

amber from the Baltic

gold, copper, tin

gold, copper, tin

copper, tin from western Mediterranean

gold

ANATOLIA

Sicily

copper, tin

glass, dye, lapis lazuli, ivory, resins

olive oil

Ulu Burun

Cape Gelidonya

copper

Mediterranean Sea

Crete

Cyprus

ostrich eggs

gold, alabaster, amethyst, ebony, jewelery, linen, ivory

☐ Mycenaean civilization, late 13th century

— Mycenaean trade route

tin source of commodity

🚢 shipwreck

that the Greeks of later times could not believe that ordinary humans had built them—a race of giants must have done so.

The Mycenaean rulers lived in great opulence. The king of Pylos kept 400 bronzesmiths and hundreds of female slaves to weave cloth. Like the Minoans, Mycenaean ships traded all round the eastern Mediterranean and as far west as Italy, Sicily, and Malta. Divers have discovered a ship that was wrecked off the Turkish coast in the 14th century BC. It probably belonged to a Mycenaean king and was found to have jewelry, copper, ivory, ebony, and even ostrich eggs from Africa on board.

THE LEGEND OF TROY

It is more than likely that the Mycenaeans raided as well as traded overseas. We know that they invaded and conquered Crete, and it is also possible that they attacked Troy. This was a powerful city on the coast of Turkey that controlled the entrance of ships into the Black Sea. The legendary story of the Trojan War is recounted by the ancient Greek poet, Homer, who tells of a Greek army, under the leadership of king Agamemnon of Mycenae, which attacked and destroyed Troy after a ten-year siege. Homer's tales of the war—the anger of Menelaus after his wife Helen had been stolen by Paris

and taken to Troy, the epic battle between Achilles and Hector outside the walls, the wooden horse built by the Greeks, and the adventures of Odysseus on his journey home—are still read and enjoyed today. Homer lived many hundreds of years after the events he described. However, archeologists have shown that Troy was attacked at least twice in Mycenaean times, and his epic poems may well have been based on folk memories of an actual incident.

THE SEA PEOPLES

During the 14th and 13th centuries BC Mycenaean civilization appears to have been exposed to increasing pressure from marauders from the north. Many strongholds, including Mycenae itself, strengthened their defenses at this time, and a wall was built across the narrow isthmus of Corinth. In about 1200 BC invaders known as the "Sea Peoples" destroyed all the major Mycenaean centers of power. Very little is known about these mysterious people who probably came from the northern Aegean. After attacking Greece, they sailed on to the Middle East and Egypt. Some of them settled in Canaan, where they were known as the Peleset, or Philistines (see page 30).

In Greece, the devastation caused by the Sea Peoples was so widespread that the Mycenaean way of life never recovered. Towns were abandoned and people even forgot how to write. For hundreds of years Greece remained in a "dark age," and very little is known about it.

(see page 30)

TIMETABLE

c.6000
The first settlement of Crete

c.2300
Bronze tools and weapons come into use in the Aegean region

c.2000
The first palaces are built on Crete and writing comes into use

c.1700
All the palaces on Crete are damaged. Knossos is rebuilt as the major palace

1626
A volcanic eruption on Thera disrupts life on Crete

c.1600
Rich burials show that a powerful royal dynasty rules at Mycenae

c.1450
The first Mycenaean palaces are built and writing comes into use

c.1450
Minoan Crete is conquered, probably by the Mycenaeans

c.1400
The Mycenaeans build defensive walls around their cities

c.1200
The Sea Peoples attack Mycenae and other strongholds in Greece

1200–800
Urban life declines and writing goes out of use in mainland Greece

THE DIVINE MOTHER

Mother goddess cults appear to have a long history in Greece and the neighboring islands of the Aegean, where enormous quantities of stone and pottery figurines of women have been found, dating back thousands of years. They vary in appearance—some are strikingly simple and geometric in form; others are more shapely with well defined figures. Very often they are nursing babies. We can only guess at their significance, but it is likely that their cult was connected to fertility, crops, and the land—crucially important matters for early farmers.

Several goddesses from later Greek mythology (for example, Ge, Hera, Rhea, Demeter, and Cybele) were associated with the divine mother or crop fertility, and are probably survivals of these earlier cults.

Female figures in Minoan and Mycenaean art often have their arms raised and breasts bared. Sometimes they hold snakes or other objects. They may represent goddesses or priestesses, and evidently had a ritual or sacred function.

__Right__ These figures, representing nursing mothers, are from Cyprus (left) and Mycenae.

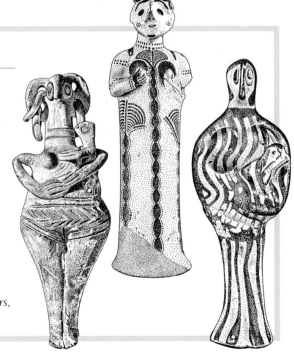

ANCIENT GREECE

THE CIVILIZATION OF ANCIENT GREECE WAS ONE OF THE MOST REMARKABLE IN HISTORY. GREEK ACHIEVEMENTS IN POLITICS, THE ARTS, LITERATURE, PHILOSOPHY, AND SCIENCE STILL HAVE INFLUENCE IN THE MODERN WORLD. YET WARFARE WAS CONSTANT BETWEEN GREECE'S RIVAL CITY STATES.

During the 9th century BC Greece began to recover from the dark age that followed the destruction of Mycenaean civilization. A new wave of invaders, the Dorians, had introduced the use of iron, and urban life revived. Towns developed into independent city-states, which were first ruled by kings. As the opportunities for trade grew, many of these city-states sent groups of citizens overseas to found trading colonies. These colonies helped solve the problem of over-population at home, caused by a shortage of suitable land for farming.

By 500 BC important Greek cities were established along the coast of Asia Minor (Anatolia), around the Black Sea, in Sicily and southern Italy, and as far as southern Spain. The only rivals to the Greeks were the Phoenicians. From their home ports on the coast of Lebanon and Syria they set up colonies in Sicily and Sardinia and along the North African and Spanish coasts.

Most of the Greek city-states had ceased to be monarchies by the 7th century BC and were ruled by hereditary clan-leaders, or aristocrats (the exceptions were Sparta and Argos). The aristocrats gradually came to be resented by other citizens, who wanted a say in how their city-states were governed. Revolutions broke out in many cities to overthrow the aristocrats. These were led by popular leaders, called tyrants, who won support by confiscating land from the aristocrats and giving it to the poor. Tyrants were often harsh rulers themselves, and they too were overthrown as citizens came to demand more power for themselves.

ATHENIAN DEMOCRACY

The city where the citizens won the largest share of power for themselves was Athens. At the end of the 6th century BC, political reforms gave rise to a new form of government, democracy ("rule of the people"). This enabled citizens to vote on all important decisions, such as whether to declare war or how to spend government money. They also elected government officials and generals, and could vote to exile anyone

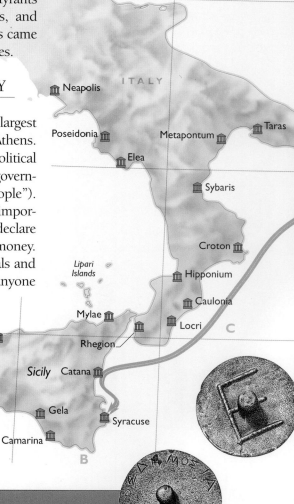

Above Counters were used for voting in the citizen assemblies.

Left The great temple of the Parthenon on the Acropolis in Athens. It was built in the 5th century BC, at the height of the city's power and prosperity.

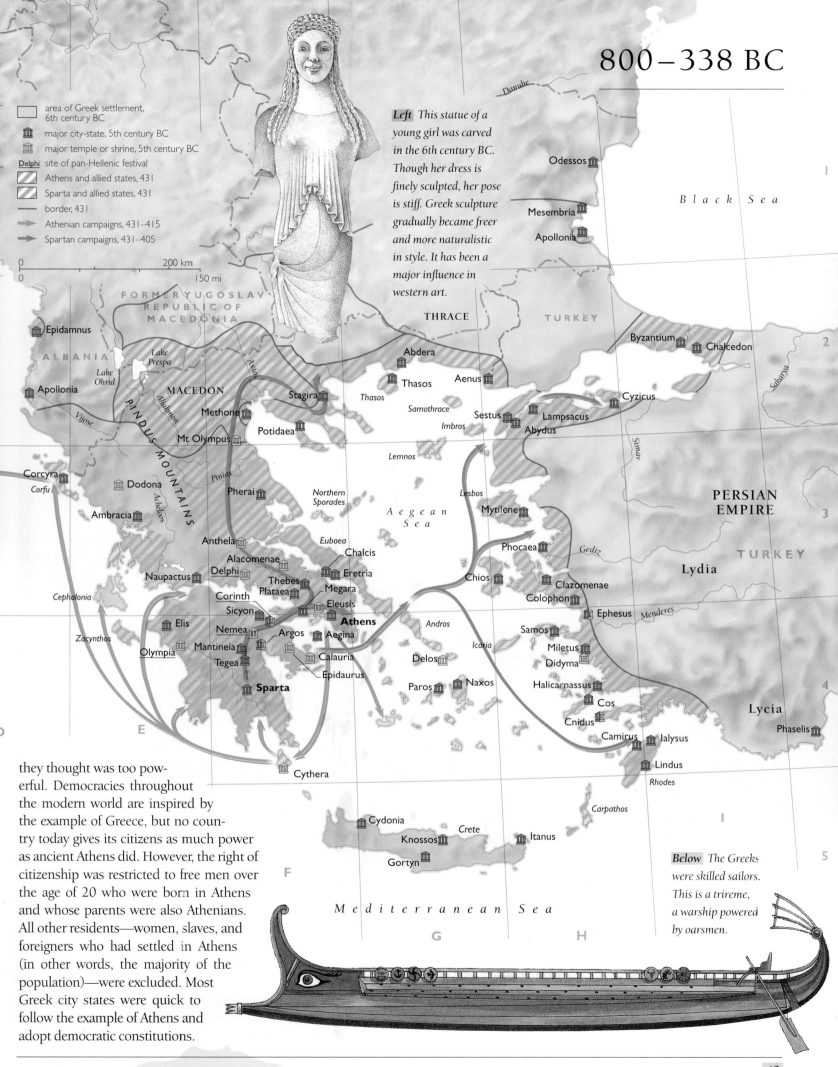

area of Greek settlement, 6th century BC

major city-state, 5th century BC

major temple or shrine, 5th century BC

Delphi site of pan-Hellenic festival

Athens and allied states, 431

Sparta and allied states, 431

border, 431

Athenian campaigns, 431–415

Spartan campaigns, 431–405

0   200 km
0   150 mi

Left This statue of a young girl was carved in the 6th century BC. Though her dress is finely sculpted, her pose is stiff. Greek sculpture gradually became freer and more naturalistic in style. It has been a major influence in western art.

Black Sea

Odessos

Mesembria

Apollonia

THRACE

TURKEY

FORMER YUGOSLAV REPUBLIC OF MACEDONIA

Epidamnus

ALBANIA

Lake Prespa

Lake Ohrid

Apollonia

MACEDON

Abdera

Aenus

Byzantium

Chalcedon

Cyzicus

Axios

Stagira

Thasos

Thasos

Samothrace

Sestus

Lampsacus

Methone

Aliakmon

Imbros

Abydus

Potidaea

PERSIAN
EMPIRE

Mt Olympus

Lemnos

Simav

Corcyra

Corfu

Pindos

Dodona

Pherai

Northern
Sporades

Lesbos

Mytilene

Phocaea

Gediz

TURKEY

Lydia

Ambracia

Achloos

*Aegean
Sea*

Euboea

Chalcis

Chios

Clazomenae

Colophon

Anthela

Alacomenae

Delphi

Thebes

Plataea

Eretria

Megara

Ephesus

Menderes

Naupactus

PINDUS MOUNTAINS

Cephalonia

Corinth

Sicyon

Eleusis

Athens

Samos

Miletus

Didyma

Elis

Nemea

Argos

Aegina

Andros

Zacynthos

Mantineia

Olympia

Tegea

Calauria

Epidaurus

Delos

Icaria

Paros

Naxos

Halicarnassus

Cos

Cnidus

Camirus

Ialysus

Lycia

Sparta

Phaselis

Lindus

Cythera

Rhodes

Carpathos

they thought was too powerful. Democracies throughout the modern world are inspired by the example of Greece, but no country today gives its citizens as much power as ancient Athens did. However, the right of citizenship was restricted to free men over the age of 20 who were born in Athens and whose parents were also Athenians. All other residents—women, slaves, and foreigners who had settled in Athens (in other words, the majority of the population)—were excluded. Most Greek city states were quick to follow the example of Athens and adopt democratic constitutions.

Cydonia

Crete

Knossos

Itanus

Gortyn

Mediterranean Sea

Below The Greeks were skilled sailors. This is a trireme, a warship powered by oarsmen.

THE GREEKS AT WAR

The city states were fierce rivals for power in Greece and the Aegean, and wars took place frequently between them. The Greeks were tough, highly disciplined soldiers. They carried spears and fought on foot in a tight, defensive battle formation called a phalanx. All fit and healthy citizens who could afford to were expected to buy their own armor and weapons and serve in their city's army when needed.

The finest soldiers in Greece came from Sparta, where all boys were taken away from their families at the age of seven and brought up by the state. Their education consisted mainly of gymnastics and training for war. When he was 20, a man could become a citizen and join a military unit. He could also marry, but he was not allowed to live with his wife and children until he was 30. Even then he had to eat with his fellow soldiers at least once a day.

Their military training stood the Greeks in good stead when the armies of the vast Persian empire tried three times to conquer Greece, by both land and sea. The weather defeated the Persians in 492 BC. Two years later, the Athenian army was victorious at the battle of Marathon. On the third occasion (480–479 BC), Xerxes' huge

Above Greek soldiers were protected by strong body armor. This bronze helmet would have been crested.

invasion force of 200,000 men and 1,000 ships was vanquished by the combined, much smaller forces of Sparta and Athens.

This show of unity was short-lived. Both Sparta and Athens wanted to dominate Greece. Hostility grew between them as they built up support among the other city states. Sparta emerged victorious from the Peloponnesian War (431–404 BC) that followed, but was not strong enough to keep control for long. As the fruitless wars continued, the city states grew steadily weaker. They were unable to resist the growing strength of Macedon, lying to the north. By 338, its king Philip II, a soldier of genius, had won control of all the Greek city states, including Athens. The classical age of Greek civilization was at an end.

THE GREEK ACHIEVEMENT

Despite their almost constant wars, the achievements of the Greeks between the 6th and 4th centuries BC were unsurpassed in the ancient world. Greek sculptors and painters created artworks of outstanding grace and beauty. The architectural styles of their great columned temples are still imitated. They invented drama and the theater. Greek literature, myths, and legends continue to inspire works of art, literature, and cinema today. The Athenian philosophers Socrates, Plato, and Aristotle are the most important early figures in the history of European thought. The Greeks wrote the first histories, were advanced in mathematics and geometry, and established medicine as a scientific discipline.

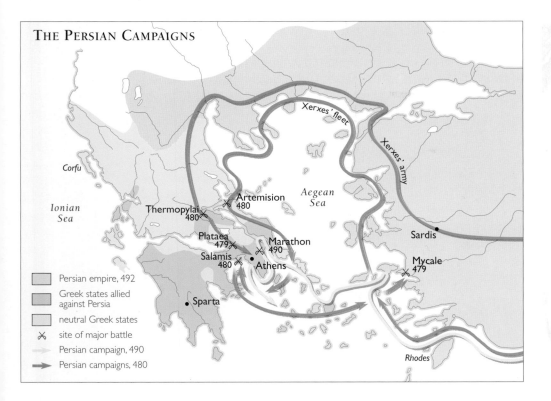

THE PERSIAN CAMPAIGNS

Corfu

Ionian
Sea

Thermopylai
480

Plataea
479

Salamis
480

Athens

Sparta

Artemision
480

Aegean
Sea

Xerxes' fleet

Xerxes' army

Sardis

Mycale
479

Marathon
490

Rhodes

- Persian empire, 492
- Greek states allied against Persia
- neutral Greek states
- ✕ site of major battle
- → Persian campaign, 490
- ➤ Persian campaigns, 480

Little of this would have been achieved without writing. Other ancient writing systems used hundreds of different symbols and took years to learn, but the Greek phonetic alphabet of only 20 chararacters was easily taught. Education had an important function in Greek democracy—politicians could not just do whatever they wanted: they had to persuade their fellow citizens to vote for their policies by skillful argument. Schools were set up to teach these skills, and literacy helped to spread ideas quickly.

High value was placed on physical education, especially athletics, wrestling, and boxing. During great sports festivals like the Olympic games, wars between rival city-states came to a stop to allow competitors and spectators to travel to them safely.

GREEK MYTHS & LEGENDS

The Greeks worshiped many gods and goddesses. Some belonged to a particular place, such as a sacred wood or spring; others had wider significance. The most important were said to live on the top of Mount Olympus in northern Greece. Chief among them were the supreme sky-god Zeus; his wife Hera; Hermes, the messenger; Apollo, the sun god; Aphrodite, the goddess of love; and Athena, the goddess of wisdom. For the Greeks, gods were powerful beings who had humanlike emotions and intervened directly in human affairs. They gave out terrible punishments to those who offended them, but were also ready to help the men and women who pleased them. The highest reward the gods could give a human was immortality. Hercules, for

example, who was endowed with extraordinary strength and performed deeds of bravery, became a god himself.

Every city-state had its own patron god or gods who gave special protection to the city under their care. Sometimes the gods quarreled among themselves over human affairs. During the Trojan War, Apollo sided with the Trojans, Athena with the Greeks. Hundreds of myths and legends were told about the gods. All Greeks were familiar with these tales and would instantly recognize a scene painted on a pottery dish or know what legendary figures were sculpted on the friezes of their great temples. The myths inspired great works of prose and poetry such as Homer's epic poems and the plays of the Athenian dramatists, Aeschylus, Sophocles, and Euripedes.

Left Athena settles an argument about the dead Achilles' armor. A vase painting of the Trojan War.

TIMETABLE

900–800
City-states develop as Greece recovers from the dark age

800–600
The Greeks found colonies around the Mediterranean and Black Sea

776
The first games are held at Olympia in honor of Zeus. They are open to all Greek males and take place every four years

c.750
The Greek alphabet is in use. Homer composes the *Iliad* and the *Odyssey*, epic poems about the Trojan War

c.600
Coinage is introduced into Greece

c.540
The first drama festival is held in Athens in honor of Dionysius

509–507
Athens becomes a democracy

490
The Athenians defeat a Persian invasion at the battle of Marathon

480–479
Xerxes' invasion force is defeated by the combined armies of Sparta and Athens

461–429
Pericles leads Athens during its golden age. The Parthenon is built; Aeschylus and Sophocles write their great tragedies

441–404
The Peloponnesian War ends in Sparta's victory over Athens

430
Herodotus writes the first major history

399
Socrates, convicted of corrupting youth by his teachings, is forced to to drink hemlock, a deadly poison

c.385
Plato founds the Academy as a school for teaching philosophy

343
The philosopher Aristotle is tutor to Alexander the Great of Macedon

338
The Greek cities become subject to Macedon after the battle of Chaeronea

ALEXANDER THE GREAT & HIS SUCCESSORS

ALEXANDER THE GREAT WAS ONE OF THE FINEST GENERALS IN HISTORY. ONLY EIGHT YEARS AFTER BECOMING KING OF MACEDON, HE HAD CONQUERED THE ENTIRE PERSIAN EMPIRE AND SPREAD THE INFLUENCE OF GREEK CIVILIZATION AS FAR AS INDIA. HIS EMPIRE, HOWEVER, DID NOT SURVIVE HIS DEATH.

Alexander became king of Macedon at the age of 18, following the murder of his father, Philip II, in 336 BC. He was well educated (the Greek philosopher, Aristotle, was his tutor), brave, bold, and violent. As a boy he dreamed of copying the deeds of the Greek heroes Hercules and Achilles, who were the legendary ancestors of the royal house of Macedon. When still a teenager, he had shown great ability fighting in his father's army. With his strong personality, Alexander had the gift of inspiring men to face great hardships and dangers.

DEFEATING THE PERSIANS

Philip II had been on the point of invading the Persian empire when he died. Alexander decided to go ahead with the plan, pausing only to put down a rebellion in Greece first. It was 150 years since the Persians had launched their last unsuccessful expedition against the Greeks, and in this time their empire had grown steadily weaker. However, the present king Darius III was far wealthier than Alexander and could raise enormous armies from his vast empire, which stretched from the Mediterranean Sea to the river Indus.

The size of the empire was not always an advantage. It could take weeks for messengers to travel from one end to the other, and months for soldiers from the provinces to join the royal army. Though huge in number, Persian armies were notoriously difficult to control in battle. By contrast, Alexander's army was well-armed, highly trained, mobile, and skilled in battle tactics. Alexander was a brilliant and inspiring general; Darius timid and unimaginative.

In 334 BC Alexander invaded and conquered Anatolia, liberating the Greek cities along the coast from Persian rule. He had only a small navy and was afraid that Darius might launch an invasion fleet against Greece behind his back. Rather than move deeper into the Persian empire, therefore,

Left *Philip II, Alexander's father, developed Macedon's military strength, making it the strongest power in Greece. He was killed at a wedding feast.*

he traveled south through Syria and along the Mediterranean coast into Phoenicia, to attack bases where the elite of the Persian fleet was anchored. Along the way he met and defeated two Persian armies, one of them led by Darius himself.

There was little other resistance to Alexander's advance. He was generous to the cities and provinces that came over to him voluntarily, undertaking not to raise taxes or allow his soldiers to plunder them. This was a wise decision as it meant most places were happy to surrender rather than risk a battle or lengthy siege.

The chief Phoenician port of Tyre was one of the few places that refused to surrender. Alexander besieged it for eight months before his soldiers broke into the city. Eight

Persian empire, 336
capital of Persian empire
Macedon, 336
allies and subject states of Macedonia, 336
empire of Alexander, 323
city founded by Alexander (with modern name)
campaign of Alexander, 334–324

0   600 km
0   400 mi

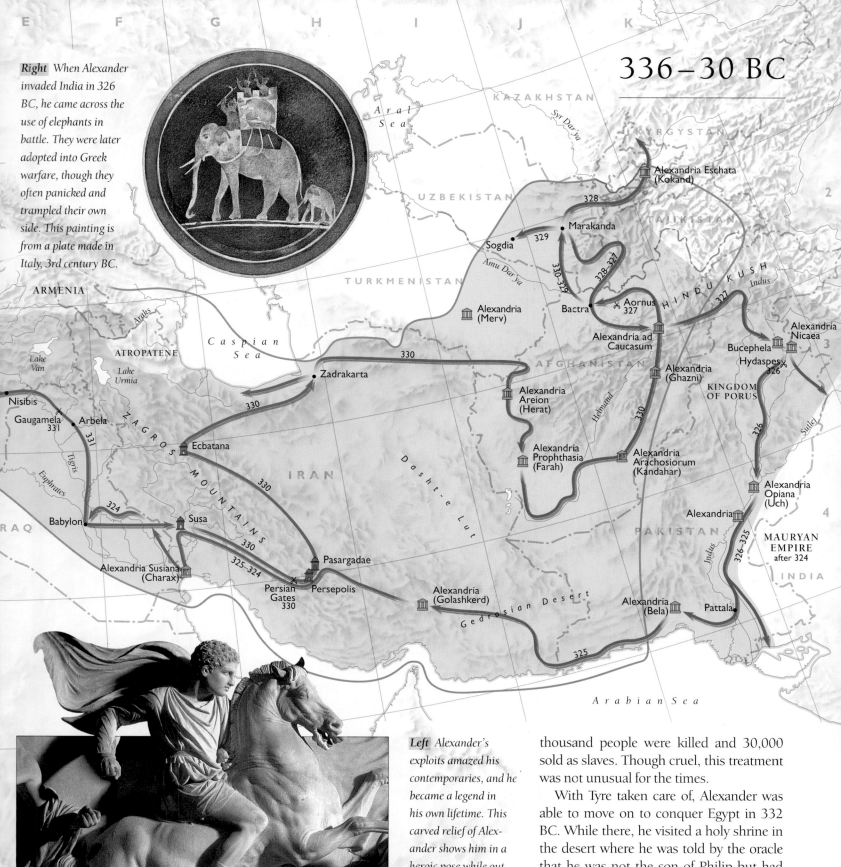

Right When Alexander invaded India in 326 BC, he came across the use of elephants in battle. They were later adopted into Greek warfare, though they often panicked and trampled their own side. This painting is from a plate made in Italy, 3rd century BC.

Map labels: KAZAKHSTAN, Aral Sea, Syr Dar'ya, KYRGYSTAN, Alexandria Eschata (Kokand), 328, Marakanda, 329, Sogdia, 330-329, 328-327, TAJIKISTAN, UZBEKISTAN, Amu Dar'ya, TURKMENISTAN, Alexandria (Merv), Bactra, Aornus 327, HINDU KUSH, Indus, 327, Alexandria Nicaea, ARMENIA, Caspian Sea, ATROPATENE, Lake Van, Lake Urmia, 330, Alexandria ad Caucasum, Bucephela, Hydaspes, 326, Nisibis, Zadrakarta, AFGHANISTAN, Alexandria (Ghazni), KINGDOM OF PORUS, Gaugamela 331, Arbela, 331, ZAGROS MOUNTAINS, 330, Alexandria Areion (Herat), Helmand, 330, Tigris, Ecbatana, 330, IRAN, Dasht-e Lut, Alexandria Prophthasia (Farah), Alexandria Arachosiorum (Kandahar), 326, Sutlej, Euphrates, 324, Babylon, Susa, 330, 325-324, Pasargadae, Alexandria Opiana (Uch), Alexandria, PAKISTAN, Indus, 326-325, MAURYAN EMPIRE after 324, IRAQ, Alexandria Susiana (Charax), Persian Gates 330, Persepolis, Alexandria (Golashkerd), Gedrosian Desert, Alexandria (Bela), Pattala, INDIA, 325, Arabian Sea

Left Alexander's exploits amazed his contemporaries, and he became a legend in his own lifetime. This carved relief of Alexander shows him in a heroic pose while out hunting. It is from the frieze of a monument raised to his memory by the king of Sidon (Phoenicia). The frieze depicts Alexander performing many deeds of courage in battle, providing a pattern for others to imitate.

thousand people were killed and 30,000 sold as slaves. Though cruel, this treatment was not unusual for the times.

With Tyre taken care of, Alexander was able to move on to conquer Egypt in 332 BC. While there, he visited a holy shrine in the desert where he was told by the oracle that he was not the son of Philip but had been fathered by Zeus, the most important of the Greek gods. Because of his remarkable achievements, many people—including Alexander himself—began to believe that he really was a god.

In 331 BC Alexander left Egypt to invade the heartland of the Persian empire. At Gaugamela in Assyria he defeated Darius a second time in battle before going on to capture Babylon. Soon afterward Alexander entered Persepolis, the chief residence and capital of the Persian kings, and burned it to the ground. Giving up all hope, Darius fled and was murdered soon after.

THE LAST CAMPAIGNS

For the next three years Alexander's army campaigned ceaselessly in central Asia to complete the conquest of the Persian empire. This was achieved by 327 BC, and Alexander then decided to invade northern India. He won a battle over an Indian king on the river Hydaspes in 326 BC, but by now his army had had enough. Alexander was forced to agree to their demands to return home. They followed the course of the river Indus to the Arabian Sea and then embarked on a grueling journey across the desert to reach Babylon in 324 BC.

Alexander was planning a new campaign in Arabia when he died suddenly in 323 BC. Aged only 33, he was an alcoholic and probably insane. Believing himself a god, he had begun to rule like a tyrant, ignoring all advice. He had given no time or thought to creating a central government to hold his vast possessions together. On his death the empire collapsed into chaos. His heirs, a mad brother and an infant son, were soon murdered and his generals, whom he had appointed provincial governors, fought each other in a series of wars to carve out independent kingdoms for themselves. The most successful and long lasting of these were the kingdoms founded by Ptolemy in Egypt and Seleucus in Syria.

ALEXANDER'S LEGACY

Alexander's conquests spread Greek civilization right across Asia to the Indus valley in the Himalayan foothills. Tens of thousands of Greeks emigrated to the dozens of new cities founded in these newly conquered lands, many of them named after Alexander himself. His soldiers grew rich on the treasure looted from the Persians.

The age of Greek cultural dominance in the Mediterranean and Near East is known as the Hellenistic period (from "Hellene," the word the Greeks used to describe themselves). Greece, however, no longer lay at the heart of the Greek world. Under the Ptolemies, Alexandria in Egypt, the most successful of the cities named for Alexander, came to replace Athens as the center of Greek culture. The rulers of the Hellenistic kingdoms were far richer than the Greek city-states had been. They spent their wealth lavishly on buildings such as

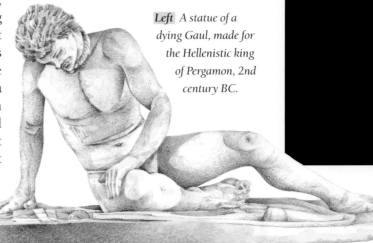

Left A statue of a dying Gaul, made for the Hellenistic king of Pergamon, 2nd century BC.

Above The ruins of Persepolis, in Iran, once the opulent capital of the Persian kings.

ALEXANDER'S SUCCESSORS 240 BC

Black Sea
L. Tuz
Pergamon
Athens
Crete
Antioch
Cyprus
Mediterranean Sea
Alexandria
Nile
Red Sea
Caspian Sea
L. Van
Tigris
L. Urmia
Euphrates
Seleucia
Persian Gulf

Macedon
Ptolemaic kingdom
Seleucid kingdom
other independent states
Hellenistic cultural or political center

the lighthouse of Alexandria, one of the Seven Wonders of the Ancient World. They encouraged new styles of art, particularly sculpture, and extended their patronage to scientists and philosophers like the mathematicians Archimedes and Euclid, and the astronomer Eratosthenes.

The Hellenistic world was overtaken by the rising strength of Rome. Greece and Macedon were conquered in the mid 2nd century. The Seleucid and Ptolemaic kingdoms survived for longer, but they too were ruled by Rome by 30 BC. The Romans had great respect for Greek civilization and borrowed many of its attributes for themselves, including its architecture, science, literature, and mythology.

CLEOPATRA: LAST OF THE PTOLEMIES

*C*leopatra, the last of the Ptolemaic rulers of Egypt and the seventh queen of that name, is remembered in history as the lover of two Roman generals, Julius Caesar and Mark Antony. But Cleopatra was ruled by more than her heart's dictates. Her actions were driven by political necessity to secure her own survival.

When the 18-year-old Cleopatra became queen in 51 BC Rome had mastery of almost the entire Mediterranean and was waiting for a chance to seize control of Egypt too. She could not hope to remain queen without powerful support, and saw her opportunity in Rome's civil wars (see page 53). Both her Roman lovers hoped to use Cleopatra to gain

Above *Cleopatra wearing Egyptian dress.*

access to Egypt's vast wealth and further their own ambitions. Her plans ended in suicide after Mark Antony was defeated in battle in 31 BC. The dynasty that had ruled Egypt for 300 years died with her, leaving Rome as ruler of Egypt.

THE RISE OF ROME

LEGEND HAS IT THAT THE CITY OF ROME WAS FOUNDED IN 753 BC. ACCORDING TO THE EARLY HISTORIES, IT WAS RULED BY KINGS UNTIL 509 BC, WHEN THE MONARCHY WAS OVERTHROWN AND THE ROMAN REPUBLIC FOUNDED. BY THE 2ND CENTURY BC ROME HAD TRANSFORMED ITSELF FROM A MINOR CITY-STATE TO THE MAJOR POWER IN THE WESTERN WORLD.

Archeologists believe that the site of the city of Rome was first occupied by Iron Age farmers in the 10th century BC. Urban life seems to have developed there in the mid 8th century BC (about the date of its traditional foundation), and it grew to become one of the largest cities in Italy. The Romans were only one of many different peoples living in Italy at this time. They used warfare and political craft to overcome their neighbors, and by the mid 3rd century BC they controlled almost all of Italy.

EXPANSION OVERSEAS

The strongest power in the western Mediterranean was Carthage, a rich trading city in North Africa originally founded by the Phoenicians. Once it had made itself master of the former Greek cities of southern Italy, Rome began to challenge Carthage for influence in Sicily. This led to a series of wars, known as the Punic Wars (from *Poeni*, Latin for Phoenicians.) Rome emerged the victor from the First Punic War (264–241 BC), with the islands of Sicily, Sardinia, and Corsica added to its possessions. War broke out again over the control of Spain (the Second Punic War, 218–202 BC). The Carthaginian general Hannibal attacked Rome by marching a large army of men and elephants from Spain into France and from there crossing the Alps to Italy. But despite a series of great victories, he was unable to force the Romans to surrender. Meanwhile, a Roman army under the command of Scipio Africanus defeated the Carthaginian armies

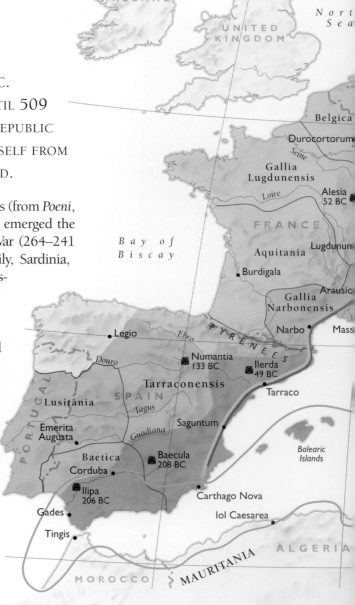

ITALY BEFORE THE ROMANS

Before the rise of Rome, the most powerful people in Italy were the Etruscans, settled in an area approximately equivalent to Tuscany today. By 800 BC they had developed the first urban civilization of western Europe. Active seafarers and traders, they had close cultural contacts with the Greeks and adopted their alphabet. Their inscriptions, however, cannot easily be deciphered, because they spoke a language unrelated to other European languages. Most of what we know about the Etruscans comes from their unique tombs. They built these like underground houses, in clusters or cities, and richly furnished them with grave goods and painted them with scenes of feasting.

Occupying the center of the peninsula were the Italics, a large group of peoples that included the Latins, Sabines, and Samnites.

Above *Tomb statues of an Etruscan couple.*

By 500 BC most still lived in tribes, but city-states had developed among the Latins, one of which was Rome. Once Rome achieved sole cultural and political dominance throughout the peninsula, all knowledge of other Italian languages and cultures disappeared.

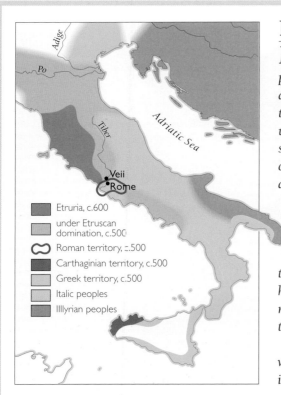

Etruria, c.600

under Etruscan domination, c.500

Roman territory, c.500

Carthaginian territory, c.500

Greek territory, c.500

Italic peoples

Illyrian peoples

750 BC – AD 14

Right *According to legend, a she-wolf suckled the twin brothers Romulus and Remus, abandoned at birth. The same legend records that Romulus later founded the city of Rome. This head of a wolf is from a bronze statue, c.500 BC.*

Map labels:

Germania 12 BC–AD 9
viomagus
Teutoburgerwald ⊠ AD 9
Colonia Agrippina
mania erior
GERMANY
Moguntiacum
Augusta Treverorum
Argentorate
Castra Regina
Augusta Vindelicorum
Vindobona
Carnuntum
Raetia
Noricum
Aquincum
Virunum
ALPS
xima egusio
Ticinus R ⊠ 218 BC
Aquileia
Pannonia
Trebia R 218 BC
Po
ITALY
Italia
Florentia
Salonae
Dalmatia
Viminacium
Singidunum
Novae
Moesia
L Trasimenus 217 BC
Telamon 225 BC
Rome
Cemenelum
Aleria
Corsica
Cannae 216 BC
Pompeii
Tarentum
Brundisium
Sardinia
Carales
Sicilia
Syracusae
Carthage
Zama 202 BC
Africa
Malta
TUNISIA
Leptis Magna
Macedonia
Pydna 168 BC
Thessalonica
Cynoscephalae 197 BC
Pharsalus 48 BC
Actium 31 BC
Achaea
Athens
Corinth
GREECE
Creta
Gortyn
POLAND
Vistula
Oder
Elbe
Danube
CZECH REPUBLIC
SLOVAKIA
Tisza
Drava
ROMANIA
Sava
BULGARIA
THRACIA
Byzantium
Nicomedia
Bithynia & Pontus
Sinope
Trapezus
Nicopolis 68 BC
Ancyra
ANATOLIA
Pergamon
Asia
TURKEY
Galatia
L Tuz
Magnesia 190 BC
Ephesus
Aphrodisias
PISIDIA
LYCIA
Cilicia
Tarsus
Antiochia
Syria
SYRIA
Palmyra
Paphus
Cyprus
Tigris
Euphrates
Carrhae 53 BC
PARTHIA
Judaea
Caesarea
Jerusalem
Mediterranean Sea
Cyrene
Cyrenaica
Alexandria
Aegyptus
LIBYA
EGYPT
SAUDI ARABIA
Nile
Thebes
Berenice
Syene

Legend:

- Roman empire, c.272 BC
- gains by 218 BC
- gains by 201 BC
- gains by 100 BC
- gains by 44 BC
- gains by AD 14
- temporary gain, with date held
- Carthaginian territory in 264 BC
- Hannibal's invasion of Italy, 218–216 BC
- ■ Roman victory
- ⊠ Roman defeat
- ⊠ Roman civil war
- Roman provincial boundary, AD 14

0 _____ 600 km
0 _____ 400 mi

---

still remaining in Spain, and then invaded North Africa. Hannibal sailed home from Italy to defend Carthage but was defeated at the battle of Zama in 202 BC. The city of Carthage itself was conquered and completely destroyed by Rome in 146 BC.

Now undisputed master of the western Mediterranean, Rome was poised to extend its influence eastward. Greece had been invaded in 197 BC, to punish Philip V of Macedon for supporting Carthage in the Punic Wars, and by 146 BC had become a Roman province. In 133 BC Rome acquired its first foothold in Asia with the acquisition of Pergamon in Anatolia (its last king left it to Rome in his will). Bit by bit, Rome took over all the kingdoms founded by Alexander's successors (see page 48). In 30 BC the last of them, Egypt, came under direct Roman control, leaving Rome in supreme command throughout the Mediterranean and Middle East.

Above From the earliest days of the Republic, any Roman citizen had the right to appeal against injustice to the people of Rome. The inscription on this coin of the 2nd century BC reads "PROVOCO" ("I appeal"), and shows a Roman addressing his fellow citizens.

ROMAN GOVERNMENT

A major factor in Rome's rise to power was its unique system of government. The city was governed by elected officers called magistrates. They ruled with the help of the Senate, an assembly of former magistrates who decided government policy. The upper classes, who were known as "patricians," dominated the government, but it was possible for talented people from the lower classes ("plebeians") to become magistrates and senators. New government policies were voted on by an assembly of all Roman citizens. The voting system in the assembly was organized in favor of the richer classes, but the plebeians had their own independent assembly and elected their own officers, called tribunes, to represent their interests. In practice, most tribunes were themselves wealthy and used the position as a stepping stone to higher office; for the most part, they had no interest in challenging the status quo. This system of government gave Rome strong leadership, ensured that there was public support for government policy, and helped make the Romans a united people during the centuries of its rise to power.

SOLDIERS & CITIZENS

War was another important factor in securing Rome's success. For the wealthy, military victory brought prestige and the chance to win political power and influence at home. For the poor, it offered plunder and a way to acquire land. Only Roman citizens could fight in the army. At first it was also necessary to be a landowner, but this requirement was abolished in 105 BC. As a result, the Romans were the first people in the ancient world to have a large professional army of well-trained, disciplined soldiers.

The Romans' unique view of citizenship was a further major factor in their success. In Greece, citizenship depended on birth and was a jealously guarded privilege: this meant that the number of politically active citizens in the Greek city-states remained small. For the Romans, however, all that mattered was residence in Rome; immigrants were welcomed as citizens, and even freed slaves could acquire citizenship. As a result, the number of Roman citizens grew rapidly, and so did the number of potential recruits for the Roman army. Later on, the Romans were prepared to grant citizenship and its privileges to the peoples it conquered in Italy and abroad, if they proved loyal and were prepared to fight for Rome; Roman identity was no longer simply confined to those living in the city of Rome itself. In this way former enemies were brought within the Roman system of government and made loyal citizens.

THE END OF THE REPUBLIC

Its rapid overseas expansion made Rome rich. But it also weakened the republican system of government. Corruption spread as officials tried to keep the wealth of the provinces for themselves. Military conquest brought a huge influx of slaves to Italy, and as a result many poor Roman farmers and laborers lost their lands and jobs. When Tiberius Gracchus, a tribune, tried to introduce reforms, he was murdered in 133 BC.

Ambitious generals became increasingly eager to conquer new provinces and plunder their riches. The wealth they won could be used to buy the support of their soldiers if they tried to win power at home. They were also expected to reward their men with grants of land when they left the army. Soon civil wars broke out between rival generals. In 44 BC the successful general Julius Caesar defeated all his rivals. In power, he abolished the republic and became dictator of Rome. His high-handed actions alarmed a number of conservative republicans, who conspired to murder him.

Caesar's death set the stage for a new civil war. The eventual victor was Caesar's ambitious young nephew, Octavian, who became sole ruler of Rome and its possessions in 31 BC. Under the new form of government he introduced in 27 BC, Octavian, now known as Augustus ("honored one"), became commander-in-chief of the army; he could make laws and reject decisions of the Senate. His official title was *princeps* ("first citizen"), but he had the power of a king. Augustus's rule restored peace and stability to the Roman empire. He was succeeded in AD 14 by his stepson Tiberius. He and all Rome's subsequent rulers used the title *imperator* ("commander"), from which our word emperor comes.

JULIUS CAESAR

Julius Caesar began his political career as tribune, going out of his way to win the support of Rome's lower classes, and then embarked on a conspicuously successful military career. His conquests included Gaul, and he acquired great wealth as well as the devotion of his men. After defeating his political enemies in the civil war of 48–45 BC, Caesar declared himself dictator and destroyed the republican system of government in his quest for power. His reforms improved the life of poorer Romans and provincials, but alienated the Senate. He was murdered by conservative republicans who feared that he was about to make himself king.

Left Caesar was the supreme Roman politician.

TIMETABLE

c.900
Earliest habitation on the site of Rome

753
Traditional date for the founding of Rome by Romulus

509
The Romans overthrow their monarchy and found a republic

390
The Gauls (Celts) sack Rome

272
The Romans capture Tarentum to complete the conquest of Italy

264–241
The First Punic War between Rome and Carthage

218–202
The Second Punic War. At the battle of Cannae (216) Rome suffers its worst defeat ever

c.200
Greek influences begin to appear in Roman art

146
The Romans destroy Carthage. It is later refounded as a Roman colony

146
Greece becomes a Roman province

105–101
Marius reforms the Roman army

73–71
Spartacus, a gladiator, leads a slave revolt. It is put down and more than 6,000 slaves are crucified

46
Julius Caesar becomes dictator of Rome

44
Julius Caesar is murdered: a new civil war breaks out

31
Octavian (Augustus) defeats Mark Antony at Actium to become sole ruler of Rome

30–19
The poet Virgil (70–19 BC) writes the *Aeneid*. Livy (59BC–AD 17) completes his history of Rome

27
Augustus introduces imperial rule

EARLY STATES OF SOUTH ASIA

THE INDIAN SUBCONTINENT HAS A COMPLEX HISTORY OF SETTLEMENT. THOUGH IT IS BORDERED ON THE NORTH BY THE HIMALAYAS, THE TALLEST MOUNTAIN RANGE ON EARTH, INVADERS AND SETTLERS HAVE ENTERED THE SUBCONTINENT THROUGH MOUNTAIN PASSES FROM CENTRAL ASIA SINCE EARLIEST TIMES. THE INDUS VALLEY WAS AN EARLY CENTER OF AGRICULTURE AND SAW THE RISE OF ONE OF THE WORLD'S FIRST CIVILIZATIONS. TWO IMPORTANT WORLD RELIGIONS, HINDUISM AND BUDDHISM, ORIGINATED IN NORTHERN INDIA.

The first civilization of South Asia developed on the flood plain of the Indus river, in Pakistan. The environment here was very similar to that of Mesopotamia (see page 22)—the climate was hot and dry, but the soils were fertile, and the river provided plentiful water for irrigation. Agriculture had an early start here, and by 2600 BC the plain was densely scattered with farming villages. In several places small towns and cities had already developed.

CITIES OF THE INDUS

Archeologists first began excavating in the Indus valley in the 1920s. Discoveries at two sites, Mohenjo-Daro and Harappa, gave the first indication that a major urban civilization had existed here more than 4,000 years ago as advanced as those of Mesopotamia and the Nile valley at around the same time. Some cities such as Mohenjo-Daro and Harappa were much larger than other settlements in the region, and may have been the capitals of kingdoms.

It is clear that the Indus civilization was highly organized. The towns and cities were neatly planned on a grid system, with different areas of the city being reserved for specific classes and occupations. They were built on mud-brick platforms to protect them from floods, and possessed a sophisticated water-supply and sewerage system.

We know very little about the people who built these cities. Though stone seals carved with pictographs (see page 18) show that the Indus people could write, the script

Left A small carved head from Mohenjo-Daro. He is thought to represent a priest or king. The bared right shoulder, headband, armring, and trefoil-patterned robe are all traditional signs of holiness in India.

UTTARAPAT

Below Mohenjo-Daro stood on a hill above the floodplain of the river Indus. Built entirely of baked mud bricks, it had a population of 30,000–40,000, making it one of the largest Bronze Age cities in the world.

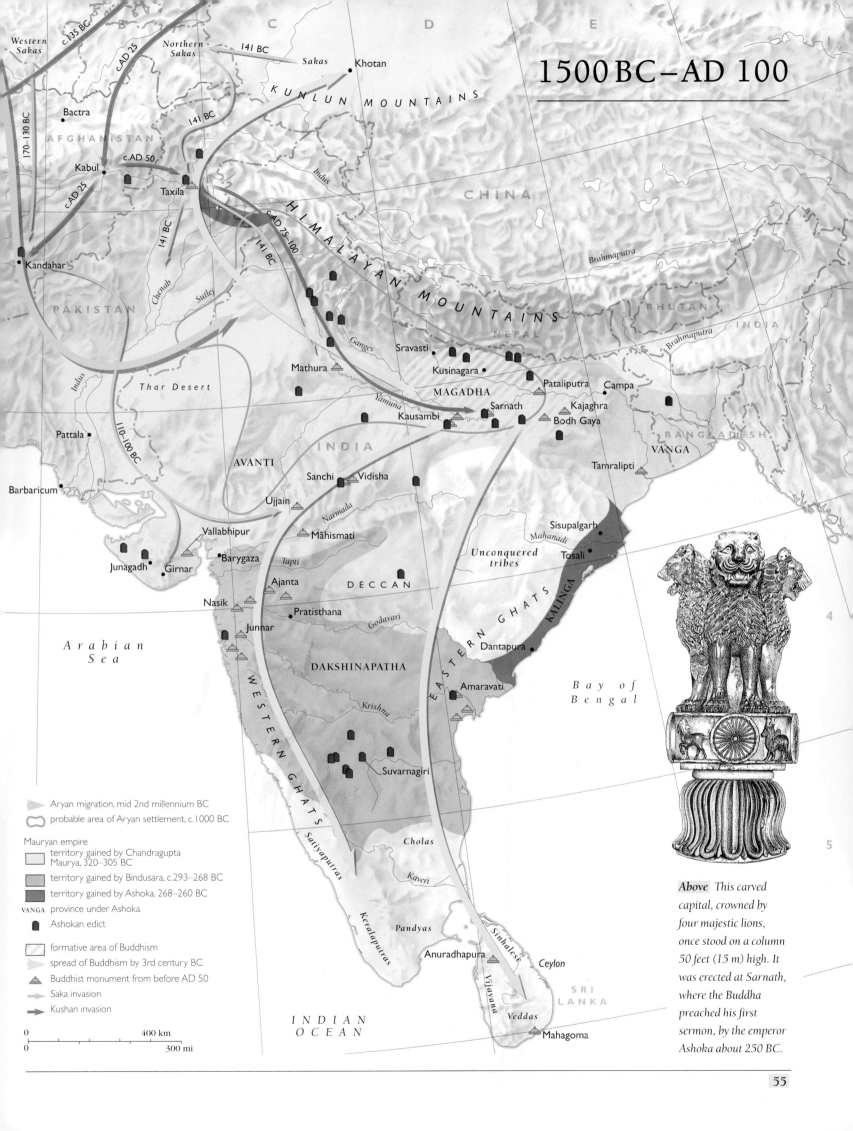

1500 BC–AD 100

Western Sakas
c.135 BC
Northern Sakas
141 BC
Sakas
170–130 BC
Bactra
AFGHANISTAN
c.AD 50
Kabul
c.AD 25
Taxila
141 BC
Kandahar

KUNLUN MOUNTAINS
Khotan
CHINA

c.AD 75–100
141 BC

Indus
PAKISTAN
Chenab
Sutlej

110–100 BC
Thar Desert
Pattala
Barbaricum

HIMALAYAN MOUNTAINS
NEPAL
Ganges
Sravasti
Mathura
Yamuna
MAGADHA
Kausambi
Sarnath
Kusinagara
Pataliputra
Campa
Kajaghra
Bodh Gaya

Brahmaputra
BHUTAN
INDIA
Brahmaputra
BANGLADESH

INDIA
AVANTI
Sanchi Vidisha
Ujjain
Narmada
Mahismati
Vallabhipur
Junagadh Girnar
Barygaza
Tapti

TAMRALIPTI
VANGA

Arabian
Sea

Ajanta
Nasik
Junnar
Pratisthana
Godavari
DECCAN
DAKSHINAPATHA
Krishna

Mahanadi
Sisupalgarh
Tosali
Unconquered
tribes
KALINGA
EASTERN GHATS
Dantapura
Amaravati

Bay of
Bengal

WESTERN GHATS

Suvarnagiri

Satiyaputras
Cholas
Kaveri
Pandyas
Keralaputras

Anuradhapura
Sinhalese
Ceylon
SRI LANKA
Vijayana
Veddas
Mahagoma

INDIAN
OCEAN

Legend

- Aryan migration, mid 2nd millennium BC
- probable area of Aryan settlement, c.1000 BC

Mauryan empire
- territory gained by Chandragupta Maurya, 320–305 BC
- territory gained by Bindusara, c.293–268 BC
- territory gained by Ashoka, 268–260 BC
- VANGA province under Ashoka
- Ashokan edict
- formative area of Buddhism
- spread of Buddhism by 3rd century BC
- Buddhist monument from before AD 50
- Saka invasion
- Kushan invasion

0   400 km
0   300 mi

Above *This carved capital, crowned by four majestic lions, once stood on a column 50 feet (15 m) high. It was erected at Sarnath, where the Buddha preached his first sermon, by the emperor Ashoka about 250 BC.*

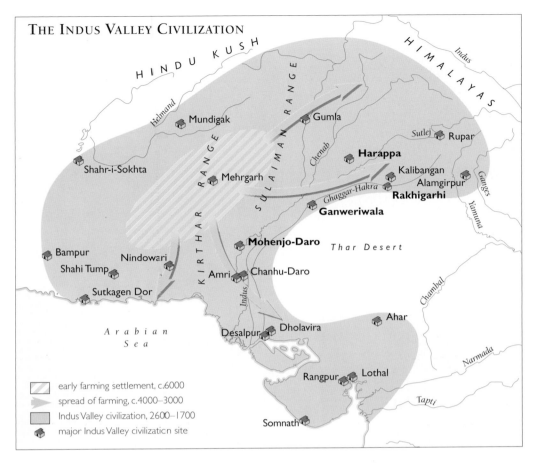

THE INDUS VALLEY CIVILIZATION

- early farming settlement, c.6000
- spread of farming, c.4000–3000
- Indus Valley civilization, 2600–1700
- major Indus Valley civilization site

has not yet been deciphered and we do not even know what language they spoke. They had extensive trading links reaching far into the subcontinent and along the coast of the Persian Gulf to Mesopotamia.

The Indus civilization appears to have gone into decline about 1800 BC, and by 1700 BC the cities had been abandoned. The reasons for this are unclear, but as life continued unchanged in the countryside, it is unlikely that invaders were responsible. It is possible that repeated flooding or some other environmental catastrophe played a part in their desertion.

VEDIC INDIA

Around 1500 BC the Aryans migrated into northern India from central Asia. They were cattle-owning seminomads, but by about 1000 BC they appear to have settled down as rice farmers on the vast, fertile Ganges plain that extends for 1,900 miles (3,000 km) west to east across the north of the subcontinent. There they developed a village-based society, loosely held together in small tribal kingdoms. By this time they had begun to use iron tools and weapons, which they had probably learned to make independently of outside influence.

The Aryans had enormous influence on Indian history. Many of the numerous languages spoken in India today have evolved from their Sanskrit language. Hinduism, the most widespread religion of modern India, is descended from the Aryan form of religion. The earliest Hindu scriptures are the Vedas, collections of hymns that tell the mythical history of the migrations and wars of the Aryans under the leadership of their god Indra. They were passed on by word of mouth and did not come to be written down until the 6th century BC.

Central to Hinduism is its caste system, or hereditary system of social ranking. This has developed from the four *varnas* or classes of Aryan society. The two highest classes were the Brahmins, the priestly caste, and the Kshatriyas, the warriors. Next came the Vaishyas, peasant farmers and merchants, with the Shudras, craftsmen, laborers, or slaves, at the bottom. Kings were always members of the warrior class, but they also had important religious duties, such as performing rituals to maintain the fertility of the fields and secure good harvests.

NEW BELIEFS

By 500 BC Hinduism had spread widely through the Indian subcontinent. It taught that each individual has to go through an endless cycle of rebirth. The Brahmins had come to hold great power, and it was partly dissatisfaction with their role that led to the development of a number of new sects, such as Jainism (still practiced by many people in India today) and Buddhism. The founder of Buddhism was Siddhartha Gautama (c.563–483 BC). His teachings gained hold in and around the Gangetic plain, where he lived and died, but did not achieve wider popularity until the reign of the emperor Ashoka (r.268–233 BC).

Below An early Buddhist stupa, or shrine.

THE BUDDHA

All we know about Siddhartha Gautama, the Buddha (or "Enlightened One"), comes from traditions written down long after his death. They relate that he was born a prince of a small kingdom in northern India. One day, age 29, he took a chariot ride outside his father's palace and saw real human suffering for the first time. Overwhelmed by sorrow, he abandoned his life of luxury. For six years he led a life of extreme austerity, fasting and meditating, until he received enlightenment while seated beneath a tree. The essence of Gautama's teaching was that by following the Eightfold Path of righteous thought and action it was possible to attain Nirvana, a state free of suffering, and end the Hindu cycle of rebirth.

__Left__ A Buddha from Gandhara, in the northwest. It is influenced by Greek art, following Alexander the Great's conquest of the Indus valley.

THE EMPEROR ASHOKA

Ashoka ruled over the Mauryan empire, founded by his grandfather Chandragupta Maurya (r.321–293 BC). Chandragupta was an able administrator and a fine soldier. He made a name for himself as a commander in the northwest of India at the time of Alexander the Great's invasion of the Indus valley (see page 46) and later seized power in Magadha, the most important kingdom in the Gangetic plain. He established strong central government and built roads, irrigation systems, and other public works. Chandragupta brought almost all of northern India under his control. His son Bindusara (r.293–268 BC) extended the influence of the Mauryan empire far into the Deccan, the central plateau of India.

Ashoka began his reign by conquering Kalinga in eastern India. This was highly valued as the source of the best war elephants. However, Ashoka was so horrified by the suffering caused by war that he converted to Buddhism and from then onward attempted to live by its teachings of non-violence and compassion for all living things. He informed the rulers of neighboring states that they would not be attacked, and gave up hunting and eating meat.

On Ashoka's orders, Buddhist teachings were inscribed on cliffs and stone pillars throughout India. He sent missionaries to Ceylon, Indonesia, and Central Asia, areas where Buddhism would later become very strong, and even as far as Syria, Egypt, and Anatolia. In this way, Buddhism took the first steps to becoming a world religion. But Ashoka also practiced religious toleration. Although many people in India followed his example and converted to Buddhism, the majority were allowed to practice their traditional Hindu beliefs unhindered.

The Mauryan empire declined after Ashoka's death and by 185 BC had split up into several independent states. They were not strong enough to resist new invaders from central Asia, the Sakas (a branch of the Scythians). After them came the Kushans, who controlled a network of states in the north and enjoyed extensive trading links with China, Persia, and Rome. These newcomers adopted the languages and religions of the people they ruled over and were fully assimilated into Indian culture. Meanwhile, thriving ports and independent kingdoms were beginning to emerge in south India as the opportunities for sea trade increased.

TIMETABLE

c.4000–3000
Settled farming begins on the flood plains of the river Indus

c.2600
Cities emerge on the Indus flood plains

c.2350
Sumerian tablets record trade in copper with the Indus valley

c.2000
Bronze tools and weapons come into use in India

c.1800
The Indus valley civilization declines

c.1500
Aryans migrate into the Indian subcontinent from Central Asia

c.1100
Ironworking begins in India

c.1000
Aryans settle down as rice farmers on the Ganges plain

1000–550
Formative period of the Hindu religion. The Vedas (hymns) are written down

563–483
Life of Siddhartha Gautama, the Buddha

321
Chandragupta Maurya founds the Mauryan empire

268–233
Mauryan empire is at its peak under Ashoka

c.260
Ashoka converts to Buddhism

c.250
Ashoka sends Buddhist missionaries to Sri Lanka

c.185
The last Mauryan king is overthrown

c.141
The Sakas invade India

AD 50–75
The Kushans invade and conquer northwest India

FIRST EMPERORS OF CHINA

FARMING BEGAN IN THE YELLOW RIVER VALLEY ABOUT 8,000 YEARS AGO.
ABOUT 3000 BC RICE FARMING SPREAD THERE FROM THE YANGTZE RIVER
FLOODPLAIN, AND IT WAS HERE THAT THE FIRST CIVILIZATION IN CHINA, THE
SHANG, DEVELOPED ABOUT 1766 BC. AS DYNASTIES CAME AND WENT, THE
BORDERS OF THE EARLY CHINESE STATE EXPANDED SOUTH AND WEST.

About 3000 BC, as agriculture became more developed and the population began to rise, the first towns and fortifications arose in the Yellow river valley of northern China. According to later legends, Chinese civilization was founded by the emperor Huang Di in 2698 BC. However, there is no archeological or historical evidence for any ruling dynasty before the Shang (c.1766–1122 BC).

During this time, cities developed and a pictographic script, the ancestor of the modern Chinese script, came into use. The Shang kings believed that they could talk to their ancestors by writing questions on special bones called oracle bones. The bones were struck with a hot metal rod, and the resulting pattern of cracks was believed to show the ancestors' answer. The kings took care not to take important decisions without ensuring they had the approval of their ancestors.

The influence of the Shang dynasty was quite widely spread across northern China. Shang rulers were extremely powerful. When a king died, hundreds of his soldiers and servants were sacrificed and buried with him. This meant that he could be sure of being guarded and looked after in the afterlife.

THE ZHOU DYNASTY

The Shang dynasty was overthrown by Wu, king of Zhou, in 1122 BC, who founded the longest lasting dynasty of Chinese history. Observing and interpreting astronomical events for the people was part of the obligations of early Chinese rulers. The Zhou kings claimed that celestial approval for their dynasty's authority was demonstrated through the "Mandate of Heaven." The stars could also predict the downfall of dynasties. All future rulers of China would claim to rule by the Mandate.

Later generations looked back to the time of the Zhou kings as a golden age. However, in 770 BC the kingdom was invaded by nomads from the west. The capital moved from Hao to Luoyang, and the kingdom disintegrated into semi-independent states. This troubled time is known as the Spring and Autumns Period (770–480 BC). It was followed by the Warring States Period (480–221 BC), when the authority of the Zhou kings declined even further.

Despite the almost constant background of warfare, important changes were taking place. Iron came into use around 600 BC, though iron weapons did not replace bronze until the 2nd century BC. Literature and philosophy flourished. The most important cultural development was the creation of Confucianism, the system of ethical beliefs that remains fundamental to Chinese thought and behavior. Its founder, Confucius (551–479 BC), was born at Qufu in Lu province to a poor but aristocratic family. He became a government official before seeking the life of a wandering

Left Early Chinese bronze working was the most advanced in the world. Skilled craftsmen could cast incredibly complicated shapes using molds made up of several separate pieces. Vessels like this one of Zhou manufacture were used to make food and drink offerings to the gods.

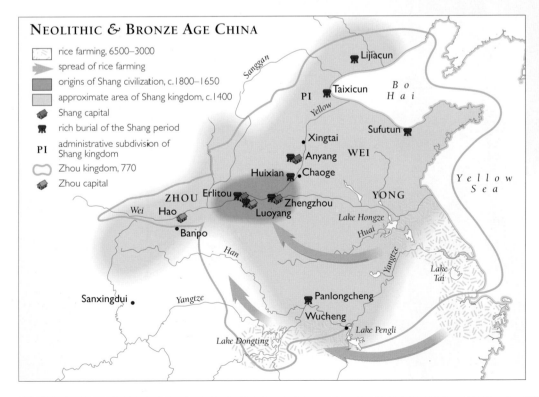

NEOLITHIC & BRONZE AGE CHINA

- rice farming, 6500–3000
- spread of rice farming
- origins of Shang civilization, c.1800–1650
- approximate area of Shang kingdom, c.1400
- Shang capital
- rich burial of the Shang period
- PI administrative subdivision of Shang kingdom
- Zhou kingdom, 770
- Zhou capital

Sanggan
Turfan
105 BC
108 BC · Dunhua
Wu-s

Lijiacun
PI · Taixicun
B o
H a i
Yellow
Xingtai
Sufutun
Anyang · WEI
Huixian · Chaoge
Y e l l o w
ZHOU · Erlitou · Zhengzhou · YONG · S e a
Wei Hao · Luoyang
Lake Hongze
· Banpo · Huai
Han
Lake Tai
Sanxingdui · *Yangtze* · Panlongcheng
Wucheng
Lake Pengli
Lake Dongting

MONGOLIA

99 BC

175–170 BC

119 BC

119 BC

315 BC

Gobi Desert

Inner Mongolian Plateau

Xiongnu (nomads)

127 BC

119 BC

201 BC

Yan wall, c.290 BC

Zhao wall, c.300 BC

YAN

Xiangping

NORTH KOREA

Luolang

Shanggu

Youbeiping

Ji

Koreans

Yue Qi (nomads)

Wuyuan

Ordos Desert

Diangxiang

ZHONG-SHAN

Bo Hai

SOUTH KOREA

Changye

ZHAO

Jinyang

QI

Yellow

Linzi

Zichuan

Yellow Sea

ILIAN MTS

Liangzhou

Lake Qinghai

Handan

Ji

Qi wall, c.450 BC

Wei wall, c.353 BC

WEI

Pingyang

Puyang

LU

Qufu

Jincheng

QIN MTS

Qin

Ping

Yong

QIN

Xianyang

Luoyang ZHOU

SONG

Shangqiu

Tibetans

Yellow

Pingyang

Chang'an

HAN

Xinzheng

Chu wall

Daliang

Chen

Lake Hongze

Guangling

Junsha (Yangtze)

Han

Juyang

Huai

Shouchun

Nanjing

Lake Tai

Wu

SHU

DABA MTS

Yanying (Ruo)

CHINA

CHU

Yangtze

Guiji

Shu

Danyang

Ying

Lake Dongting

Pengli

Lake Pengli

East China Sea

Ba

Yalong

Dadu

Independent mountain tribes

Lingling

Guiyang

Viets

TAIWAN

Yizhou

Thai-speaking tribes

Xi

Nanhai

Lancang (Mekong)

Viets

Red

Black

VIETNAM

South China Sea

Jiaozhi

Zhuyai

LAOS

Juizhen

Hainan

Mekong

sage and teacher. Confucius's moral teachings stressed respect for authority, family, and tradition. He instructed rulers to act virtuously so as to set a good example for their subjects to follow.

THE FIRST EMPEROR

After the Warring States Period, the province of Qin, in the west, emerged as the strongest power in China. Its mountainous borders made it hard to attack, and from about 350 BC onward it steadily expanded its territory by conquering the tribal peoples on its western borders. Between 230 and 221 BC the Qin king Zheng, in a series of lightning campaigns, rapidly conquered the other states of China. To mark his success he adopted the title Shi Huangdi, or "First Emperor."

As a defense against nomad invasions, Shi Huangdi linked the border ramparts built in the Warring States Period into a continuous earth barrier that stretched for more than 1,000 miles (1600 km). This was the beginning of the Great Wall of

THE TERRACOTTA ARMY

In 1974, peasants digging a well near the ancient Qin capital of Xianyang broke into a pit containing thousands of lifesize clay soldiers. They had been placed there to guard the body of Shi Huangdi, who is buried in a massive mound about 1 mile (1.6 km) away. Records state that more than 700,000 men were conscripted from all over the empire to build it.

Archeologists uncovered more than 7,000 soldiers belonging to the Terracotta Army, together with their horses and war chariots. Enormous care had been taken in sculpting the figures: the head of each soldier is different, with a wide range of facial expressions, beards, and hairstyles being seen. They include archers, infantrymen, and cavalry, and provide invaluable information about ancient Chinese armor and weaponry.

Right Terracotta soldiers stand ready for battle.

Top A checkerboard of fields in the Yellow river valley. From the Shang civilization to the Han dynasty, this fertile region formed the heartland of the early Chinese state.

Above Horses, first domesticated in southern Russia, were highly prized by the Chinese, who would capture fine specimens on their campaigns in the west. This bronze horse and rider from Gansu is of Han origin.

China, though the stone wall that can be seen today is of much later date.

Shi Huangdi adopted forceful measures to unite his empire. Local customs were banned; everyone had to obey the same laws and use the same coins, weights, measurements, and style of writing. Even the width of axles on wagons had to be the same. The emperor appointed all officials. Opposition to his policies was ruthlessly punished, usually by death.

For a man who did not care how many people he killed, Shi Huangdi was terrified of dying himself. He ordered doctors to try to discover a medicine to make him immortal. They failed, of course, and Shi Huangdi died in 210 BC. The cost of his policies had been enormous. Peasant farmers had been taxed heavily to pay for them, and forced to join the army or work on building projects. In 206 BC a rebellion broke out and the entire Qin royal family was massacred.

THE HAN DYNASTY

Although the downfall of the Qin dynasty sparked off a ferocious civil war, the empire did not break up. The eventual winner was Gaozu, the first emperor of the Han dynasty (202 BC–AD 220). Gaozu recognized that the Qin dynasty had been overthrown because it had been too brutal. He therefore reduced taxes, gave land to the peasants, and passed other reforms to increase prosperity. The law was made less harsh and the death penalty used much less.

China continued to expand under the early Han emperors, who conquered large territories in the south and much of the Korean peninsula. In the west, seizure of the strategic Gansu corridor opened the way to central Asia, where a protectorate was set up. Xiongnu nomads invaded China many times from Mongolia but were eventually defeated in 36 BC. The Han's constant military campaigns drained the economy, and in AD 9 the dynasty was overthrown by a rebel called Wang Mang.

Though the Han won back their throne just 14 years later, they were unable to revive their former greatness. Peasant rebellions became common. The emperors were figureheads only, isolated from their subjects by the ceremonies of court ritual. Actual power passed into the hands of their generals and officials. In 220, the last Han emperor was deposed and the empire broke up into three separate kingdoms.

THE MEDIEVAL WORLD 2

The maps in this section trace nearly 1,500 years between the birth of Christ (the end of the ancient world) and Christopher Columbus' historic voyage to the Americas in 1492 (the prelude to the modern world). It was an eventful period in human history, which saw the the rise of Christianity and Islam, the most recent of the world's five major religions.

In the 1st century AD, the Roman empire was at the height of its dominance and prosperity, and people believed it would last for ever. It actually survived for another 400 years in the west before falling to Germanic invaders. After its collapse, Europe entered a long period of economic and political decline, now known to us as the Dark Ages. When they came to an end, about AD 1000, almost all of Europe was Christian.

From the 7th century on, the dynamic Arab empire spread the new religion of Islam through the Middle East into North Africa and Spain, along the coast of East Africa, and across Central Asia as far as India, building a civilization that in terms of art, literature, science, and philosophy far outshone that of early medieval Europe. Islam's cultural life was matched in richness and sophistication only by that of China, whose technology was the most advanced in the medieval world: papermaking, printing, gunpowder, and the magnetic compass were among the many inventions in use in China long before they were known in Europe.

In the 13th century, the Mongols—nomadic warriors who swept out of Central Asia to conquer the largest land empire the world has ever seen— inflicted terrible damage on both the Islamic and Chinese civilizations. In part as a result of this, Europe in the late Middle Ages was beginning to catch up with Asian culture and technology. Art, architecture, and scholarship flourished, trade expanded rapidly, and by the mid 15th century, European seafarers were voyaging around the coast of Africa to India and across the Atlantic to the Americas, which they called the New World.

The globe had started to shrink. Europeans learned that civilizations such as they had never dreamed of existed in this strange New World, with large cities, complex buildings, and advanced astronomical knowledge. Above all, the New World possessed vast wealth—gold, silver, and copper—and this the Europeans envied. Within a short time the Aztec and Inca empires had been conquered and pillaged. Europe's impact on the rest of the world was just beginning.

Left *Window from Chartres Cathedral, France, c.1200.*

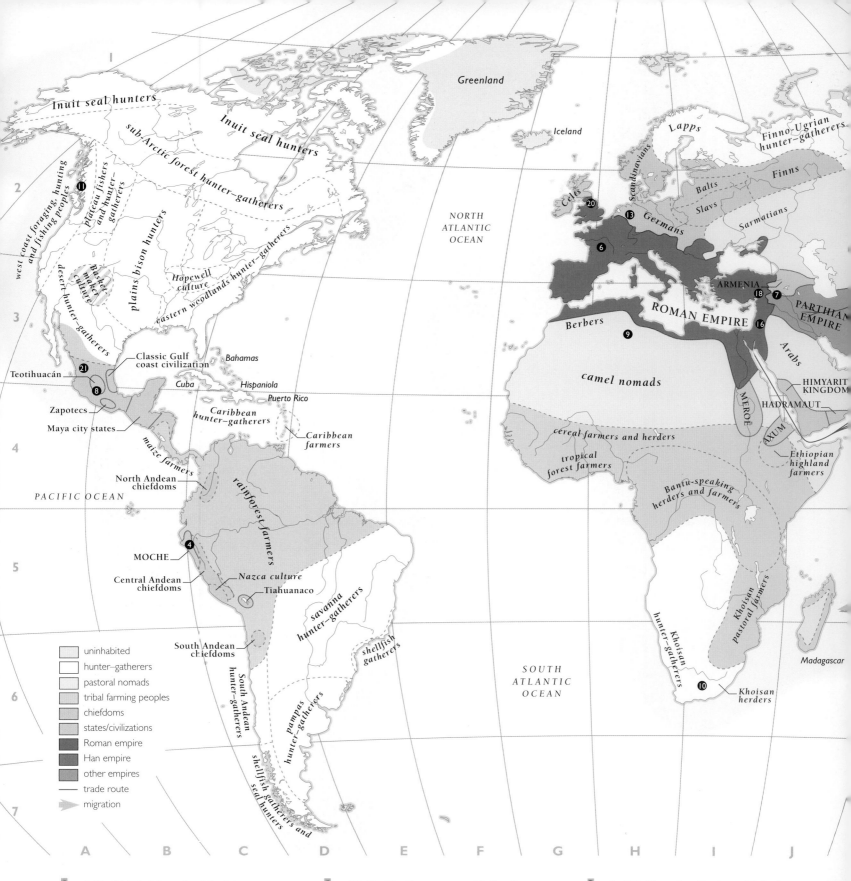

uninhabited
hunter–gatherers
pastoral nomads
tribal farming peoples
chiefdoms
states/civilizations
Roman empire
Han empire
other empires
trade route
migration

Map labels:

Inuit seal hunters
Greenland
Iceland
Lapps
Finno-Ugrian hunter–gatherers
Scandinavians
Finns
Balts
Slavs
Celts
Germans
Sarmatians
ARMENIA
PARTHIAN EMPIRE
ROMAN EMPIRE
Berbers
Arabs
HIMYARIT KINGDOM
HADRAMAUT
MEROË
AXUM
Ethiopian highland farmers
camel nomads
cereal farmers and herders
tropical forest farmers
Bantu-speaking herders and farmers
Khoisan pastoral farmers
Khoisan hunter–gatherers
Khoisan herders
Madagascar
NORTH ATLANTIC OCEAN
SOUTH ATLANTIC OCEAN

west coast foraging, hunting and fishing peoples
Inuit seal hunters
sub-Arctic forest hunter–gatherers
Plateau fishers and hunter–gatherers
Basket maker culture
desert hunter–gatherers
plains bison hunters
Hopewell culture
eastern woodlands hunter–gatherers
Teotihuacán
Classic Gulf coast civilization
Zapotecs
Maya city states
Bahamas
Cuba
Hispaniola
Puerto Rico
Caribbean hunter–gatherers
Caribbean farmers
maize farmers
North Andean chiefdoms
rainforest farmers
MOCHE
Central Andean chiefdoms
Nazca culture
Tiahuanaco
savanna hunter–gatherers
shellfish gatherers
South Andean chiefdoms
South Andean hunter–gatherers
pampas hunter–gatherers
shellfish gatherers and seal hunters
PACIFIC OCEAN

① c.140–94 BC A branch of the Sakas, a nomadic people of Central Asia, migrates into northwest India

② 128–36 The Han rulers of China subdue the Xiongnu nomads of the eastern steppes

③ 113 The Chinese expand into Vietnam

④ c.100 South America's first state develops in the Moche valley of coastal Peru

⑤ 57 According to tradition, Silla, the earliest state in Korea, is founded

⑥ c.58–51 The Roman general Julius Caesar conquers the Celts of Gaul (France)

⑦ c.53 The Parthians inflict a crushing defeat on a Roman army at the battle of Carrhae

⑧ 31 The "long count" calendar, the earliest known calendar of Mesoamerica, is devised, possibly by the Toltecs

⑨ c.AD 1–100 The camel is introduced from Asia to the Sahara, opening up trade routes across the desert to sub-Saharan and tropical Africa

⑩ c.1–100 Sheep-herding is established among the Khoisan nomads of southern Africa

⑪ c.1–100 Complex societies develop among the hunter–gatherer peoples living on the Pacific coast of North America

⑫ c.1–100 Pottery skills die out among the Polynesians of the Fiji-Samoa-Tonga triangle

⑬ 9 In Germany, a Roman army is defeated in the Teutoburgerwald. No further attempts are made to extend the empire north of the Rhine

THE WORLD BY AD 120

THE 1ST CENTURY AD WAS AN AGE OF EMPIRES. IN EUROPE, THE ROMAN EMPIRE WAS AT ITS HEIGHT, WHILE IN CHINA THE HAN DYNASTY HELD SWAY. TRADE WAS EXPANDING BY LAND AND SEA, AND THESE TWO GREAT IMPERIAL POWERS KNEW OF EACH OTHER'S EXISTENCE THROUGH TRAVELERS' TALES. EARLY CIVILIZATIONS IN MESO- AND SOUTH AMERICA WERE ALSO ESTABLISHING CONTROL OVER THEIR NEIGHBORS.

By AD 1, the start of the Christian era, Rome controlled nearly all the land around the Mediterranean as well as most of the Iberian peninsula and France. After a Roman army was annihilated in the Teutoburgerwald in Germany in AD 9, the emperor Augustus (r.27 BC–AD 14) warned against new territorial conquests, believing that the empire had reached its natural limits. His successors, however, ignored his advice, and it continued to grow for another century. In Europe, most of Britain was conquered between AD 43 and AD 78 and Dacia (modern Romania) fell in 106. The emperor Hadrian (r.117–38) ended further expansion and strengthened the empire's defenses. He even built stone and turf walls to protect the most vulnerable frontiers in Britain and Germany. His policy was a wise one: the Germanic tribes living on the other side of the Rhine and Danube frontiers were

Below *The province of Britain, the northern-most part of the empire, as shown on a late Roman document.*

---

⑭ c.9–23 An economic crisis causes a rebellion that results in the temporary overthrow of the Han dynasty in China

⑮ 25–50 The Kushan state comes into being under Kujala Kadphises

⑯ 30 Jesus of Nazareth (Jesus Christ) is crucified in Jerusalem

⑰ 50–100 The kingdom of Funan is founded on the Mekong river in Cambodia and prospers from the sea trade between China and India

⑱ 115–17 The Roman empire is at its greatest extent following Trajan's short-lived conquest of Armenia and Mesopotamia

⑲ c.120–30 The Kushan empire reaches its greatest extent under king Kanishka, extending from the Aral Sea in Central Asia to the Ganges

⑳ 122–28 The emperor Hadrian builds a defensive wall across northern Britain

㉑ 150 The Pyramid of the Sun is built at Teotihuacán in Mexico

growing stronger and better organized. The wealth of the empire would come to have great attraction for them, and in the late 2nd century they would begin to make frequent raids into Roman territory. In 167 they would even campaign as far as northern Italy. For the time being, however, the Roman empire was secure, peaceful, and more prosperous than ever before.

THE MIDDLE EAST

The Roman empire had been dominant in the Middle East for more than two hundred years, following the collapse of the Seleucid empire. The kingdom of Arabia was added to the empire in the 1st century AD, and a Jewish rebellion in Judea in 66–70 was put down with such firmness that it ended all further resistance. The Middle Eastern provinces were one of the richest parts of the empire because they had trading links with Asia. Only the Parthians, who had overrun Persia and Mesopotamia in the 2nd century BC, were a serious challenge to Rome's power. At first the Romans thought the Parthians were little more than barbarians but came to respect their military skills after a Parthian army won an overwhelming victory at Carrhae in 53 BC. Wars between Rome and Parthia were frequent, although neither side had the upper hand for long. However, the emperor Trajan (r.97–117) had ambitions to conquer the Parthians, and seized control of Armenia and Mesopotamia in 115. His successor Hadrian considered them to be undefendable and gave them up as soon as becoming emperor.

SOUTH ASIA

Parthia was at the western end of the Silk Route, the long overland trade route that crossed Asia from China. It passed through lands controlled by the Kushans who, like the Parthians, were originally nomads from the steppes of Central Asia. Late in the 1st century AD the Kushan leader Kujala Kadphises had created a kingdom in Bactria (northern Afghanistan). From there he went on to invade India, conquering most of the upper Ganges plain. Control of the valuable Silk Route trade enriched the Kushans, and in 120 their empire was at its height. King Kanishka, its most powerful ruler, issued coins that used Chinese, Parthian, Indian,

and Roman titles to proclaim his greatness. Many goods traveling along the Silk Route to Parthia were destined for Rome. Wealthy citizens delighted to wear silk clothes and flavor their food with spices from the east. But they resented having to buy them from their enemies, the Parthians. To avoid this, Roman merchants in Egypt opened up a new route to the east by sailing through the Red Sea and across the Indian Ocean to ports in southern India.

CHINA

By 120 China was the largest and most populated state in the world. The Han dynasty had ruled it since 206 BC. At first Han rule was beneficial; taxes were reduced and the people prospered. During the 1st century BC the powerful Xiongnu nomads, who regularly made raids into northern China, had been subdued in a long series of campaigns. Han control extended as far as the

Left The ancient Silk Route ran for 4,000 miles (6,400 km) across Asia. Merchants did not travel the entire length—goods were passed on by middlemen who exacted large sums of money for their services. Ideas also traveled along the Silk Route—it was the way by which Buddhism entered China from India in the 1st century AD. At Bezeklik, in the foothills of the Tien Shan mountains, Buddhist temples carved into the rock recall the time when travelers, merchants, and missionaries were frequent visitors.

Below Caravans, long strings of pack camels, carried consignments of goods across the arid wastes and deserts of the Silk Route. Travelers rested overnight at inns known as caravanserais.

northern Korean peninsula. A number of major territorial gains also took place in the west and the south, and the first Chinese expansion was made into Vietnam. However, the economic costs of these policies were high, leading to rebellion and the overthrow of the dynasty from AD 9–23. Although the Han rulers were restored, they failed to stop the abuse of peasants by rich landowners, and discontent continued to spread.

AFRICA

By AD 44 the entire North African coast from Egypt to Morocco was in the hands of the Romans. It was a prosperous region that supplied the empire with grain and olive oil. The introduction of the camel from Asia, about 100 BC, opened up trade across the Sahara, while the kingdom of Axum on the Red Sea grew wealthy from exporting ivory and other goods to Rome. As Bantu-speaking farmers continued to move out of the rainforests of tropical Africa onto the central grasslands, they introduced arable farming and the use of iron to the nomadic herders and hunter–gatherers already living there. Bantu languages and customs soon became predominant among them. In the far south of the continent, Khoisan hunter–gatherers used stone tools and weapons. During the 1st century AD voyagers from Indonesia, probably traders on their way to East Africa, settled the previously uninhabited island of Madagascar.

THE AMERICAS

While the civilizations of the Old World knew of each other through trade and war, they were completely ignorant of the New World and the civilizations that had developed there. At the end of the 1st century AD the city of Teotihuacán was the most powerful state in the Americas. It dominated central Mexico and had strong cultural influence over its neighbors, the Zapotecs and Maya. The Teotihuacáns had probably developed an early form of writing but no inscriptions of theirs have survived. We know that the Maya understood advanced mathematics and astronomy and used a form of hieroglyphic writing. The first organized state in South America arose in the Moche valley in northern Peru around 100 BC; by AD 120 it controlled several hundred miles of the coastal lowlands. The Moche were fine craftsmen in gold, silver, and copper and produced fine pottery and textiles. They built vast ceremonial centers of adobe (mud brick). Farther south on the Peruvian coast the Nazca culture was flourishing. It is best known for its "geoglyphs," vast drawings of geometrical patterns and animals that were laid out on the ground as a means of communicating with the gods.

THE ROMAN EMPIRE

THE ROMAN EMPIRE WAS AT ITS PEAK IN THE 2ND CENTURY AD. IT STRETCHED FROM BRITAIN TO ARABIA, UNITING A MULTITUDE OF RACES, CULTURES, AND RELIGIONS. ALTHOUGH THE EMPIRE WAS CREATED BY WAR AND CONQUEST, IT PROVIDED THOSE LIVING WITHIN ITS WELL-DEFENDED FRONTIERS WITH PEACE, STABILITY, AND PROSPERITY. BUT INCREASING PRESSURE FROM THE PEOPLES LIVING JUST BEYOND ITS BORDERS WEAKENED IT, BRINGING ABOUT ITS EVENTUAL DOWNFALL.

The emperor Augustus (r.23 BC–AD 14) restored peace to the Roman empire after a long period of civil war, bequeathing to it a strong and efficient system of provincial government. This contributed to the steady growth and stability of the empire over the next 200 years. The authority of the emperors was weakened, but not fatally damaged by, the scandals of Caligula's reign (37–41) and the despotic rule of Nero (54–68). The latter was deposed by an army rebellion, and from then on the army had ultimate control over the choice of emperor. Their preference was often given to a professional soldier rather than a high-born Roman. The empire reached the height of its prosperity during the 2nd century when it had the fortune to be ruled by an unparalleled succession of able and efficient emperors—the Spanish-born Trajan (r.97–117), Hadrian (r.117–38), Antoninus Pius (r.138–61), and Marcus Aurelius (r.161–80).

A FAR-FLUNG EMPIRE

The vast Roman empire was divided into provinces, each with its own legal administration. It was Roman policy to persuade leading native provincials to take part in local government and loyal service was rewarded with Roman citizenship. Although there was a state religion, many hundreds of gods were worshiped by the different peoples living within the empire; the Romans were ready to tolerate any religion that did not involve human sacrifice. All citizens were expected to observe the official cult of the emperor and make sacrifices to the Roman gods; refusal to do so was seen as a sign of disloyalty. Because Jews and Christians held back, they were often persecuted.

INFLUENCES FROM THE EAST

During the 1st century AD a number of religious mystery cults from the eastern Mediterranean became hugely popular throughout the Roman empire: there is evidence that they were practiced even in northern Britain by the soldiers garrisoning Hadrian's Wall. One of the earliest was the cult of the wine god Dionysus (Bacchus to the Romans), which involved riotous drinking and dancing. It was officially frowned on as a danger to public order, but its followers met in secret—no doubt that was part of its attraction. The cult of the Egyptian mother goddess Isis also won many followers. Initiates into its mysteries took part in long fasts during which they received visions of the goddess and were given a foretaste of the delights of the afterlife.

The cult of the Persian sun god Mithras was open only to men. Mithras killed the cosmic bull of creation, symbolizing victory over death and evil. It was very popular with soldiers throughout the empire because it laid great stress on loyalty, self-sacrifice, courage, and strength.

All these cults were overtaken in the 4th century by Christianity, like them a mystical religion that originated in the eastern Mediterranean.

Left *A painting from the temple of Isis in Pompeii shows a mythological scene associated with her cult.*

Legend:

- Roman empire, AD 14
- gains by AD 120
- temporary gain, with dates held
- border of Roman empire, AD120
- division between Greek and Latin languages
- major city
- frontier wall or rampart

goods traded within Roman empire
- grain
- glass
- pottery

goods imported from outside Roman empire
- main road
- sea trading route

0   600 km
0   400 mi

Map labels:

viomagus (imegen)
Colonia Agrippina (Cologne)
Augusta Treverorum (Trier)
GERMANY
POLAND
UKRAINE
RUSSIA
Castra Regina (Regensburg)
Carnuntum (Petronell)
CZECH REPUBLIC
SLOVAKIA
AUSTRIA
HUNGARY
CARPATHIAN MTS
ROMANIA
Olbia
Panticapaeum (Kerch)
GEORGIA
Aquileia
Mediolanum (Milan)
Genua (Genoa)
Ravenna
Ancona
ITALY
ALPS
Singidunum (Belgrade)
Salonae (Solin)
Naissus (Nis)
Sarmizegethusa
Tomi (Constanta)
Black Sea
Sinope (Sinop)
Trapezus (Trabzon)
ARMENIA AD 115–117
Corsica
Rome
Ostia
Puteoli (Pozzuoli)
Sardinia
BULGARIA
Dyrrachium (Durres)
Brundisium (Brindisi)
Thessalonica (Thessaloniki)
Byzantium (Istanbul)
Nicomedia (Izmit)
Ancyra (Ankara)
Megalopolis (Sivas)
ANATOLIA
TURKEY
Amida (Diyarbakir)
Edessa (Urfa)
Pergamon (Bergama)
Smyrna (Izmir)
Ephesus
GREECE
Athens
Corinth
Tarsus
Antiochia (Antakya)
MESOPOTAMIA AD 115–117
Dura Europus (Qal'at as Salihiyah)
Sicily
Syracusae (Syracuse)
Carthage
Malta
Crete
Rhodes
Cyprus
Palmyra (Tadmur)
SYRIA
IRAQ
Mediterranean Sea
Tyrus (Tyre)
Damascus
Caesarea
Jerusalem
Gaza
Cyrene (Shahhat)
Leptis Magna
TUNISIA
LIBYA
Alexandria
Memphis
EGYPT
Petra
SAUDI ARABIA
Mycs Hormus
Thebes
Berenice
Nile

Rivers and features:
Rhine, Danube, Elbe, Oder, Vistula, Po, Sava, Dnieper, Euphrates, Tigris

Trade goods labels:
amber
animal skins
slaves
grain, honey
animal skins
flax, iron, wine
wild animals from Asia
silk from China
aromatic resins from Arabia
muslin, perfume and spices from India
ebony, ivory, slaves and wild animals
slaves and wild animals
animals from central Africa

All the peoples of the Roman empire were encouraged to adopt Roman styles of living. Whether in Britain, beside the Danube, in Palestine, or North Africa, towns were built on an identical grid pattern with aqueducts for a piped water supply, baths, theaters, and all the other amenities the Romans thought essential for a civilized life. The army also helped to spread the Roman way of life. Provincials could enlist in "auxiliary," or support, regiments. Men serving in the army learned Latin, the common language of the Roman empire, and were given Roman citizenship on retirement. In this way, they began to think of themselves not as conquered peoples but as Romans. In AD 212 Roman citizenship was granted to all the empire's free inhabitants. Latin came to replace most local languages in the west (Celtic survived in Britain and Basque in the Pyrenees). The Romance languages (Italian, French, Spanish, Catalan, Portuguese, and

Romanian) have all developed from regional Latin dialects. Latin did not make the same inroads in the eastern provinces of the empire; there Greek remained the most widely spoken language.

ECONOMY & DEFENSE

Within the empire's borders, trade flourished without the threat of war or piracy, and the Roman coinage was the basis of all transactions. The empire was self-sufficient in all essential resources. A large agricultural trade developed to feed its growing cities: Rome, by far the largest city in the empire, imported 400,000 tons of grain annually in large ships from Egypt, Africa, and Sicily. The army consumed more than 100,000 tons of grain each year, while the hides of 54,000 calves were required to make the tents for one legion alone. Rome's network of paved roads, built to move the army quickly from place to place as needed, was the most developed in the ancient world, covering more than 55,000 miles (88,500 km), but road transportation was always slow and expensive and goods usually traveled by sea or river boat. Most people were peasant farmers. Their tools, utensils, pottery vessels, baskets and everyday clothes were made at home or by local craftsmen. But expensive luxuries for the rich, such as spices, silks, perfumes, ivory, and precious

Above Roman roads were built to withstand use by troops and heavy wheeled vehicles in every kind of weather.

Left Legionaries had to be engineers as well as fighting soldiers. Here an army crosses the river Danube on a bridge of boats.

stones, were imported from as far away as China, India, and East Africa.

The prosperity of the empire began to decline in the 3rd century. Mounting pressure on the empire's frontiers forced it to strengthen its border defenses. To find the money to pay the army, the amount of silver in the coinage was reduced. People began to charge more for all goods, and inflation soared. If an emperor failed to win success and booty on the battlefield, the soldiers following him might easily be led to depose and execute him. Armies serving in different parts of the empire would then elect rival emperors to succeed him. Civil wars were common. The Germans and Persians were able to invade the empire at will. Of the 26 emperors who ruled between 235 and 284, all but one died violently.

THE EMPIRE DIVIDES

The empire was saved by Diocletian (r.284–305), who realized that it was too large to be ruled by one man and divided it into eastern and western halves, each with its own emperor. In time, there came to be two capitals: Rome in the west and Constantinople in the east. Diocletian doubled the size of the army. Taxes had to be raised to pay for it, and this created more long-term problems: in many parts of the empire the tax burden forced peasant farmers below subsistence level. There was a fall in manpower numbers, and German mercenaries had to be recruited into the army to fill its ranks.

In 313 Constantine the Great (r.306–37) extended toleration to Christians. Although he only accepted baptism on his deathbed, throughout his reign he ordered churches to be built in many parts of the empire. Christianity came to influence all aspects of Roman life. In 391 the emperor Theodosius (r.379–95) put an end to traditional pagan worship and recognized Christianity as the empire's official religion.

Left Born a pagan, Constantine the Great believed that the God of the Christians intervened to give him a decisive victory at the battle of the Milvian Bridge in 312. He issued the Edict of Milan, which freed Christians from the threat of persecution.

In the late 4th century the Huns, mounted nomads from central Asia, migrated into eastern Europe. They caused panic among the Germanic tribes already living there, sending waves of uprooted peoples across Rome's weak defenses. Some received land within the empire in return for military service but proved unreliable allies. The western empire, poorer and less populated than the east, was unable to resist the continuing waves of invasions into Gaul, Spain, and North Africa. Under Attila (r.434–53), "the scourge of God," the Huns, too, ravaged the empire until they were defeated by an army of Romans and Germans at the Catalaunian Plains. It was too late to save the western empire, which had already collapsed by the time the last emperor was deposed in 476. The eastern empire hung on to become the Byzantine empire (see pages 76–79).

(see pages 76–79)

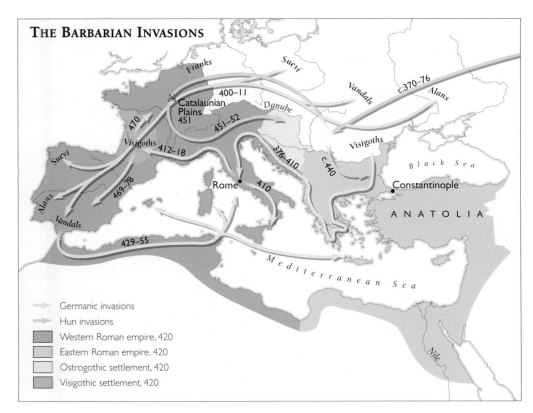

THE BARBARIAN INVASIONS

Legend:
- Germanic invasions
- Hun invasions
- Western Roman empire, 420
- Eastern Roman empire, 420
- Ostrogothic settlement, 420
- Visigothic settlement, 420

Map labels: Franks, Suevi, Vandals, c.370–76, Alans, 400–11, Catalaunian Plains 451, Danube, 470, 451–52, Visigoths, 412–18, Visigoths, 376–410, Suevi, 469–78, c.440, Black Sea, Alans, Rome, 410, Constantinople, Vandals, ANATOLIA, 429–55, Mediterranean Sea, Nile

TIMETABLE

14
Augustus is succeeded by his stepson Tiberius (d.37)

43
The emperor Claudius begins the conquest of Britain

64
Nero blames the Christians for a fire that destroys Rome, and orders a mass execution

68–69
Civil war as Rome has four emperors in one year, ending in the accession of Vespasian

115–17
Trajan annexes Armenia and Mesopotamia. The Roman empire is at its greatest extent

133
A defensive stone wall is built across northern Britain on the orders of the emperor Hadrian

212
Roman citizenship is granted to all inhabitants of the empire, regardless of birth

235–84
Civil war, invasions, and economic crisis bring the empire to the brink of collapse

286
The emperor Diocletian divides the empire into western and eastern halves

313
The emperor Constantine grants toleration to Christians

324
Constantine founds Constantinople as a new capital for the empire

410
An army of Visigoths led by Alaric sacks Rome

453
The Huns cease to threaten the empire following the death of Attila

455
Vandal pirates from North Africa attack Rome

476
Romulus Augustulus, the last emperor of the west, is overthrown by Odoacer, a German general

EUROPE IN THE DARK AGES

AFTER THE COLLAPSE OF THE ROMAN EMPIRE, WESTERN EUROPE ENTERED A LONG PERIOD OF DECLINE, OFTEN CALLED THE "DARK AGES." RECOVERY BEGAN AMONG THE FRANKS. THEIR GREATEST KING, CHARLEMAGNE, CONTROLLED MOST OF WESTERN EUROPE IN THE EARLY 9TH CENTURY, BUT HIS EMPIRE BROKE UP AFTER HIS DEATH. BY THE LATE 10TH CENTURY, POWER HAD PASSED INTO THE HANDS OF THE GERMAN EMPERORS.

With the fall of the Roman empire, western Europe reverted to a simpler pattern of life. Trade declined and towns almost died out, especially in the north. Rule was in the hands of local kings who tried to keep order as best they could, but for most people life was less secure than it had been under the emperors. Instead of a standing army, the new rulers maintained bands of soldiers in their households at their own expense. They had to be ready to do battle at any time, and if successful were rewarded with a share of the plunder. Peasant farmers looked to powerful local lords for protection, surrendering their freedom, ownership of the land they farmed, and part of their annual harvest in return. This was known as serfdom.

THE CHRISTIAN SURVIVAL

Except within the Christian church, literacy all but disappeared. For administrative purposes the church was organized into dioceses under the rule of a bishop, and in many places this structure survived the end of the Roman empire. Although the city of Rome lay in ruins, it remained important as the seat of the bishop of Rome, the pope, who came to be recognized as the leader of the church in western Europe.

The rulers of the new Germanic kingdoms were nearly all Christian, but they followed a form of the religion, Arianism, that most of their Catholic subjects considered heretical. The Franks were an exception to

Left This helmet, found at Sutton Hoo in east England, belonged to a powerful 7th-century king. He was buried inside a ship, and was surrounded by splendid treasures: fine armor, gold ornaments, silverware, and a purse of coins. Some were of Anglo-Saxon workmanship, others from as far away as Byzantium.

this. They had settled in an area approximating to modern Belgium, and did not become Christian until Clovis (r. 481–511) was baptized about 503 as a Catholic. This made him more acceptable to his new subjects, and he was able to expand the boundaries of his kingdom southward, overcoming the Germanic leaders already settled there. By 600 the kingdom of the Franks was the strongest power in western Europe.

The peoples of north Europe, living outside the former limits of the empire, were still pagan. Angles, Jutes, and Saxons from Denmark and north Germany migrated to Britain in the 5th century and settled wherever there was good land for farming; the native Celts were confined to mountainous parts of the north and west. The Anglo-Saxons, as they are known, were converted to Christianity in the 7th century by missionaries who were sent from Rome by Pope Gregory the Great and by Celtic monks from Ireland, which had been Christian since the 5th century.

In 711 a new threat appeared in Europe when a Muslim army of Arabs and Berbers from North Africa invaded Spain and easily conquered the Visigothic kingdom. Except for the small Christian kingdom of Asturias in the northern mountains, the Iberian peninsula became absorbed into the Umayyad caliphate (see pages 80–83).

c.AD 500–1000

Above Kings and warlords maintained bands of warriors to fight for them. It was from these household soldiers that the knights of medieval Europe developed. This stone carving, made at the end of the 7th century, comes from Germany.

North Sea

NORWAY
Norse
Trondheim
Svear
SWEDEN
Finns
FINLAND
L Ladoga
Vänern
Kaupang
Birka
Vättern
Götar

ESTONIA
Lake Peipus
LATVIA

Danes
Ribe
Baltic Sea
Reric
Wolin
Grobin
Balts
LITHUANIA
Western Dvina
Elbing
BELARUS

Hamburg
Bremen
GERMANY
Dorestad
Paderborn
Magdeburg
POLAND
Vistula
Aachen
Cologne
Fulda
Elbe
Oder
Kiev
UKRAINE
eims
Mainz
Frankfurt
Lorsch
Prague
CZECH REPUBLIC
Dnieper
Metz
Rhine
Regensburg
SLOVAKIA
Langres
Danube
Vienna
Salzburg
Lorch
HUNGARY
Goths

Besançon
St Gall
L Balaton
CARPATHIAN MTS
MOLDOVA
ALPS
-yon
Aquileia
CROATIA
ROMANIA
Black Sea
Vienne
Milan
Sava
BULGAR KHANATE
Pavia
Venice
Belgrade
Danube
Bobbio
Ravenna
BOSNIA HERZEGOVINA
Pliska
les
Pisa
ITALY
Split
YUGOSLAVIA
BULGARIA
Marseille
Spoleto
Ragusa
Corsica
Patrimony of St Peter
Farfa
Dyrrachium
Constantinople
Rome
Monte Cassino
Bari
Thessalonica
ANATOLIA
Naples
Benevento
Abydos
TURKEY
Sardinia
GREECE
BYZANTINE EMPIRE
(Eastern Roman empire before 610)
Cagliari
Ephesus
Palermo
Reggio
Corinth
Athens
Sicily
Tunis
Syracuse
Rhodes
Cyprus
Malta
Mediterranean Sea
Crete

AGHLABID EMIRATE

TUNISIA

LIBYA

Frankish/Carolingian empire	borders, 814
Frankish kingdom at death of Clovis, 511	Anglo–Saxon kingdoms, 814
gains by 768	Byzantine empire, 814
gains under Charlemagne, 768–814	Celtic kingdoms, 814
Holy Roman empire, c.1000	Muslim states, 814
	Slavic peoples, 814
	✠ seat of papacy
	✛ archbishopric
	⌂ monastery

0 ——— 600 km
0 ——— 400 mi

*M*onasteries—houses where monks (or nuns) lived secluded lives dedicated to prayer—formed scattered centers of learning and culture in Dark Age Europe. In the west, monastic life was governed by the Rule of St. Benedict (c.480–547), a nobleman who had chosen a life of religious austerity and founded a monastery for like-minded companions at Monte Cassino in Italy. His rule divided the monk's day into periods for physical work, study, and prayer. Monks had to be obedient to the abbot, could own nothing, and could not marry. Rulers supported monasteries because they believed the monks' prayers would benefit their kingdoms. Most monasteries had schools attached to them where monks were trained to copy the Gospels and other books. These were beautifully decorated and illustrated, and given covers of gold encrusted with jewels.

By the 10th century monastic life had become lax. An abbey founded at Cluny in France in 910 introduced a return to strict observance of the Benedictine Rule. Reform spread to other monasteries and helped to bring about a revival in Christian enthusiasm in the next century.

Left A decorated page from the Book of Kells, a lavish 9th-century Gospel Book.

CHARLES THE GREAT

The most successful of the Frankish kings was Charlemagne (r.768–814); his name means simply "Charles the Great." He halted the Muslim advance in Spain and, in 30 years of unbroken campaigning, he all but doubled the size of the Frankish kingdom. Charlemagne believed he had restored the "golden age" of the Roman empire and was crowned emperor in Rome by the pope on Christmas Day 800.

Charlemagne was a devout Christian. He believed that God would hold him personally responsible for his subjects' behavior, and passed laws to ensure that people lived a Christian life. He encouraged attempts to improve the quality of the clergy and personally sponsored a revival of monastic learning. We owe much of our knowledge of classical Roman literature to the copying of their works by Frankish monks. Charlemagne also sent missionaries to north Germany to convert the pagan Saxons.

THE VIKINGS

Charlemagne's reign saw a recovery of economic activity in western Europe, and with it a revival of seaborne trade. During the 790s Viking pirate ships from Denmark and Norway were seen along the Frankish and British coasts, creating terror wherever

Above A portrait of Charlemagne sitting at God's right hand, from a medieval French medallion.

Left This head of a fierce Viking warrior decorates a wagon from a royal burial. The Vikings were not only raiders; they were also farmers and merchants. Craftsmen fashioned intricate patterns in wood and metal. At feasts, skalds (court poets) were famed for their skill at rhyming and storytelling.

they landed. Rich, undefended monasteries were the targets for their raids. Their attacks increased in the 830s during the civil wars that followed Charlemagne's death. Their fast longships gave them terrifying mobility. By the time an army had been raised against them, they had moved on to their next raid.

Late in the 9th century Vikings began to settle in Britain, Ireland, and northwestern France. Sailing farther west than any before, they colonized the Faroe Islands, Iceland, and Greenland, and even reached North America around 1000, but did not found a permanent settlement there. Vikings from Sweden pioneered trade routes down the rivers of eastern Europe to reach the Black Sea and Constantinople. Known as "Rus," they founded the ruling dynasty of Kiev, the origin of the medieval Russian state.

In England, Wessex under its king Alfred the Great (r.871–99) halted the advance of the Viking armies. His successors expelled them by 954. In so doing, they united all of England under one crown. The Frankish empire did not recover its former strength. Disunity continued among its rulers, and in 889 it broke up for good, with France and Germany emerging as the largest kingdoms.

Europe now faced new invasions from the Magyars (Hungarians), mounted nomadic warriors from central Europe. Their raids caused great damage in the east until they were halted by the German king Otto I (r.936–73) at the battle of Lechfeld in 955. In 961 Otto annexed northern Italy. He was by now the most powerful ruler in Europe. The following year he was crowned emperor, to found the Holy Roman empire.

THE VIKING INVASIONS

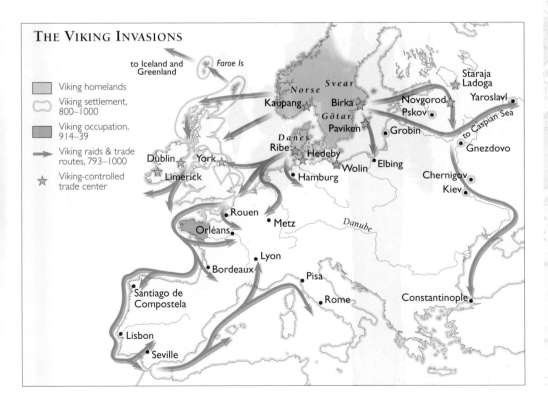

to Iceland and Greenland · Faroe Is

- Viking homelands
- Viking settlement, 800–1000
- Viking occupation, 914–39
- → Viking raids & trade routes, 793–1000
- ★ Viking-controlled trade center

Norse · *Svear* · Staraja Ladoga
Kaupang · Birka · Novgorod · Yaroslavl
Götar · Pskov
Paviken · Grobin · to Caspian Sea
Danes · Gnezdovo
Ribe · Hedeby
Dublin · York · Wolin · Elbing
Limerick · Hamburg · Chernigov
Rouen · Kiev
Orléans · Metz · *Danube*
Lyon
Bordeaux · Pisa
Santiago de Compostela · Rome · Constantinople
Lisbon
Seville

THE BYZANTINE EMPIRE

WITH ITS CAPITAL AT CONSTANTINOPLE, THE BYZANTINE EMPIRE WAS THE DIRECT DESCENDENT OF THE ROMAN EMPIRE IN THE EAST. IN THE 5TH CENTURY ITS LANDS INCLUDED GREECE, ANATOLIA, SYRIA, PALESTINE, AND EGYPT. THE EMPIRE SURVIVED FOR MORE THAN A THOUSAND YEARS AFTER THE FALL OF THE WESTERN EMPIRE, ONLY COLLAPSING WHEN CONSTANTINOPLE WAS CAPTURED BY THE TURKS IN 1453.

In 324 Constantine the Great (r.306–37) chose Byzantium, a Greek port on the western shore of the Bosporus, the narrow strait between Turkey and Europe, as the site for a new capital in the east, which he renamed Constantinople. Trade flourished as a result of its excellent communications by sea with the Mediterranean and Black Sea, and the city grew fast. It was surrounded on three sides by the sea and was strongly defended on its landward side by a fortified wall built in the 5th century.

Below *The great domed cathedral of St. Sophia in Constantinople was built by Justinian in the 6th century; it is now a mosque. The patriarch of Constantinople was leader of the eastern Orthodox church as the pope was of the western Catholic church.*

- —— border, 628
- Byzantine empire, 628
- Byzantine empire, 1025
- Byzantine empire, 1204
- ■ semi-autonomous Byzantine enclave, with date of loss
- --- border of Byzantine *themes*, 1025
- Bulgar khanate, 986
- Norman kingdom of Sicily, c.1090
- ▮ major fortified city
- <u>Mistra</u> major Byzantine cultural center
- ➔ attacks on Byzantine empire
- ➔ Arab campaigns

The eastern empire, which was wealthier and more populated than the west, had greater resources to resist the impact of the Germanic invasions (see page 71). Justinian (r.527–65) even managed to recapture lost land in North Africa, Italy, and southern Spain. At the end of the 6th century attacks from the Slavs and Avars, who lived north of the Danube, weakened the empire. In the east, the Sasanian Persians overran Syria, Palestine, and Egypt before being defeated in 627 by the emperor Heraclius (r.610–41). He saved the empire from collapse and introduced much-needed reforms.

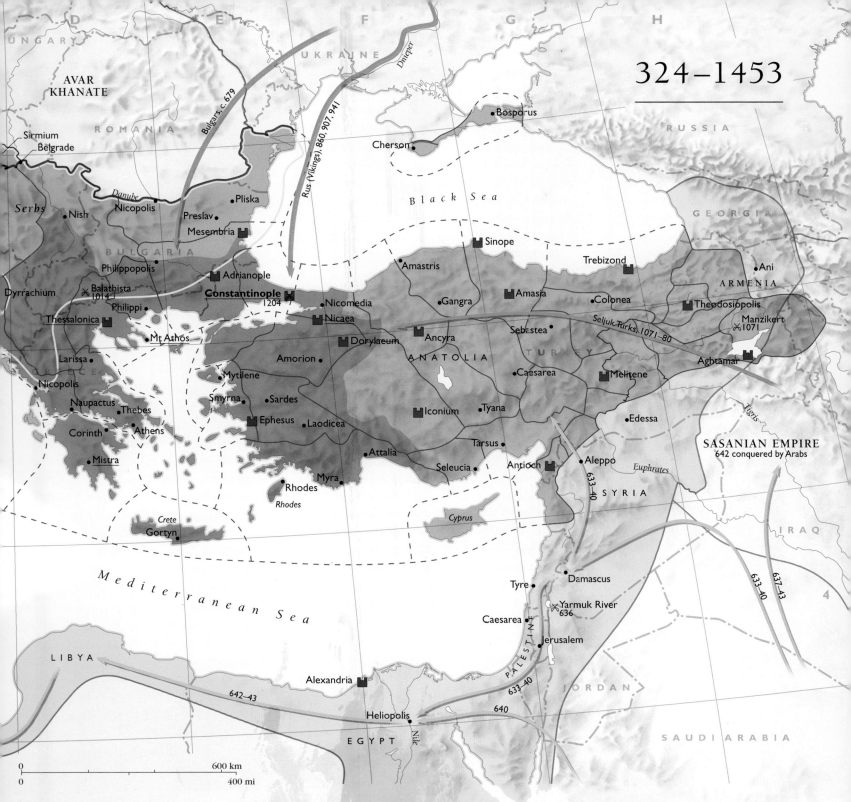

A GREEK EMPIRE

Heraclius's reign is usually taken to mark the beginning of the Byzantine empire. As most people in the east were Greek speakers, he replaced Latin with Greek as the official language of government. However, the Byzantine emperors continued to call themselves Roman. Heraclius's most important reform was to introduce a system of military recruitment districts called *themes*. Soldiers were settled on land as free peasant farmers, growing their own food and paying taxes to the state. In wartime, the soldiers of each *theme* formed a single military unit. The system greatly improved the empire's defenses by providing a reliable supply of soldiers who could be swiftly mobilized.

In 633, before it had had time to recover from the recent war with Persia, the Byzantine empire was attacked by a new enemy, the Muslim Arabs (see pages 80–83). They overran Syria and after a decisive victory at the Yarmuk River (636) went on to conquer Palestine, Egypt, and much of North Africa. A little while later, around 679, the Bulgars crossed the Danube to establish an independent state in Byzantine territory, from which the modern state of Bulgaria gets its name. As a result of Heraclius's reforms, the empire was able to survive and rebuild its military strength, in spite of these territorial losses. In 1014 Basil II "the Bulgar-slayer" (r.976–1025) defeated the Bulgars at Balathista, pushing the frontier back to the river Danube. Byzantium was now the greatest power in the Middle East and Europe.

In the course of the 11th century Seljuk Turks from central Asia conquered much of the Arab empire and were converted to Islam. In 1071 they invaded the Byzantine empire. The welfare of the army had been

Left Icons (painted images of saints) were objects of prayer and contemplation. In every Orthodox church, they were fixed to the screen that divided the people from the clergy in the sanctuary. Spiritual serenity was suggested by the stylized postures of the figures. The Virgin in this icon gazes out at the viewer with an expression of watchful calm.

Below left Saladin, the most feared of Muslim warriors, and King Richard the Lionheart of England, a leader of the Third Crusade, meet in battle; an encounter fancifully recreated here by an English artist.

excommunicated each other. The Byzantine emperors saw themselves as the legitimate rulers of the territories of the former western Roman empire. Southern Italy and Sicily remained within the Byzantine sphere of influence, but it was here that landless Norman adventurers established an independent kingdom in the late 11th century.

Urban's calling of the First Crusade met a mood of spiritual fervor in the western church (see page 86). Thousands of knights made the long journey to the Holy Land, and in 1099 Jerusalem was captured by a Crusader army. Relations between Byzantium and the west worsened as a result of the Crusades. After making some gains in Anatolia, the Byzantines would not follow the crusading army to Palestine. This was seen in the west as a sign of their lack of religious zeal: many Crusaders believed their Greek allies were not truly Christian at all. They refused to hand back to the Byzantines the territory they gained in Syria and Palestine from the Seljuks, but established independent states of their own. The Italian ports of Genoa and Venice, benefiting from the increased traffic with the crusading kingdoms, took over control of Mediterranean trade from the Byzantines.

neglected by Basil's successors, and the Byzantines were crushingly defeated at the battle of Manzikert. The Seljuk occupation of Anatolia was a crippling blow, as this was the most populated part of the empire, providing most soldiers. Byzantium's days as a great power were ended. In the aftermath of the disaster, the emperor Alexius I Comnenus (r.1081–1118) appealed to the west for help in recovering his lost lands. Pope Urban II responded by calling faithful Christians in the west to join a crusade to free the Holy Land from Muslim control.

THE CRUSADES

In many ways, Urban's action was a surprising one. For centuries, the Catholic and Orthodox churches had been drifting apart. Distrust had hardened into outright hostility as the two competed for influence in eastern Europe: missionaries from Constantinople converted the Balkan Slavs, Bulgars, and Russians to the Orthodox faith, while Hungary and Poland became Catholic. In 1054 the breach became permanent after the pope and the patriarch had mutually

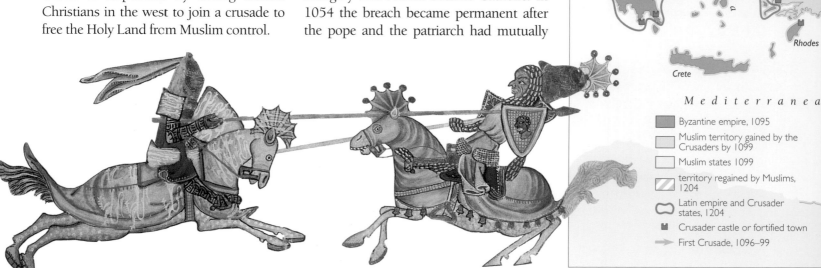

BYZANTIUM & THE CRUSADER STATES

Thessalonica

Constantinople

Aegean Sea

Athens

Rhodes

Crete

Mediterranea

▨ Byzantine empire, 1095

☐ Muslim territory gained by the Crusaders by 1099

☐ Muslim states 1099

▨ territory regained by Muslims, 1204

◠ Latin empire and Crusader states, 1204

▣ Crusader castle or fortified town

➛ First Crusade, 1096–99

RUSSIA CONVERTS

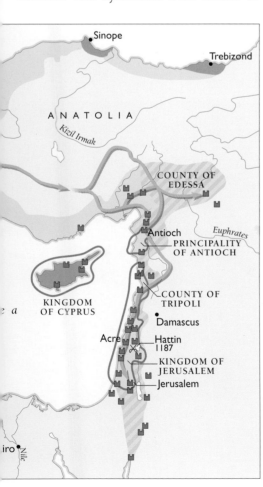

Vladimir, prince of Kiev, was a pagan descended from the Vikings who founded the first political state in Russia. Both the Byzantines and Germans, who wanted to win converts among the Slavs of eastern Europe, tried to bring him over to their side. In 988 the emperor Basil II offered Vladimir his sister Anna in marriage on condition that he was baptized into the Orthodox faith. Vladimir agreed, and ordered all the idols in Kiev and Novgorod to be thrown into the river Dnieper. A later chronicle shows a picture of his baptism.

Further Crusades were made to defend the Holy Land against Muslim attacks. Much territory, including Jerusalem itself, was lost after a defeat at Hattin in 1187. In 1204 the Fourth Crusade was held up in Constantinople while it sought funds for a new campaign in the east. When these were withheld, the Crusaders sacked the city and created a Latin empire in Greece and the Balkans. The Byzantines were unable to regain their capital and empire until 1261. Thirty years later the Turks destroyed the last of the Crusader states in Palestine.

Weakened by civil wars, the Byzantine empire never recovered. The Turks seized control of Anatolia in the 14th century and gradually reduced the empire to no more than a small area around Constantinople. In 1453 they took the city, marking the end of the Roman empire in the east.

THE BYZANTINE LEGACY

Despite its slow and painful collapse, the legacy of the Byzantine empire was a splendid one. While western Europe had fallen into intellectual and cultural decline, it preserved the cultural traditions of late Roman times. Art, music, literature, and architecture flourished. The mosaics that decorated its churches were especially noted for their brilliant colors. One account says that Vladimir of Kiev (see box) decided to embrace the Orthodox faith after his ambassador declared that no other religion could match the cathedral of St. Sophia for beauty.

The influence of Byzantine culture was spread more widely by the Greek missionaries who converted the Slavs. The Cyrillic alphabet devised by the brothers Saint Cyril and Saint Methodius is the basis of the Russian and other Slavic alphabets. After Constantinople fell, the Russian prince Ivan III (r.1462–1505) believed that his capital, Moscow, would carry on the traditions of the Roman empire. As a sign of this he adopted the double-headed eagle in 1472.

THE RISE OF ISLAM

IN THE 7TH CENTURY ARAB ARMIES SWEPT OUT OF THE DESERT. THEY CARRIED WITH THEM A NEW RELIGION, ISLAM, WHOSE FOLLOWERS ARE KNOWN AS MUSLIMS. IN LESS THAN A CENTURY THE ARABS CONQUERED A VAST EMPIRE FROM SPAIN TO CENTRAL ASIA. THEIR CIVILIZATION WAS MORE SOPHISTICATED THAN THAT OF WESTERN EUROPE. CONTROL OF MUCH OF THE ARAB EMPIRE LATER PASSED INTO THE HANDS OF THE TURKS, WHO WERE CONVERTS TO ISLAM.

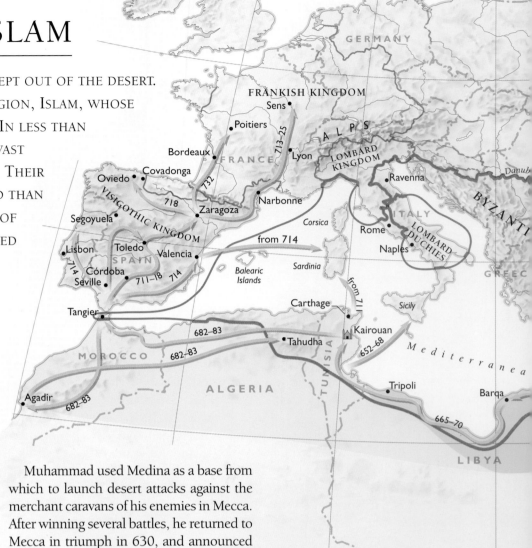

Islam (which means "submission to the will of God") was founded by the Prophet Muhammad (c.570–632). He was a merchant from the city of Mecca in Arabia. As a result of a vision he experienced in a cave in the mountains outside Mecca, he began to preach that there was only one God and that he was His messenger. At this time the Arabs worshiped many gods, and Mecca was an important cult center. The people of Mecca feared that this new religion would lessen their city's wealth and prestige. They turned against Muhammad, and in 622 forced him to flee with a band of followers to the city of Medina.

Muhammad used Medina as a base from which to launch desert attacks against the merchant caravans of his enemies in Mecca. After winning several battles, he returned to Mecca in triumph in 630, and announced that the city's pagan shrine, the Ka'aba, was now sacred to Islam.

THE WORD OF GOD

Muhammad's teachings are contained in the Koran, the holy book of Islam. He taught that Muslims have five basic duties: to know that there is only one God and that Muhammad is His prophet; to pray five times a day facing Mecca; to give alms to the poor; to observe the fast of Ramadan; to make the pilgrimage to Mecca once in their lifetime if able to afford it and physically capable of making the journey. Because it was the word of God, the Koran could only be written in Arabic script. Muslim artists could not depict themes from nature, so they put their creative energies into forming beautiful calligraphy (writing) and intricate patterns as an expression of devotion.

Right *A decorated page from the Koran.*

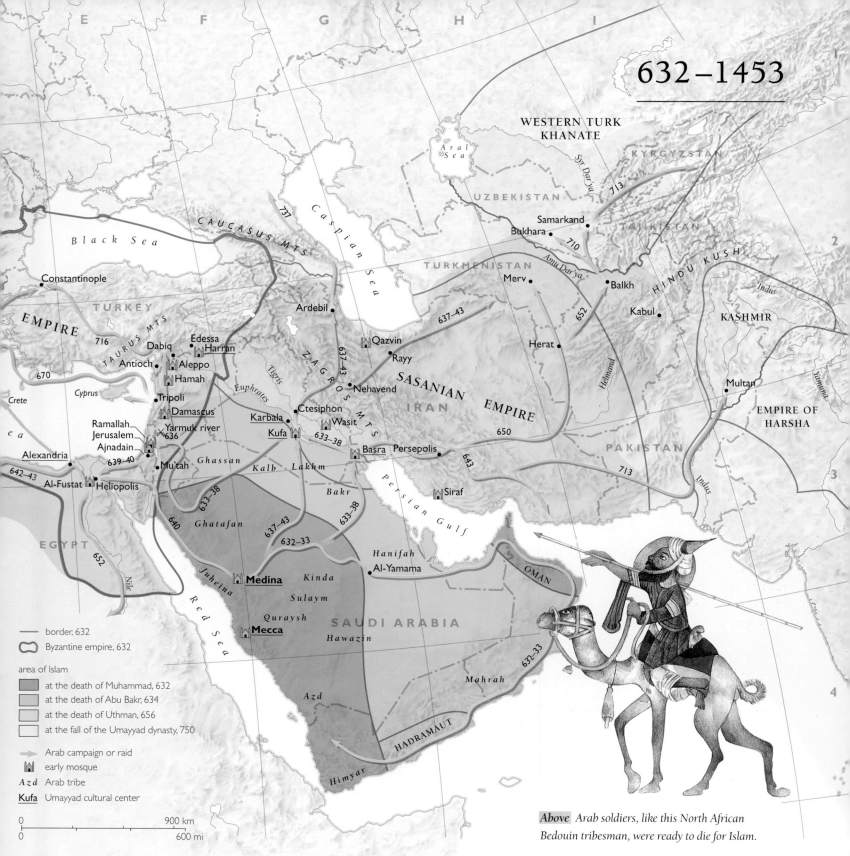

WESTERN TURK KHANATE

KYRGYZSTAN

Aral Sea

UZBEKISTAN

Samarkand
Bukhara

TAJIKISTAN

713

710

TURKMENISTAN

HINDU KUSH

Merv
Balkh

Amu Dar'ya

Indus

Caspian Sea

Black Sea

Constantinople

TURKEY

Ardebil

652

Kabul

KASHMIR

Herat

Helmand

Multan

EMPIRE

716

TAURUS MTS

Qazvin

Rayy

737

SASANIAN

EMPIRE

IRAN

EMPIRE OF HARSHA

670

Dabiq
Antioch
Aleppo
Hamah

Edessa
Harran

Tigris

ZAGROS MTS

637–43

Yamuna

Crete
Cyprus

Tripoli
Damascus

Euphrates

Nehavend

650

PAKISTAN

713

Karbala
Kufa
Ramallah
Jerusalem
Ajnadain
636

Ctesiphon
Wasit

633–38

Basra
Persepolis

643

Indus

Alexandria

Yarmuk river

639–40

Mu'tah

Ghassan

Kalb

Lakhm

Siraf

642–43

Al-Fustat
Heliopolis

640

Bakr

633–38

Persian Gulf

EGYPT

652

Ghatafan

637–43

633–38

632–33

Hanifah
Al-Yamama

OMAN

Nile

Juheina

Medina

Kinda

Sulaym

Red Sea

Quraysh

Mecca

SAUDI ARABIA

Hawazin

Mahrah

632–33

Azd

HADRAMAUT

Himyar

Legend:

— border, 632

⌒ Byzantine empire, 632

area of Islam
- at the death of Muhammad, 632
- at the death of Abu Bakr, 634
- at the death of Uthman, 656
- at the fall of the Umayyad dynasty, 750

→ Arab campaign or raid

🕌 early mosque

Azd Arab tribe

Kufa Umayyad cultural center

0 — 900 km
0 — 600 mi

Above *Arab soldiers, like this North African Bedouin tribesman, were ready to die for Islam.*

Muhammad was a political as well as a religious leader. His ambition was that all Muslims should live within a single community or state (*ummah*), ruled by the laws of Islam. He made Medina the center of this community. During the last two years of his life he converted many of the other tribes of Arabia to Islam. One reason for Islam's success is that Muhammad's teachings, contained in the "five pillars" of Islam, are simple and easily understood (see box).

THE ARAB CONQUESTS

Muhammad had no male heirs to carry on his work. His followers chose his father-in-law Abu Bakr (r.633–44) to be his first successor, or caliph. He completed the task of converting the Arab tribes. War was traditionally extremely important to the Arabs as it gave individuals the chance to win prestige and wealth. But Muhammad had united the Arabs behind the common cause of

Islam, and put an end to intertribal conflicts. He taught that it was every man's sacred duty to fight in the *jihad* ("holy war") and that anyone who died in the service of Islam would immediately enter paradise. As a united people, the Arabs were able to put far larger armies into the field than they had ever done before. During the reigns of the next two caliphs, Umar (634–44) and Uthman (644–56), they began to expand northward. Their raids were so successful that they were encouraged to attempt to conquer new lands and peoples.

The Persian and Byzantine empires were taken completely by surprise by the huge, well-organized Arab forces that poured out of the desert in the 630s. They had just ended a damaging 20-year war with each other (see page 77), and did not have the resources or might to resist such a strong enemy. Palestine, Egypt, Libya, Syria, and all of Persia were conquered in only 20 years. During the late 7th century expansion continued into the rest of North Africa

Right Islamic science was well in advance of the west. One astronomer is using dividers, another a sextant, while two more examine an astrolabe, used to calculate the positions of the planets and the stars.

Left At the center of every Islamic community was the mosque where prayer was held on Fridays. The mosque also served as a school and public meeting place. Islamic rulers showed their devotion by spending great sums on elaborate mosques. This, in Isfahan, was begun by the Seljuk Malik Shah c.1085.

(670–98) and Spain (711–18), and as far as the Indus river and into Central Asia. Defeat by the Byzantines at the gates of Constantinople in 716–17 and by the Franks at Poitiers in 732 halted the Arabs' advance into Europe.

Internal divisions within the Byzantine empire aided the Arabs' success. The Orthodox church was the official religion of the empire, but most people in Syria, Palestine, and Egypt were Monophysite Christians: they did not believe that Christ was true man as well as true God. They were frequently persecuted for their beliefs and, as a result, welcomed the Arabs as liberators. Similarly, the Visigothic kings of Spain were Arian Christians while their subjects were Catholic (see page 72). This created a wide gulf between them and people felt little loyalty to the ruling class. Islamic rule met with hardly any resistance once the monarchy had been toppled.

It was not long before conflicts began to appear within the community of Islam. Discontent with the caliph Uthman led to his assassination and he was succeeded by Muawiya (r.661–80). On his death, many believed that Husain, Muhammad's grandson, had a better claim to the caliphate than Yashid, Muawiya's son (r.680–83). This led to a civil war, in which Husain was killed. His followers regarded him as a martyr and broke away from the main body of Islam, who became known as Sunnites, to form the smaller Shiite branch. Today, this division still exists within Islam.

ISLAMIC CULTURE

Muawiya founded the Umayyad dynasty of hereditary caliphs. They modeled the government of their vast empire on the Byzantine system, and the capital was transferred from Medina to Damascus in Syria, nearer to its center. The populations ruled by the Arabs were not forced to convert to Islam, but tax and social advantages encouraged them to do so. The Arabic religion, language, and culture soon became widespread. But the Arabs in their turn were heavily influenced by the civilizations they conquered. From desert dwellers, they became highly urbanized and sophisticated. Literary styles, decorative arts, music and

END OF THE CALIPHATE

The conflict between Sunnites and Shiites gradually undermined the authority of the Umayyads. In 750 they were overthrown by the Abbasid dynasty, who ruled over the Islamic empire from Baghdad. Every member of the Umayyad family was massacred, with the exception of one, Abd al-Rahman I (r.756–88). He escaped to Spain, where he established an independent state, or emirate, with its capital at Córdoba. Under his successors it was made a caliphate, claiming authority over North Africa.

The ideal of a single Muslim community under one caliph had been broken for all time. The authority of the Abbasid caliphs gradually withered away as province after province rebelled against them. By 1000 they were purely religious leaders who did not even control Baghdad. Political power lay in the hands of the Seljuk Turks, a people from Central Asia who had converted to Islam and entered the Abbasids' service as mercenary soldiers. By the end of the 11th century they had seized control of much of the Arab empire and conquered Anatolia from the Byzantines (see page 78).

Trade and war continued the spread of Islam. By 1000 it had reached west Africa. During the 12th and 13th centuries Muslims from Afghanistan overran much of the Indian subcontinent. By the 15th century Islam had begun to spread into Southeast Asia. In the west, the Ottoman Turks had expanded into southeast Europe and were poised to destroy the Byzantine empire.

gardening were learned from the Persians. Byzantine and Persian architecture influenced building styles. Literacy and learning were greatly valued at a time when they had almost disappeared from Europe, and Arab scholars preserved and added to the geographic, mathematical, medical, and scientific knowledge of the ancient world.

DECLINE OF THE ABBASIDS

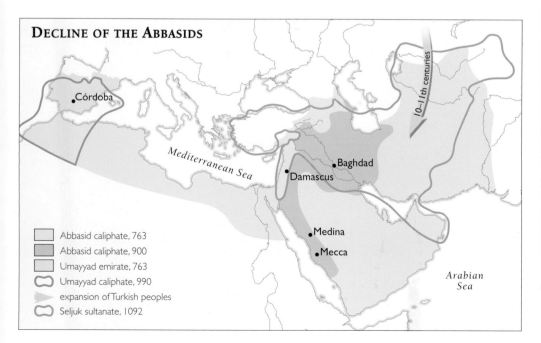

Córdoba

Mediterranean Sea

10–11th centuries

Baghdad
Damascus

Medina

Mecca

Arabian
Sea

- ▢ Abbasid caliphate, 763
- ▨ Abbasid caliphate, 900
- ▢ Umayyad emirate, 763
- ⬭ Umayyad caliphate, 990
- ➤ expansion of Turkish peoples
- ⬭ Seljuk sultanate, 1092

TIMETABLE

622
Muhammad flees from Mecca to Medina. Known as the *hijra* ("emigration"), it marks the first year of the Muslim calendar

632
Following Muhammad's death, Abu Bakr becomes the first caliph, or successor

635–38
An Arab army defeats the Byzantines at the Yarmuk river (modern Jordan) and conquers Syria and Palestine

637–42
The Arabs overrun the Persian empire

656
The standardized text of the Koran is completed

698
Carthage, the last Byzantine possession in North Africa, falls to the Arabs

711
A Muslim army invades Spain

750
The Umayyad caliphate is overthrown by the Abbasids

786–809
Abbasid power is at its peak under caliph Harun al-Rashid of Baghdad

c.970
The Seljuk Turks of central Asia convert to Islam

1055
The Seljuks seize power in Baghdad

1175–1200
Northern India is conquered by Muslims from northwest Aghanistan

1258
A Mongol army destroys Baghdad and executes the last Abbasid caliph

1389
An Ottoman army crushes the Serbs at Kosovo in the Balkans

1453
The Ottomans take Constantinople to complete their conquest of the Byzantine empire

MEDIEVAL EUROPE

AS THE UNCERTAINTIES OF THE DARK AGES DISAPPEARED, STABILITY AND PROSPERITY RETURNED TO WESTERN EUROPE. FEUDALISM GAVE MEDIEVAL RULERS NEW SOURCES OF AUTHORITY, AND STRONG KINGDOMS AND DUCHIES BEGAN TO EMERGE. AS PEOPLE FOUND RENEWED CONFIDENCE AND OPTIMISM, RELIGION AND INTELLECTUAL LIFE FLOURISHED. THROUGHOUT EUROPE, THE POPULATION BEGAN TO RISE, TRADE REVIVED, AND TOWNS GREW RAPIDLY.

Left The duke of Austria does homage to his feudal lord, the Holy Roman emperor.

In medieval Europe, most kings were feudal monarchs: they held power by granting lands, known as fiefs, to their nobles. In return, the nobles became the king's vassals by swearing an oath of loyalty. This obliged them to fight for the king when needed, either in person or by supplying armies of knights—mounted soldiers—at their own expense. Nobles in their turn rewarded their followers with small grants of land. Relations between kings, nobles, and knights were governed by a common code of chivalry, based on honor and bravery. The chivalric code also included courtesy to women and a willingness to defend the Christian religion.

Kings often had difficulty controlling their most powerful vassals. This particularly affected the German rulers of the Holy Roman empire. Great families such as the Welfs of Bavaria possessed vast estates and were able to ignore the emperor's wishes when it suited them. The emperors tried to counter the power of the dukes by seeking the support of the bishops, who also held large estates in Germany. However, during the 11th century a reform movement in the church (at first encouraged and led by the German emperors) made the popes in Rome more powerful than before. They demanded, and won,

Left Medieval abbeys and cathedrals soared upward to heaven. Colored light poured into their lofty interiors through stained-glass windows. The Gothic style of architecture, which originated in France, spread through Europe in the 12th and 13th centuries, a witness to the spiritual energy of the age.

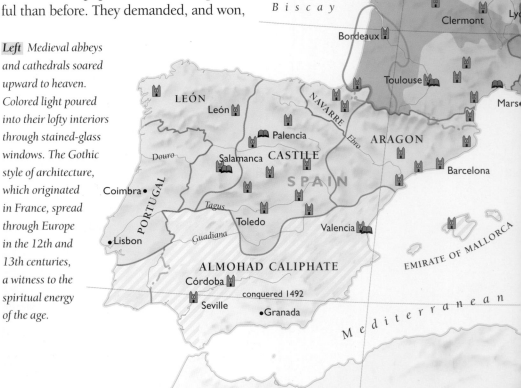

Legend:
- borders, c.1175
- kingdom of Sicily, c.1175
- Holy Roman empire, c.1175
- French royal demesne, c.1175
- other French lands, c.1175
- lands belonging to English crown, c.1175
- lands nominally controlled by England, c.1175
- lands in France controlled by England, 1216
- Iberian Christian states, c.1175
- Christian reconquest of Iberia by 1230
- Italian Lombard league of city-states, 1167
- university founded 1088–1250
- Gothic cathedral or church, c.1135–1500
- expansion of German influence

0 _____ 600 km
0 _____ 400 mi

the right to appoint bishops instead of the emperor. This struggle is known as the Investiture Contest, and it freed the 12th-century popes from political control.

The German emperors emerged from this contest far weaker, especially in northern Italy (the richest part of the empire), where leagues of city-states twice rebelled against imperial rule. They were encouraged by the popes, who were intent on creating a territorial base for themselves in Italy. In the 13th century the empire began to break up into a federation of semi-independent kingdoms, duchies, city-states, and bishoprics. Yet its influence steadily expanded eastward as German settlers established themselves in farming villages and trading towns among the Slavs of Poland and Hungary.

FRANCE & ENGLAND

At the beginning of the 11th century the French king ruled only a small area around Paris: many of his vassals were more powerful than he was. In 1066, one of them, William the Conqueror, duke of Normandy, defeated King Harold of England at the battle of Hastings to seize the English throne. Around the same time, landless adventurers from Normandy established a kingdom for themselves in Sicily and southern Italy.

By the middle of the 12th century the greatest landowner in France was the count of Anjou. In 1154 he inherited the English throne to become, as Henry II (r. 1154–89), the most powerful monarch in Europe. However, England's possessions in France

Below *In medieval Europe, the land was mostly farmed by serfs, bound laborers who worked a strip of land on a manor (estate). They paid part of their annual harvest to the lord of the manor as rent; another part went to the church. The lord protected them in war, and acted as a judge in disputes with their neighbors. Conditions were hard, but peasant living standards were rising steadily. The introduction of better plows and a threefold system of crop rotation meant that more food was grown, which they could sell at local markets.*

had been lost by 1214, and the defeat of the Holy Roman emperor shortly after at the battle of Bouvines confirmed France as the major power in Europe. English kings never abandoned hope of regaining their French possessions. Meantime, the French kings steadily extended their authority over their vassals in southern and eastern France.

Ireland was invaded by the English in the 12th century, but was not strongly held at this time. Wales was overrun in the 13th century, and Scotland was also invaded. However, under William Wallace (c.1274–1305) and Robert Bruce (r.1306–129), the Scots won back their independence.

THE AGE OF CRUSADES

In 1096, Pope Urban II appealed to western Christians to recapture the Holy Land from the Muslims (see page 78). The crusades were an outlet for the popular religious enthusiasm of the time, but were also

THE SPREAD OF THE BLACK DEATH

Left *Hasty burials were an everyday occurrence while the Black Death raged through Europe. The plague was carried by the fleas that live on rats. The earliest outbreaks occurred in east Asia in the 1330s and it spread along the Silk Route to reach the Black Sea port of Kaffa in late 1346. Ships' rats carried it to the ports of Venice, Genoa, and Marseille, and from there it spread rapidly along the main trade routes. Victims suffered terrible swellings and internal bleeding, which turned their skins black.*

seen as a chance to win fortune and prestige. The same motives inspired the campaigns against the Muslims in Spain, which led to the gradual reconquest of the Iberian peninsula and the setting up of Christian kingdoms such as Aragon, Castile, and Portugal. The French king and his northern nobles promoted the Albigensian crusade against heretics in the south of France to extend their authority into the region. The Teutonic Knights, a German and Danish crusading order, were active in converting the Slavs and Balts of the eastern Baltic, the last stronghold of paganism in Europe, while creating a trading power base there.

Throughout Europe, rising commerce and trade led to a growth in towns. An important boost to urban prosperity was the right to hold weekly or seasonal fairs. Cathedrals were built as monuments to God and

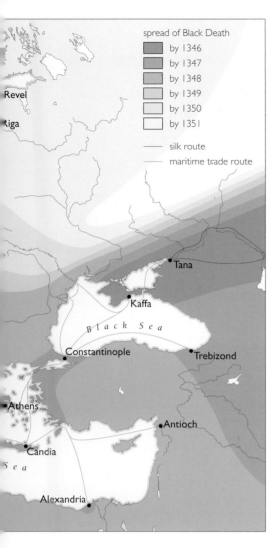

spread of Black Death
- by 1346
- by 1347
- by 1348
- by 1349
- by 1350
- by 1351

— silk route
— maritime trade route

Revel

Riga

Tana

Kaffa

Black Sea

Constantinople

Trebizond

Athens

Antioch

Candia

Sea

Alexandria

There was widespread depopulation. In many places labor became so scarce that wages rose and serfs were able to abandon their manors to find paid work, or became tenant farmers. But because there was nobody to sell goods or produce to, prices fell. Landowners therefore limited wages and imposed harsher conditions on their tenants. Popular uprisings such as the English Peasants' Revolt (1381) were the result. Churchmen, who were considered corrupt and greedy, were prime targets for attack. Heretical movements gained support. They were put down, but the church failed to introduce reforms, storing up future trouble.

THE RENAISSANCE

The independent city-states of northern Italy, such as Florence and Milan, were the richest areas of Europe at this time. Their wealth came from international trade and banking. It was here that the cultural movement known as the Renaissance (meaning "rebirth") began to emerge in the mid 14th century as interest revived in the literature, art, architecture, and science of the ancient Greek and Roman world.

The rulers of the Italian city states competed with each other to employ the leading artists, architects, and musicians of the day. In the 15th century the patronage of the powerful Medici family of bankers made Florence pre-eminent. The new technique of printing, which was developed in Germany in the 1450s, made books more readily available and by the end of the century the new learning and artistic styles of the Renaissance were beginning to spread outside Italy to the rest of Europe.

civic pride. Cathedral schools and universities grew up as centers of learning.

Despite the growth of towns, about 95% of medieval Europeans were farmers. Most peasants were serfs, unable to leave their village without the permission of their lord. Things changed in the mid 14th century when the Black Death, a virulent plague epidemic, swept through Europe, killing a third of the population within four years.

JOAN OF ARC: THE MAID OF ORLEANS

In the 1420s France's fortunes in the Hundred Years War (1337–1453) with the English were at their lowest point. The English claimed the French crown and their troops occupied much of northern France. It was a teenage peasant girl, Joan of Arc, who changed the course of the war. Joan claimed that the voices of Saints Michael, Catherine, and Margaret spoke to her, urging her to save her homeland. Her simple message breathed new hope and energy into the French forces.

Dressed in armor, she rode at the head of an army to defeat the English at Orleans in 1429. The dauphin Charles was crowned king of France at Reims and by 1453 the English had been driven from nearly all their lands in France. Joan, however, was captured by her enemies, tried as a heretic, and burned at the stake in 1430. She has been a symbol of national pride to the French ever since.

Right *A tapestry of Joan arriving at Castle Chinon.*

TANG & SUNG CHINA

THE TANG WERE ONE OF THE MOST SUCCESSFUL DYNASTIES EVER TO RULE CHINA. THEY EXTENDED CHINESE RULE FAR INTO CENTRAL ASIA; THE ARTS AND TRADE FLOURISHED UNDER THEIR REGIME. THE DYNASTY LATER FELL INTO DISORDER AND WAS SUCCEEDED BY THE SUNG. PROSPERITY WAS HIGH AND CHINA MADE GREAT TECHNOLOGICAL ADVANCES BEFORE FALLING TO THE ONSLAUGHTS OF THE MONGOLS.

The Tang dynasty (618–907) was founded by a military governor named Li Yuan, who seized power to save the Chinese empire from collapse but was later forced to abdicate by his ambitious son Taizong (r.626–49). Taizong became one of China's most able rulers. At the time he came to power, China had been reunited for only 30 years after nearly four centuries of civil war and division following the end of the Han dynasty (202 BC–AD 220).

Taizong's greatest achievement was to give China a strong system of government. The emperor stood at its head and below him were three departments: the Imperial Secretariat; the Imperial Chancellery; and the Department for State Affairs. The latter was charged with overseeing the ministries responsible for administration, finance, religion, justice, the army, and public works.

The empire was divided into 15 administrative regions or "circuits." Officials were usually chosen by examinations. This system was originally introduced by the Han emperors. They were supposed to be open to everyone but only rich landowners could afford to be educated to the high level needed to secure a pass.

Under Taizong, land was given to the poor and taxes were reduced. This brought about an increase in agriculture and craft production, and internal trade flourished,

BUDDHISM IN TIBET

A powerful kingdom first emerged in Tibet under the Buddhist ruler Sron-btsan-sgampo (r.608–50). He and his successors established a military empire in Central Asia, where it came into conflict with the territorial ambitions of Tang China before going into decline in the 9th century. The Indian missionary Atisa was responsible for reviving Tibetan Buddhism in the 11th century, and from then on it dominated every aspect of Tibetan life. Numerous sects developed, and there was a great outburst of monastic building and literary activity. The Mongols, who conquered Tibet in 1247, ruled it through a succession of powerful priests, or lamas.

Left *Shalu monastery, Tibet, founded c.1040.*

Map labels

D E F G I

Gobi Desert

MONGOLIA

Altai Mts

Tingzhou 791

rfan

KOGURYO
Chinese
protectorate
668–76

645–47, 660–68

630

Khitans

Pyongyang

SOUTH KOREA

660

Kyongju

SILLA

Sheng

Feng

Yun

You

Jojun (Beijing) 755

Hebei

874

Hedong

Heng

Henan

Yellow Sea

Suzhou

QILIAN MTS

Gansu Corridor

Liang

Taiyuan

Yan

787

791

Shan

Guannei

Lake Qinghai

Pu

Bianzhou

Luoyang

Yangzhou

Wei

Qin Jingji

Shan

Duji

Caizhou

Su

Longyou

Chang'an

Han

Huainan

An

859

East China Sea

3

Liang

Shanan-Xi

Shanan-Dong

Yangtze

Jiannan

Li

Hong (Nanchang)

Tibetans

Chengdu

Ya

Qianzhong

868

Jiangnan-Xi

Tanzhou

Jiangnan-Dong

Fu

Lhasa

620–50

Li

c.760

Mekong

763

63–68, 763

Sui

751

Yaozhou

Longyu

Lingnan

Guangzhou

Brahmaputra

NAN CHAO

Irrawaddy

Mekong

Red

VIETNAM

MYANMAR

Salween

Hainan

South China Sea

4

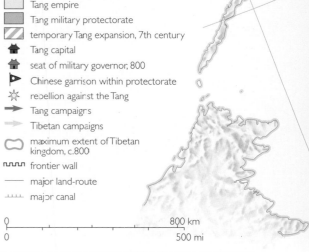

Below A model of an early Chinese junk. These high-prowed sailing vessels were developed in the Sung dynasty to make long ocean voyages.

Body text

carried on the canals that were built to link the Yellow and Yangtze rivers. Silk and fine pottery were exported. Many new inventions, including porcelain, canal locks, and gunpowder, were made.

The Tang were successful in waging war and established a military protectorate over the nomads on their western border. This brought them into contact with the newly unified kingdom of Tibet, which was also expanding into Central Asia. For a time, Tang authority extended as far as Ferghana and Soghd, on the eastern limits of the Arab empire. However, because of the great distances involved, the Central Asian empire was difficult to defend. In 751 the Chinese suffered a serious defeat by the Arabs at the Talas river near Samarkand. Forty years later, defeat by the Tibetans at Tingzhou ended their control of the Gansu Corridor and signaled the total collapse of the Chinese Central Asian empire. Tang advances into Korea proved as difficult to hold. Although a protectorate was set up in Koguryo, in the north of the country, from 668–76, the Chinese were defeated and expelled by Silla, the ruling kingdom in the south.

A rebellion led by the general An Lushan from 755–63 contributed to the loss of Central Asia, as garrisons were withdrawn from

Legend

border, 750

'circuits' of Tang empire, c.750

Tang empire

Tang military protectorate

temporary Tang expansion, 7th century

Tang capital

seat of military governor, 800

Chinese garrison within protectorate

rebellion against the Tang

Tang campaigns

Tibetan campaigns

maximum extent of Tibetan kingdom, c.800

frontier wall

major land-route

major canal

0 — 800 km
0 — 500 mi

the northwest to deal with it. Though the rebellion was put down, Tang authority declined and disorder increased as military governors in the provinces seized power for themselves. In 907 the Tang dynasty was overthrown and China broke up into nearly a dozen rival kingdoms.

THE SUNG DYNASTY

China was united again by two brothers, Sung Taizu (r.960–76) and Sung Taizong (r.976– 97). They met with little serious resistance because the years of Tang rule had given most people the idea that China should be a single state under one emperor. In the intervening years, however, powerful kingdoms had formed to the north and

Below *A Tang painting shows the imperial court fleeing to the mountains from An Lushan's revolt.*

west. These were strong enough to prevent the Sung from reconquering the border lands that had belonged to the Tang empire.

The Sung dynasty is divided into two periods: Northern Sung (960–1127) and Southern Sung (1127–1279). The Northern Sung capital was at Kaifeng, a large commercial center in the Yellow River plain. In 1127 it was captured by the Jürchen, invaders from Manchuria who conquered northern China to establish an empire of their own under the Jin dynasty. The Sung emperors moved their capital south to the port of Hangzhou. The south was now the richest and most densely populated part of China so the loss of territory was not crippling, and the Sung did not attempt to reconquer the northern provinces.

During the 13th century Mongol warriors, recently unified by Ghengis Khan (see pages 92–95), began campaigning in the

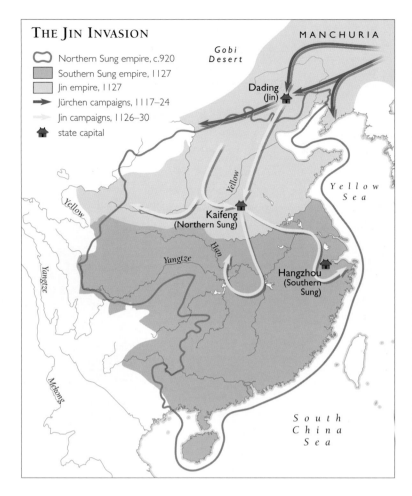

THE JIN INVASION

- Northern Sung empire, c.920
- Southern Sung empire, 1127
- Jin empire, 1127
- → Jürchen campaigns, 1117–24
- → Jin campaigns, 1126–30
- 🏯 state capital

TIMETABLE

618
Li Yuan becomes the first emperor of the Tang dynasty

640–59
The Tang empire expands its borders into Central Asia

755–63
A rebellion led by the general An Lushan permanently weakens Tang government

791
A Tibetan victory at Tingzhou ends Chinese power in Central Asia

c.850
Gunpowder first comes into use

907–60
On the fall of the Tang dynasty, China is divided—a period known as the Five Dynasties and Ten Kingdoms

936
The foundation of the kingdom of Koryo leads to the unification of Korea

960–79
Sung Taizu, founder of the Sung dynasty, reunites China

969
Gunpowder rockets are used for the first time in warfare

1090
A water-driven mechanical clock is built for the Sung court

1127
On the capture of Kaifeng by the Jürchen, the Sung capital moves to Hangzhou

c.1150
The magnetic compass is in use with Chinese navigators

1234
The Jin empire is conquered by the Mongols; first Mongol attacks take place on the Sung empire

1271
Khubilai Khan, the Mongol leader, adopts the Chinese dynastic title, Yuan

1276
Hangzhou is captured by the Mongols

1279
The last Sung emperor is drowned following a naval battle off the island of Yaishan. The Mongols rule all China

east from the steppes of Central Asia. At first the Jin empire acted as a buffer zone between them and the Sung, who even supplied the Mongols with troops. But when Jin fell in 1234, the Sung received the full fury of the Mongol attacks. China was finally conquered in 1279 and remained part of the Mongol empire for nearly a century.

AN AGE OF INVENTION

Although the Sung empire was the smallest in Chinese history, its achievements were considerable. The Sung rulers were more humane and capable than most, and China prospered under their rule. The population rose rapidly. Fast-growing varieties of rice, introduced from Vietnam, meant that two crops could be harvested a year, nearly doubling the food

Right This elegant ceramic vase was made in China during the years of Mongol rule, an indication that the traditional arts continued to flourish.

supply. In order to finance the increase in trade, banking and the world's first paper money came into use.

The Sung period was one of amazing inventiveness in all sorts of ways. Large junks—high-sterned sail ships with projecting bows—were built with watertight bulkheads that made them capable of withstanding heavy seas. They were navigated using a magnetic compass (unlike those developed later in Europe, the needle pointed south rather than north). Man-powered paddlewheels were used to drive riverboats. In warfare, the invention of gunpowder led to the development of incendiary rockets and the world's first simple guns made from bamboo tubes. Movable type came into use for printing some 200 years before it did in Europe, and watermills were used to power bellows for furnaces and spinning machines. Most of these inventions eventually found their way to Europe, where they contributed to the technological and commercial advances of the late Middle Ages.

THE MONGOL EMPIRE

THE MONGOLS WERE ONE OF THE MOST DESTRUCTIVE FORCES THE WORLD HAS KNOWN. IN THE 13TH CENTURY THEY SWEPT OUT OF THE ASIAN STEPPES TO TERRORIZE THE SETTLED PEOPLES OF EURASIA FROM CHINA TO HUNGARY. YET WITHIN LESS THAN A CENTURY THE MONGOL EMPIRE HAD BEGUN TO DISINTEGRATE INTO A NUMBER OF INDEPENDENT STATES (KHANATES). BY THE END OF THE 15TH CENTURY IT HAD ALL BUT DISAPPEARED FROM HISTORY.

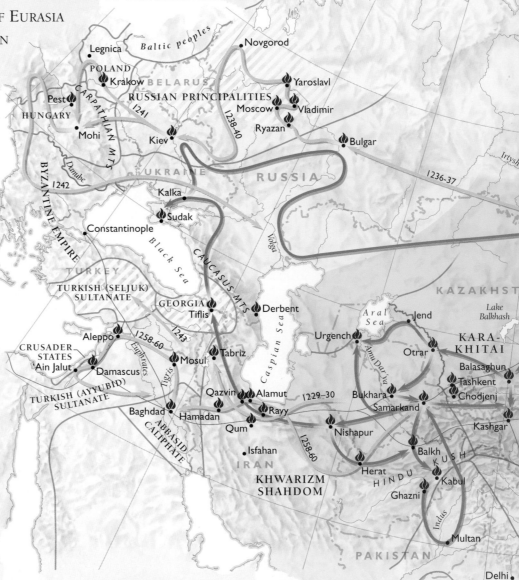

The steppes, vast grasslands similar to the North American prairies, run from the Danube plain of eastern Europe across south Russia and Central Asia to Manchuria in the east, a distance of more than 3,000 miles (5,000 km). The climate is harsh, with bitterly cold winters and arid summers. The steppes were inhabited by tribes of nomadic pastoral farmers who moved their herds of horses, sheep, and cattle vast distances in search of fresh pastures and traded with the settled peoples living around their borders.

From time to time through history, warbands like that of Attila the Hun, whose raids spread terror though Europe in the 5th century AD, burst out of the steppes to attack the peoples living on their borders. They caused widespread fear, but their territorial empires never lasted long. This was

LIFE ON THE STEPPES

There were no permanent settlements on the steppes: even today nomadic farmers use hide tents called "yurts." Life was hard—anyone too old or sick to travel was simply left to die when it was time to move the herds on. These conditions bred a tough, ruthless people. Interclan warfare was a way of life, especially in times of drought when there was fierce competition for the best grazing lands. Mounted warriors fired bone-tipped arrows from powerful bows. They relied on the speed of their horses to take the enemy by surprise.

Right *A nomadic pastoralist's yurt in Mongolia.*

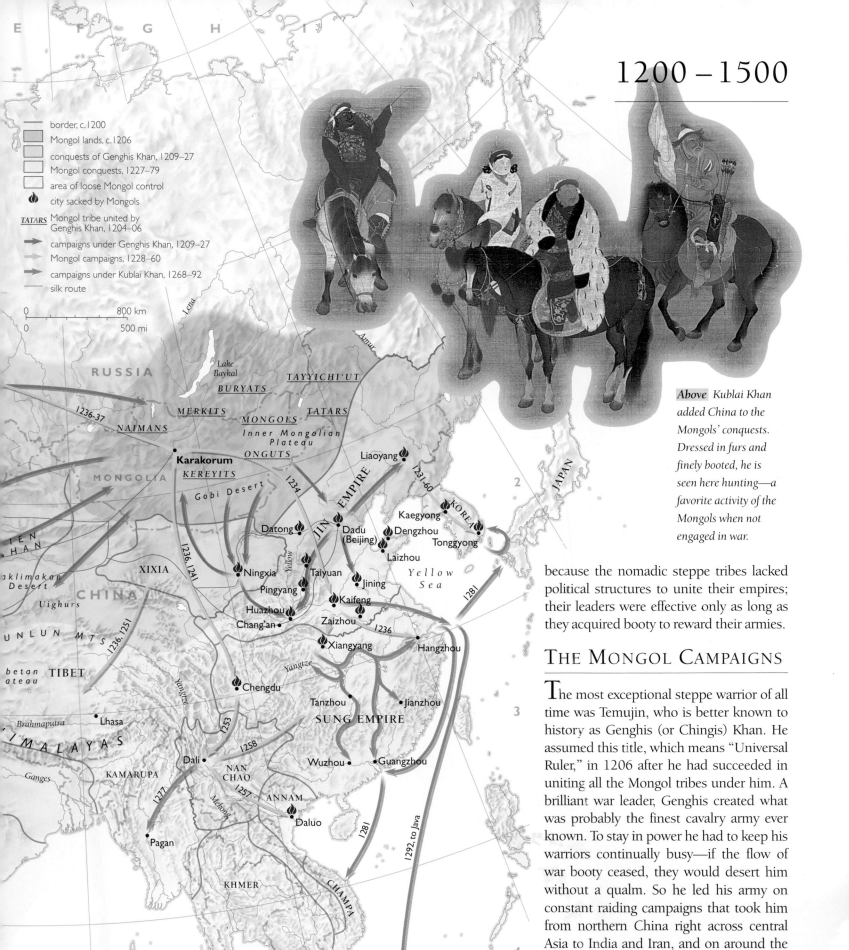

Map legend

- border, c.1200
- Mongol lands, c.1206
- conquests of Genghis Khan, 1209–27
- Mongol conquests, 1227–79
- area of loose Mongol control
- 🔥 city sacked by Mongols
- *TATARS* Mongol tribe united by Genghis Khan, 1204–06
- campaigns under Genghis Khan, 1209–27
- Mongol campaigns, 1228–60
- campaigns under Kublai Khan, 1268–92
- silk route

0   800 km
0   500 mi

Above *Kublai Khan added China to the Mongols' conquests. Dressed in furs and finely booted, he is seen here hunting—a favorite activity of the Mongols when not engaged in war.*

because the nomadic steppe tribes lacked political structures to unite their empires; their leaders were effective only as long as they acquired booty to reward their armies.

THE MONGOL CAMPAIGNS

The most exceptional steppe warrior of all time was Temujin, who is better known to history as Genghis (or Chingis) Khan. He assumed this title, which means "Universal Ruler," in 1206 after he had succeeded in uniting all the Mongol tribes under him. A brilliant war leader, Genghis created what was probably the finest cavalry army ever known. To stay in power he had to keep his warriors continually busy—if the flow of war booty ceased, they would desert him without a qualm. So he led his army on constant raiding campaigns that took him from northern China right across central Asia to India and Iran, and on around the Black Sea to southern Russia, conquering a territorial empire that far exceeded that of Alexander the Great.

No other army could match the battle tactics of the Mongols. Highly skilled horsemen, they could ride away from danger in

The Mongols committed horrific atrocities in their wars of conquest: for example, more than 200,000 prisoners were slaughtered when Baghdad was captured in 1251. Their terror tactics cost millions of lives and caused lasting damage to the two most advanced civilizations of the age, those of Islam and China. The devastated ancient trading cities of Central Asia never recovered their former prosperity. Vast areas of northern China, Persia, and Iraq were depopulated, and Russia was left isolated from the mainstream of European cultural development for almost two centuries.

One result of Mongol rule, however, was an increase in trade and cultural contacts between China and the rest of the world. The Mongols were less hostile to Christian Europeans than the Muslims who had previously controlled the trade routes across central Asia. This allowed European merchants such as Marco Polo to travel east for the first time and bring back knowledge of Chinese technology.

BREAK UP OF THE EMPIRE

In 1235, the capital of the Mongol empire was established at Karakorum, once Genghis Khan's favorite campsite in Mongolia. But their extensive territories proved too

an instant and shoot their arrows at the gallop to inflict long-range casualties on their enemies. A favorite tactic was to pretend to retreat and then ambush any opponents rash enough to pursue them. They were at their most effective in the open country of the steppes, and could not operate far beyond them as they needed pasture land on which to graze their vast herds of horses.

Genghis was succeeded as Great Khan (ruler) by his son Ogedai (r.1229–41) and his grandsons Küyük (r.1246–48), Möngke (r.1251–59), and Kublai Khan (r.1260–94). Their armies overran Tibet, Korea, Persia, Iraq, and much of Russia and Hungary. In 1279, after more than a decade of campaigning, Kublai Khan finally conquered Sung China and took the dynastic title of Yuan (see page 91). This was the last great Mongol gain—his campaigns in Southeast Asia brought no lasting successes, and he twice failed to invade Japan (see page 99).

CONQUESTS OF TIMUR

Volga

KHANATE
THE GOLD
HORDE

Danube

Black Sea

New Sarai

Old Sarai

Mediterranean Sea

Caspian Sea

Maragha

Sultaniyya

Samarkand

Mongol territory, 1279

border of khanate, 1279

campaign of Timur, 1369–1405

empire of Timur, 1405

Mongol capital

ILKHANATE

GENGHIS KHAN

Genghis Khan did not seem destined for the role of world conqueror. The son of a minor chieftain, the murder of his father left him without tribal protection. However, his military skill soon won him a band of followers, and through a combination of cunning and murder, he exploited interclan rivalries to claim authority over all the Mongolian tribes. Even as the ruler of a vast empire, he never abandoned the life of a nomad. He was constantly on campaign for more than 20 years. Traveling with a great entourage, he received ambassadors and advisers in his richly decorated yurt.

Left A Persian miniature shows a crowned Genghis Khan holding court in his yurt.

vast to be ruled effectively from one place, so subordinate khanates were created to govern the western conquests: the khanate of the Golden Horde (thought to be named for the color of the first khan's tent) in Russia; the Ilkhanate in Persia; the Chagatai khanate in the central steppes. Their leaders were supposed to be subject to the Great Khan, but they had all broken away from direct rule by the time that Kublai became khan in 1260. The Mongols had no outstanding rulers after Kublai. As their power began to wane, even nominal control of the western khanates slipped out of their grasp as they broke up into rival clanships and states. The Mongols of the Golden Horde converted to Islam, alienating them from their Christian Russian subjects. In the east, Tibet regained its independence by 1294. China was liberated by a rebel leader of peasant stock, Zhu Yuanzhang, between 1356 and 1368. After taking Beijing, which had been the capital of the Great Khanate since 1266, he proclaimed himself to be the first emperor of the Ming dynasty (1368–1644). The power of the Great Khanate was restricted to the Mongolian heartland of the eastern steppe.

TIMUR'S CAMPAIGNS

Timur (r.1361–1405), emir of Samarkand in the Chagatai khanate and a notoriously brutal leader, was the last of the Mongol conquerors. Although he was a Muslim and Turkish speaker, he claimed to be descended from Genghis Khan and was a nomad who spent most of his life on campaign in Central Asia and the Middle East. Craftsmen were enslaved and brought to Samarkand to enrich it with several of the Islamic world's finest mosques, but according to folklore he built towers with the skulls of his victims. Timur's empire, like those of his predecessors, died with him. His campaigns left the Islamic world in ruins and fatally weakened the western khanates.

THE RISE OF JAPAN

THE HEREDITARY MONARCHY OF JAPAN WAS FOUNDED BY THE YAMATO KINGS WHO BROUGHT THE WHOLE COUNTRY UNDER THEIR RULE AND ESTABLISHED AN IMPERIAL COURT. CHINESE INFLUENCES WERE STRONG AT FIRST, BUT JAPAN SOON DEVELOPED A RICH COURT CULTURE OF ITS OWN. HOWEVER, REAL POWER CAME TO BE HELD BY RIVAL WARRIOR CLANS. BY 1500 JAPAN HAD BROKEN UP INTO HUNDREDS OF SMALL FEUDAL STATES.

Owing to their geographical isolation, the first Japanese people lived by hunting and gathering long after farming had begun on the Asian mainland. Pottery vessels were made from a very early date (c.8000 BC), but rice farming, iron-working, and textiles were not known until about 300 BC, when they were introduced by immigrants from Asia who settled on Kyushu, the southernmost island. From there, the Yayoi culture, as it is known, spread through Japan except for Hokkaido. This mountainous island in the north, inhabited by hunting–gathering Ainu people, remained apart from the rest of Japan until the 17th century.

UNIFICATION OF JAPAN

Around AD 300, powerful warrior chiefs living around the Inland Sea of southern Japan began to build themselves massive keyhole-shaped tombs containing quantities of pottery, weapons, armor, jewelry, and other rich objects. Little is known about them, but by the end of the 4th century the rulers of a kingdom on the Yamato plain of Honshu appear to have had power over a wide area.

By the end of the 6th century the Yamato rulers had extended their rule over most of Japan. For a time they controlled part of the Korean peninsula. Chinese culture was an important influence at this time. Chinese writing and the Chinese calendar were in use, and in 604 Prince Shotoku adopted a constitution that was modeled on that of the Chinese court and gave the emperor total power over the nobility. Shotoku also imported craftsmen from China and promoted Chinese art styles. In 646 all land in Japan was brought under imperial ownership, as it was in China, and in 710 a permanent imperial capital was built at Nara.

Buddhism, which spread to Japan from Korea in around 552, was gradually adopted as the state religion. Buddhist monks gained so much influence in government that they began to erode the power of the emperor, though Buddhism did not entirely replace belief in the traditional Shinto religion of Japan, with its many gods.

THE HEIAN COURT

In 794 the emperor Kammu moved the imperial capital from Nara to Heian to escape the influence of the increasingly powerful Buddhist monasteries. Heian (which came to be known as Kyoto from the 11th century) remained the imperial and administrative capital until the 19th century. It was also the cultural and social center of the country. Its way of life was dominated by the court nobles, who made up one-tenth of the population of 100,000. For these leisured aristocrats, court life itself became a kind of art. Fine handwriting, elegant dress, and an ability to compose poetry or music were the keys to success in court politics, for both sexes. Art and literature—written at first in Chinese, later in Japanese—flourished. Many works of literature, including *The Tale of Genji*, claimed by many to be the world's first novel, were written by

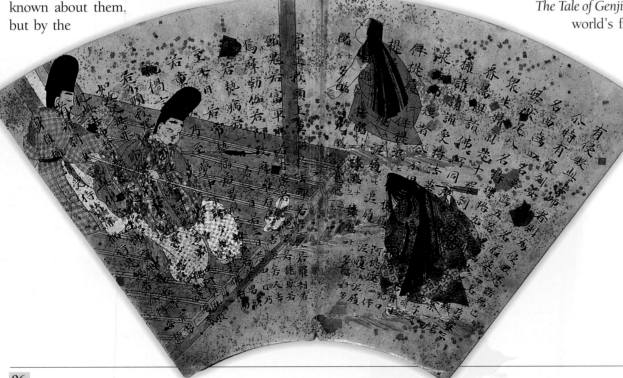

Left This 12th-century fan is painted with a scene showing court servants cleaning a temple veranda, overwritten with a passage from a sacred Buddhist text. The fan, with its elegant calligraphy, decorative paper techniques, and delicate color painting, captures the gracious manners of the Heian court.

THE WAY OF THE GODS

Shinto, Japan's traditional religion, had literally countless gods and spirits, called "kami." They were thought to be present not just in all living things but also in objects of the natural world, such as waterfalls, rocks, and trees. The "kami" were not universal gods, but were associated with particular people, ancestral spirits, or places. After the introduction of Buddhism into Japan, the two beliefs intermingled: Shinto gods came to be seen as protective deities and manifestations of Buddhist saints. The most important form of Japanese Buddhism was Zen, which emphasized the need for meditation. To create suitable settings, Zen monks became skilled gardeners and landscape painters.

Above The Golden Pavilion temple, Kyoto, in its Zen-inspired garden.

Left The protective Shinto deity Zao Gongen wards off evil.

Ainu (hunter–gatherers)

Hokkaido

c.1000

Osore

Nie

Kuriyagawa

Akita

c.800

Izawa

Ogachi

Tamatsukuri

Taga

Okuma

Miyanouchi

c.600

Sado

Noto

Utsunomiya

Kannonyama
Inariyama

Matsumoto

Tone

Hida

Kiso

Edo

Shinano

Chimori

Matsubara

Fuji

Kamakura

Numaza

Odawara

Sea of Japan

Oki

Matsumoto
Myorenjiyama

Misasa

Kokubunji

Heian
from 794

Himeji

Osaka

Ichigodani

Jinguji
Komorizuka

Yamato
plain

Nara
710–794

Honshu

Iwasakiyama

Tokushima

*PACIFIC
OCEAN*

Andong

from China via Korean peninsula

Nakdong

Kyongju

Chokojiyama

Iya

Yokokurayama

Shikoku

Pusan

Takehara

Dannoura
1185

*Inland
Sea*

Tsushima

Dazaifu

Hososhima

*Goto
Islands*

Mike

Sekijinyama

Funayama

Yamanoshita

from China

Shimo

Kyushu

Shimazu

from China via Ryukyu Islands

Shibushi

*Osumi
Islands*

Legend

→ probable routes for introduction of rice farming and Yayoi culture into Japan

keyhole tombs, 4th–8th centuries
- single
- multiple

▲ sacred mountain

🏯 Ainu hilltop fort

🏰 early fortress

■ imperial capital

🏛 shoen of the Fujiwara family, 9th–12th century

— imperial frontier, with date

area under control of warrior clans
- Northern Fujiwara, 1183
- Minamoto Yoritomo, 1183
- Minamoto Yoshinaka, 1183
- Taira, 1183
- furthest extent of Yoritomo's control, 1189

0 — 300 km
0 — 200 mi

women. Practical abilities, such as skill as a warrior, brought little prestige. Elaborate rituals of dress and etiquette set the court elite apart from the common people.

The Heian emperors came increasingly under the influence of aristocratic families like the Fujiwara, who built up a powerful presence at court by marrying their daughters to members of the imperial family. The great families and Buddhist temples persuaded the emperors to grant them tax-free estates called *shoen* as rewards for good service. Government was neglected and there was growing disorder in the provinces. As a result, wealthy landowners and temples began to raise their own armies of warriors, known as *samurai*, for protection. Like the knights of medieval Europe, the *samurai* were a hereditary warrior class, who were granted estates in return for military service. As bands of *samurai* became increasingly independent, long private wars and rivalries disrupted the life of the countryside, sometimes dragging on for years.

THE SHOGUNS

During the 12th century clans of *samurai* became involved in the politics of the court. The influence of the Fujiwara family came to an end as the Taira and Minamoto clans began a struggle for power. Civil war broke out in 1180–85. Under the generalship of Minamoto Yoritomo (the family name came first in medieval Japan), the Minamoto clan destroyed the Taira at the battle of Dannoura. Yoritomo, who by now was the most powerful man in Japan, was given the title of shogun ("supreme commander") by the emperor in 1192.

Yoritomo was a highly skilled administrator. His castle at Kamakura in eastern Honshu became an alternative center of government and to strengthen his authority in the provinces, he created the office of *shugo*, or local military governor. The imperial court remained at Heian, but real power was exercised by the shogun: the emperor was reduced to a mere figurehead. Yoritomo

Left A scroll painting
showing the Heiji
uprising in 1159,
which brought the
Taira clan to power.
Mounted samurai are
fighting a pitched battle
with a Minamoto army.
Their principal weapon
is the longbow: The
long, curving, deadly
"tachi" sword—prized
as "the soul of the
samurai"—had not
yet come into use.

JAPAN UNDER THE SHOGUNS

key to *daimyo* house

1	Akamatsu	11	Ouchi
2	Ashikaga	12	Satake
3	Date	13	Shiba
4	Hatakeyama	14	Shimazu
5	Hosokawa	15	Shoni
6	Imagawa	16	Takeda
7	Isshiki	17	Toki
8	Kyogoku	18	Uesugi
9	Mogami	19	Yamana
10	Otomo		

border, c.1467
major *daimyo* house
capital of Shogun
late medieval castle, c.1300–1600

was succeeded as shogun by his two sons in turn, but when the Minamoto line died out in the early 13th century, the office passed into the hands of the Hojo clan. They soon became extremely powerful, intervening in affairs at all levels of society.

The Mongol leader Khubilai Khan (see page 94) twice attempted to invade Japan from Korea, in 1274 and 1281. The Hojo government took urgent steps to resist him, but on both occasions the Mongol invasion fleet was scattered by typhoons and shipwrecked before a major battle had taken place. The Japanese attributed these near-miraculous escapes to *kamikaze* or "divine wind" and came to regard them as a sign that their country was under the special protection of the gods.

THE RISE OF THE DAIMYO

In 1338, after a civil war caused by the attempt of the emperor Go-Daigo to take back power, a new succession of shoguns, the Ashikaga, took over from the Hojo. By now the *shugo* had more power in their localities than the shoguns did, and strong government had all but disappeared. Another civil war, the Onin war (1467–77), caused widespread discontent in the provinces, and this allowed a new class of feudal warlords, the *daimyo* ("domain lords"), to seize power for themselves.

The *daimyo* surrounded themselves with large armies of *samurai* vassals and were constantly at war. Their castles, which were strongly fortified, attracted large numbers of merchants and craftsmen. Markets sprang up, leading to a sudden growth in urban development. By 1500 the shoguns were as powerless as the emperors, and Japan had effectively split up into nearly 400 independent warlord states.

THE WAY OF THE WARRIOR

Samurai lived by the code of "bushido" (The Way of the Warrior). This prized above all things skill with weapons, especially the sword and the bow, physical fitness, and courage in battle. A samurai should live simply, behave honestly, and show kindness and respect to his parents. However, his supreme obligation was to serve his lord loyally and, if necessary, sacrifice his life for him. To flee from battle, or to surrender, was the ultimate disgrace: it was more honorable to commit suicide than be taken captive. But the ideal warrior should not merely be a master of the military arts: he should be skilled in the composition of poetry and sensitive to human emotions.

Left The body armor of a samurai.

TIMETABLE

c.300 BC
Rice farming and iron-working spread to Japan from Asia

c.AD 300–400
Yamato rule is established

369
According to an 8th-century source, a Japanese army invades Korea

552
Buddhism is introduced to Japan from Korea

593–622
Prince Shotoku creates a centralized Japanese state on Chinese lines

562
The Japanese are expelled from Korea

646
All land comes under imperial control

708
The earliest official coinage is introduced in Japan

794
The imperial court is established at Heian (Kyoto)

858
Fujiwara Yorifusa becomes regent, marking the rise of the Fujiwara clan and the decline of imperial authority

1010
The Tale of Genji is written by Lady Murasaki Shikibu

1156–59
The Taira clan is dominant at court

1185
Minamoto Yoritomo destroys the power of the Taira and becomes shogun

1333–38
Emperor Go-Daigo overthrows the shogun and attempts to rule directly

c.1360
The Japanese school of Noh drama comes into being

1467–77
The Onin war leads to the rise of the *daimyos*

1573
Fall of the Ashikaga shogunate

KINGDOMS OF AFRICA

THE FIRST AFRICAN KINGDOMS DEVELOPED IN THE NILE VALLEY IN EGYPT AROUND 3000 BC AND IN NUBIA AROUND 1700 BC, BUT FEW ORGANIZED STATES HAD EMERGED SOUTH OF THE SAHARA BEFORE THE 1ST MILLENNIUM AD. THE DEVELOPMENT OF TRANS-SAHARAN CARAVAN ROUTES AND THE INCREASE IN LONG-DISTANCE TRADE IN THE INDIAN OCEAN HELPED STIMULATE THE GROWTH OF WEALTHY CITIES AND KINGDOMS IN BOTH WEST AND EAST AFRICA BEFORE AD 1000.

For thousands of years the Sahara desert was a near-impassable barrier that divided the peoples of North Africa from those living in the rest of the continent. In the vast expanses south of the Sahara, most people were farmers, nomadic herders, or hunter–gatherers. Around 2000 BC Bantu-speakers began to spread into central and east Africa from their original homeland in southern Nigeria and Cameroon and by AD 500 had reached southern Africa.

Contact with cultures outside Africa was made only by way of the river Nile into Egypt, or with Indian Ocean traders who regularly called at places along the east coast to exchange pottery and other goods for cargoes of gold, ivory, aromatic resins, and slaves. When, before AD 100, camels were introduced into North Africa from Arabia, traders were able to cross the desert more easily, bringing the agricultural societies of sub-Saharan Africa into the orbit of the Mediterranean world for the first time.

CITIES OF THE SAHEL

The Sahel, the region of dry grasslands that fringes the south and west of the Sahara, had been home to farmers for thousands of years. It was ideally suited to rearing cattle, while areas along rivers and by waterholes and lakes were used for growing crops. As agriculture intensified, the population rose. An early iron-using culture, the Nok, noted for its sophisticated terracotta sculptures, had emerged in northern Nigeria around

Right This statuette of a king and queen comes from Ife, a kingdom in west Africa famous for its pottery and bronze sculptures.

500 BC. Local trade in salt (a vital necessity in hot climates), metals, and food gained in importance, leading to the growth of trading centers such as Jenne-jeno in present-day Mali, which had been encircled by a defensive wall by AD 400. Ghana, which was situated some 400 miles (650 km) northwest of the modern state of that name, was one of several early kingdoms that grew up in the western Sahel in the late 1st millennium. Its rulers were buried in great mounds, surrounded by human sacrifices and lavish grave goods.

Islam became widely established in the Sahel after Berber traders from North Africa introduced it about 1000. There was no stone available for building, so enormous beehive-shaped mosques were constructed out of dried mud bricks. At the western and southern ends of the trans-Saharan trade routes, gold, ivory, and slaves, transported there from places deeper in tropical Africa, were exchanged for goods such as salt, glass, and pottery. Horses were especially highly prized, as they could not be bred locally.

Right The Great Mosque at Jenné, Mali, is the largest mud building in the world.

AD1–1500

Tangier
Fez
MOROCCO
ATLAS MOUNTAINS
Tunis
Tripoli
Ghadames
ALGERIA
LIBYA
Mediterranean Sea
EGYPT
Alexandria
Cairo
Nile
El Kharga
Aswan
Red Sea
Jiddah
Mecca
SAUDI ARABIA
SABAEA
YEMEN
Ghat
Zuwaylah
SAHARA DESERT
Al Kufrah
Faras
Selima
erhazza
Taoudenni
Djado
Sherda
Bilma
Ain Galakka
Old Dongola
NUBIA
Meroë
Soba
Dahlak
Timbuktu
AIR
NIGER
KANEM-
BORNU
CHAD
DARFUR
El Fasher
Sennar
Axum
Aden
Koumbi
Saleh
Gao
Agadez
SAHEL
SUDAN
FUNJ
Lalibela
Saylac
Ras
Xaafuun
Jenné
Jenne-jeno
Niger
Katsina
Lake Chad
ETHIOPIAN
HIGHLANDS
Berbera
Ouagadougou
MOSSI
STATES
HAUSA
CITY
STATES
Kano
Ngarzagamu
ADAL
Zaria
NIGERIA
ETHIOPIA
Nok
Begho
OYO
White Nile
Old Oyo
Ife
CENTRAL
AFRICAN
REPUBLIC
AKAN
STATES
Benin
Lake
Turkana
Jasiira
Mogadishu
IFE
BENIN
Baraawe
Congo
KENYA
Bigo
RIFT VALLEY
Shanga
Ungwana
Manda
Gedi
Malindi
Lake
Victoria
Mombasa
INDIAN
OCEAN
Mbanza Congo
CONGO
RIFT VALLEY
Lake
Tanganyika
TANZANIA
Pemba Island
Zanzibar
NDONGO
Mafia
Island
Kilwa Kisiwani
Lake
Malawi
ANGOLA
ZAMBIA
Zambezi
MOZAMBIQUE
MWENEMUTAPA
Okavango
ZIMBABWE
Khami
Great
Zimbabwe
Sofala
TORWA
NAMIBIA
Chibuene
BOTSWANA
Limpopo
MADAGASCAR
Kalahari
Desert
SOUTH
AFRICA
Orange

Legend

area of Bantu farmers and herders
by AD 500

Early states

Alwa, c.350–1505

Axum, c.AD1–975

Ghana, c.700–1205

Makkura, c.600–1317

Takrur, c.800–1100

Arab Muslim states , c.750

Later states

Ethiopia, founded c.1100

Mali, c.1200–1500

Songhai, c.1450–1590

other areas of state formation by 1500

🏛 city by the 15th century

🌴 oasis

trans-Saharan trade route

desert

tropical rainforest

0   1200 km
0   800 mi

The kingdom of Mali (c.1200–1500) developed as a result of this trade. Its armed horsemen controlled a vast area of the western Sahel. Mali was very wealthy. It had rich farmlands along the Niger river and controlled access to the rich goldfields of west Africa. It was later overtaken by Songhai, while the nomadic Kanem-Bornu dynasty established an empire in the central Sahel.

By 1300 well-organized kingdoms had developed among the rainforest farmers of west Africa. At a number of places such as Oyo, Ife, and Benin in present-day Nigeria, craftsmen made finely carved heads and sculptures in terracotta, iron, and bronze.

NUBIA & AXUM

Nubia (which was known as Kush to the ancient Egyptians) lay on the upper Nile in the region of modern Sudan. An early state grew up here under the influence of Egypt, which later conquered it as a source of slaves and gold. In the 8th and 7th centuries BC a Nubian dynasty ruled as pharaohs of Egypt. The kings and queens of Nubia were buried in pyramids, and a hieroglyphic script was employed for official inscriptions. Meroë, its later capital, was a populous city with palaces and temples, but in the 1st century AD Nubia was increasingly cut off from Roman Egypt and went into decline. Meroë was destroyed by raiders from Axum around 350, and Nubia split into three successor states: Nobatia, Makkura, and Alwa.

The kingdom of Axum, on the Red Sea coast, rose to prominence during the 1st century AD. Through the port of Adulis, Axum was in close contact with Sabaea on the opposite shore of the Red Sea. Sabaea—present-day Yemen—was the Sheba of the Bible, and the kings of Axum claimed descent from King Solomon and the Queen of Sheba. Sabaea's wealth was based on the export of ivory, rhinoceros horn, tortoiseshell, semiprecious stones, and aromatic resins, commodities that were highly valued by the citizens of the Roman empire.

CHRISTIANS & MUSLIMS

The kingdom of Axum went into decline after 600 and was destroyed by invaders around 975. Carved granite obelisks, the tallest of them 69 feet (21 m) high, are all that remain of its ancient capital today. One records the baptism of a king of Axum around 350, the earliest known Christian convert in sub-Saharan Africa. Monks from Syria and Egypt spread Christianity into Nubia and Axum between the 4th and 6th centuries, but the Arab conquest of Egypt (see pages 80–83) isolated the Christian communities in Africa from the rest of the world. By then a successor state to Axum had arisen in the highlands to the south

GREAT ZIMBABWE

Great Zimbabwe, with its massive stonewall enclosures, is one of the most visited sites of southern Africa. Built between 1270 and 1450, it appears to have been the capital of a large cattle-owning empire of the Shona people, who controlled the grazing lands between the Zambezi and Limpopo rivers.

The most impressive of the ruins is the "Great Enclosure." This may have been where young men and women were initiated into marriage. Nearby was a sacred enclosure where the king called on the ancestral spirits of the Shona people. The royal palace included special courtyards where the king could display his wealth to visitors. His wives lived in their own enclosure: it has been estimated that he had a total of about 300—an indication of his wealth and high status. Commoners lived in the surrounding town, and the whole complex would have been home to some 18,000 people. Objects found during excavations show that Great Zimbabwe had trading links with the Islamic cities on the east African coast and, through them, with the Middle East and as far away as China.

Left The massive walls of the Great Enclosure.

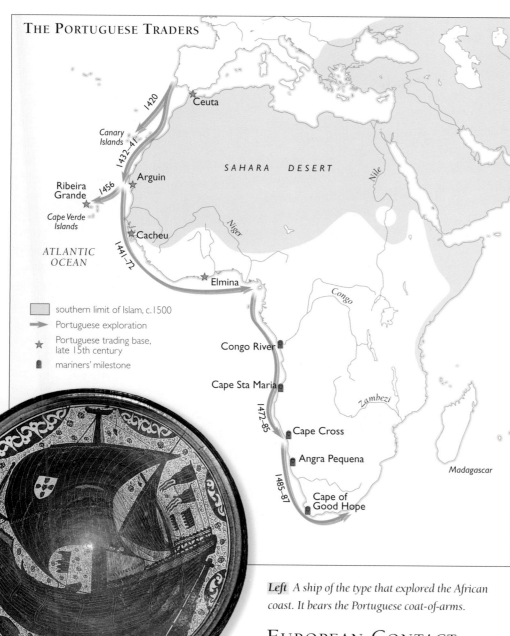

THE PORTUGUESE TRADERS

southern limit of Islam, c.1500

Portuguese exploration

Portuguese trading base, late 15th century

mariners' milestone

Left A ship of the type that explored the African coast. It bears the Portuguese coat-of-arms.

EUROPEAN CONTACT

The Muslim monopoly of trade with India and the far east led European navigators to look for new routes to the Indian Ocean. European sailors had never dared venture far along the west coast of Africa because the prevailing north winds threatened their return journey. However, early in the 15th century the Portuguese discovered that by sailing far out into the Atlantic it was possible to find southerly winds to bring them safely home. Bit by bit they traveled further south, leaving stone columns ("mariners' milestones"), carved with the date, to mark where they had been. In 1487 the first Portuguese ship rounded the Cape of Good Hope into the Indian Ocean. By the 1480s the Portuguese had begun to export slaves from west Africa and had already built a number of trading forts.

around Lalibela, famous for its rock-cut churches, and it was here that the kingdom of Ethiopia emerged in the 12th century. By the 15th century nearly all the Ethiopian highlands were under its control. Because the Ethiopian church grew in isolation from other Christian communities, many of its beliefs and practices are unique to it.

As the Arabs who controlled trade in the Indian Ocean spread the influence of Islam along the Red Sea coast and into the Horn of Africa, some peoples, such as the Funj, became nominally Muslim. Farther south, many coastal market centers developed into city-states under Muslim ruling elites, and were strongly Islamic in character.

TIMETABLE

c.AD 1–100
The kingdom of Axum develops on the Red Sea coast

c.350
Monks from Syria convert king Ezana of Axum to Christianity

c.400
Defensive walls are built at Jenne-jeno in west Africa

c.540
The Nubians are converted to Christianity

c.700
The ancient kingdom of Ghana emerges in the western Sahel

738
First Arab slave raid on west Africa

c.800
Trading towns develop on the east African coast

c.1250
The kingdom of Benin emerges in equatorial west Africa

c.1250
Mali is the dominant kingdom of west Africa

c.1260–77
Mansa Uli, king of Mali, makes a pilgrimage to Mecca

c.1270
The Great Enclosure is built at Great Zimbabwe

1270
The Solomonid dynasty comes to power in Ethiopia (rules until 1777)

1432
Portuguese navigators begin to explore the west coast of Africa

1450–1500
Songhai supplants Mali as the chief power in the western Sahel

1487
Bartolomeu Dias rounds the Cape of Good Hope and enters the Indian Ocean

1490
In the Congo, Nzinga Nkuwu, a chieftain, is converted to Christianity by the Portuguese

THE MAYA & THE AZTECS

FOR ALMOST 2,000 YEARS A SOPHISTICATED CIVILIZATION FLOURISHED IN MESOAMERICA. ELABORATELY CARVED STONE PYRAMIDS WERE BUILT FOR RELIGIOUS RITUALS AND WRITING WAS DEVELOPED. TENOCHTITLÁN, THE CAPITAL CITY OF THE POWERFUL AZTEC EMPIRE, WAS LARGER AND RICHER THAN ANY 15TH-CENTURY EUROPEAN CITY. THIS REMARKABLE CULTURE WAS SWEPT AWAY BY SPANISH INVADERS IN THE 1520S.

The origins of civilization in Mesoamerica lie in the adoption of corn farming around 2700 BC. Reliable rainfall and year-round warmth made it possible for people to grow four crops a year on the fertile river plains of southeastern Mexico. By 1250 BC chiefdoms and small states had emerged among the Olmecs, who built large ceremonial centers with earth pyramid mounds and monumental stone sculpture; they later devised the first astronomical calendars. Complex societies also formed among the Zapotec peoples of the Oaxaca valley. The earliest writing script in the Americas, using glyphs (picture symbols), developed here around 800 BC. One of their most important centers was at Monte Albán, which flourished between 400 BC and AD 700.

During the 1st century AD a major settlement arose at Teotihuacán in the Valley of Mexico. Covering an area of over 8 square miles (20 sq km), it was larger than ancient Rome, though it was not as densely populated. Designed on a grid pattern, it contained ceremonial centers, palaces, a large

urban settlement, craft workshops, and a quarter for foreign merchants. The Pyramid of the Sun (c.150) was the largest building in pre-Columbian America. Teotihuacán's influence had been declining for a century when it was sacked by invaders about 750.

The Maya originated in the highlands of Guatemala. Around 1000 BC they began to spread into the lowlands of the Yucatán peninsula, where they dug canals to drain the swamps to grow food. By the 7th century BC they were building monumental temple pyramids, and city-states began to form. Writing, the use of the astronomical calendar, and the sacred ball game were probably adopted from the Olmecs and Zapotecs as long-distance trade developed.

EARLY STATES IN MESOAMERICA

Gulf of Mexico

- Tectihuacán
- Xochicalco
- Acatlan
- Tres Zapotes
- La Venta
- San Lorenzo
- San José Mogote
- Monte Albán

Pacific Ocean

- ◼ Zapotec states, c.1400 BC–AD 700
- ◼ Olmec states, c.1250–400 BC
- ◼ Teotihuacán, c.AD 1–700

Map labels

Las Flores
Tamuin
METZTITLÁN
Moctezuma
Tolteca-Chichimeca
Zimapan
Tiayo
El Tajín
Atlacomulco
Tula
Tollantzinco
Tzintzúntzan
✕ 1520
Teotihuacán
Xocotla
Villa Rica
Tenayuacan
Texcoco
Cempoala
Azcapotzalco
TLAXCALLAN
Jalapa
Calixtlahuaca
Tenochtitlán
Tlaxcala
Ixhuacan
Vera Cruz
Tlacopán
Culhuacan
Spanish settlement from 1519
Chapultepec
Cholula
Tepeacac
Malinalco
Tepoztlan
Orizaba
Huetamo
Xochicalco
Mexiquito
SIERRA MADRE DEL SUR
Zacatollan
Teloloapan
TEOTITLAN
Zacatula
Balsas
Teotitlan
Petatlan
Tetela
YOPITZINCO
Nochcoc
Tetzmoliuhuacan
Yanhuitlan
Acapulco
Ayutla
Quetzaltepec
Monte Albán
Mitla
Ixtayutlán
MIXTEC KINGDOM
Atoyac
Tututepec
PACIFIC OCEAN
Pochutlan

A   B   C

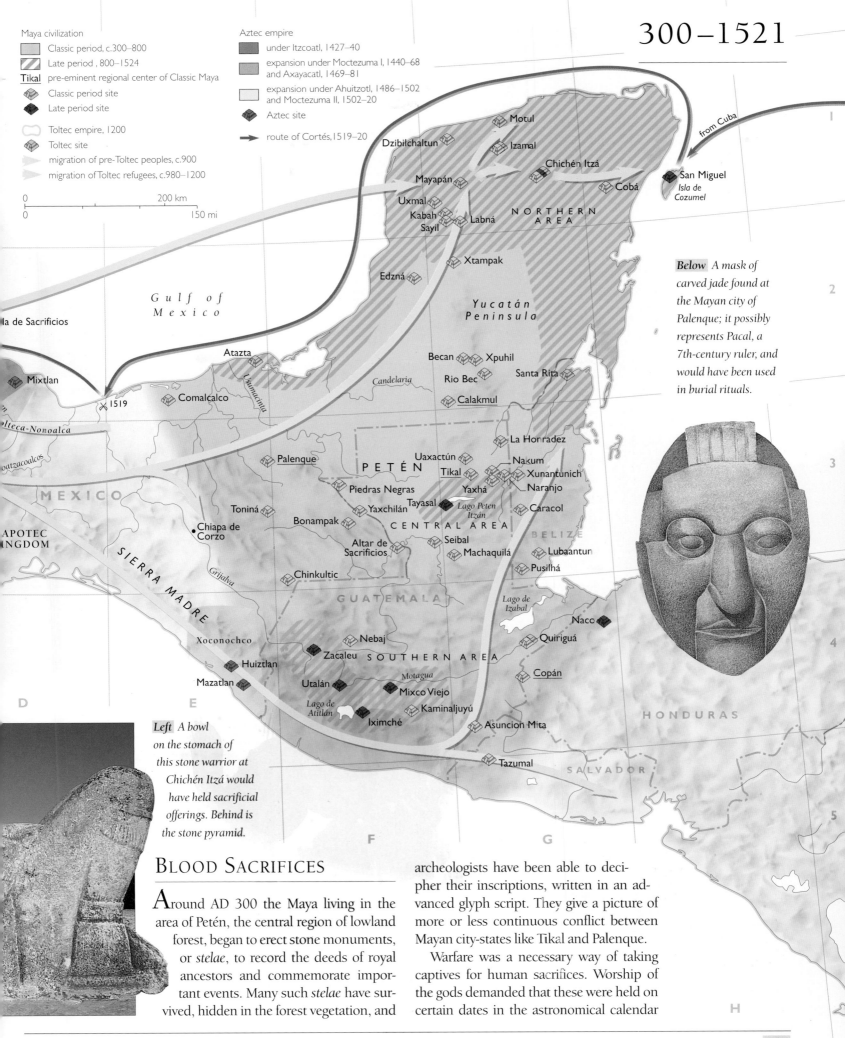

Maya civilization

- Classic period, c.300–800
- Late period, 800–1524
- **Tikal** pre-eminent regional center of Classic Maya
- Classic period site
- Late period site
- Toltec empire, 1200
- Toltec site
- migration of pre-Toltec peoples, c.900
- migration of Toltec refugees, c.980–1200

Aztec empire

- under Itzcoatl, 1427–40
- expansion under Moctezuma I, 1440–68 and Axayacatl, 1469–81
- expansion under Ahuitzotl, 1486–1502 and Moctezuma II, 1502–20
- Aztec site
- route of Cortés, 1519–20

0   200 km
0   150 mi

Below *A mask of carved jade found at the Mayan city of Palenque; it possibly represents Pacal, a 7th-century ruler, and would have been used in burial rituals.*

Left *A bowl on the stomach of this stone warrior at Chichén Itzá would have held sacrificial offerings. Behind is the stone pyramid.*

BLOOD SACRIFICES

Around AD 300 the Maya living in the area of Petén, the central region of lowland forest, began to erect stone monuments, or *stelae*, to record the deeds of royal ancestors and commemorate important events. Many such *stelae* have survived, hidden in the forest vegetation, and archeologists have been able to decipher their inscriptions, written in an advanced glyph script. They give a picture of more or less continuous conflict between Mayan city-states like Tikal and Palenque.

Warfare was a necessary way of taking captives for human sacrifices. Worship of the gods demanded that these were held on certain dates in the astronomical calendar

Above *Lady Wak Tun, in a trance, has a vision of a serpent—a scene from a Mayan glyph carving.*

THE WARLIKE AZTECS

The Aztecs were the last great civilization of central Mexico. They claimed descent from the Toltecs, whom they believed must have been extremely strong and wise super-humans to have built such enormous stone monuments. They took over many aspects of Toltec culture, including the worship of many gods such as Quetzalcoatl, the feathered serpent. In fact, the Aztecs migrated into the Valley of Mexico after the decline of the Toltec empire. In 1325, they settled at Tenochtitlán on an island in Lake Texcoco and served as mercenary soldiers in neighboring states before establishing a military empire in the Valley of Mexico during the reign of king Itzcoatl (r.1427–40). The empire grew under his successors, reaching its peak in the reign of Moctezuma II (r.1502–20). Like the Maya, the Aztecs needed to wage continual war, as their religion required the constant taking of prisoners for human sacrifices. The Aztecs took care not to conquer all their enemies; some states, such as Tlaxcallan, were allowed to survive so that they could be regularly raided for sacrificial victims.

The Aztecs had a very complex and well-defined class system: an individual's status could instantly be known from their hairstyle and other details of dress. At the top was the king, whose official title was "great speaker." Below him was an elite rank of nobles who all claimed descent from the first Aztec king. Commoners belonged by birth to one of 20 clans, each of which lived

or to mark important events, such as royal funerals. Victims were tortured and mutilated before having their hearts cut out. Mayan kings themselves were expected to participate in painful rituals; for example, their tongues were pierced with the spines of stingrays to allow them to communicate with ancestral spirits.

The Maya used a complex and highly accurate calendar, based on precise astronomical observations. They later produced written sacred books of bark, which they illustrated with intricate paintings. These, and their stone carvings, tell us something of their violent cosmos and powerful gods.

Wars and famine brought about by over-cultivation of the land may have caused the rapid collapse and desertion of the lowland Mayan cities after 800. Those in the highlands survived longer, but were conquered by the Spanish in the 16th century.

THE TOLTECS

Early in the 10th century the Toltecs, consisting of two groups of people who migrated into central Mexico during the power vacuum after the fall of Teotihuacán, formed their capital at Tula. From here they extended their influence throughout the Valley of Mexico. Archeologists believe that a band of Toltec adventurers invaded Yucatán around 987 and founded a dynasty that ruled the Mayan city of Chichén Itzá for 200 years—many of its buildings were modeled on those of Tula. In the late 12th century Tula was destroyed and the Toltec people scattered. Great temple pyramids and stone statues of warriors were all that remained of their former presence.

APPEASING THE GODS

*H*uman sacrifice lay at the heart of Aztec religion. At the Great Temple of Tenochtitlán, priests performed sacrifices every day, cutting the hearts out of their victims to offer them to the war god Huitzilopochtli. If this was not done, he would lack the strength to battle with the forces of the dark, and the sun would fail to rise the next day. Other gods also demanded terrible sacrifices. To honor Xipe Totec, a god of springtime, captives were killed in mock battles by Aztec warriors. The skins were flayed from their bodies and worn by their victors to invoke the bursting of the corn seed from its husk.

Left *A figure of Xipe Totec wearing the flayed skin of a sacrificial victim.*

in a particular quarter of Tenochtitlán, with its own temples and schools. Members of the clan owned and farmed land in common, while in wartime, the men of the clan fought together. Warriors could win fame and glory by capturing prisoners. No man was considered an adult until he had taken a prisoner in battle. Below the commoners in rank was a class made up of conquered peoples, who worked as tenant farmers and laborers. There were also slaves (prisoners-of-war and criminals) and a class of merchants, who might be very rich but could not display their wealth.

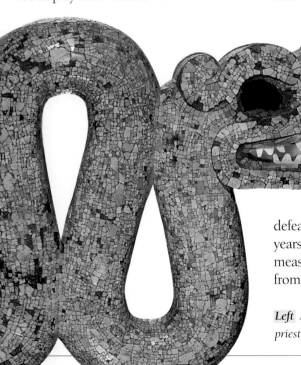

THE FALL OF THE AZTECS

T he Aztecs believed that the god Quetzalcoatl would one day come back in human form from the east. When a Spanish army landed on the east coast of Mexico in 1519 under the leadership of Hernán Cortés, it was rumored that the god—whom the legends described as fairhaired and bearded—had returned. If this was so, the king was obliged to treat him with honor and respect. Moctezuma invited the Spaniard to a meeting in Tenochtitlán, but Cortés, who had made an alliance with Moctezuma's enemies, responded by taking him prisoner. The Aztecs resisted the invaders bravely, but weapons of wood and stone were no match for firearms, armor, swords, and horses. Though only a tiny band, the Spanish conquistadors had defeated the Aztecs by 1521. Within a few years European diseases like smallpox and measles had reduced the Aztec population from ten to only one million.

Left *A turquoise ornament worn by an Aztec high priest, probably part of a treasure sent to Cortés.*

THE INCA EMPIRE

**THE INCAS CREATED THE LAST GREAT EMPIRE OF THE ANCIENT AMERICAS.
IT EXTENDED FOR SOME 3,000 MILES (4,800 KM) ALONG THE ANDES FROM
ECUADOR TO CENTRAL CHILE AND WAS LINKED BY A NETWORK OF ROADS
AND ROPE SUSPENSION BRIDGES. DESPITE ITS WEALTH AND SPLENDOR, IT
LASTED BARELY A CENTURY BEFORE IT WAS CONQUERED BY THE SPANISH.**

The Incas were the heirs of cultural traditions stretching back to the first fishing and farming communities that emerged on the coastal lowlands of Peru around 1800 BC. Archeologists have identified a succession of cultures here, for example the Chavín (c.850–200 BC), whose art, with images of strange animal-gods, is found throughout northern and central Peru. Around 100 BC the Moche began to build a powerful state on the coast. They were ruled by warrior-priests and created marvelous objects in gold, semiprecious stone, pottery, and textiles. They were conquered around AD 600 by the Huari, who overcame other states, such as the Nazca, to build an empire that extended into the Andean highlands. Its presence there blocked the northward expansion of the Andean empire of Tiahuanaco, a city close to Lake Titicaca, which had some 20,000–40,000 inhabitants and contained temples, tombs, and palaces of well-worked stone. Around 1000 both empires collapsed into small local states. The most powerful was Chimú, based in the Moche Valley, which emerged around 1200 and came to control over 600 miles (1,000 km) of the Peruvian coastal plain.

INCA ORIGINS

Little is known about the early history of the Incas. According to legend, they were led out of mountain caves by Manco Capac to settle in Cuzco, in a fertile valley high in the Andes. We do not know if Manco Capac was a real person; if he was, he probably lived around 1200, at the time that the Chimú state was being formed. Until the time of Pachacutec (r.1438–71) and his son Tupac Yupanqui (r.1471–93), there was little to distinguish the Incas from other early Andean states. Both

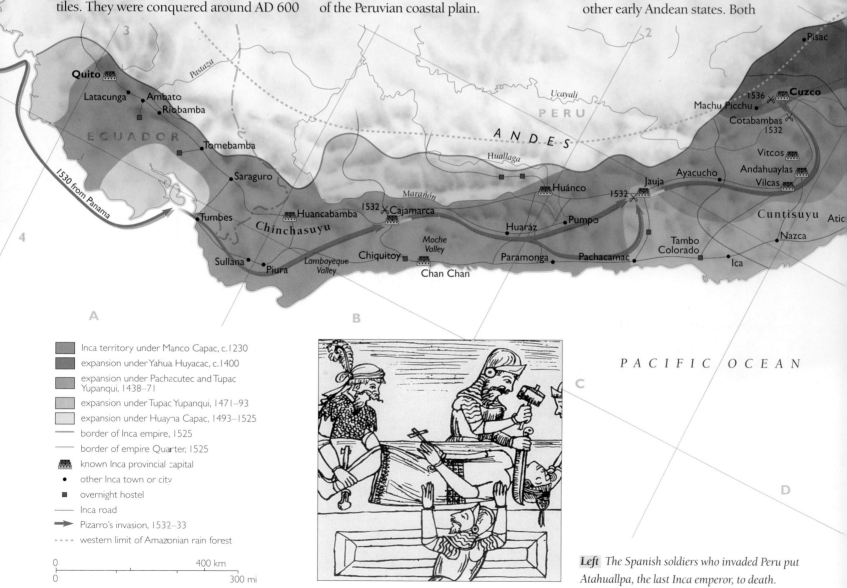

Inca territory under Manco Capac, c.1230
expansion under Yahua Huyacac, c.1400
expansion under Pachacutec and Tupac Yupanqui, 1438–71
expansion under Tupac Yupanqui, 1471–93
expansion under Huayna Capac, 1493–1525
border of Inca empire, 1525
border of empire Quarter, 1525
known Inca provincial capital
other Inca town or city
overnight hostel
Inca road
Pizarro's invasion, 1532–33
western limit of Amazonian rain forest

0 — 400 km
0 — 300 mi

Left *The Spanish soldiers who invaded Peru put
Atahuallpa, the last Inca emperor, to death.*

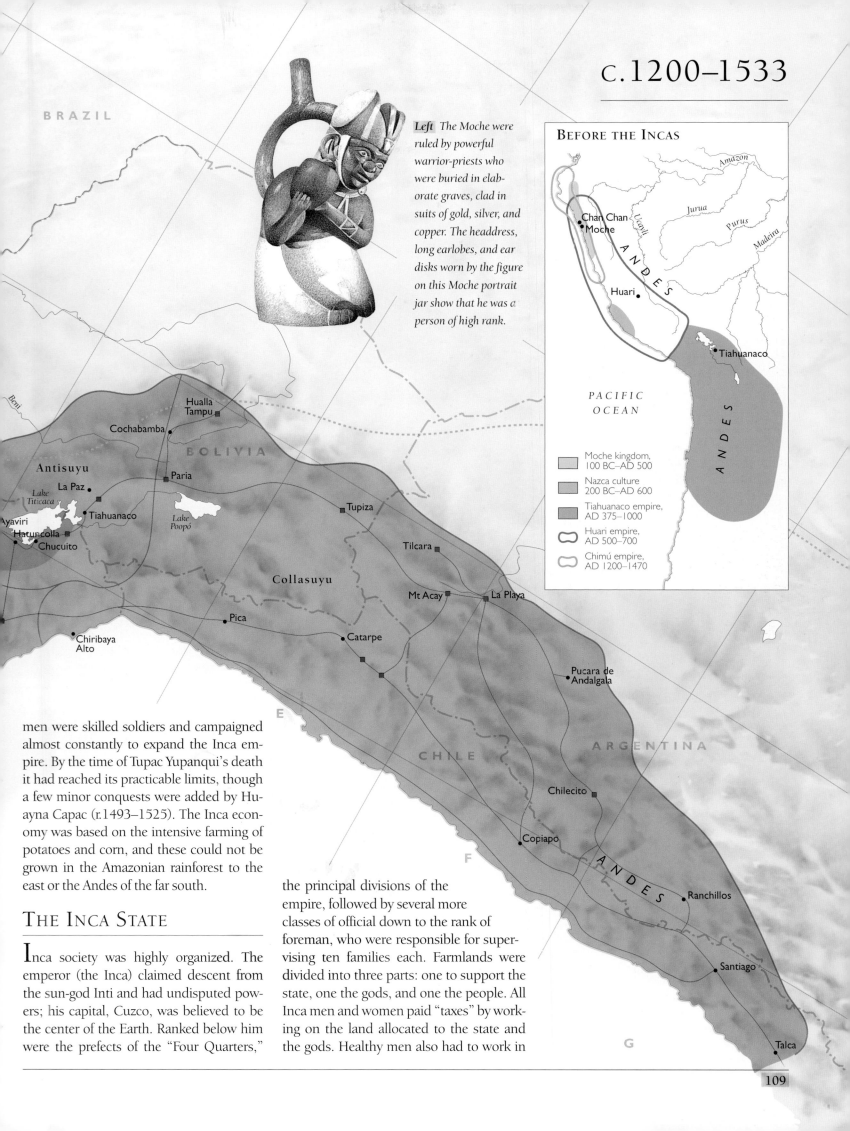

BRAZIL

Left *The Moche were ruled by powerful warrior-priests who were buried in elaborate graves, clad in suits of gold, silver, and copper. The headdress, long earlobes, and ear disks worn by the figure on this Moche portrait jar show that he was a person of high rank.*

BEFORE THE INCAS

Amazon

Jurua

Purus

Madeira

Chan Chan
Moche

A N D E S

Ucayli

Huari

Tiahuanaco

PACIFIC
OCEAN

A N D E S

Moche kingdom,
100 BC–AD 500

Nazca culture
200 BC–AD 600

Tiahuanaco empire,
AD 375–1000

Huari empire,
AD 500–700

Chimú empire,
AD 1200–1470

Beni

Hualla
Tampu

Cochabamba

B O L I V I A

Antisuyu

La Paz

Lake
Titicaca

Paria

Ayaviri

Tiahuanaco

Lake
Poopó

Hatuncolla

Chucuito

Tupiza

Tilcara

Collasuyu

Mt Acay

La Playa

Pica

Catarpe

Chiribaya
Alto

Pucara de
Andalgala

E

ARGENTINA

CHILE

Chilecito

men were skilled soldiers and campaigned almost constantly to expand the Inca empire. By the time of Tupac Yupanqui's death it had reached its practicable limits, though a few minor conquests were added by Huayna Capac (r.1493–1525). The Inca economy was based on the intensive farming of potatoes and corn, and these could not be grown in the Amazonian rainforest to the east or the Andes of the far south.

Copiapo

F

Ranchillos

THE INCA STATE

Inca society was highly organized. The emperor (the Inca) claimed descent from the sun-god Inti and had undisputed powers; his capital, Cuzco, was believed to be the center of the Earth. Ranked below him were the prefects of the "Four Quarters,"

the principal divisions of the empire, followed by several more classes of official down to the rank of foreman, who were responsible for supervising ten families each. Farmlands were divided into three parts: one to support the state, one the gods, and one the people. All Inca men and women paid "taxes" by working on the land allocated to the state and the gods. Healthy men also had to work in

A N D E S

Santiago

G

Talca

labor drafts known as *mit'a*—they might be required to construct roads and fortresses, terrace steep hillsides for new fields, or build irrigation canals. This system allowed the Incas to keep a large full-time army in the field for long periods, giving them an edge over their opponents. Women had to do craft work such as weaving—fine textiles were highly prized and regarded as more precious than gold. This complex tax system was run without the

Right A gold burial mask of the Chimú, symbolizing power. After their defeat by the Incas, Chimú goldsmiths were taken to work in Cuzco.

use of writing. Records were kept by an elaborate system of knotted strings called a *quipu*. Strings of different color represented different kinds of goods, while the number of knots on each string stood for the quantities owed or issued as rations.

The Incas' network of over 12,500 miles (20,000 km) of roads allowed armies and messengers to travel quickly to all parts of the empire. Steep gorges were crossed by rope suspension bridges, and short tunnels found a way through rock obstacles. In the absence of the wheel, freight was carried on the backs of llamas and alpacas. Overnight hostels were provided for travelers.

Conquered peoples were forced to adopt Inca ways and speak the Inca language, Quechua, which is still widely spoken in the Andes. Rebels were deported to the heart of the empire, where they could be closely guarded, and their lands resettled by loyal subjects.

The Inca religion centered on worship of the sun-god Inti. His temple in Cuzco was completely covered in

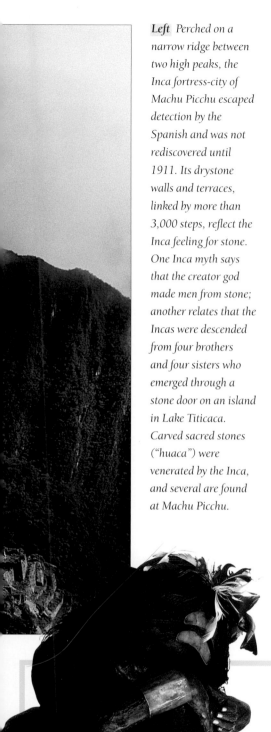

Left Perched on a narrow ridge between two high peaks, the Inca fortress-city of Machu Picchu escaped detection by the Spanish and was not rediscovered until 1911. Its drystone walls and terraces, linked by more than 3,000 steps, reflect the Inca feeling for stone. One Inca myth says that the creator god made men from stone; another relates that the Incas were descended from four brothers and four sisters who emerged through a stone door on an island in Lake Titicaca. Carved sacred stones ("huaca") were venerated by the Inca, and several are found at Machu Picchu.

gold, the symbol of the sun. Mama Cocha ("Mother Earth"), who was the source of fertility and crops, and Viracocha, who created the world, were also worshiped. There were many religious festivals, when the people took part in feasts.

THE END OF THE INCAS

After Huayna Capac's death a bloody civil war broke out between his sons Atahuallpa and Huáscar. Atahuallpa finally defeated his brother in 1532 but the empire had been seriously weakened. Far worse was soon to come. The Spanish conquistador Francisco Pizarro, who had set sail from Panama a year earlier, landed on the coast of Peru. Although he had a force of only 180 men at his disposal, he took Atahuallpa captive in a surprise attack. Without the emperor at their head, the Incas could take no important decisions, so Pizarro's action paralyzed the empire. Atahuallpa paid a huge sum of gold for his freedom, but Pizarro had him executed all the same. By 1536 Cuzco was in Spanish hands.

Resistance continued for some years in remote mountain areas, but smallpox and other imported diseases wiped out thousands of people, while many others were enslaved. The Spanish looted and destroyed Inca temples, banned their religion, and imposed Christianity. Yet Inca customs survive among the Andean peoples, and Inca gods find a place in Christian rituals today.

TIMETABLE

c.100 BC
The Moche state emerges on the coast of northern Peru

AD 375–700
Tiahuanaco is dominant in the southern Andes

c.850
The Chimú state comes into being

c.1200–30
The Incas establish themselves at Cuzco

1438
Pachacutec begins the rapid expansion of the Inca empire

1470
The Incas conquer the Chimú empire

1525
Death of the Inca, Huayna Capac: the Inca empire is at its height.

1525–32
Atahuallpa defeats his brother Huáscar in a civil war

1532
Francisco Pizarro invades the Inca empire and captures Atahuallpa

1533
Pizarro executes Atahuallpa

1572
The last Inca resistance is suppressed by the Spanish

Above The mummified body of an 8-year-old child found on a mountain in Chile.

THE CHILD MUMMIES OF THE ANDES

The Spanish claimed that the Incas commonly sacrificed children. They recorded that the most beautiful boys and girls were selected from their villages to go to Cuzco, where they were ritually "married" to the Inca to ensure health and fertility. They were then taken to a sacred mountaintop, made drunk with liquor, and buried alive. Until the mummy of a young girl was uncovered on a mountain in Chile in 1994, these stories were thought to be anti-Inca propaganda to justify the destruction of their religion. The mountain was sacred to the Inca deity who brought rain and good harvests, and she was found at a height of 20,000 feet

(6,000 m), preserved by the dry climate. Her hair was worn in a long braid tied to her belt by a thread of black alpaca wool, and she had a cap of feathers. Leather slippers protected her feet. Her shawl was fastened with silver pins, from which hung a miniature box and two drinking vessels. Two more children were later found on the same mountain, buried with small dolls and tiny silver models of llamas and alpacas. They may have been a boy and girl who were sacrificed together. While we cannot know the full meaning of these sacrificial burials, they may represent the symbolic relationship between the Inca and the Earth, the living and the dead.

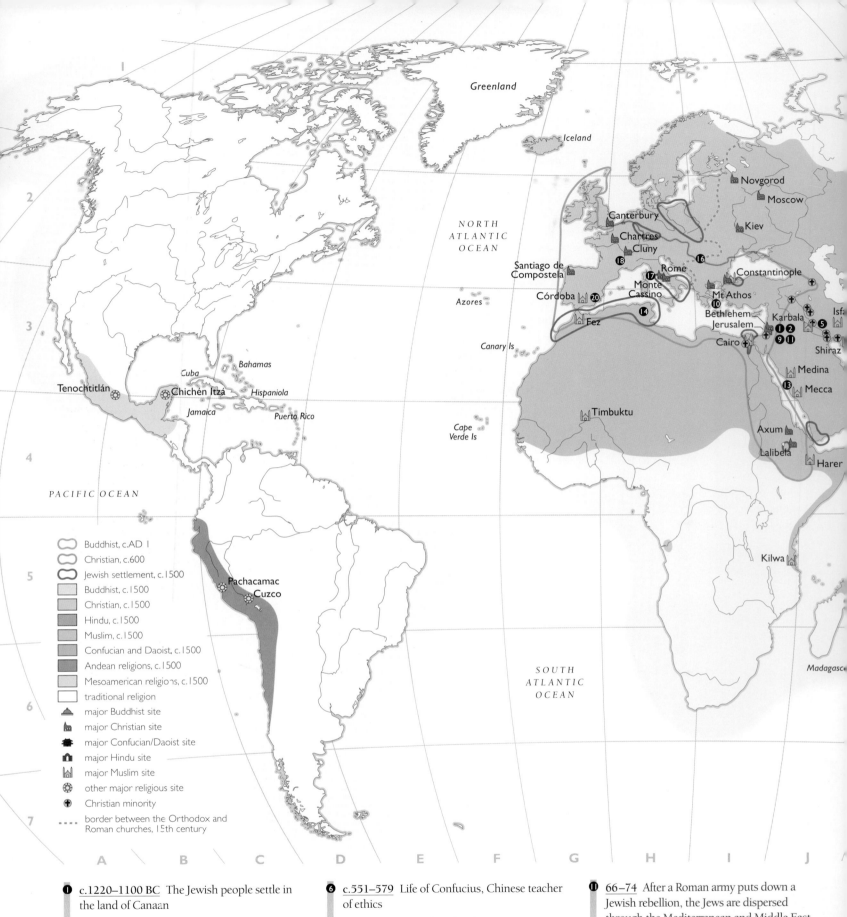

Greenland

Iceland

NORTH
ATLANTIC
OCEAN

Novgorod
Moscow
Canterbury
Kiev
Chartres
Cluny
Santiago de
Compostela
Rome
Constantinople
Córdoba
Monte
Cassino
Mt Athos
Fez
Bethlehem
Jerusalem
Karbala
Cairo
Shiraz
Medina
Mecca

Azores

Canary Is

Cape
Verde Is

Timbuktu

Axum
Lalibela
Harer

PACIFIC OCEAN

Tenochtitlán
Chichén Itzá
Cuba
Bahamas
Hispaniola
Jamaica
Puerto Rico

SOUTH
ATLANTIC
OCEAN

Madagascar

Kilwa

Pachacamac
Cuzco

Buddhist, c.AD 1
Christian, c.600
Jewish settlement, c.1500
Buddhist, c.1500
Christian, c.1500
Hindu, c.1500
Muslim, c.1500
Confucian and Daoist, c.1500
Andean religions, c.1500
Mesoamerican religions, c.1500
traditional religion
major Buddhist site
major Christian site
major Confucian/Daoist site
major Hindu site
major Muslim site
other major religious site
Christian minority
border between the Orthodox and
Roman churches, 15th century

❶ **c.1220–1100 BC** The Jewish people settle in the land of Canaan

❷ **c.1000** King David makes Jerusalem the capital of Israel

❸ **c.800** The *Upanishads,* sacred Hindu texts, are written down

❹ **c.630–553** Life of Zoroaster, founder of the Zoroastrian religion of Iran

❺ **c.587** The Jews are deported to Babylon by King Nebuchadnezzar II

❻ **c.551–579** Life of Confucius, Chinese teacher of ethics

❼ **c.528–461** Life of Siddhartha Gautama, founder of Buddhism

❽ **c.260** The first Buddhist missionaries arrive in Ceylon

❾ **c.6 BC–AD 30** Life of Jesus of Nazareth, founder of Christianity

❿ **AD 44–62** St. Paul makes missionary journeys to Asia Minor, Greece, and Rome

⓫ **66–74** After a Roman army puts down a Jewish rebellion, the Jews are dispersed through the Mediterranean and Middle East

⓬ **c.100** Buddhism reaches China

⓭ **c.570–632** Life of the Prophet Muhammad, founder of Islam

⓮ **632–750** The Arab conquests spread the Islamic religion from Spain to Persia

⓯ **791** Buddhism becomes the state religion of the kingdom of Tibet

THE WORLD'S RELIGIONS

By 1500 THE FIVE MAJOR "WORLD RELIGIONS" OF HINDUISM, BUDDHISM, JUDAISM, CHRISTIANITY, AND ISLAM WERE WIDELY SPREAD THROUGH ASIA, EUROPE, AND MUCH OF NORTHERN AFRICA, WHERE THEY OFTEN EXISTED ALONGSIDE, AND INTERMINGLED WITH, EARLIER BELIEFS. BUT MUCH OF THE WORLD STILL LAY OUTSIDE THE REACH OF THEIR INFLUENCE.

Religion has probably been a characteristic of all societies in all parts of the world from the beginning of human history; there is evidence of ritual burial even among some of our early human ancestors such as the Neanderthals. Most traditional societies of hunter-gatherers and tribal farmers have systems of belief that recognize a relationship between the natural and supernatural worlds: the landscape is inhabited by gods or by good and evil spirits, often the souls of ancestors or animals, who have influence over human affairs. They can bring about calamities such as death, sickness, or famine, or ensure good fortune and success. Holy men (more rarely women)—known as shamans, witch doctors, or medicine men—may claim the power to communicate with the spirit world and to influence it through rituals passed down over generations. Sometimes gods or spirits are believed to inhabit a particular site such as a waterfall, tree, or cave. If they are given food or other offerings, they may bring about good results such as the birth of a child or a plentiful harvest. Belief systems of this kind are still found in every part of the world. They vary greatly in their beliefs and practices, and are known as animist or traditional religions.

Map labels: Naimans and Keraits, Samarkand, Herat, Beijing, Kyongju, Mt Fuji, Luoyang, Kaifeng, Heian, Chang'an, Nanjing, Hangzhou, Gangotri, Mt Kailas, Hardwar, Lhasa, Varanasi, Bodh Gaya, Konarak, Pagan, Somnath, Dagon, Vijayanagara, Angkor, Philippine Is, Madurai, Polonnaruva, Ceylon, Malacca, Celebes, Sumatra, Borneo, New Guinea, Java, Borobudur, Timor, INDIAN OCEAN

Right Many religions, including Hinduism, Christianity, and Islam, encourage pilgrimage: a long or hard journey made to a sacred site or shrine will win the traveler special merit. St. James is shown here as a Christian pilgrim.

As societies developed, religion became more structured. Organized states had the resources to build and maintain central temples or shrines. Rulers often had a special religious function, which was the basis for their power: their performance of certain set rituals ensured the safety of the state and bound the people to them. A great number of gods might be worshiped, some of whom were associated with a particular city or shrine. Religions of this kind had developed in the early agricultural societies of Europe and Asia, and in 1500 could be found among many of the settled farmers of Mesoamerica and the Andes.

WORLD RELIGIONS

Over time, some religions claimed universal status: they held that their teachings had relevance for all people and sought to win converts from other religions. The societies in which these religions developed were literate, and their beliefs were usually written down in divinely "revealed" sacred books. They define the basic teachings of that religion in a precise form for future generations to interpret and live by. Others spread from their original place of origin because of the uprooting and dispersal of their followers.

By the year 1500 the "world religions," as they are known, were widely established in Asia and Europe. That did not mean that all earlier beliefs had disappeared. Often local gods or sacred sites became part of the new religion (a process often known as syncretism). There were also many smaller religions like Zoroastrianism, many of whose followers had settled in western India after being expelled from Persia.

ONE GOD OF ALL

Three world religions—Judaism, Christianity, and Islam—believe in a single creator God, though they do not worship him in the same way. These religions are called monotheistic. The oldest is Judaism, the faith that grew up among the ancient Jewish people. They believed that God had given them the land of Canaan (modern Israel and Lebanon) to live in for ever. Their complex set of laws and beliefs, contained in the Old Testament books of the Bible, set them apart from others and sustained their sense of cultural and ethnic identity after they had

been scattered by conquest and migration. Many Jewish communities were established around the Mediterranean and Middle East, but Jews were often persecuted by other religions, particularly Christians. Persecution increased during the Middle Ages. In 1492 the Inquisition was used against the Jews of Spain, and all those who refused to convert to Christianity were driven from the country their families had lived in for centuries.

Christianity shares some of the Biblical foundations of Judaism. It is based upon the teachings of Jesus of Nazareth, a Jewish teacher who rebelled against the current religious practices of the Jews and was put to death. His followers became known as Christians, and after his death Christianity became a missionizing religion that sought to convert people throughout the Mediterranean world. The Romans persecuted the early Christians but after Christianity was made the official religion of the empire in 391, it spread rapidly. By 1500 it was recognized throughout Europe but was split into two: the western Catholic church in Rome and the eastern Orthodox church in Constantinople. The Crusades against the Muslims of Spain and the Middle East, led

THE EASTERN RELIGIONS

The origins of Hinduism, the main religion of the Indian subcontinent in 1500, stretch back at least 3,000 years, based on the Vedas and other ancient scriptures. A complex system of ideas and rituals, it has no formal beliefs but has at its center the idea of reincarnation, or rebirth in a new form after death. It embraces the worship of numerous gods and spiritual beings, and its devotees often make pilgrimages to holy sites such as the river Ganges. The cultural influence of Hinduism spread outside India to parts of Southeast Asia, but by 1500 it was declining here, except in Bali.

Buddhism, based on the teachings of Siddhartha Gautama, the Buddha, taught that people could attain nirvana, a state free of suffering, by correct living. At one time widespread in India, where it originated in the 5th century BC, it had nearly died out there by 1500. However, missionaries had spread it outside India to all parts of east Asia. By AD 300, Buddhism had divided into two main traditions. Mahayana or Tantric Buddhism, practiced in Tibet, China, Korea, and Japan, believes in the existence of supernatural deities; Theravada Buddhism, followed in southeast Asia, does not.

In China Buddhist ideas were assimilated into Taoism, an indigenous philosophical system. Traditional worship of ancestors also continued, as did the ethical code based on the teachings of Confucius (551–479 BC). Japanese Buddhism blended with Shinto, which recognizes the sacred power of *kami*, gods and spirits that were believed to inhabit rocks, trees, streams, and many other natural sites.

by the popes, were the cause of increasing hostility between Christianity and Islam.

Like Judaism and Christianity, Islam grew up in the Middle East: it also teaches that there is only one God and is based upon a sacred text, the Koran, which contains the divine revelations of the Prophet Muhammad. Conquest and the expansion of trade spread the religion he founded in 7th-century Arabia throughout the Middle East and northern Africa and into central and southeast Asia. By 1500 Islam was the most successful of the world religions, both numerically and by geographical spread.

Above Angkor Wat in northern Cambodia was a 12th-century Hindu temple dedicated to the cult of Shiva. Built by a ruler of the Khmer kingdom, it shows the strong Indian cultural influence in southeast Asia at this time. It later became a Buddhist shrine.

Left Shiva is the most powerful and terrifying of the Hindu gods. He is contradictory in character: he both saves the world and destroys it. Here he is shown as the Lord of the Dance, depicted within a circle of flames as he tramples the demon of ignorance beneath his feet.

THE AGE OF DISCOVERY

In the three centuries from 1492 to 1815 the world became a smaller place. European navigators and explorers charted the world's oceans and coastlines; by the end of the period all the continents, and most of the major island groups, had been written on to the maps. The period also saw a great shift in global power.

Before the Spanish set foot in the New World, Europe had been overshadowed by the more advanced civilizations of the Middle East and East Asia, who dominated international trade. The quantities of American gold and silver sent back to Europe brought a ready stream of wealth, and the opening of a direct sea route meant that European traders could buy silk and spices directly from Southeast Asia and the Far East. By the end of the 18th century Europeans controlled most of Asia's maritime trade. More shameful was the inhuman trade in slaves they had established between Africa and the Caribbean.

Europe itself underwent great religious and social upheavals between 1492 and 1815. It was split into opposing Catholic and Protestant camps by the Reformation and subsequently divided by frequent political wars, caused in part by rivalry for colonial trade. The French Revolution of 1789 threw Europe into turmoil. Napoleon emerged from the political chaos in France to make himself emperor, but his attempt to create an empire in Europe ended in his defeat in 1815. The French revolutionaries shared many of the ideals of liberty and democracy that inspired the thirteen American colonies to throw off British rule in 1776. By 1815, the young United States had established itself territorially and politically. The colonial empires of Latin America were also moving toward independence.

For all its success, Europe did not dominate the world in 1815. Most people in Asia, Africa, and the Pacific region had never seen or heard of Europeans. The largest empire was China, which controlled many neighboring states in Central and East Asia and had, like Japan, turned its back on contact with Europe. Closer to home, the Ottoman empire was still a challenge to European power, though it was obviously in decline. But western technological and scientific knowledge had seen rapid advances, and large-scale industrial production was just beginning in Britain. The global economy was set to grow as industrialization spread to the rest of Europe and the United States in the coming century.

Left *Seventeenth-century Flemish still-life.*

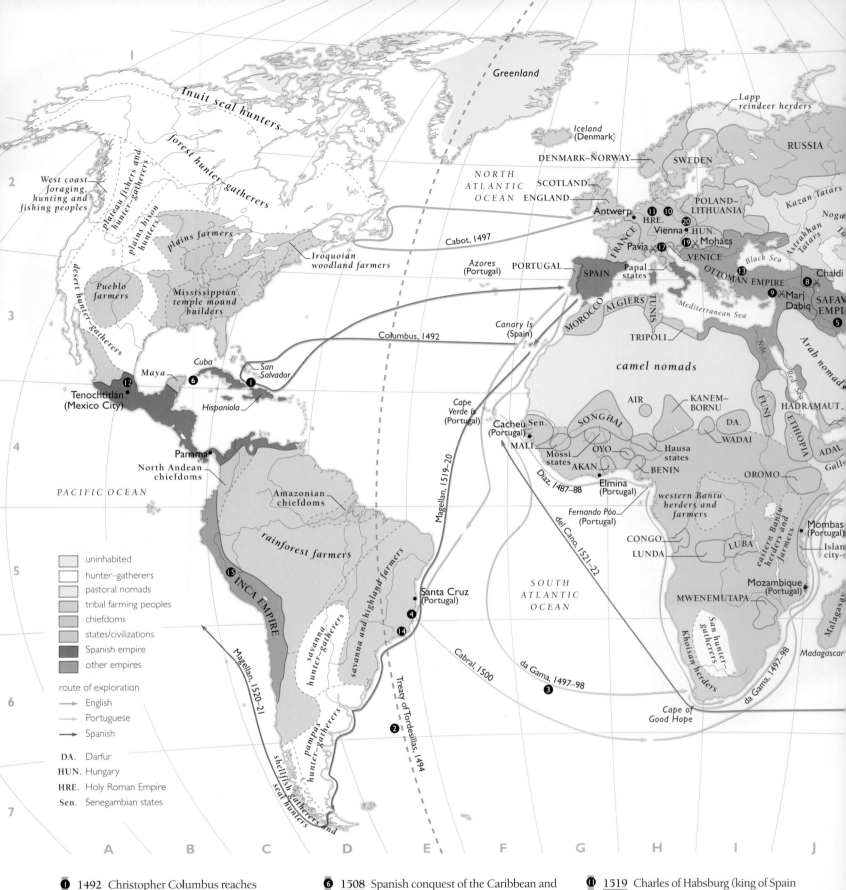

1492 Christopher Columbus reaches Hispaniola and Cuba in the Caribbean

1494 The Treaty of Tordesillas gives all land west of an imaginary line in the Atlantic to Spain, and all land east of it to Portugal

1497–98 Vasco da Gama makes the first return voyage from Portugal to India

1500 Pedro Alvarez Cabral discovers Brazil for Portugal, while sailing to India

1501 The Safavid dynasty is set up in Persia

1508 Spanish conquest of the Caribbean and Central America begins

1511 The Portuguese capture Malacca

1514 The Ottoman Turks defeat the Safavids at the battle of Chaldiran

1516 The Ottoman Turks defeat the Mamluke rulers of Egypt at the battle of Marj Dabiq

1517 Martin Luther publishes his 95 Theses in Wittenberg, Germany, an act that leads to the Protestant Reformation

1519 Charles of Habsburg (king of Spain since 1516) is elected Charles V, Holy Roman emperor, on the death of his grandfather

1519 The Spanish adventurer Hernán Cortés begins the conquest of the Aztec empire

1520 Suleiman I becomes the reigning sultan of the Ottoman empire

1521 The Portuguese begin to colonize Brazil

1521–25 The Inca empire in Peru reaches its greatest extent

THE WORLD BY 1530

IN THE LATE 15TH CENTURY, THE WORLD'S GREATEST CIVILIZATIONS WERE ALL IN ASIA; EUROPE WAS BACKWARD BY COMPARISON. YET BY 1530 EUROPEANS CONTROLLED THE INDIAN OCEAN, AND WERE ON THE WAY TO CONQUERING THE GREAT EMPIRES OF THE AMERICAS. ONE SHIP, COMMANDED BY FERDINAND MAGELLAN, HAD SAILED AROUND THE WORLD. THE IMPLICATIONS FOR WORLD HISTORY WERE ENORMOUS.

Trade in the rich cloths, jewels, and spices of Asia was the chief goal of the European explorers. Such luxury goods had great value in Europe. However, western traders did not have direct access to the profitable markets of Asia—their way was blocked by hostile Muslim states such as the Ottoman Turks who by 1530 controlled the Black Sea and eastern Mediterranean ports at the western end of the overland route from China and India, as well as the sea route from the Indian Ocean to the Red Sea and Egypt.

During the 15th century, European navigators had begun looking for other routes to Asia. They were led by the Portuguese who learned to build ships that were capable of making the long sea voyage down the Atlantic coast of Africa; in 1497–98 Vasco da Gama sailed from Portugal to India and back around the Cape of Good Hope. More daring still, in 1492 Christopher Columbus ventured west across the Atlantic with a Spanish fleet in an attempt to reach China. But instead of arriving in Asia, he had found

Map labels

Inuit seal hunters
Siberian hunter–gatherers
Siberian reindeer herders
Ainu hunter–gatherers
...ir Tatars
Central Asian khanates
Mongols
Kirghiz
...egs
Kalmyks
Beijing
KOREA JAPAN
Kabul
MUGHAL EMPIRE
TIBET
MING CHINESE EMPIRE
Nanjing
Panipat
Islamic and Hindu states
Shan states
...GHARRA
...OMAN
BENGAL
Burmese kingdoms
Taiwan
...AHRA
...EMEN
Goa (Portugal)
ORISSA
PEGU
LAOS
ANNAM
Philippine Is
VIJAYANAGARA
...ma, 1497–98
SAYLAN
Ceylon
Lopez de Sequeira, 1509–10
ACEH
AYUTTHAYA
CAMBODIA
Magellan 1520–21
Cabral, 1500
Colombo (Portugal)
Perestrello, 1514–16
del Cano, 1521
Malacca (Portugal)
Borneo
MALACCA
Sumatra
Malaysian Islamic states
New Guinea
Papuan farmers
Java
Timor (Portugal)
Melanesians
INDIAN OCEAN
Australian Aboriginal hunter–gatherers
del Cano, 1521–22
Polynesians
Tasmanian hunter–gatherers
Maori chiefdoms

L M N O P

16 **1522** Magellan's voyage around the world (begun in 1519) is completed by Sebastian del Cano

17 **1525** Francis I of France is captured by the Spanish at the battle of Pavia in northern Italy

18 **1526** Babur defeats the sultan of Delhi at the battle of Panipat and conquers northern India

19 **1526** An Ottoman army defeats the Hungarians at Mohács

20 **1529** The Ottomans besiege Vienna

Right The "Santa Maria," flagship of the small fleet with which Columbus sailed in 1492, resembled this tiny vessel. The crossing from the Canary Islands to landfall at San Salvador (Bahamas) took almost six weeks.

the way to a new continent, soon to be called America. Other explorers followed and a few years later John Cabot sailed from England to Newfoundland. In 1520 Ferdinand Magellan entered the Pacific Ocean around the tip of South America. Although he died en route, his crew returned to Europe having made the first circumnavigation of the globe.

EUROPE

By 1530 Spain was the wealthiest kingdom in Europe, profiting from the gold that the Spanish conquerors discovered in the Americas and shipped home in vast quantities. In 1519 the Spanish king became, as Charles V, the Holy Roman emperor. This gave him control of Spain, Germany, the Netherlands, and much of Italy, and created a Habsburg power bloc that would dominate Europe for 200 years. Spain's only political rival was France. Since the start of the century they had been fighting a long war for control of the rich city-states of northern Italy. By 1530 it was clear that Spain would be the eventual winner.

The greatest event in Europe in the first half of the 16th century was the controversy over religious reform. Many Christians felt that the Catholic church, and the popes in particular, had become corrupt. In 1517, a German monk, Martin Luther, launched a movement of protest against church abuses. It fueled religious and political unrest in Germany and led to the Protestant Reformation, which divided Europe into bitterly opposed camps for 150 years. By 1530 the Reformation had spread to Sweden, and would soon reach England and Scotland.

THE MIDDLE EAST

In 1530 the Ottoman Turks dominated the Middle East. They had begun to expand out of Anatolia (mainland Turkey) into the Balkans in the 13th and 14th centuries; the city of Constantinople (Istanbul) was taken in 1453. In 1514 they seized Mesopotamia (modern Iraq) from the Safavid rulers of Persia, and the invasion of Egypt two years later laid the way open for further expansion in North Africa and Arabia. The Ottomans continued, too, to make inroads into Europe. After the Hungarians were defeated in 1526, an Ottoman army reached Vienna,

one of the leading cities of Europe and the seat of the Habsburg emperors, in 1529. It failed to capture the city, but few believed the threat to Europe was over. In 1530 the sultan Suleiman I ("the Magnificent") was the most powerful man in the world.

AFRICA

Before the European discovery of America, tropical west Africa had been the main source of gold for Europe and the Middle East. Caravans of camels conveyed it across

the Sahara desert to ports on the North African coast. This trans-Saharan trade was controlled by the kingdom of Songhai, but when the Portuguese set up a string of bases on the west African coast in the late 15th century, they took trade away from the Saharan routes, thus weakening Songhai. Defeat by the neighboring state of Hausa in 1517 hastened its decline.

Portuguese traders were steadily developing their activities in Africa. By 1502 they were sending African slaves to the Americas. They used their warships to attack the

Left *A Venetian ambassador is received by the Ottomans, in a painting by Giovanni Bellini. Venice had once been the most powerful naval and trading power in the Mediterranean, but its days were numbered. The Ottomans had taken over many of its island fortresses, and with the opening up of the new ocean-going trade routes, Antwerp replaced it as the main European market for the spice trade.*

Below *This silver alpaca was made as a ritual offering by the Incas. South America had vast natural and mineral wealth before the arrival of the Europeans. Herds of alpacas – which gave thick, soft wool – and llamas, providing food, power, cloth and hides, made the steep Andean mountainsides productive. Peru's vast reserves of gold and silver proved irresistible to European explorers.*

Mongols. The Ming rulers were resistant to outside influences and foreign trade, and as a result, China had begun to lose its technological lead over the rest of the world.

In Central Asia, the growing power of the Ottomans and the Russians was beginning to push the nomadic tribes of the steppes eastward after several centuries of movement in the opposite direction. One nomadic tribal leader, Babur, captured Kabul in Afghanistan in 1504 and went on to invade India. He defeated the sultan of Delhi in 1526 and founded the Mughal dynasty that ruled much of India until the 18th century.

In 1510 the Portuguese founded a trading base at Goa in India. The following year they seized the important Malayan port of Malacca, thereby laying the foundations for what would become a powerful trading empire in the East Indies.

THE AMERICAS

European impact in Central and South America had disastrous consequences for the indigenous peoples. The colonists and adventurers who followed Columbus west were greedy for gold and wasted little time in plundering the wealth of the Aztec empire in Mexico. Virtually all of Central America had been conquered by 1530, and Francisco Pizarro was preparing to invade the Inca empire from the Spanish colony in Panama. By 1533 it, too, would have fallen to the conquistadors.

The Spanish showed little or no interest in the civilizations they found in the New World. Horrified by the practice of human sacrifice, they suppressed native religions and imposed Christianity, usually by force. Entire groups of Amerindians in the Caribbean islands and on the mainland were destroyed in epidemics of diseases introduced by Europeans. Those who survived were forced to work in the mines and on the plantations established by Europeans.

Arab traders who had controlled trade in the Indian Ocean for centuries, and Muslim trading ports on the east African coast were brought under their influence. The Portuguese also helped the Christian kingdom of Ethiopia defeat its Muslim neighbor, Adal.

SOUTH & EAST ASIA

China was the world's largest state in the 16th century. Since 1368 it had been ruled by the Ming dynasty, which had come to power after a century of devastation by the

THE SPANISH–AMERICAN EMPIRE

IN 1492, THE ITALIAN-BORN NAVIGATOR CHRISTOPHER COLUMBUS SAILED WEST ACROSS THE ATLANTIC IN SEARCH OF A SEA ROUTE TO CHINA. SPONSORED BY THE CATHOLIC MONARCHS, FERDINAND AND ISABELLA, HE SAILED UNDER THE FLAG OF SPAIN. HE MADE LANDFALL ON AN ISLAND IN THE CARIBBEAN, THE FIRST EUROPEAN CONTACT WITH THE AMERICAS SINCE THE VIKINGS. AS WORD OF COLUMBUS'S DISCOVERIES IN THE "NEW WORLD" SPREAD, OTHER EUROPEAN EXPLORERS FOLLOWED IN HIS FOOTSTEPS.

Columbus made four journeys across the Atlantic to the Caribbean. He claimed all the islands he visited for Spain and founded a settlement on Hispaniola. In 1499 a Spanish fleet explored along the coast of South America. One ship was captained by a certain Amerigo Vespucci; an early map-maker ascribed his forename (Americus in Latin) to the new continents, and they have been known as the Americas ever since.

The New World held out unparalleled opportunities for personal enrichment and national conquest. Spanish military adventurers, known as conquistadors, followed on the heels of the early explorers. Rumors of the vast wealth possessed by the Aztec rulers of Mexico led the conquistador Hernán Cortés, at the head of an army of only a few hundred, to invade and conquer their empire in 1519–24. An even smaller force under the command of Francisco Pizarro overcame the far larger Inca empire of the Andes in 1531–35. Huge quantities of gold and silver were plundered from both empires and shipped back to Europe. Stories of a fabulously rich city, El Dorado ("The Golden"), buried deep in the jungle, traveled back with the treasure ships. Many expeditions were sent to look for it, but they all failed. Instead, the conquistadors met with disease, starvation, and the poisoned arrows of hostile Amerindians. But their quest resulted in large areas of the Americas being explored and mapped by Europeans.

THE IMPACT OF CONQUEST

As a result of the Spanish presence, the indigenous New World peoples suffered a huge loss of life. More died in epidemics than in war—the native Amerindian population lacked immunity to European diseases such as smallpox. The Carib and Arawak peoples of the Caribbean, who were treated with extreme harshness, were nearly extinct by 1550, while the numbers of Aztecs, Incas, and other South American peoples had more than halved by 1600 and continued to decline throughout the next 100 years. The Spanish imported African slaves to make up for the loss of workers on the sugar plantations they established in the Caribbean. The Amerindians of Central and South America were forced to work in the rich silver mines of Mexico and Peru.

Above A Dominican friar supervises an Inca woman at her loom.

The Spanish believed they had a divine duty to convert the Amerindians to Christianity. They refused to tolerate pagan worship; in banning it, they suppressed many aspects of native culture. Dominican and Franciscan friars set up schools where European farming methods and crafts were taught. Though harshly run, they offered some protection against the cruelty of the conquistadors. Later, the Jesuits founded

Portuguese territory, 1650
Portuguese territory, 1750
Spanish territory, 1650
Spanish territory, 1750
Jesuit mission state to 1767
British territory, 1750
Dutch territory, 1750
French territory, 1750

early settlement or trading post, with date of foundation
Portuguese
Spanish
archbishopric
line of Treaty of Tordesillas, 1494
route of explorer
route of conquistador
slaving expedition of the Paulistas
circumnavigation by Francis Drake, 1577–80

0   1400 km
0   1000 mi

NORTH
ATLANTIC
OCEAN

Bermuda Islands
to Britain

Columbus, 1492

Columbus, 1493

Columbus, 1498

Vespucci, 1499

Lake Ontario

Lake Erie

St Augustine
1565

Florida

Ponce de Leon, 1512–13

New Orleans

Bahamas

San Juan
1511

Puerto Rico

Lesser Antilles

ulf of exico

Matanzas

Havana
1515

Cuba

Hispaniola

Santo Domingo
1496

s, 1519

Jamaica

Columbus, 1502–4

Cumaná
1521

Caracas
1567

Paramaribo

Cayenne

Georgetown

Ceará

Orinoco

VENEZUELA

Guiana Highlands

São Luis do Maranhão
1615

Natal
1597

Olinda
1537

igua
1542

Guatemala

Cartagena
1533

Porto Bello
1597

Nombre de Dios
1510

Panama
1519

Pizarro, 1526–27

Santa Fe de Bogota
1538

COLOMBIA

Negro

Japura

Putumayo

Amazon

Tapajos

Xingu

Tocantins

São Francisco

Bele do Para
1616

Manaus
1674

BRAZIL

Portuguese Spanish

Recife
1563

Bahia
1549

Santa Cruz

PACIFIC
OCEAN

Quito
1534

Guayaquil
1535

Amazon Basin

Jurua

Purus

Madeira

Brazilian Highlands

Villa Rica
1698

PERU

ANDES

Ucayali

Pizarro, 1533

Cuzco

Mato Grosso Plateau

Rio de Janeiro
1565

São Paulo
1532

São Vicente
1530

Callao

Ciudad de los Reyes
(Lima)
1535

La Paz

BOLIVIA

Chuquisaca
(Charcas/La Plata)
1538

Arica
1537

Potosí

Asunción
1538

PARAGUAY

Paraguay

Parana

Banda Oriental

Córdoba
1573

Buenos Aires
1536

ARGENTINA

ANDES

Valparaiso
1541

Santiago
1541

SOUTH
ATLANTIC
OCEAN

Spanish

Portuguese

Valdivia
1552

Patagonia

mission states in the frontier regions. Spanish gradually replaced native languages.

The whole of Central America was made the Viceroyalty of New Spain. Another viceroyalty was established in Peru shortly after Pizarro's conquest. Both viceroyalties expanded as settlements were founded in California, Texas, and Florida, and east of the Andes, and were later divided into smaller administrative regions.

Above African slaves were sent in large numbers to the New World. This heavily armed "mulatto," the term used for people of mixed African and European descent, was painted by a visitor to Brazil in the 1630s.

Above Colonial life
in Brazil and Spanish
America reproduced
the patterns of life at
home. Towns were built
in European archi-
tectural styles to serve
the local neighborhood.
In this 17th-century
Brazilian town, the
main square is the site
of the slave market:
plantation owners
stroll up and down to
inspect the most recent
consignments. The
slave trade was made
illegal in the Spanish
colonies by the 1820s,
but continued in the
coffee plantations of
Brazil until the late
19th century.

The conquistadors were given parcels of
land called *encomienda*. Each *encomendero*
(lord) was entitled to collect taxes and use
local labor in return for keeping soldiers to
defend the empire, in much the same way
as the Aztecs and Incas had maintained
their empires. In time, the Spanish created
large farming estates (*haciendas*). Colonists
were always in short supply, the more so as
emigration from Spain was restricted in the
17th century to a limit of 2,000 a year to
stem falling population levels at home. The
Spanish in South America became absentee
landlords, staying in the towns, or returning to Europe, for long periods. Amerindians were made to leave the land to become
wage laborers, or peons, on the *haciendas*.
This system remains in force in many parts
of Central and South America.

EUROPEAN RIVALS

Its American empire turned Spain into the
greatest power in Europe. The silver that
was shipped back in huge quantities helped
to finance its wars, and the flow of precious
metal stimulated the whole European economy. Other European countries were eager
to grab a share of the New World's riches.
The Treaty of Tordesillas between Spain and

END OF THE SPANISH & PORTUGUESE EMPIRES

UNITED STATES OF AMERICA

MEXICO 1821

ATLANTIC OCEAN

Cuba

HAITI 1804

Jamaica

Puerto Rico

British Honduras

Mosquito Coast

UNITED PROVINCES OF CENTRAL AMERICA (1821–23 to Mexico) 1823

REPUBLIC OF GRAN COLOMBIA 1819

British Guiana
Dutch Guiana
French Guiana

PACIFIC OCEAN

BRAZIL 1822

PERU 1821

BOLIVIA 1825

PARAGUAY 1811

CHILE 1818

ARGENTINE CONFEDERATION (United Provinces of La Plata, 1816–25) 1816

Patagonia

Malvinas (Falklands)

Portuguese territory, early 19th century

Spanish territory, early 19th century

remaining Spanish territory in the Americas, 1825

borders, 1825

1818 date of independence

Portugal in 1494 had drawn an imaginary line to bisect the Atlantic west of the Cape Verde islands: the Portuguese were free to settle all land to the east of it, the Spanish all land to the west. In effect, this restricted the Portuguese to a small area of coastal Brazil, which they began to settle in large numbers in the 1530s. Portuguese slavers, known as *Paulistas*, frequently raided into the Brazilian jungle, where they attacked the Spanish Jesuit mission states. In the late 17th century, to avoid war with Spain, Portugal cracked down on such raids, banning the enslavement of Native Americans. To provide labor in their mines and plantations they imported black slaves from Angola on the west coast of Africa.

For a long time, other European countries such as the Netherlands, England, and France had to confine their activities in the New World to attacking Spain's ships and coastal ports. Piracy and smuggling were common; so too was privateering, in which the captain of a commercial ship was authorized to carry out piracy on behalf of a hostile government. The English privateer Sir Francis Drake was particularly famous for his daring raids around the Caribbean. But even he failed to capture the heavily guarded treasure fleet that carried quantities of recently mined American silver back to Spain every year. It was seized only once, by the Dutch admiral Piet Heyn in 1628.

Spanish Decline

In the 17th century, the Spanish-American economy collapsed, partly through labor shortages caused by the dramatic fall in the Amerindian population. The Netherlands, England, and France seized advantage of Spain's weakness to set up small colonies of their own in Central and South America: the English capture of Jamaica in 1655 was a particularly expensive loss. Spanish territory in North America was also threatened by the success of French and English colonies (see pages 126–129). At the end of the Seven Years War (1756–63) Britain gave up Havana (captured in 1762) for Florida, but had lost it again by 1783.

In spite of these losses, the Spanish and Portuguese American empires were mostly intact at the end of the 18th century. However, independence movements were starting to develop, fueled partly by the ideals of the American and French Revolutions. The Napoleonic wars in Europe, when Spain and Portugal were under French occupation (see pages 138–141), provided the catalyst for revolt. The battle for independence started in Mexico in 1810. In 1811 Simón Bolívar (the "Liberator"), an inspired military leader, began the struggle to free South America from Spanish rule. Within 15 years the Spanish empire had broken up, and Brazil was also independent.

The Catholic Legacy

Although it was imposed by force, Roman Catholicism put down deep roots among the native peoples of Latin America. Today, half the world's Catholics live there. Many traditional beliefs and customs were assimilated into Catholicism, giving it a distinctive Amerindian character. In the Andes, sacrifices were made to Christian saints to placate the mountain gods. The figure of Christ was associated with the Sun-god and the Virgin Mary with Mama Cocha, the Inca earthgoddess. In Mexico, belief in the sacredness of ancestors remains alive in the vivid celebrations on the Day of the Dead (November 1st), the Christian remembrance of All Souls.

Right Guatemalan villagers celebrate the feast of St. Thomas by carrying his statue through the streets.

TIMETABLE

1492
Christopher Columbus lands on Hispaniola

1496
The first permanent European settlement in the Americas is founded at Santo Domingo on Hispaniola

1513
Vasco Núñez de Balboa is the first European to sight the Pacific Ocean

1517
The first African slaves arrive in the Americas

1531–35
Francisco Pizarro conquers the Inca empire of Peru

1539–43
Francisco Vázquez de Coronado explores the North American West

1545
The world's richest silver mine is discovered at Potosí in the Andes

1630
The Dutch briefly occupy eastern Brazil

1655
The English capture Jamaica

1697
Tayasal, the last independent Maya state, is conquered by Spain

1708–09
Portugal suppresses the *Paulista* slave raiders

1716
Spain occupies Texas

1762
Britain captures Havana. Spain cedes Florida to get it back

1780–81
Spain recaptures West Florida from Britain during the American Revolution

1810–11
Miguel Hidalgo leads an unsuccessful revolt in Mexico

1817–24
The wars of independence are led by Simón Bolívar and José de San Martin

1823
The United States recognizes the newly independent states of South America

COLONIAL NORTH AMERICA

IN 1500 NORTH AMERICA WAS INHABITED BY SCATTERED GROUPS OF NATIVE AMERICAN FARMERS AND HUNTER–GATHERERS. THE FIRST EUROPEANS WHO CAME HERE HAD NO IDEA OF THE CONTINENT'S TRUE SIZE AND DIVERSITY, AND FOUND IT AN ALIEN, ENIGMATIC PLACE. SATISFIED THAT IT HELD NO RESERVES OF GOLD OR SILVER, SPAIN MADE LITTLE ATTEMPT TO COLONIZE IT, AND IT WAS LEFT FOR THE NORTHERN EUROPEAN NATIONS TO DO SO.

In 1497, John Cabot, an Italian-born seafarer sailing under the English flag, set out from Bristol across the Atlantic in the hope of finding a northern sea route to China. He reached Newfoundland, becoming the first European to arrive in North America since the Vikings had made a temporary camp there 500 years earlier. He found the waters were teeming with cod, and English fishing fleets visited the island regularly thereafter, but no permanent settlement was established there until 1610.

Giovanni da Verrazano sailed the length of the Atlantic seaboard in 1524, and the French sailor, Jacques Cartier, explored the St. Lawrence river in 1535–36, searching for a way through the heart of the northern continent; others tried to sail around it. The sheer scale of North America was beyond any European's ability to imagine.

Early visitors reported that it was covered in forest and inhabited by hostile peoples. The first attempts at colonization ended in failure. Eventually, in 1607, an English settlement took root at Jamestown, Virginia. Quebec was founded a year later by the French, and by 1650 there was a scattering of colonies along the eastern seaboard, Swedish and Dutch among them.

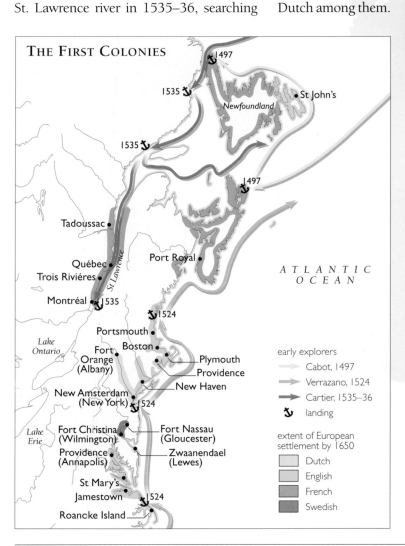

THE FIRST COLONIES

1497

1535

Newfoundland

St John's

1535

1497

Tadoussac

Québec

Port Royal

Trois Riviéres

ATLANTIC OCEAN

Montréal · 1535

1524

Portsmouth

Lake Ontario

Fort Orange (Albany)

Boston

Plymouth

Providence

New Haven

New Amsterdam (New York) · 1524

Lake Erie

Fort Christina (Wilmington)

Fort Nassau (Gloucester)

Providence (Annapolis)

Zwaanendael (Lewes)

St Mary's

Jamestown · 1524

Roancke Island

early explorers

→ Cabot, 1497

→ Verrazano, 1524

→ Cartier, 1535–36

⚓ landing

extent of European settlement by 1650

☐ Dutch

☐ English

☐ French

☐ Swedish

Above The artist John White took part in several expeditions to North America and for a time was governor of Sir Walter Raleigh's shortlived colony on Roanoke Island (1587). His paintings are among the earliest pictures of Native American society. The "towne of Pomeiock" depicts a stockaded village of bark longhouses.

TRADE & COEXISTENCE

The first French settlers in North America were fur trappers. They were soon trading with the local people, exchanging firearms, iron implements, and brandy for animal skins. There was a huge European demand for North American furs; beavers, in particular, were highly valued by the hat trade. French explorers made their way down the St. Lawrence, discovering the Great Lakes. They traveled into the interior, and followed the Mississippi river to the Gulf of Mexico.

The French aside, colonists from north Europe tended to be farmers, who cleared the forests to exploit the rich farmlands of the Atlantic seaboard and quickly developed a European-style agricultural economy. The native peoples welcomed settlers

D E F G H I J K

Coats Island

Mansel Island

Inuit

Naskapi

Inuit

Hudson Bay

Belcher Islands

Fort Churchill

Port Nelson

Fort York

Fort Severn

Eastern Cree

Montagnais

Newfoundland

St John's

Rupert's Land
(Hudson's Bay Company)

Fort Albany

Moose Factory

Fort Rupert

Ile Royale
(Cape Breton I)

Louisbourg

CANADA

Cree

Tadoussac

Ft Beausejour

Nova Scotia

Halifax

Port Royal

Lake Winnipeg

Fort La Tourette

Ojibwa

Québec

New France

Trois Riviéres

Fort Maurepas

Fort Népigon

Fort St Pierre

Fort Kaministiquia

Lake Superior

Fort Michipicton

Huron

Montréal

St Lawrence

Iroquots

Fort La Reine

Fort St Charles

Sault St Marie

Crown Point

Ticonderoga

New Hampshire

Portsmouth

Gros Ventre

Lake Huron

Fort Frontenac

Fort William Henry

Fort George

Boston

Massachusetts

Plymouth

Fort St Croix

Fort Oswego

Fort Ontario

Albany

Providence

Mandan

Winnebago

Fort Rouillé

Fort Niagara

Lake Ontario

New York

New Haven

Connecticut

Sioux

Fort St Joseph

Ottawa

Lake Erie

Fort Presqu'isle

Delaware

Pennsylvania

New York City

New Jersey

ATLANTIC OCEAN

Lake Michigan

Fort St Croix

Fort Beauharnais

Mississippi

Fort Pontchartrain

Fort Duquesne
(Fort Pitt)

Philadelphia

Delaware

Fort Necessity

Baltimore

Maryland

Miami Wyandot

Annapolis

Fort St Louis

Fort Crevecoeur

Fort Pickawillany

Shawnee

Virginia

Richmond

Jamestown

Williamsburg

Missouri

Kaintuck

Tuscarora

Fort Vincennes

Ohio

North Carolina

New Bern

Fort Orléans

Fort Chartres

Cherokee

APPALACHIAN MTS

South Carolina

Georgetown

UNITED STATES OF AMERICA

Chickasaw

Fort Augusta

Charleston

Fort Prudhomme

Choctaw

Creek

Wilmington

Savannah

Fort King George

Georgia

Mississippi

Louisiana

Alabama

Yamassee

St Augustine

Fort Rosalie

Fort Condé

Pensacola

Florida

Natchez

New Orleans

Gulf of Mexico

settlement or trading post
founded since 1650

British

French

extent of European settlement in 1713

British

French

Spanish

extent of European settlement, 1750

British

French

Spanish

French and Indian War, 1754–63

fort or settlement captured by the British

fort or settlement captured by the French

exploration by La Salle, 1681–82

colonial road

native American trade route

Ute native American peoples

0   600 km

0   400 mi

for the trade they brought, but prevented expansion inland; the Appalachian mountains also posed a formidable barrier. The first settlers in New England were mostly Puritans, strict Protestants who had left England to avoid religious persecution, and hoped to create a truly godly society in the New World. Hardworking people, many became prosperous through farming and commerce, and enjoyed a higher standard of living and higher life expectancy than most people in England.

The Virginian settlements of the south were mostly sponsored by English aristocrats as a form of investment. They hoped to establish plantations using the labor of servants, wage laborers, African slaves, and convicted criminals who had chosen emigration to America as an alternative to jail. Virginia's subtropical climate was unfamiliar to the first settlers, and many died from disease or starvation. The cultivation of tobacco, a native American plant, for export to Europe later made Virginia as wealthy as the New England trading ports.

GROWING CONFLICTS

From the start, women and children had numbered among the colonists beginning new lives in North America. The European settlers on the eastern seaboard soon outnumbered the Native American peoples. As their towns and villages expanded, they took over new areas of land, making conflict inevitable. Relations between the settlers and Native Americans worsened in the course of the 17th century as attacks on European settlements grew. The colonists

responded by driving the Native Americans from their traditional territories. As in Spanish America, the native peoples lost huge numbers to mass epidemics of European diseases, reducing their relatively small and fragmented tribes still further.

Europe's wars often spilled over into the North American colonies, leading to armed skirmishes and warfare. New Sweden (Delaware) was captured by the Dutch in 1655, but they lost it to the English in 1664, along with their settlement of New Amsterdam, which became New York.

As English settlement began to extend inland to the St. Lawrence and Great Lakes, tensions built up with the French. From 1686, the French attacked English trading posts on Hudson Bay and, in alliance with the Huron Indians, raided New England. Rivalry was even stronger in the 18th century. In the French and Indian War (1754–63) the British used their navy to blockade France's colonies in North America. After the capture of Quebec (1759) and Montreal (1760) the British took control of all settlement east of the Mississippi river. More than 60,000 French settlers were left under British rule, but were allowed to continue living under French laws.

Ætatis suæ 21 Aᵒ 1616

POCAHONTAS

Many legends surround the figure of Pocahontas, a Native American Powhatan who befriended the English settlers at Jamestown and is supposed to have intervened to spare the life of the colony's founder, John Smith. She was later baptized and married an Englishman, John Rolfe. This early portrait shows her in European dress during her stay in England in 1616. Advertised as an Indian princess, she became an instant celebrity, but died there of smallpox.

Left *The labor of the early settlers transformed the New England landscape to give us the familiar vistas we see today. Forests were cleared and swamps drained for agriculture, creating a close patchwork of small farms and rural communities.*

Below *This 1710 print of an armed, tobacco-smoking frontiersman presents a typical image of Canadian life. French fur trappers relied on native guides and formed closer links with Native Americans than the English colonists did.*

A DISTINCT SOCIETY

By 1775 the population of the 13 colonies of British North America was about 2.25 million, more than a quarter of Britain's. In Virginia, slave numbers had increased from 15,000 in 1700 to 190,000 by 1775, almost half the population. Owners, fearful of rebellion, treated them harshly.

The American colonists were still strongly influenced by British culture: the well-off liked to wear the latest London fashion. But there were growing differences. People were more self-reliant, and the lack of an aristocracy made it easier for all classes to succeed. There was no state church to impose uniformity of religion, as was the case in Britain. A large influx of Germans, Scots, and Irish settlers since the 1720s had radically altered the English character of some of the colonies. Along with an American dialect of English, a distinctly American society was emerging.

TIMETABLE

1497
John Cabot is the first European to visit North America since the Vikings

1535–36
Jacques Cartier explores the St. Lawrence river

1584–90
Sir Walter Raleigh founds a settlement on Roanoke island, but it fails

1607
The first permanent English colony is established at Jamestown, Virginia

1608
Champlain, "founder of Canada," establishes a settlement at Quebec and explores Lake Champlain

1620
The Pilgrims, an extreme Puritan sect, land at Plymouth, Massachusetts

1622
Native Americans kill 350 colonists at Jamestown after their lands are taken

1626
The Dutch found New Amsterdam

1636
Harvard University is founded

1664
The English capture New Amsterdam and rename it New York

1675–76
King Philip's War is waged between Native Americans and colonists

1681–82
La Salle explores the Mississippi river

1732
Georgia is founded as the 13th British American colony

1754–63
The French and Indian War is fought

1759
The British defeat the French at the Plains of Abraham, leading to the capture of Quebec

1763
The British suffer initial defeats by the Native Americans in Pontiac's War

1763
The Treaty of Paris confirms British control of French America

THE AMERICAN REVOLUTION

GREAT BRITAIN'S VICTORY OVER FRANCE IN 1763 MADE IT THE STRONGEST COLONIAL POWER IN THE WORLD. BUT WITHOUT THE IMMEDIATE THREAT OF FRENCH INVASION, THE THIRTEEN AMERICAN COLONIES HAD LESS REASON FOR REMAINING LOYAL TO BRITAIN. THE IMPOSITION OF TAXES AND RESTRICTIONS ON OVERSEAS TRADE LED TO INCREASING DISSATISFACTION WITH BRITISH RULE. IN 1776 THE THIRTEEN COLONIES DECLARED THEIR INDEPENDENCE FROM BRITAIN. WAR FOLLOWED, AND IN 1783 THE UNITED STATES OF AMERICA WAS BORN.

Most people in Britain believed that the main purpose of colonies was to further the interests of trade in the home country by supplying cheap raw materials for manufacturing and providing an export market for goods. During the 17th century laws were passed to prevent the American colonies from trading with countries other than Britain. This had the effect of creating a flourishing illegal trade with the Spanish, French, and Dutch colonies of the Caribbean. During the French and Indian War, merchants in New England began to export goods directly to Europe in their own ships, and once peace was signed the British government increased customs controls in an attempt to halt the trade. This caused great resentment. Plantation owners in the south were also afraid that Britain's increasing opposition to slavery would cause the collapse of their plantation economy .

Yet another cause of resentment was the Proclamation Line of 1763, which forbade colonial settlement west of the Appalachian mountains. The intention was to prevent clashes with the uprooted Native American groups forced inland from their traditional lands by European settlement. But the continued flow of immigrants and overcrowding of the coastal colonies meant that there was relentless pressure to keep pushing the frontier westward, and many colonists simply ignored the law.

Right Benjamin Franklin drew this cartoon to show the dangers of colonial disunity in the French and Indian War. He argued for the same unity against Britain.

Below One of the most famous events in American history: a group of angry colonists, dressed as Native Americans, sneaked aboard a British ship and dumped its cargo of tea in Boston Harbor.

"NO TAXES!"

The war with France had been expensive, and the British government decided to raise money by taxing the colonists. The Stamp Act, introduced in 1765, imposed a tax on legal documents and newspapers. The colonists, who had never been directly taxed before, were outraged. British goods were boycotted and representatives of all 13 colonies met in a special congress to oppose the move. Taking as their slogan "No taxation without representation," they declared they would not pay the tax because they had no voice in the British Parliament.

The Stamp Act was quickly withdrawn but replaced almost immediately with taxes on tea, glass, lead, paint, and paper. Once again the government backed down in the face of boycotts, and all but the tea tax were withdrawn. Protests mounted and turned violent. In 1770 British soldiers shot dead five people during a riot in Boston, an event that came to be immortalized as the Boston Massacre and heightened popular feeling against the British still further.

In December 1773, the Boston Tea Party occurred. The British responded to this act of defiance by passing a series of punitive measures, called the Intolerable Acts. They united all the colonies against Britain. Some people wanted an immediate break with Britain, but others argued that this step should be taken as a last resort.

In September 1774 the Continental Congress met in Philadelphia to debate this and other options.

D E F G H

Fort Albany
Fort Rupert
Moose Factory
Albany
Harricana

Rupert's Land
(Hudson's Bay Company)

CANADA

Quebec
created 1763

Québec

Fort Népigon

Fort William

Lake Superior

Sault St Marie

Montréal

Burgoyne, 1777

Falmouth

Montgomery, 1775

St Leger, 1777

1775

1775

Nova Scotia

Halifax

Arnold, 1775

William Howe, 1776

William Howe, 1776

Lord Howe, 1776

Fort Ticonderoga

Bunker Hill 1775

Lexington 1775

Boston

Lake Huron

Lake Michigan

Canada
1774 to Quebec

Fort Niagara

Butler, 1778

Fort Stanwix

Fort Oswego

Oriskany 1777

Saratoga 1777

Bennington 1777

Providence

Rochambeau, 1780

Rochambeau, 1780

Lake Erie

Lake Ontario

White Plains 1776

New York

Long Island 1776

Monmouth 1778

Washington, 1777

Trenton 1776

Princeton 1777

Germantown 1777

Philadelphia

Valley Forge

Brandywine 1777

de Barras, 1781

ATLANTIC
OCEAN

Fort Pontchartrain

Hamilton, 1778

Fort Sandusky

Fort Pitt

Baltimore

Washington, 1781

Lafayette, 1781

William Howe, 1777

Fort Vincennes

Clark, 1778–79

Ohio

Boonesborough

Harrodsburg

St Louis
Cahokia

Kakaskia

Native American Territory

Yorktown 1781

Richmond

Petersburg

Chesapeake Capes 1781

Cornwallis, 1781

Thirteen
Colonies

de Grasse, 1781

A P P A L A C H I A N   M T S

Cornwallis, 1781

Guilford
Court House 1781

Greene, 1781

Cornwallis, 1781

Wilmington

Tennessee

King's Mountain 1780

Cowpens 1781

Hobkirk's Hill 1781

Camden 1780

Eutaw Springs 1781

Clinton & Cornwallis, 1780

Louisiana
'63 to Spain from France

Augusta

Lincoln 1779

Charleston

Campbell, 1778

Arkansas Post

Savannah

Prevost, 1778–79

Mississippi

Alabama

Chattahoochee

West Florida
created 1764

Pensacola

Fort Rosalie

Baton Rouge

New Orleans

East
Florida

St Augustine

British possessions in North America, 1763
 the Thirteen Colonies
 Rupert's Land
 Quebec
 Nova Scotia
 Native American Territory
 Florida
 other

· · · · · British Proclamation Line of 1763
 fort or trading post
⊗ American victory
⊗ British victory
⊗ French victory
→ American campaign, with commander
→ British campaign, with commander
→ French campaign, with commander
── border of United States of America, 1783

0 600 km
0 400 mi

Above The Declaration of Independence is signed in Philadelphia, July 4, 1776. Its principal author was Thomas Jefferson, a wealthy planter and slave owner who attended the Congress as the representative for Virginia. He later became president (1801–09) and presided over the Louisiana Purchase.

WAR WITH THE BRITISH

Before the issue had been decided fighting had broken out. Skirmishes between rebel forces and British troops at Lexington and Concord in April 1775 led to a general uprising. On July 4, 1776, the 55 delegates at the Second Continental Congress met to sign the Declaration of Independence.

The British believed that the majority of Americans would remain loyal and that the rebellion would soon be at an end. However, the British generals lacked an effective strategy and failed to make the most of their advantages. The forces the colonists could raise were smaller and vastly more inexperienced, and their morale was often lowered by lack of pay. But the longer the fighting lasted, the more hostile most Americans became to British rule.

In December 1776, Washington led his troops across the frozen Delaware river in a daring raid on the garrison at Trenton. Success began to slip away from the British, who were struggling to supply an army from 3,000 miles away. In 1778 France joined the war against Britain. Their defeat of a British fleet off Chesapeake Capes in 1781 cut off supplies to the British in York-town. Its surrender brought the war to an end. At the Treaty of Paris in 1783, Britain recognized the United States of America.

THE U.S. CONSTITUTION

Once the war was ended, debate started on the way the government of the United States should be organized. In 1786–87 the Constitutional Convention met at Philadelphia to debate these issues. Collectively known as the Framers of the Constitution, the delegates included Benjamin Franklin and George Washington. At the heart of the debate was the question of how much power should be given to the national government, and how much freedom the individual states should have to govern themselves. It was probably the first time in history that the nature and function of government had been so fully discussed.

A system of "checks and balances" was devised that prevented any single part of the government from growing too powerful. There would be an elected executive head of state (the president), who would not have power to make laws—this would be the prerogative of the two Houses of Congress (the legislature), whose representatives would also be elected. The Supreme Court (the judiciary), independent of both the executive and the legislature, would interpret American law.

The American constitution was one of the first written constitutions of the 18th century. Four years after it was ratified, the first ten amendments, collectively known as the Bill of Rights, were made to the constitution. Some legal scholars consider this to be the most important document in American history as it defines the rights of individual citizens and puts specific limits on government power over the citizen. Today, these issues are once again the subject of debate and controversy as the pressure of social change makes the problems of government more complicated.

THE UNION GROWS

The new constitution was ratified in 1788, and took effect in 1789, with George Washington as the first president. All 13 colonies had joined the republic by 1790; Rhode Island was the last to do so. Expansion was soon taking place westward along the Ohio river, and Kentucky was incorporated into the Union in 1792, followed by Tennessee and two other states. In 1800 the Mississippi basin was ceded back to France by Spain. In 1803, Napoleon, short of cash to fight his European wars (see pages 146–149), sold the entire territory to the United States. The Louisiana Purchase all but doubled the size of the fledgling republic.

U.S. EXPANSION TO 1803

Upper Canada to Britain
Lower Canada to Britain
Rupert's Land to Hudson's Bay Company
Lake Superior
Lake Huron
Lake Michigan
Lake Ontario
Lake Erie
Vermont 1791
to Massachusetts
New Hampshire 1788
Massachusetts 1788
New York 1788
Rhode Island 1790
Connecticut 1788
New York 1785–90
Pennsylvania 1787
Philadelphia 1790–1800
New Jersey 1787
Washington from 1800
Delaware 1787
Maryland 1788
Virginia 1788
Ohio 1803
Northwest Territory
Louisiana
Mississippi
Missouri
Platte
Ohio
Kentucky 1792
North Carolina 1789
Tennessee 1796
South Carolina 1788
Arkansas
Mississippi
Red
Mississippi Territory
Georgia 1788
Florida to Spain
Gulf of Mexico

ATLANTIC OCEAN

expansion of the United States
- Thirteen Colonies
- 1783 settlement and Native American cessions
- Louisiana Purchase, 1803
- **1787** date of admission of state to the Union
- ■ United States capital
- borders, 1803

TIMETABLE

1765
The Stamp Act imposes direct taxation on the American colonies

1770
British soldiers kill five Bostonians during a riot

1773
The Boston Tea Party provokes the Intolerable Acts

1774
The first Continental Congress meets in Philadelphia

1775
Fighting breaks out in Lexington and Concord (near Boston)

July 4, 1776
Congress passes the Declaration of Independence

1776
On Christmas night, Washington crosses the Delaware river to seize Trenton

1777
The Articles of Confederation are passed to create the United States of America

October 17, 1777
British army of General Burgoyne surrenders at Saratoga

1777–78
Washington's Continental Army reorganizes at Valley Forge

1778
France declares war on Britain in support of the Americans

1779
Spain joins war against Britain and retakes west Florida the next year

1781
The British army surrenders at Yorktown

1783
The Treaty of Paris confirms American independence

1787
The Constitution of the United States is adopted

1789
George Washington becomes the first president of the United States

1800
Washington DC is chosen as the capital of the United States

THE EUROPEAN REFORMATION

BY THE 16TH CENTURY THE CATHOLIC CHURCH, WHICH HAD DOMINATED WESTERN EUROPE FOR A THOUSAND YEARS, HAD BECOME CORRUPT. INDIVIDUAL VOICES CALLED FOR REFORM, WHILE POWERFUL MONARCHS CHALLENGED ROME'S POLITICAL AUTHORIT THE RELIGIOUS AND CIVIL CONFLICTS OF THE TIME SET NEIGHBOR AGAINST NEIGHBOR.

Kings in 16th-century Europe were more powerful than their predecessors. The 15th century had been a time of dynastic civil wars, but the rise of an educated class of professional bureaucrats had increased the efficiency of royal governments, while international bankers made it possible for kings to pay for fulltime armies with which to coerce their subjects. European culture was changing as Renaissance humanist thinkers challenged the certainties of medieval theology and questioned the role of rulers.

Right A satirical cartoon showing the head of Martin Luther being used as a bagpipe to play the Devil's tune.

ROYAL RIVALS

In an age of fierce competition between monarchs, the most powerful ruler in Europe was Charles V (Charles I of Spain). He was only 19 years old when he was elected Holy Roman emperor on the death of his grandfather Maximilian I in 1519, and so added to his Spanish possessions those of the Habsburg empire—Austria, Bohemia, Hungary, Burgundy, the Netherlands, and much of Italy. His wealth was made still greater by the steady stream of silver and gold that entered his coffers from the Spanish empire in Mexico and Peru.

Not unnaturally, other European rulers resented his superiority. His greatest rival was the French king Francis I (r.1515–57), whose lands were almost entirely surrounded by Habsburg territories. Francis had unsuccessfully opposed Charles in elections for Holy Roman emperor, and his attempts to extend French influence into northern Italy were fiercely resisted by Charles; their wars threatened to destroy the achievements of the Italian Renaissance. For a year, after the battle of Pavia (1525), Francis was Charles' prisoner. Francis had a highly competitive relationship with Henry VIII of England (r.1509–47). The two came face to face at a meeting called the Field of the Cloth of Gold (1520), when Francis' entourage far outshone Henry's in wealth and splendor. A great Renaissance prince, Francis employed Italian artists and architects, including Leonardo da Vinci, to build and embellish his palaces.

Above The ideas of the Reformation spread quickly through the new printing presses.

RELIGIOUS CONFLICT

Charles V's greatest problems lay within his own empire. He was a devout Catholic, but the church, especially in Germany, had become deeply unpopular with many of his subjects. Priests used their positions for

Legend:
- borders, 1600
- predominantly Catholic, 1598
- Protestant lands reverting to Catholicism by 1600

Protestant/Reformed
- predominantly Calvinist/Huguenot, 1598
- predominantly Church of England, 1598
- predominantly Lutheran, 1598
- lands with mixed Calvinist/Catholic/Lutheran faiths, 1598

- Ottoman empire, 1492
- Ottoman gains by 1600
- major center of St Bartholomew massacre, 1572
- major printing center, 15th–16th centuries
- Ottoman offensive against Christian Europe
- campaign of Don John, 1571

0 — 600 km
0 — 400 mi

Map labels: North Sea, SWEDEN, Vänern, Vättern, Gotland, Baltic Sea, ESTONIA, Lake Peipus, Livonia, LATVIA, Courland, LITHUANIA, PRUSSIA, DENMARK–NORWAY, Emden, Hamburg, Netherlands, Deventer, Amsterdam, Utrecht, HOLY ROMAN EMPIRE, Elbe, Brandenburg, Berlin, Vistula, Warsaw, POLAND, London, Antwerp, Brussels, Cologne, GERMANY, Anhalt, Wittenberg, Leipzig, Lusatia, Bonn, Nassau, Hesse-Kassel, Saxony, Silesia, BELGIUM, Mainz, Frankfurt, Bamberg, Prague, Bohemia, Moravia, Luxembourg, Rouen, Lower Palatinate, Nuremberg, Ansbach, Upper Palatinate, Meaux, Paris, Troyes, Strasbourg, Bavaria, Augsburg, Munich, Danube, Vienna, Austria, IMPERIAL HUNGARY, 1529, Guns, Buda, Orléans, Bourges, Charolais, Franche-Comté, Basel, Zürich, Berne, Swiss Confederation, Geneva, Tyrol, SLOVENIA, 1532, 1526, HUNGARY, TRANSYLVANIA, FRANCE, Lyon, Savoy, Milan, Venice, CROATIA, ROMANIA, Rhine, Po, Parma, VENICE, Genoa, Modena, BOSNIA HERCEGOVINA, Belgrade, WALLACHIA, Avignon, Aix, Genoa, Florence, Tuscany, PAPAL STATES, URBINO, Ravenna, YUGOSLAVIA, Montenegro, Bulgaria, Black Sea, Toulouse, ANDORRA, Corsica to Genoa, Siena, ITALY, Rome, Subiaco, Bulgaria, OTTOMAN EMPIRE, Barcelona, Sardinia, SARDINIA, Naples, NAPLES, BENEVENTO, 1537, Thessalonica, Rumelia, ANATOLIA, TURKEY, Balearic Islands, 1543–44, Reggio, Lepanto 1571, Morea, 1522, Algiers, SICILY, Sicily, Malta, 1543, 1530, Mediterranean Sea, Rhodes, Crete to Venice, GREECE, Constantinople

---

personal gain, and the popes themselves were seen to be more concerned with politics than with spiritual leadership. One of the most detested abuses was the sale of "indulgences," which allowed the rich to buy forgiveness of their sins. In 1517 a former monk and theologian, Martin Luther

(1483–1546), composed a lengthy protest against these practices, which he nailed to the door of the university church in Wittenberg for everyone to read; they are known as the 95 Theses. It was a courageous act: those disagreeing with the church could be condemned as heretics and burned alive.

Printed copies of the 95 Theses spread quickly, and soon Germany and all Europe was immersed in the religious debate of the Reformation. Luther was outlawed by an imperial court at Worms in 1521, but support for his views continued to grow. Other reformers inside and outside Germany took his ideas in new directions. The most influential of them was the Frenchman John Calvin (1509–64), founder of Calvinism.

By the 1530s a great number of German princes were Protestants (the name given to members of the reformed churches). This was often more for reasons of politics than religion: it enabled them to declare their independence from the emperor, and made them rich from the seizure of church lands. Charles failed to bring the princes back to the Catholic faith, and at the Peace of Augsburg (1555) conceded their right to decide what faith their subjects should follow. Believing he had failed in his religious duty, he divided his empire in two and retired to a monastery. His son Philip II was given Spain, the Netherlands, Naples, Sicily and Sardinia, his brother Ferdinand II Austria, Hungary, and Bohemia.

REFORM SPREADS

The weakening of papal authority was evident in the willingness of many European rulers to break with Rome for reasons of state. One of the first to do so was king Gustavus Vasa of Sweden, who took all church property in his kingdom into his own hands in 1527. In 1534 Henry VIII made himself supreme head of the church in England after the pope had refused to grant him a divorce so that he could marry Anne Boleyn, the second of his six wives.

The Catholic Church had been comparatively slow to meet the challenge of the new reformed ideas, but in 1545 a general council met at Trent in southern Austria to launch the Counter Reformation. Catholic teaching was redefined, Protestant literature banned, and in Catholic countries the medieval Inquisition was revived to track down and interrogate Protestants. The missionary Jesuit order, founded in Spain in 1540, had particular success in bringing people back to the Catholic faith, especially in Bavaria, Austria, and Poland.

Despite this, Protestantism continued to spread. In the 1560s Calvinism, more radical and uncompromising in its beliefs than Lutheranism, gained hold in the Netherlands, Switzerland, Scotland, and much of France (where its followers were known as Huguenots). In England, Puritanism was also influenced by Calvinism. The Counter Reformation needed a new champion.

WARS OF RELIGION

It found its champion in Philip II of Spain (r.1556–98). A dour, earnest ruler, he was more than ready to take up his father's war against Protestantism. His harsh measures led to rebellion in the Netherlands. By 1566 this had became an outright struggle for Dutch independence, effectively gained in 1609. The Dutch were aided by Elizabeth of

THE MONSTROUS REGIMENT OF WOMEN

Men in the 16th century were often unwilling to accept women as rulers, believing that God had endowed them with natural authority over women. One of those most opposed to women rulers was the Scottish Calvinist preacher, John Knox (1514–72). In the 1550s three women occupied European thrones—Mary I of Scotland (Mary Queen of Scots), Mary Tudor in England, and Catherine de Medici in France. All three were Catholic monarchs, set on persecuting

Left Elizabeth I of England, painted in 1588.

Protestants in their realms. Knox furiously condemned them in a pamphlet entitled "The First Blast of the Trumpet against the Monstrous Regiment of Women," but unfortunately for him, its publication coincided with the death of Mary Tudor and the accession of her formidable Protestant sister, Elizabeth. She once famously said "I know I have the body of a weak and feeble woman, but I have the heart and stomach of a king." Incensed by Knox's misogyny, Elizabeth had him banned from England for life.

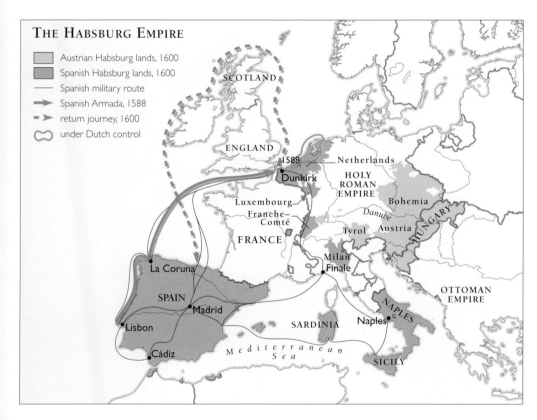

THE HABSBURG EMPIRE

- Austrian Habsburg lands, 1600
- Spanish Habsburg lands, 1600
- Spanish military route
- Spanish Armada, 1588
- return journey, 1600
- under Dutch control

England (r. 1558–1603), who had restored Protestantism after Mary Tudor's brief and bloody reimposition of Catholicism (1553–58). In retaliation, Philip sent a huge fleet, the Spanish Armada, to invade England in 1588. It was a complete failure, destroyed more by bad weather than the English navy.

In France, a long civil war broke out after the Huguenots took up arms in 1562. The Catholics, who had the support of the king, Philip II, committed one of the very worst atrocities of the European wars of religion

Left Protestant nobles, in Paris for the wedding of Henry of Navarre, are massacred by Catholics.

by killing thousands of Huguenots in the St. Bartholomew's Day Massacre (1572). In 1598 Henry IV, a Protestant who became Catholic in order to pacify the kingdom, granted Huguenots freedom of conscience through the Edict of Nantes.

The same year Philip died. Spain by now was bankrupt, its supplies of silver exhausted by Philip's wars. Some 40% of Europe's population was Protestant. Despite a spectacular naval victory at Lepanto by Philip's half-brother Don John in 1571, the Turks were still a threat to Europe (see page 154). Tunis was lost three years later, and their attacks continued in eastern Europe.

(see page 154)

TIMETABLE

1517
Martin Luther nails his 95 Theses to the door of Wittenberg cathedral

1519
Charles of Habsburg, king of Spain since 1516, is elected Holy Roman emperor

1521
Charles V outlaws Luther at a formal church council in Germany called the Diet of Worms

1529
The Ottoman Turks lay unsuccessful siege to Vienna

1534
Henry VIII makes himself head of the Church in England

1536
John Calvin publishes *The Institutes of the Christian Religion*

1545–63
The Council of Trent launches the Counter Reformation

1555
The Peace of Augsburg allows German princes to decide the religion of their subjects

1559
The Treaty of Cateau-Cambresis ends Italian wars between France and Spain

1572
On St. Bartholomew's Day, French Catholics massacre Huguenots

1576
Spanish troops slaughter 7,000 people at the siege of Antwerp

1580
Philip II becomes king of Portugal

1587
Mary Queen of Scots is executed on the order of Elizabeth I of England

1588
Philip II sends the Spanish Armada against England

1598
The Edict of Nantes grants Huguenots toleration in France

1609
A 12-year truce is agreed between the Netherlands and Spain

EUROPE IN CONFLICT

RELIGIOUS CONFLICT CONTINUED TO AGITATE EUROPE IN THE 17TH
CENTURY AND WAS THE CAUSE OF THE CATACLYSMIC THIRTY YEARS WAR
(1618–48). BY THE CENTURY'S END, RELIGION WAS LOSING ITS DIVISIVE
NATURE. THE FRANCE OF LOUIS XIV WAS NOW THE MAJOR POLITICAL FORCE
IN EUROPE, DOMINATING ITS NEIGHBORS BY WAR AND INTIMIDATION.

The split between Roman Catholics and
Protestants dominated all other issues in
Europe at the start of the 17th century—
both sides were resolutely hostile and con-
spiracies were seen everywhere. The Peace
of Augsburg (1555), intended to establish
the means of coexistence between Catholic
and Protestant rulers in the Holy Roman
empire, had failed because neither side
trusted the other. The immediate cause of
the Thirty Years War was the attempt by the
Habsburg rulers of Austria to reimpose
Roman Catholicism in their territories in
Bohemia in 1618. The war dragged on until
1648 and drew in most of Europe.

In the first stage of fighting (1618–23)
the Spanish Habsburgs invaded the Lower
Palatinate, the leading Protestant state in
Germany, in support of Austria. Then Denmark intervened on the side of the German
Protestants until defeated at Lutter (1625–
29). Gustavus II Adolphus of Sweden fared

better for a time and briefly carried the war
to the heart of Catholic Germany (1630–
35). In the war's final phase (1635–48)
France, a Catholic country surrounded by
Habsburg lands, supported the Swedish–
Protestant side. In France's foreign affairs,
political differences had more weight than
religion, but Huguenots were still disadvan-
taged at home, despite the Edict of Nantes.

The Thirty Years War had lasting disastrous consequences for Germany. Most soldiers in the war were mercenaries, often left
unpaid for long periods. They destroyed
vast areas of the countryside, leaving the
population to starve—it fell by 7 million.

Spain's days as Europe's leading power
were finished. France won some major battles, but domestic rebellions prevented it
from exploiting its gains. The only beneficiary of the war was the Netherlands. Spain
finally recognized its independence in the
Treaty of Westphalia, which ended the war.
Dutch ships had taken over Spanish and
Portuguese trade routes, and Amsterdam
was now the financial center of Europe.

*Below A military skirmish during the Thirty Years
War—the conflict caused tremendous devastation.*

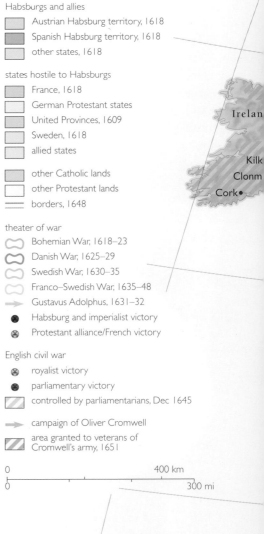

Habsburgs and allies
- Austrian Habsburg territory, 1618
- Spanish Habsburg territory, 1618
- other states, 1618

states hostile to Habsburgs
- France, 1618
- German Protestant states
- United Provinces, 1609
- Sweden, 1618
- allied states

- other Catholic lands
- other Protestant lands
- borders, 1648

theater of war
- Bohemian War, 1618–23
- Danish War, 1625–29
- Swedish War, 1630–35
- Franco–Swedish War, 1635–48
- Gustavus Adolphus, 1631–32
- Habsburg and imperialist victory
- Protestant alliance/French victory

English civil war
- royalist victory
- parliamentary victory
- controlled by parliamentarians, Dec 1645
- campaign of Oliver Cromwell
- area granted to veterans of Cromwell's army, 1651

0   400 km
0   300 mi

1600–1715

A   B   C   D   E   F   G

Scotland
• Aberdeen

North Sea

SWEDEN
Vänern
Vättern
• Stockholm

Baltic Sea

• Edinburgh

Philiphaugh 1645
1650-51

Ister
Belfast
Drogheda
Dublin

Marston Moor 1644 • York
• Hull

England

Nottingham

Naseby 1645
Edgehill 1642
Gloucester •
Oxford
Bristol •
London
Roundway Down 1643
Newbury 1643
Turnham Green 1643
Lostwithiel 1644

exford

DENMARK–NORWAY

• Copenhagen

Holstein

West Pomerania • Stralsund

Mecklenburg

East Pomerania
• Königsberg   PRUSSIA
• Danzig

Bremen

Brandenburg

Vistula

UNITED PROVINCES
• Amsterdam

Ravensberg
Westphalia
Kleve
Mark

Hesse

Anhalt
Saxony

Lutter 1626
Lützen 1632
Breitenfeld 1631

Frankfurt

Elbe

POLAND

Dunkirk
Brussels •
Spanish Netherlands

HOLY ROMAN EMPIRE
Frankfurt

Bayreuth

White Mountain 1620
Bohemia • Prague

Oder

Silesia

• Krakow

Rocroi 1643

Rouen •

Lower Palatinate
Rhine
Württemberg

Ansbach

CZECH REPUBLIC

Moravia

• Paris

Breisach •

Munich •
Bavaria

Austria
• Vienna

AUSTRIA

• Orléans

Loire

Franche-Comté

SWISS CONFEDERATION

Tyrol

Salzburg

Styria

Carinthia

IMPERIAL HUNGARY
• Gran
• Buda
TRANSYLVANIA

• Nantes

Bourges •

Charolais

Geneva •

FRANCE

Lyon •

SAVOY

MILAN
• Milan
• Mantua

Carniola

CROATIA

HUNGARY

ay of iscay

• Bordeaux

Rhône

Turin •

Po
Genoa •
PARMA
MODENA

• Venice
VENICE

OTTOMAN EMPIRE

• Toulouse

Avignon •

GENOA

PAPAL STATES

• Ravenna

• Ragusa

Bilbao
• Pamplona
ANDORRA

Marseille •

Perpignan
Roussillon 1642 to France

Florence •
TUSCANY

PIOMBINO

ITALY

• Montenegro

• Barcelona

Corsica to Genoa

• Rome

ALBANIA

Valencia •

Palma •

Balearic Islands

Sardinia
SARDINIA

• Cagliari

BENEVENTO
Naples •

NAPLES

Mediterranean Sea

• Palermo
Messina •

SICILY

Sicily

MALTA

139

Left Oliver Cromwell failed to find an alternative to royal power and finished up almost a king himself.

ENGLAND'S CIVIL WAR

Although England stayed out of the Thirty Years War, it did not avoid religious and political dispute. Like other European monarchs, Charles I (r.1625–49) believed that kings ruled by divine right. His attempts to govern without Parliament alienated many of his subjects; his religious policies offended English Puritans and Scots Calvinists. The result was civil war. Charles lost, and was executed in 1649. A Commonwealth was set up under Oliver Cromwell, who later took the title of Lord Protector (1653) and ruled as a military dictator. The monarchy was restored in 1660, two years after his death, but on terms that Parliament dictated to the new king, Charles II.

The Glorious Revolution of 1688–89 set the Dutch king William of Orange (married to James II's daughter Mary) on the English throne and barred Catholics from succeeding. At the same time, the Bill of Rights put further restrictions on royal power. In 1707 the Act of Union formally joined the kingdoms of England and Scotland to form the United Kingdom of Great Britain.

IN THE COURT OF THE SUN KING

Louis XIV's title of the "Sun King" owed much to the splendor of the vast palace he built for himself at Versailles, near Paris. The cost of this project, one of the masterpieces of European architecture, accounted for 5% of France's gross annual income—it has been compared to the expense of constructing a modern airport. The palace was embellished by the finest architects and artists of the day. More than 1,400 fountains played in the palace's grounds. Spectacular ballets, lavish concerts, and firework displays added to Versailles' glories.

From 1682 Louis lived most of the time at Versailles, and expected his nobles to do so too. The king was continually on display at Versailles, which became the center of the French universe. The great nobles of France scrambled with each other for the privilege of attending the semipublic ritual of his rising in the morning and going to bed at night. To be asked to hold the king's shirt was considered a great honor. This fierce competition for the king's favor enabled Louis to play off rivalries between courtiers and keep even his most powerful subjects firmly in check. Despite Versailles' surface brilliance, however, basic amenities for courtiers were few, and living quarters were notoriously cramped.

Right The landscaped gardens at Versailles were one of the glories of the age.

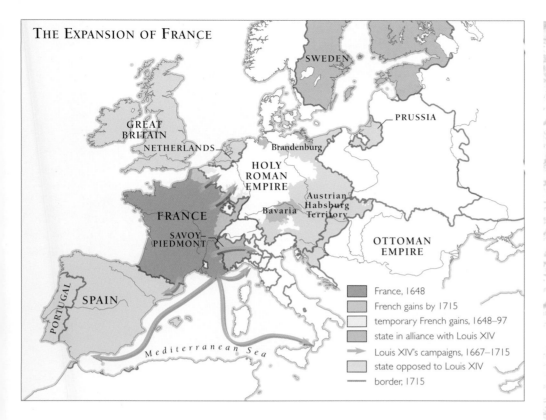

THE EXPANSION OF FRANCE

SWEDEN

PRUSSIA

GREAT
BRITAIN

NETHERLANDS

Brandenburg

HOLY
ROMAN
EMPIRE

Austrian
Habsburg
Territory

FRANCE

Bavaria

SAVOY–
PIEDMONT

OTTOMAN
EMPIRE

PORTUGAL

SPAIN

Mediterranean Sea

France, 1648
French gains by 1715
temporary French gains, 1648–97
state in alliance with Louis XIV
Louis XIV's campaigns, 1667–1715
state opposed to Louis XIV
border, 1715

THE RISE OF FRANCE

In contrast to England, the power of the French monarchy grew much stronger during the reign of Louis XIV (1643–1715, the longest in European history). He succeeded to the throne at the age of four, and his early years were made wretched by civil war and intrigue among the French aristocracy. He determined that the crown should exercise absolute authority to prevent this ever happening again.

Louis had ambitions to make France the greatest power in Europe. In 1661 he took the rule of the kingdom into his own hands and, with the help of skilled advisers, set about reforming the government, the army, and the navy. He then successfully attacked Spain and the Netherlands, winning valuable new territories for France.

Other European states were made nervous by Louis' aggression. Any chance he had of forming military alliances with Protestant countries was spoiled when he outlawed the Huguenots in 1685 by revoking the Edict of Nantes. This caused general alarm as no one wanted to see the old religious wars start up once more. Some 200,000 Huguenots fled abroad, to the detriment of the French economy. Most were skilled craftsmen and merchants; a large number of them took their skills and expertise to England and the Dutch Republic.

Louis' subjects were heavily taxed to pay for his wars. Resentment of the king began to grow but, isolated at Versailles and convinced of his divine right to rule, he ignored it. His successors carried on in the same way, adding to the grievances that led to the French Revolution (see pages 142–145).

THE SPANISH SUCCESSION

Louis' last and most ambitious scheme was in Spain. He managed to persuade the childless Spanish king Charles II to accept Louis' teenage grandson Philip as his heir. When he became king on Charles' death in 1700, Louis refused to exclude him from the succession to the French throne. The fear that France would eventually control Spain, its American empire, the Spanish Netherlands, and much of Italy led almost all Europe, including Britain, to back the Austrian Habsburg candidate in the War of the Spanish Succession (1701–13). Louis suffered a number of military defeats and sought to end the war. The Treaty of Utrecht ended Spain's role as a European power. Philip was confirmed as Spanish king, but had to give up all territories outside Spain to Austria. Louis was forced to promise that the French and Spanish crowns would never be united. Britain took possession of Spanish and French trading bases in the Caribbean, boosting its overseas empire.

(see pages 142–145).

TIMETABLE

1610
Henry IV of France is assassinated
by a fanatic

1618
The Thirty Years War begins

1624
Cardinal Richelieu becomes chief
minister of France

1632
Gustavus II Adolphus of Sweden is killed
at the battle of Lutzen

1648
The Treaty of Westphalia ends the
Thirty Years War

1649
Charles I of England is executed by
Parliament and a Commonwealth
established

1660
Charles II is restored as king of England

1661
Louis XIV begins to rule France directly

1666
Much of the city of London is destroyed
in a great fire

1669
Portugal regains its independence
from Spain

1672
William of Orange floods much of the
Dutch Netherlands to save them from
French invasion

1683
A Polish army led by John Sobieski
breaks the Turkish siege of Vienna

1685
Louis XIV revokes the Edict of Nantes,
ending toleration of Huguenots

1699
Austria annexes Hungary from the Turks

1707
The Act of Union unites Scotland and
England as Great Britain

1713
The Treaty of Utrecht ends the War of
Spanish Succession

1715
Louis XIV dies and is succeeded by his
5-year-old great-grandson, Louis XV

THE AGE OF ENLIGHTENMENT

POLITICAL AND ECONOMIC DEVELOPMENTS IN 18TH-CENTURY EUROPE CHANGED THE COURSE OF WORLD HISTORY. THE FRENCH REVOLUTION THREW THE WHOLE CONTINENT INTO POLITICAL CHAOS AND WARFARE FOR OVER 20 YEARS, WHILE THE BEGINNING OF THE INDUSTRIAL REVOLUTION IN BRITAIN BROUGHT NOT ONLY MACHINES AND FACTORIES BUT ALSO SOCIAL CHANGES AS PROFOUND AS THOSE OF THE FRENCH REVOLUTION.

The 18th century is often called the Age of the Enlightenment—the name given to a cultural movement that developed partly in reaction to the religious conflicts of the previous century. The study of science (or natural philosophy as it was called) provided experimental proof of a world governed by physical rather than divine laws and seemed to offer a more rational basis for understanding the world than religious belief. The Royal Society of London (1660) was the first body in Europe to be founded for the study of science. A similar society was soon set up in Paris.

Dynastic wars divided the continent in the 1730s and 40s. Austria began to win territory back from the Ottomans, as did Russia later in the century. The Seven Years War (1756–63) saw France, Austria, and Russia joined against Britain and the rising kingdom of Prussia. Although France lost most of its overseas colonies to Britain, it

Above *By the end of the 18th century, the "sans-culottes" ("man without breeches") had become the symbol of the new revolutionary forces in France.*

remained a major power on the continent. It took its revenge by aiding the American colonies in their independence wars against Britain. In eastern Europe, Poland—much reduced in size—ceased to exist as a sovereign state in 1795, having been partitioned between Russia, Prussia, and Austria.

ABSOLUTIST RULERS

Prussia's rise was engineered by its third king, Frederick the Great (r.1740–86), a talented military strategist who was admired for his achievements and loathed for his excessive ambition. Frederick was passionately interested in art, music (he played the flute) and philosophy, and was the first European ruler to advocate public education and universal religious tolerance. He was typical of his age, however, in his failure to modify Prussia's rigid social structure. Aristocrats, the new middle classes, and the

THE INDUSTRIAL REVOLUTION

The Industrial Revolution began in the 18th century with the invention of mechanized means of spinning yarn. At about the same time, iron manufacture was transformed by the development of the blast furnace. Industrial centers grew up around coalfields and canals were built to move goods in bulk. The coming of steam power speeded up the pace of change still further. Improvements in agriculture meant fewer people were needed to work the land. These events radically altered the way people lived in Britain and parts of northern Europe as more and more people left the countryside to work in the emerging industrial cities.

Above *A cast iron bridge, built in 1779, spans the river Severn, Britain.*

La Coruña

Oporto

PORTUGAL

Lisbon 1779

Guadia

Gibraltar to Britain

Cádiz

Tangier

Ceuta to Spain

A B C D E F G H I

1

Revel

2

RUSSIAN EMPIRE

Lake Peipus

Christiania

SWEDEN

Uppsala 1710

Stockholm 1741

Vänern

Vättern

Gotland

Baltic Sea

Riga

Western Dvina

Samogitia

Lithuania

Minsk

3

BELARUS

Black Russia

DENMARK–NORWAY

North Sea

Hamburg

Hanover

Berlin 1700

Warsaw

Great Poland

POLAND

Mazovia

Little Poland

Podlesia

Volhynia

GREAT BRITAIN & IRELAND

Falkirk

Glasgow

Edinburgh 1739

Bolton Bury

Iron Bridge

Dudley

Cromford

Birmingham 1766

blin 1731

London 1660

Plymouth

Haarlem 1752

Rotterdam 1773

NETHERLANDS

GERMANY

Göttingen 1736

HOLY ROMAN EMPIRE

Prague

Bohemia

Moravia

Silesia

Vistula

Red Russia

Galicia and Lodomeria

Bukovina

Jassy

Jemappe

Amiens 1750

Reims 1776

Mannheim 1755

Danube

Rhine

Austria

Vienna

Styria

Carinthia

Buda

Hungary

Transylvania

4

Rouen 1736

Caen 1705

Paris 1666

Plassey

Nancy 1736

Munich 1759

Brest

Orléans 1753

Dijon 1723

FRANCE

Loire

Nantes

Geneva 1776

SWISS CONFEDERATION

Tyrol

Carniola

Croatia

Slavonia

Banat

ROMANIA

Danube

Bay of Biscay

Clermont-Ferrand 1705

Lyon 1700

Milan

SARDINIA–PIEDMONT

Padua 1779

Venice

VENICE

Sava

Bordeaux 1712

Venaissin to Papal States

Genoa

Parma

Florence 1752

MONTENEGRO

BULGARIA

5

Toulouse 1782

Avignon

GENOA

TUSCANY

PAPAL STATES

RAGUSA

OTTOMAN EMPIRE

Constantinople

ANDORRA

Ebro

Corsica

Rome

ITALY

Naples

TURKEY

SPAIN

Madrid 1713

Barcelona

SARDINIA–PIEDMONT

Sardinia

Naples 1779

KINGDOM OF NAPLES AND SICILY

GREECE

Valencia

Balearic Islands

6

Palermo

Sicily

Oran

Melilla to Spain

Malta

Mediterranean Sea

Crete

7

borders, 1789

Austrian Habsburg territory, 1789

France, 1789

Brandenburg–Prussia, 1789

Great Britain & Hanover, 1789

Ottoman empire, 1789

Spanish Bourbon territory, 1789

Russian empire, 1789

Brandenburg–Prussian gains by 1795

Russian gains by 1795

Austrian Habsburg gains by 1797

scientific society, with date of foundation

observatory

important industrial site

0 600 km

0 400 mi

peasantry were firmly fixed in their established places. Most European rulers were absolutists, who supported religious conformism and protected aristocratic privileges. New agricultural techniques (particularly improved methods of crop rotation and livestock breeding) were revolutionizing farming in Britain and the Netherlands but had only limited impact elsewhere; in most of Europe, the labor-intensive institution of serfdom still tied peasants to the land and prevented innovation.

In France the conservative social order, headed by the monarchy and supported by the church, was known as the *ancien régime* (the old regime). The rising middle class, though wealthy and numerous, was excluded from centers of power, which continued to revolve around the court life of Versailles. Increasingly, the narrow, aristocratic values of the *ancien régime* were challenged by the leaders of the Enlightenment, which had its roots among the French middle class. Leading intellectuals such as the great French philosopher-essayist Voltaire attacked the repressive nature of the Catholic church, and tried to persuade rulers to introduce progressive reforms such as the abolition of serfdom and the use of torture.

A passionate belief in the dignity of people—not as the subjects of kings, but as individuals—was one of the touchstones of the Enlightenment, and was strengthened by the success of the American Revolution, which the French had supported. These ideas found their fullest expression in the political and philosophical writings of Jean-Jacques Rousseau (1712–78). His ideas on education profoundly influenced parental attitudes to childcare, and his political treatises, the *Social Contract* (1762) in particular, with its emphasis on individual liberty, helped shape the intellectual background to the debates of the French revolutionaries. Rousseau's attitudes to nature pointed the way ahead to the Romanticism of the early 19th century.

REVOLUTION IN FRANCE

The cost of France's participation in the American Revolution was a high one. It bankrupted the government, and soaring prices and food shortages caused hardship and panic, giving rise to demands for political reform. The Estates-General, France's representative assembly, had not been summoned since 1614, but in 1789 Louis XVI called it to approve his plans to raise taxes. The Estates-General was made up of three estates, or assemblies: that of the clergy, the nobles, and the commoners. Following an argument about the voting power of each of the estates, the entire Third Estate withdrew and set up a rival National Assembly in Paris to institute reforms.

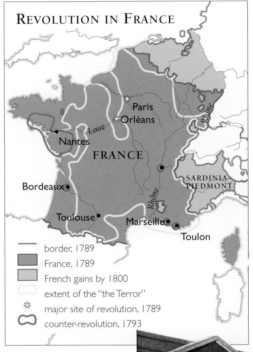

REVOLUTION IN FRANCE

Paris
Orléans
Loire
Nantes
FRANCE
Bordeaux
SARDINIA
PIEDMONT
Rhône
Toulouse
Marseille
Toulon
Rhine

— border, 1789
France, 1789
French gains by 1800
extent of the "the Terror"
✳ major site of revolution, 1789
counter-revolution, 1793

Right The execution of Marie Antoinette, queen of France, in October 1793. Born into the Habsburg dynasty of Austria, she lived in splendor and isolation from her French subjects, who resented both her nationality and her extravagant lifestyle. Her secret negotiations with Austria against the revolutionaries were the chief factor that led to her execution and that of the indecisive King Louis XVI.

The assembly received widespread popular support. On July 14, 1789, as rumors spread that the king's army was planning to attack it, an angry crowd gathered to storm the fortress of the Bastille, a hated symbol of royal tyranny. It was taken easily and found to hold only a few prisoners, but it proved a rallying point for popular rebellion.

Under the slogan of *Liberté, Egalité, Fraternité* ("Liberty, Equality, Fraternity") the revolution spread rapidly. Widespread famine and unemployment in the countryside helped foment panic, leading to the "Great Fear" (July 20–August 6, 1789) when armed peasants destroyed aristocratic property in a frenzy of hatred. In Paris, the National Assembly proclaimed the Declaration of the Rights of Man, promising freedom of conscience, property, and speech. Serfdom was outlawed, church property confiscated, and hereditary titles abolished.

At first the National Assembly tried to work with the king, but he proved to be an unwilling partner. In 1791 he tried to flee the country with his wife, the even more unpopular Marie Antoinette, but they were stopped and brought back to Paris. Exiled French aristocrats persuaded Prussia and the Austrian empire to invade France. The king and

VOLTAIRE & THE ENLIGHTENMENT

Voltaire, real name François-Marie Arouet (1694–1788), was the embodiment of the Enlightenment. One of France's greatest writers, he devoted his life to criticizing tyranny, intolerance, and injustice. His sharp wit got him into trouble; he was imprisoned in the Bastille twice, and spent nearly 30 years in exile from Paris, part of it in England, which he admired for its freedom of thought. In the 1750s, Frederick the Great of Prussia sheltered him in his palace at Sans Souci, and he also corresponded with Catherine the Great of Russia. From 1754 he lived in Switzerland. After the Revolution his remains were reinterred in the Panthéon.

Above *Voltaire dictates a letter as he dresses.*

queen were accused of plotting to betray France and were imprisoned. Moderates within the National Assembly tried to spare them the death sentence, but radical sentiment was too strong. Both were guillotined, along with hundreds of aristocrats.

Royalist revolts broke out in the west and parts of southern France. They were quickly suppressed, whereupon the revolutionaries turned on each other in fierce political feuding. As many as 200,000 people may have died during the Terror of 1793 and 1794, most of them in the civil wars, others on the guillotine or in prison. Two prominent victims of the Terror were Georges Danton and Maximilien de Robespierre, leaders of the extreme Jacobin faction, both of whom had been active in setting it up.

THE REVOLUTION ABROAD

Fear of French agents fomenting popular uprisings abroad hardened European opposition to revolutionary France, and Britain, the Netherlands, and Spain joined Prussia and Austria in a military alliance against the new republic (the Revolutionary Wars, 1792–1802). In spite of its internal chaos, France held out against its enemies, first of all repelling the invasion attempt to restore the monarchy in 1792, and then going on to the offensive itself. A series of victories in 1794–95 culminated in the successful invasion of the Netherlands (ruled by France as the Batavian Republic until 1806). Prussia and Spain made peace, leaving Britain and Austria to carry on the war. Britain maintained its naval supremacy with a series of victories over France, but by 1797 the general Napoleon Bonaparte (see pages 146–149) had emerged as the greatest of the French commanders after brilliant campaigns in Italy and Austria.

TIMETABLE

1712
Thomas Newcomen designs a steam pump for use in mines

1721
Robert Walpole is the first British prime minister (to 1742)

1733–35
The War of the Polish Succession leads to Austrian and Russian domination of Poland

1740
Frederick the Great of Prussia introduces religious and economic reform

1740–48
The War of the Austrian Succession; Prussia gains Silesia from Austria

1751
Publication begins in France of the *Encyclopédie*, one of the chief works of the Enlightenment

1756–63
France supports Austria, Spain, and Russia against Britain and Prussia in the Seven Years War

1758
Voltaire publishes *Candide*, a satirical novel, his best-known work

1769
Richard Arkwright patents a water-powered spinning frame and opens the first textile factories in Britain

1781
Joseph II abolishes serfdom throughout the Austrian empire

1789
The storming of the Bastille begins the French Revolution

1791
The composer Wolfgang Amadeus Mozart (b.1756) dies in Vienna

1793
Louis XVI and Marie Antoinette are executed in Paris

1798
France backs an unsuccessful revolt by the United Irishmen against British rule

1799
Napoleon Bonaparte becomes First Consul of France

EUROPE UNDER NAPOLEON

A NATIONAL HERO IN FRANCE, NAPOLEON BONAPARTE WAS SEEN BY SOME AS
AN IDEALIST AND REFORMER, BY OTHERS AS A RUTHLESS TYRANT. HIS MILITARY
GENIUS BROUGHT FRENCH POWER TO ITS PEAK BUT HIS HUGE AMBITION
SUCCEEDED IN UNITING EUROPE'S MAJOR POWERS AGAINST HIM. AFTER
15 YEARS OF WAR, NAPOLEON WAS DEFEATED AND SENT INTO EXILE.
AT THE CONGRESS OF VIENNA (1815) THE VICTORIOUS ALLIES
REDREW THE BOUNDARIES OF EUROPE IN
THEIR OWN FAVOR AND STRIPPED FRANCE
OF ITS OVERSEAS COLONIES.

Napoleon was born on the Mediterranean island of Corsica in 1769, the year that it became part of France. After graduating from the Paris military academy, he joined an artillery regiment in the French army. The French Revolution provided an opportunity for the brilliant young officer to rise. He aligned himself with the more radical revolutionaries and came to notice at the siege of Toulon (1793) when, commanding the artillery, he forced the withdrawal of an Anglo-Spanish fleet. Three promotions in four months made him a brigadier general at age 24, but the fall of the radical leader Robespierre led to Napoleon's arrest and brief imprisonment the next year.

In October 1795 Napoleon suppressed a royalist rebellion in Paris and was rewarded with the command of an army in the continuing war against France's enemies. Leading campaigns in northern Italy and Austria (1796–97), his military and strategic skills were displayed to the full as he took on and defeated Austria's forces. Britain now stood alone as France's most implacable enemy. The government urged Napoleon to launch an invasion across the Channel, but instead he led an expedition to Egypt, from where he planned to strike at Britain's most valuable colony, India. He won a decisive battle over the Mamluke rulers of Egypt, but the defeat of his fleet at the battle of the Nile (1798) by the British admiral Nelson cut off supplies to the French army, forcing it to surrender. Despite this debacle, Napoleon's prestige stood higher than ever in France, where there was great public enthusiasm for all things Egyptian. Austria, Russia, and Turkey, encouraged by the defeat, were led to resume the war against France.

Left "Bonaparte crossing the Alps," a painting by Jacques Louis David, Napoleon's official artist, that glorifies his successful invasion of Italy in 1796–97.

CONSUL & EMPEROR

The foundations of the French republic were extremely shaky. The Directory, the committee that had governed since 1795, was weak and unpopular, and in November 1799 Napoleon conspired with others to overthrow it and replace it with a three-man consulate. He justified this by claiming that only a firm hand could hold France together after the chaos of the revolutionary years. As First Consul, Napoleon was in effect the military dictator of France. The nature of his power was only partly concealed by a new constitution, which was approved by popular vote in 1800.

Further campaigns in Europe, culminating in the defeat of Austria at Marengo (1800), brought the Revolutionary Wars to an end. With all its allies in Europe defeated, Britain was compelled to sign the Treaty

1799–1815

Below The Legion d'honneur (Legion of Honor) was created by Napoleon to reward civilian and military achievements. It is still in use today.

Left Moscow burns in 1812, set on fire by its citizens to deprive Napoleon of booty and supplies.

Below Delegates to the Congress of Vienna (1814–15) were entertained at night with lavish balls. In this French satire, Russia, Prussia, and Austria dance to the bidding of Castlereagh, the British delegate (in red).

of Amiens (1802). Napoleon appointed himself consul for life. In 1804 he went a step further and assumed the hereditary title of emperor, securing the succession in the event of his death.

TYRANT OR REFORMER?

Napoleon had fought for the revolution, but he had a low opinion of the masses. He ignored the slogans "liberty, equality, fraternity" and "the rights of man." However, as First Consul and then emperor, he introduced a program of reforms that still influence France today: local government and the university system were restructured, a national bank founded, and the tax system made more equitable. The reform of French law, begun by the National Convention in 1790, was completed. The Code Napoleon of 1804 built on some of the old revolutionary ideals—a secular state, individual liberty, freedom of conscience—but it also maintained traditional property rights and offered little protection to workers. Women were granted few rights, though they had been active participants in the revolution.

THE NAPOLEONIC SYSTEM

No sooner had the Revolutionary Wars ended than Napoleon began to increase French influence in the Netherlands, Switzerland, and Italy. He also tried to extend the French empire overseas and attempted to restrict British trade rights. These expansionist policies caused Britain to declare war again in 1803. Austria, Sweden, and Russia followed suit in 1805 but were rapidly defeated. Napoleon proceeded to occupy most of Germany and abolished what was left of the Holy Roman Empire. Prussia joined the war in 1806 but was also beaten. Napoleon now placed his brothers on royal thrones throughout Europe—an action that was much resented and helped to create nationalist resistance. In 1810 Napoleon divorced the childless Josephine in order to marry the 18-year-old archduchess Marie-Louise, daughter of Francis I of Austria, who duly gave birth to a son, the king of Rome (nicknamed L'Aiglon, or the Eaglet).

By 1807 Britain was on its own. British control of the sea left Napoleon unable to attack Britain directly, so he tried to prevent

the rest of Europe from trading with it. His efforts proved by and large ineffectual; illicit trade continued and Britain retaliated by blockading European ports. When Portugal refused to comply with the French ban, Napoleon ordered his army to invade. This sparked off revolt in Spain, and a British army commanded by Wellington landed in

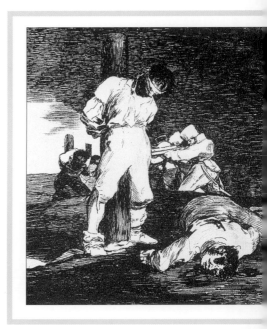

THE DIVISION OF EUROPE, 1815

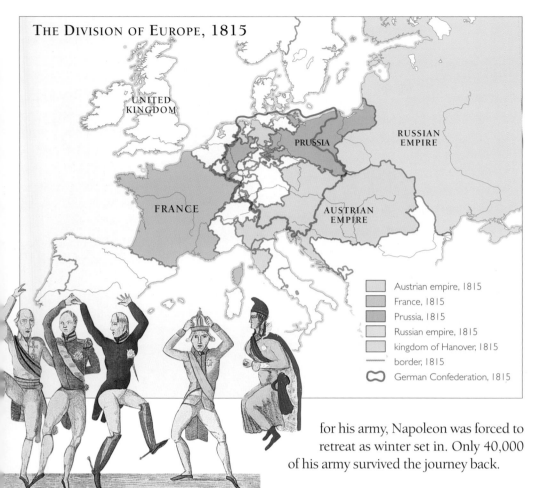

- Austrian empire, 1815
- France, 1815
- Prussia, 1815
- Russian empire, 1815
- kingdom of Hanover, 1815
- border, 1815
- German Confederation, 1815

for his army, Napoleon was forced to retreat as winter set in. Only 40,000 of his army survived the journey back.

DEFEAT & EXILE

Napoleon had been welcomed into many parts of Europe because he was seen as a liberator, spreading the ideals of the French Revolution. But his treatment of the territories he conquered, which were systematically drained of taxes, supplies, and conscripts for the French army, turned the popular mood against him. The catastrophe in Russia persuaded Prussia, Austria, Sweden, and Spain back into the war. As the allies approached Paris, Napoleon abdicated and was exiled to the Italian island of Elba. The French monarchy was restored while the victorious allies met in Vienna to redistribute Napoleon's conquests. Russia eventually emerged with the biggest prize, in the shape of Poland, but Prussia and Austria also made substantial gains.

In March 1815, before the Congress had completed its sessions, Napoleon escaped and returned to France, where he seized power once more. A little more than three months later he was defeated by the British and Prussians at the battle of Waterloo. This time he was exiled to St. Helena in the southern Atlantic, too remote for escape or intrigue, where he died in 1821.

the peninsula to support the rebels. His campaigns succeeded in tying down a large part of the French army. When Russia also ignored the ban Napoleon invaded the country at the head of an army of 600,000 men. He narrowly escaped defeat at Borodino, and went on to capture Moscow, but found it deserted. Unable to find supplies

THE DISASTERS OF WAR

When Napoleon put his brother Joseph on the Spanish throne in 1808, Madrid rebelled. For the next six years, locally organized militia groups fought the French in a series of skirmishes and raids. The term "guerrilla war" (little war) was invented in this conflict, which was often brutal, with vicious reprisals on both sides. The great Spanish painter Francisco Goya (1746–1828) expressed his feelings of horror in a series of engravings, "The Disasters of War" (1810–14).

Left *"There is no way out," by Francisco Goya.*

TIMETABLE

1793
Napoleon wins Toulon from the royalists and is made brigadier general

1796–97
Napoleon's victories in Italy and Austria win him glory and prestige

1799
Napoleon overthrows the Directory and becomes First Consul

1802
Napoleon becomes consul for life

1803
Britain resumes the war against France. Napoleon threatens to invade Britain

1804
Napoleon crowns himself emperor of France in the presence of the pope

1805
Nelson's victory at Trafalgar deprives the French of a fleet. Napoleon beats Austria and Russia at Austerlitz

1806
Napoleon dissolves the Holy Roman Empire and replaces it with the Confederation of the Rhine

1807
The Continental System is introduced

1808
Joseph Bonaparte, elder brother of Napoleon, is crowned king of Spain

1809
Napoleon enters Vienna and defeats the Austrians at Wagram

1810
Napoleon marries Marie-Louise of Austria

1812
Napoleon retreats from Russia

1813
Napoleon is defeated at Leipzig and leads his army back to France

1814
Napoleon abdicates and is exiled to Elba

1814–15
The Congress of Vienna meets to reorganize post-Napoleonic Europe

1815
After defeat at Waterloo, Napoleon is exiled to St. Helena

THE EXPANSION OF RUSSIA

FOR 250 YEARS, FROM ABOUT 1240 TO 1480, THE RUSSIAN PRINCIPALITIES
WERE SUBJECT TO THE MONGOLIAN TATARS. INDEPENDENCE CAME IN THE
REIGN OF IVAN III, GRAND PRINCE OF MOSCOW FROM 1462–1505. HE
UNITED THE OTHER PRINCIPALITIES UNDER HIS LEADERSHIP AND BEGAN
EXPANDING RUSSIA'S FRONTIERS. BUT RUSSIA REMAINED WEAK AND BACK-
WARD BY COMPARISON WITH WESTERN EUROPE. MODERN RUSSIA WAS
CREATED BY PETER THE GREAT LATE IN THE 17TH CENTURY.

During the centuries of Tatar rule, Moscow looked east, to Persia and central Asia.
But the Russians' Orthodox faith linked
them to the Byzantine empire. After Byzantium fell to the Ottomans in 1453, Moscow came to be seen as the Third Rome in
succession to Constantinople. When Ivan
III, grand prince of Moscow, married Zoe,
niece of the last Byzantine emperor, he took
the double-headed eagle of the Byzantine
empire as his own symbol.

The association was made even more
explicit by Ivan IV (r.1533–84), who had
himself crowned czar (caesar, or emperor)
of Russia in 1547. Russia nearly doubled in
size during his reign. The Tatars were conquered and Russian control extended into
Siberia. However, Ivan's attempts to expand
west to the Baltic were resisted by Sweden
and Poland. Ivan reduced the power of the
nobility (the *boyars*) and took over their
estates. During a reign of terror, thousands
were killed by his personal bodyguards.
This earned him the nickname of "Ivan the
Terrible," though "Awe-inspiring" is a more
accurate translation of the Russian.

The "Time of Troubles" (1604–13) saw
much of western Russia devastated by a
civil war, which was ended by the accession
of the first Romanov czar (the dynasty that
ruled Russia until 1917). Settlement continued to spread eastward down the rivers
of Siberia, and Russians had reached the
Pacific by 1637. Trading posts were set up
and furs became Russia's most valuable
export. However, Russia's vast size was not
to its advantage; though rich in natural
resources, there were enormous problems
of communication and transportation, and
labor was short. To meet this, serfdom was
introduced; peasants lost their traditional
right to change employers once a year and
were bound for life to one owner or estate

under conditions little different from
slavery. Russian nobles were virtually
the serfs of the czars. Trade and cultural
contact with Europe rose during the 16th
century, and there was a flourishing community of westerners—merchants, craftsmen, artists, clergy, and intellectuals—living in Moscow. But, in economic and political terms, Russia still lagged far behind its
European neighbors.

Above *Peter the Great ordered the nobles to shave.*

PETER THE GREAT

The reign of Peter the Great (1682–1725)
proved a turning point in Russian history.
Although he was not the first czar to introduce westernizing measures (his three predecessors had each done so in a small measure) Peter was the first to attempt to turn
Russia into a modern European power, and
had the energy and ruthlessness to realize
his ambition. In 1697–98 he made a tour

RUSSIA'S PROGRESS EAST

ARCTIC OCEAN

Russian
America

Bering Strait

Nizhnekolymsk
1644

Turukhansk
1607

Tobolsk
1587

Ob

Yenisey

Lena

Yakutsk
1632

1648

Tomsk
1604

Yeniseysk
1619

Krasnoyarsk
1628

Olekminsk
1635

Petropavlovsk
1740

Semipalatinsk
1718

Irkutsk
1652

Amur

returned to China
following 1689 Treaty
of Nerchinsk

MANCHU CHINA

Beijing

- Russia, 1689
- Russian expansion under Peter the Great, 1689–1725
- Russian expansion, 1725–1796
- Russian expansion, 1796–1826
- border, 1826
- new Russian town, with date of foundation
- major trade route

Barents Sea

SWEDEN

Karelia

Finland

Lake Onega

Lake Ladoga

Ingria

Olonets

Helsinki

St Petersburg
1703

Stockholm

Revel

Estonia

Narva

Vänern

Vättern

Lake Peipus

Pskov

Livonia

Novgorod

Riga

Pskov

Tver

penhagen

Libau

Baltic Sea

Vitebsk

Western Dvina

to Europe

Moscow

Danzig

Königsberg
June–July 1697

Smolensk

Minsk

Mogilev

Vistula

POLAND

Oder

Warsaw

USSIA

Ukraine

Kiev

CZECH
EPUBLIC

Krakow

Lemberg
(Lvov)

UKRAINE

Podolia

TRIA

Vienna
June–July 1698

AUSTRIAN EMPIRE

HUNGARY

ROMANIA

Jassy

Sava

Danube

KHANATE OF CRIMEA

Kinburn

Kaffa

Kerch

Azov

Sevastopol
1783

Varna

Black Sea

BULGARIA

Constantinople

PLES

GREECE

OTTOMAN EMPIRE

TURKEY

to Europe

Archangel
1583

Eastern Dvina

Yarensk

Ustyug

Kargopol

Vyatka

Vologda

Yaroslavl

Nizhniy Novgorod

Volga

Tula

Orel
1564

RUSSIA

Voronezh
1586

Tambov
1636

Simbirsk
1648

Kazan

Kharkov
1654

Don

Dnieper

Tsaritsyn
1589

Saratov
1590

Astrakhan

Georgia

Batum

Tiflis

Yerevan

Tabriz

CAUCASUS MTS

URAL MOUNTAINS

Obdorsk
1595

Berezov
1593

Ob

Surgut
1594

Ob

Pelym
1592

Tobolsk
1587

Irtysh

Solikamskaya

Verkhotyure
1598

Ishim
1670

Omsk
1716

Tyumen
1586

Yegoshika
(Perm)

Ufa
1586

Orenburg
1743

Ural

Ishim

KAZAKHSTAN

Turgay

Guryev
1645

Volga

Aral Sea

UZBEKISTAN

Khiva

Amu Darya

Derbent

Caspian Sea

Baku

TURKMENISTAN

Gorgan

Meshed

Tehran

PERSIA

IRAQ

IRAN

Legend:

- Russia, 1505
- Russia by 1689
- Russian expansion under Peter the Great, 1689–1725
- Russian expansion by the death of Catherine II, 1796
- Russian expansion, 1796–1815
- Polish territory at maximum extent, 1618–34
- borders, 1815
- new Russian town, with date of foundation
- route of Peter the Great, 1697–98
- major trade route

0 ___ 600 km
0 ___ 400 mi

of Prussia, the Netherlands, England, and Austria to teach himself about the technology of the west, particularly shipbuilding (he even worked as a shipwright in England and Holland). On returning home, he set about reorganizing the Russian army and in 1700 went to war with Sweden to win an outlet on the Baltic, where he founded his new capital of St. Petersburg. English and Dutch shipwrights were imported to supervise the building of a modern navy, while Italian architects introduced the fashionable baroque style to Russia. State-run copper and ironworks were founded in the Urals to exploit the region's rich mineral deposits. Peter even transformed the way Russians looked—he ordered his courtiers to wear western clothes, and nobles to shave off their traditional Russian beards. Anyone who refused had to pay a tax.

Peter's programs were aimed at making Russia competitive with the west. He did not attempt to reform Russia's deeply conservative society, and introduced repressive measures of control such as censorship of the press. Serfs were subjected to new restrictions, taxed heavily to pay for Peter's schemes, and forced to work on the construction of St. Petersburg; thousands died in terrible conditions. Serfdom was even extended to industrial workers in Peter's newly built factories.

MIGHTY RUSSIA

During the 18th century, Russian's frontiers expanded slowly. The Ottoman Turks were driven from the Crimea and southern Ukraine, and with the fall of Sevastopol in 1783 the Black Sea was opened to Russian trade. Russian fur traders crossed the Bering Sea to North America and founded the first permanent European settlements in Alaska in 1784. But the most significant gain was on its western frontier, where Russia benefited from Poland's weakness to share with Austria and Prussia in the partition of the kingdom between 1772 and 1795. After the Napoleonic wars (see pages 146–149), the Congress of Vienna (1815) ceded the rest of Poland to Russia.

Many of these territorial gains were made in the reign of the German-born empress Catherine the Great (1762–96), who came to the throne upon the death of her highly unpopular husband, Peter III, grandson of Peter the Great. Catherine was suspected by many of being implicated in his murder, and she has won great notoriety for her love affairs. However, she ruled Russia firmly

SAINT PETERSBURG

Peter the Great chose a marshy site on the Neva river, at the head of the Gulf of Finland, to be his "window on Europe." He laid the foundations for the Peter-Paul Fortress in May 1703, and in 1712 the city became his capital. A wave of building followed, all according to an elegant plan centered on Peter's vast Admiralty building and shipyards. Later rulers added to its splendors with new buildings in a variety of baroque and neoclassical styles, among them the magnificent Winter Palace (now the Hermitage). Known as Leningrad during the period of Soviet rule, the city's original name was restored in 1991.

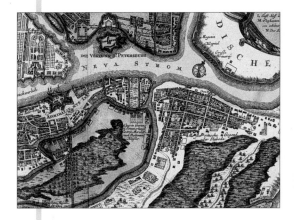

Above A map of St. Petersburg in 1728.
Right View from the river about the same time.

and well. An autocrat, she was also keenly interested in the cultural movements of the day in art, music, and architecture. Her collection of paintings forms the core of the great national collection now in the Hermitage Museum in St. Petersburg. At her invitation, many Germans settled in Russia, particularly in the newly conquered areas north of the Black Sea, where they introduced efficient agriculture.

In common with her fellow European monarchs, Catherine was alarmed by the outbreak of the French revolution in 1789. As the revolutionaries tried to spread their ideas across Europe, Russia joined Austria, Spain, Prussia, and Britain in the struggle against France (see pages 146–149). Catherine was succeeded by her son Paul in 1796, but his erratic policies (he sent a Cossack army to conquer India) led to his murder in 1801. His son Alexander I seized Finland from Sweden (1808). Napoleon invaded Russia in 1812 but was defeated by its unmanageable size. As the French retreated, Alexander placed himself at the head of the pursuing Russian army, entering Paris with the allies in 1814. Russia was now established as one of the great powers of Europe.

Above Catherine the Great, whose expansionist foreign policy brought new gains to Russia.

THE MUSLIM WORLD

BETWEEN 1500 AND 1800, ASIA WAS DOMINATED BY THREE GREAT ISLAMIC STATES: THE OTTOMAN IN THE MIDDLE EAST AND THE BALKANS, THE SAFAVID IN PERSIA, AND THE MUGHAL IN INDIA. ALL THREE HAD AMBITIONS TO ESTABLISH AN ISLAMIC WORLD EMPIRE AND WERE CONTINUALLY PUSHING TO EXPAND THEIR BOUNDARIES OUTWARDS. AT THE SAME TIME, THEY ARGUED AMONG THEMSELVES OVER CLAIMS TO GOVERN THE MUSLIM WORLD.

Left *Ottoman sea power struck at the heart of Venice's maritime empire. The defeat of the Ottoman navy at the battle of Lepanto (1571) marked a revival in European fortunes, but the eastern Mediterranean remained a closed Ottoman lake for another century.*

At the beginning of the 16th century the Ottomans were the most powerful Muslim dynasty. In the 14th century, as the Byzantine empire declined, they had expanded from their base in Anatolia (Turkey) to conquer Bulgaria, Greece, and Serbia. Edirne (formerly Adrianople), 140 miles northwest of the Byzantine capital, was their center of government until Constantinople itself fell to the armies of Mehmet II in 1453. The ancient capital of the eastern Roman empire and the seat of the Orthodox patriarch now became the capital of the Ottoman sultans and the administrative center of their highly organized empire. The church of St. Sophia was converted to a mosque.

The Balkan parts of the empire were crucially important to its success. The sultan's Christian subjects had to send a tribute of children to Constantinople each year (the *devshirme*). Here, they were brought up as Muslims and educated to serve in the government or fight in the highly trained elite corps of Janissaries, the sultan's personal guard. Although slaves, the Janissaries were well treated and could rise to high positions of wealth and authority in the empire. Constantinople at this time was a more cosmopolitan and tolerant city than most European capitals; many of its citizens were Greek Christians and Jews.

Selim I (r.1512–20) was the most successful of the Ottoman sultans; during his reign, Syria and Kurdistan were conquered from the Safavids and the holy city of Mecca taken into Ottoman control. His successor, Suleiman the Magnificent (r.1520–66), added Hungary, Iraq, and the North African coast. Expansion started to slow from then on: long supply lines hindered military campaigns. The authority of the sultans began to weaken, and the Janissaries, who had developed into a hereditary privileged class that meddled in politics, ceased to be a powerful fighting force.

The Muslim empires no longer dominated trade with India and the Far East. The British and Dutch controlled the Indian Ocean trade, while the opening up of Siberia had created a land route to China that bypassed Ottoman and Safavid territories. The Ottomans were in economic and military decline. In 1683 a last great campaign in Europe ended in crushing defeat at the gates of Vienna. Hungary was won back by Austria in 1699. Further losses followed, and by 1800 the draining away of territory in the Balkans, and in North Africa, had become a steady and irreversible process.

Ottoman empire, 1512
gains under Selim I and Suleiman I, 1512–1566
gains 1566–1683
Ottoman empire, 1815
Safavid empire, 1722
Ottoman territory effectively
independent by 1815
Ottoman administrative center
Ottoman campaign
borders, 1815

800 km
600 mi

PRUSSIA
BELARUS
RUSSIA
Volga
Kazan
Moscow
POLAND
Kiev
Cossacks
Dnieper
1571–72
1521
Astrakhan
Cossacks
AUSTRIAN EMPIRE
1502, 1519
Krakow
Podolia
UKRAINE
Jedisan
Azov
1527, 1543
Khanate of the Crimea
1774–83 independent
1579–80
Caspian Sea
TURKMENISTAN
Derbent
Baku
1529
Buda
Transylvania
Jassy
Bessarabia
1532
Hungary
ROMANIA
Moldavia
Akkerman
Kaffa
CAUCASUS MTS
Daghestan
Mohács
1526
Belgrade
Wallachia
Bucharest
Danube
Silistria
Varna
Black Sea
Georgia
Batum
Tiflis
Karabagh
Bosnia
Sarajevo
Niš
Bulgaria
Serbia
Sofia
1526
Edirne
(Adrianople)
Amasra
Sinope
Trabzon
Kars
Yerevan
Armenia
Chaldiran
1514
Tabriz
Ragusa
MONTENEGRO
Rumelia
Constantinople
Bursa
Ankara
Sivas
Kurdistan
Azerbaijan
ZAGROS
Herat
AFGHANISTAN
Taranto
Gallipoli
OTTOMAN
EMPIRE
ANATOLIA
TURKEY
Kayseri
Urfa
Mardin
Mosul
Hamadan
Tehran
SAFAVID
EMPIRE
Reggio
Lepanto
1571
Morea
Athens
Izmir
Konya
Adana
Aleppo
Qasr-i-Shirin
Luristan
Qum
IRAN
ALTA
1543
MALTA
Rhodes
Candia
Crete
1574
Cyprus
Syria
Euphrates
Tigris
Baghdad
Iraq
MTS
Isfahan
PERSIA
1551
Mediterranean Sea
Tripoli
Damascus
Jerusalem
Basra
1554
Bandar Abbas
Hormuz
Benghazi
CYRENAICA
semi-independent 1714
Alexandria
Damietta
1521
El Hasa
TRIPOLI
semi-independent
1714
LIBYA
Cairo
Suez
EGYPT
semi-independent
1805
Hejaz
Arabs
ind
BAHRAIN
QATAR
independent
1780
1521
Muscat
OMAN
ndependent 1650
Asyut
Quseir
Medina
SAUDIA
OMAN
El Kharga
Aswan
SUDAN
Jiddah
Mecca
Red Sea
Selima
Suakin
FUNJ
Massawa
Sana
YEMEN
independent
1635
ETHIOPIA
Aden

THE SAFAVID EMPIRE

Safavid Persia, on the Ottoman empire's eastern border, was established by
Shah Ismail I (r.1501–24) who expanded from a power base in Azerbaijan to
occupy the area between the Caspian
Sea and the Persian Gulf. This growth
was abruptly halted when his army was
defeated by the Ottomans at the battle of
Chaldiran in 1514. The Ottomans continued to make inroads into Safavid territory
until Shah Abbas the Great (r.1588–1629)
revived the Safavid fortunes. After strength-
ening the army by replacing the old military
elite with a slave caste of Muslim converts
similar to the Ottoman corps of Janissaries,
he won back most of the land in western
Persia lost to the Ottomans and captured
Kandahar (Afghanistan) from the Mughals

Right *Suleiman the
Magnificent was
painted by the Venetian
artist Titian. He was
known to the Turks as
the "Law Giver."*

of northern India. Abbas made Isfahan the Persian capital in 1587, which he adorned with many mosques. Persian poetry, painting, and architecture flourished under his rule. He was followed by a succession of mediocre rulers, but the Safavid empire survived until 1722 when it was overrun by Afghan raiders. Persia briefly revived during the reign of Nadir Shah (1736–47), a bandit turned general who conquered Afghanistan and raided Delhi in 1739.

THE MUGHALS

Muslim invaders from Afghanistan had established the first Islamic state in India in the 11th century. By the 14th century the sultanate of Delhi ruled most of northern India and had extended its control far into central India (the Deccan), but it was in decline when the Mughals—a central Asian dynasty claiming descent from the Mongols—invaded India under Babur (r.1501–30) in 1519. After defeating the sultanate of Delhi at the first battle of Panipat (1526), he went on to conquer most of northern India. Rebellions broke out after his death but his grandson Akbar (r.1556–1605) took Mughal rule into the Deccan.

Akbar was a competent and wise ruler. Although a devout Muslim, he encouraged religious toleration among his Hindu subjects for the sake of stability. His empire was prosperous. Its grain harvests were larger

Above The Taj Mahal, the garden tomb built by the Mughal Shah Jahan for his favorite wife, 1632–54.

than all of Europe's together, it possessed the world's largest textile industry, and produced high-quality steel and cannon. The weapons employed by the Mughals' professional army of a million soldiers were the equal of any used in the west at that time.

The Mughal empire was at its greatest under Aurangzeb (r.1658–1707), who conquered all but the far south of India. By now, Mughal rule had become less tolerant, and Aurangzeb asserted his Islamic faith by destroying Hindu temples and holy places.

From the mid 17th century resistance to Mughal rule was headed by the Marathas, a military Hindu state based in the western Deccan. Mughal power declined after Aurangzeb's death, and the Marathas were able to drive them from the Deccan and attack the north. Meanwhile, Nadir Shah of Persia took advantage of their weakness to sack Delhi in 1739. In a humiliating gesture, he took away the Peacock Throne of the Mughal emperors. Provincial governors began to rule like independent princes.

The opening up of trade with the west had led a number of European nations to establish trading bases on the Indian coast. The Mughals had welcomed the influx of European money to pay for their exports of spices, silk, cotton, and dyes, but the European trading companies now took advantage of Mughal weakness to increase their influence. Wars in Europe spilled over into colonial possessions. The Seven Years War (1756–63) greatly strengthened the position of the British East India Company. It possessed its own army and heavily armed ships and was able to intimidate and neutralize Indian opposition through a network of favorable alliances. By 1765 the British had won control of the rich Bengal cotton trade; by 1815 they dominated India and the Mughal emperor was a mere puppet.

Below The Persian general Nadir Shah (r.1736–47) invaded the declining Mughal empire in 1739.

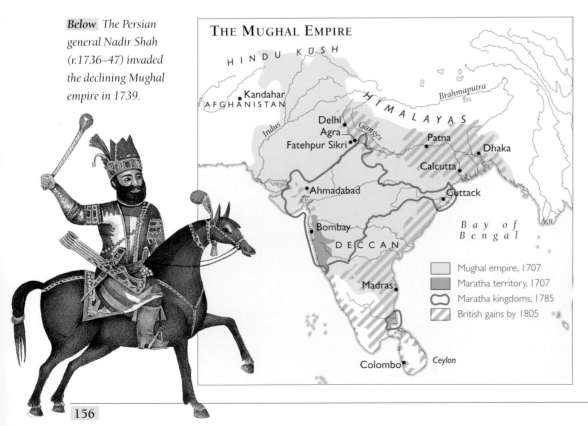

THE MUGHAL EMPIRE

HINDU KUSH

Kandahar
AFGHANISTAN

Brahmaputra

HIMALAYAS

Indus

Delhi
Agra
Fatehpur Sikri
Ganges
Patna
Dhaka
Calcutta

Ahmadabad
Cuttack

Bombay

Bay of Bengal

DECCAN

Madras

Mughal empire, 1707
Maratha territory, 1707
Maratha kingdoms, 1785
British gains by 1805

Colombo   Ceylon

THE ART OF MUGHAL INDIA

Mughal emperors were rich patrons of the arts, and they encouraged artists from Safavid Persia to their court, where they set up royal workshops. Persian artists excelled in creating books lavishly illustrated with miniature drawings and paintings in a formal, highly decorated style, which made brilliant use of color. Indian artists, Hindu and Muslim, were trained in the Mughal studios, and while they continued to work in the Persian style, they added to it a distinctly Indian view of life. Mughal art is especially noted for its delicate portraiture and its natural history paintings—two subjects largely ignored by the Safavids.

Under the patronage of the emperor Jahangir (r.1605–27), Mughal painting reached its richest expression. He prized individuality above all things, and rewarded one exceptional artist, the nature specialist Abu'l Hasan, with the title "Wonder of the Age."

Architecture and landscaping were also highly prized by the Mughals. The first emperor, Babur, was an avid maker of gardens—an interest he brought to India from Central Asia. The emperor who has left the greatest architectural legacy is Shah Jahan (r.1628–66). He oversaw the construction of the Peacock Throne, rebuilt Lahore and Agra, laid out a new capital at Delhi, and built the Taj Mahal as a tomb for his favorite wife.

Below Shah Jahan on the Peacock Throne.

TIMETABLE

1512
Selim I becomes sultan of the Ottoman empire

1514
The Ottomans defeat the Safavids at Chaldiran

1517
The *sharif* of Mecca surrenders to Selim

1526
Babur founds the Mughal empire in India. The Ottomans defeat Hungary at the battle of Mohács

1536
Suleiman the Magnificent forms an alliance with Francis I of France

1566
Suleiman dies campaigning in Hungary

1571
A European fleet defeats the Ottoman navy at Lepanto (Greece)

1598
The Mughals establish a new capital in Agra

1603–23
Abbas the Great regains Safavid territories from the Ottomans

1639
The Ottoman tribute of Christian children (*devshirme*) is abolished

1669
The Ottomans capture Crete from the Venetians after a 25-year war

1683
The Ottoman siege of Vienna is defeated

1707
The Mughal empire begins to disintegrate on the death of Aurangzeb

1720s
The Marathas begin to expand into northern India

1722
The Afghans overthrow the Safavid dynasty in Persia

1818
British defeat of the Marathas establishes their supremacy in India

1805
Egypt becomes independent of the Ottoman empire

IMPERIAL CHINA

CHINA HAS ALWAYS BEEN OPEN TO INVASION FROM THE NORTH. THE MING DYNASTY, WHO EXPELLED THE MONGOLS AND RULED CHINA FROM 1368–1644, BUILT THE 2,000-MILE-LONG GREAT WALL TO PROTECT THIS VULNERABLE FRONTIER. BUT IT PROVED A FAILURE. DURING A CIVIL WAR IN 1644, MANCHU TRIBESMEN FROM THE NORTH WERE ABLE TO INVADE THE EMPIRE AND CAPTURE BEIJING. AS THE QING DYNASTY, THEY WERE TO BE THE LAST RULERS OF IMPERIAL CHINA.

Under the Ming emperors, China began a period of stable government. Chinese rule extended farther than ever before, into Vietnam and Burma in the south and Mongolia and Korea in the north. But Ming China was inward looking. Early in the 15th century, the admiral Zheng He sailed as far as east Africa, but maritime expeditions ended with his death in 1433. The decision to move the capital back to Beijing from the thriving ports of the south reflected the lack of enthusiasm for overseas trade. A Portuguese trading base was founded at Macau in 1557, and a Dutch settlement on Taiwan in 1622, but Ming relations with European merchants remained distant.

THE MANCHUS IN POWER

By the early 17th century Ming authority had begun to crumble. Liaodong, the Chinese enclave north of the Wall, was protected by a wooden defensework with gate towers (the Willow Palisade) but this did not prevent it being seized by a new rival power, the Manchus, Jürchen tribesmen from the north. When civil war broke out in China, the Manchus stepped in. Dorgun (r.1628–50) won control of Beijing in 1644 and acted as regent to his nephew who was installed as the first Qing emperor. It took several years to bring southern China under control: Manchu rule was never popular

Below A vase of the Ming period. At this time, the secret of making porcelain was unknown in Europe, where there was a huge demand for quality items such as this. Many articles were produced in China especially for the export market.

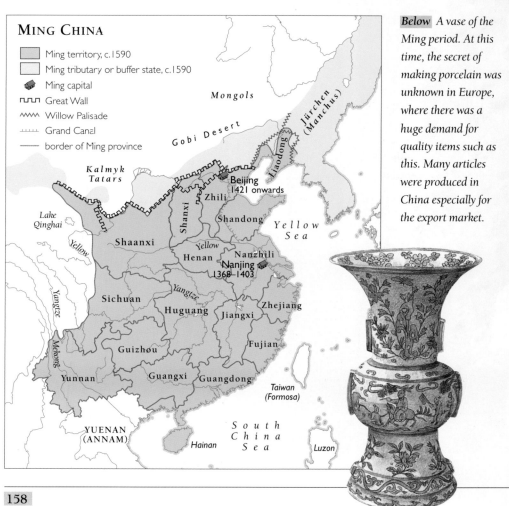

MING CHINA

- Ming territory, c.1590
- Ming tributary or buffer state, c.1590
- Ming capital
- Great Wall
- Willow Palisade
- Grand Canal
- border of Ming province

Manchu legend
- Manchu homeland, early 17th century
- Manchu expansion to 1644
- Manchu expansion, 1644–1697
- Manchu expansion, 1697–1800
- state paying tribute to Manchu China at some time between 1637 and 1800
- Manchu provincial capital
- trade route of the Manchu empire
- **silk** commodity traded
- internal migration of Han Chinese during the 18th century
- borders, c.1800
- Great Wall
- Willow Palisade
- Grand Canal

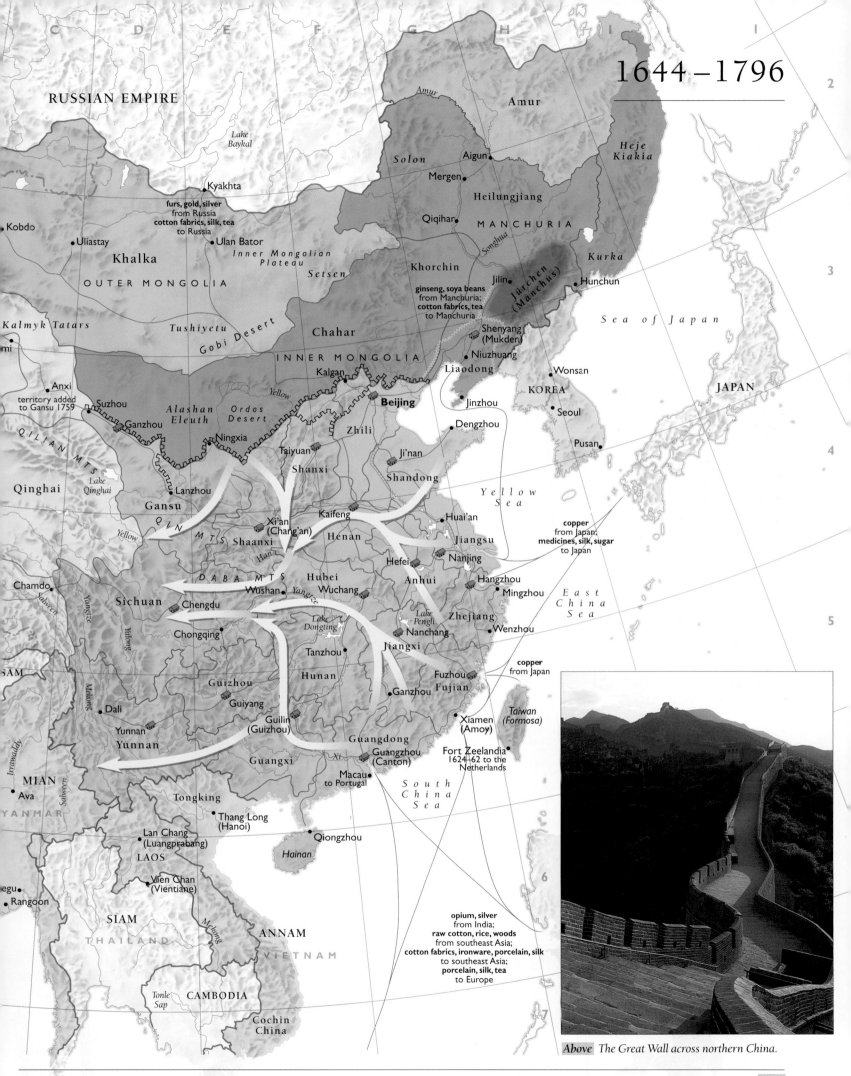

RUSSIAN EMPIRE

Amur

Amur

Lake Baykal

Heje Kiakia

• Kyakhta

furs, gold, silver
from Russia
cotton fabrics, silk, tea
to Russia

• Kobdo

• Solon

Aigun •

Mergen •

Heilungjiang

• Uliastay

Qiqihar •

MANCHURIA

Ulan Bator •

Inner Mongolian Plateau

Setsen

Khalka

OUTER MONGOLIA

Khorchin

Songhua

Kurka

• Jilin

Jürchen (Manchus)

Hunchun •

Kalmyk Tatars

Tushiyetu

Chahar

ginseng, soya beans
from Manchuria;
cotton fabrics, tea
to Manchuria

Sea of Japan

mi

Gobi Desert

INNER MONGOLIA

Shenyang (Mukden) •

• Niuzhuang

• Anxi

Kalgan •

Liaodong

• Wonsan

KOREA

JAPAN

territory added
to Gansu 1759

Suzhou •

Alashan Eleuth

Ordos Desert

Beijing

• Jinzhou

Seoul •

Ganzhou •

Yellow

Zhili

• Pusan

QILIAN MTS

Ningxia •

Taiyuan •

• Dengzhou

Qinghai

Lake Qinghai

• Lanzhou

Shanxi

• Ji'nan

Shandong

Yellow Sea

copper
from Japan;
medicines, silk, sugar
to Japan

Gansu

QIN MTS

Xi'an (Chang'an) •

Kaifeng •

Henan

• Huai'an

Yellow

Shaanxi

Han

Jiangsu

DABA MTS

Hubei

Hefei •

Nanjing •

Chamdo •

Salween

Wushan •

Wuchang •

Yangtze

Anhui

• Hangzhou

East China Sea

Sichuan

Chengdu •

• Mingzhou

Chongqing •

Ydlong

Lake Dongting

Lake Pengli

Zhejiang

Yangtze

Nanchang •

• Wenzhou

SAM

Mekong

Tanzhou •

Jiangxi

copper
from Japan

Hunan

Fuzhou •

Fujian

Guizhou

Taiwan (Formosa)

Guiyang •

• Ganzhou

• Dali

Guilin (Guizhou) •

Yunnan

• Xiamen (Amoy)

Yunnan

Guangdong

Fort Zeelandia
1624–62 to the
Netherlands

Irrawaddy

Guangxi

Xi

Guangzhou (Canton) •

MIAN

• Ava

Macau
to Portugal

South China Sea

YANMAR

Salween

Tongking

Lan Chang (Luangprabang) •

Thang Long (Hanoi) •

LAOS

• Qiongzhou

Hainan

Vien Chan (Vientiane) •

egu

• Rangoon

SIAM

Mekong

ANNAM

opium, silver
from India;
raw cotton, rice, woods
from southeast Asia;
cotton fabrics, ironware, porcelain, silk
to southeast Asia;
porcelain, silk, tea
to Europe

THAILAND

VIETNAM

Tonle Sap

CAMBODIA

Cochin China

Above *The Great Wall across northern China.*

there. Once firmly established in power, the Qing set about the conquest of Mongolia, Turkestan, and Tibet. Qing expansionism made China a greater territorial power in east Asia than at any previous period in its history. Neighboring states such as Ladakh, Nepal, Bhutan, Laos, Burma, and Annam (Vietnam) were forced to make regular payments of tribute. Military protectorates in the northeast ended Russian expansion into Central Asia.

STABILITY & GROWTH

After a five-year uprising was put down in 1681, China enjoyed more than a century of peace and stability under Qing rule. The most obvious change they introduced was the custom of wearing the hair in a queue, or single braid, in the traditional Manchu style; they showed their authority by making their Chinese (Han) subjects wear the same. Manchus were not allowed to marry Chinese. The only occupations open to them were the army and civil service.

The Manchus brought new efficiency to Chinese military and political life, but did not attempt to reform the thousand-year-old system of administration. In all but

the most senior posts, civil servants and soldiers continued to be drawn from the landowning class, who were recruited for their knowledge of ancient Chinese classics rather than their demonstration of practical skills. Peasant revolts during the late Ming period had virtually ended serfdom, but millions of tenant farmers lived at subsistence level. They could not afford the education to enter the imperial bureaucracy, but carried most of the tax burden.

Between 1650 and 1800 the population rose from 100 million to 300 million. The agricultural heartlands of the Yangtze basin and southeast were by now overpopulated, and this forced large numbers of peasants to migrate. The Qing forbade Han Chinese to settle in the Manchu homelands north of the Great Wall, so movement was principally to the less crowded western provinces.

WIDER CONTACTS

While the Qing pursued their expansionist policies in Asia, they showed as little interest in trading on equal terms with Europe as their Ming predecessors had. As long as the Chinese economy was self-

Left *The emperor Qianlong (r.1735–96) had the longest reign in Chinese history. Highly educated and a patron of the arts, he regarded China as the only powerful and civilized country in the world. He declined the innovations of the west, while appreciating its technical skills.*

Right *A Chinese 17th-century lacquer screen decorated with pictures of Portuguese ships and sailors. All Europeans were known as "foreign devils" because they wore trousers. This form of apparel was traditionally worn by the actors playing demons in the Chinese theater, but was otherwise unknown.*

BEIJING: NORTHERN CAPITAL

Beijing had been a frontier town for centuries before the Mongol leader, Kublai Khan, founder of the Yuan dynasty, made it his capital in 1267 and gave it its present name, which means "northern capital." It has remained China's capital ever since, with two brief interruptions when Nanjing was used: from 1368–1421 by the Ming; and from 1929–49 by the nationalist Kuomintang government.

The buildings seen today were mostly constructed under the Ming and Qing. As the capital grew under the Ming, they built

Left *A lion guards the Forbidden City, Beijing.*

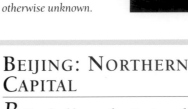

sufficient and bolstered by the payment of tribute from its weaker neighbors, it had little incentive to trade abroad. China was the world's most advanced civilization; westerners were regarded as barbarians who had nothing to offer by way of material goods or technological knowledge, though there was a thriving trade in furs from Russia through the Mongolian trading city of Kyakhta.

Seventeenth-century Europe saw a growing fashion for all things Chinese, particularly porcelain, cotton, silks, and tea. As European traders had nothing the Chinese wanted to buy, they paid for their exports with New World silver, which proved very expensive. All European trade was restricted to the port of Guangzhou (Canton) in the south. Jesuit priests were also active in China during the 17th century. They were tolerated for their knowledge of physics and astronomy—though these were considered amusing trifles—but won few converts. Christianity was later banned because it conflicted with ancestor worship.

CHINA'S SWIFT DECLINE

In 1793, the emperor Qianlong (r.1735–96) snubbed a British trade delegation. Its leader, Lord Macartney, had refused to prostrate himself in the traditional kowtow, or deferential bow, to the emperor, but this was probably just a pretext for breaking off relations. Notes taken by the delegation of Chinese methods of silk and tea production were passed to the British East India Company, which quickly set up in competition to the Chinese. At the end of Qianlong's reign there were obvious signs of Chinese decline. The civil service had become corrupt, and tax increases provoked a new wave of peasant rebellions. European technological superiority was becoming obvious even to the Qing court, but it was too conservative to contemplate modernization. By the mid 19th century, as China came closer to collapse, the west was able to impose its own terms for trade.

Right Fishermen using cormorants for catching fish on the Yangtze river.

---

a new wall to enclose Kublai Khan's original walled city. Imposing gates marked the entrance at each wall. The new outer city became Beijing's thriving commercial and residential district, while the old inner city of the Mongols became the Imperial City, the heart of the Chinese bureaucracy. Within the Imperial City, behind yet another wall, lay the Forbidden City, the compound of private palaces and gardens where the imperial family lived. Beijing escaped destruction in the wars of the early 20th century, and today the Forbidden City, which is not used by the Communist government, is open to the public as a museum.

TIMETABLE

1421
The Ming capital is transferred from Nanjing to Beijing

1556
The worst earthquake in Chinese history kills over 850,000 people

1557
A permanent Portuguese trading base is established at Macau

1644
The Ming dynasty is overthrown in a civil war; the Manchus capture Beijing

1674–81
The Qing suppress a rebellion in south China

1689
The Russians withdraw from the northern province of Amur in exchange for trading rights in China

1697
Mongolia is occupied by Chinese troops

1723
Christianity is banned in China

1751
Chinese invade Tibet and establish control over the succession of the Dalai Lama

1757
Foreign traders are restricted to the port of Guangzhou

1793
The emperor Qianlong snubs a British trade mission led by Lord Macartney

1796
Peasant rebellions break out on the death of Qianlong

THE EMERGENCE OF AFRICA

ALTHOUGH THE ARRIVAL OF EUROPEAN TRADERS HAD GROWING CONSEQUENCES FOR AFRICAN SOCIETIES AND CULTURE IN THE CENTURIES AFTER 1500, THEIR INFLUENCE DID NOT EXTEND EVERYWHERE IN THE CONTINENT AND SEVERAL IMPORTANT INDIGENOUS AFRICAN STATES EMERGED DURING THIS PERIOD. ELSEWHERE, THE MASS TRANSPORTATION OF AFRICANS TO THE AMERICAS, IN CONDITIONS OF GREAT CRUELTY, HAD DEVASTATING IMPACT. BY THE TIME THE SLAVE TRADE WAS ABOLISHED IN THE 1800S, SOME 10–15 MILLION PEOPLE HAD BEEN SHIPPED FROM AFRICA TO PLANTATIONS IN THE NEW WORLD.

Left An ivory mask from the west African state of Benin.

Trade in gold and ivory, rather than conquest, was the aim of the Portuguese who first began to build fortified bases around the African coast in the late 15th century. Soon slaves were also being traded from Africa and exported as forced labor to the plantations of Brazil and the Caribbean (see pages 122–125). Dutch, French, and English traders founded bases alongside the Portuguese, attracted by the profitable trade in human lives. Their arrival had considerable impact in some areas, disrupting existing patterns of trade and cultural exchange. The creation of new coastal networks for trade in west Africa drew commerce away from the wealthy trading kingdoms of the upper Niger. The powerful Songhai empire, which controlled the trade routes across the western Sahara, began to decline in the 16th century and was overthrown by a Moroccan army in 1591, which established a governorship in the region. The successor states of Segu and Kaarta were never able to match Songhai's former influence.

A number of small states, such as the Mossi, Oyo, and Benin, emerged in equatorial west Africa during the 16th and 17th centuries. Asante and Dahomey, dominating the coast, had become powerful and well-organized centralized kingdoms by the late 18th century, partly as a result of their involvement in the the slave trade.

South of the Equator, Portuguese traders exploited rivalry between the kingdoms of Congo and Ndongo to establish a colony at Luanda (Angola) by 1575. Njinga, queen of the Ndongo (r.1624–63), fought a long war to stop Portuguese slavers from extending their activities, but was forced to submit.

The Portuguese founded a string of bases on the east coast of Africa to dominate the Indian Ocean trade. Their presence upset the existing balance of power. Mwenemutapa, the most powerful state of southern Africa in the 16th century, asked the Portuguese for help in suppressing a rebellion, but found itself unable to resist their extortionate demands for trade and mining privileges. By the 1630s it had become a puppet state, and was later eclipsed by the neighboring kingdom of Rozwi.

ISLAMIC STATES

Many parts of Africa were unaffected by the presence of European traders, and several important African states emerged at this time that owed nothing to their influence. Kanem-Bornu, on the southern edge of the Sahara, was the leading Islamic state in Africa and built up its power by importing firearms from the Ottomans. Farther to

Below A camel caravan crosses the western Sahara from Morocco. By the 16th century this route was declining in importance.

1508–1807

Mediterranean Sea

MOROCCO
ALGIERS
Tunis semi-independent
Cyrenaica semi-independent
Tripoli semi-independent

LIBYA

SAHARA DESERT

TIBESTI MASSIF

Ghat
Murzuq
Al Kufrah
to the Middle East

Alexandria
Egypt
Asyut
El Kharga
Aswan
Selima
Red Sea

Medina
Jiddah
Mecca
BAHRAIN
QATAR
SAUDI ARABIA
ARABIA

MALI
Gao
SONGHAI
NIGER
AIR
Agadez

Timbuktu
SEGU
né

MOSSI STATES
Say
Ouagadougou

KONG EMPIRE
Kong

ASANTE
Kumasi
Axim
Accra
Ouidah
Elmina
to the Netherlands
DAHOMEY
Lagos
Porto Novo
OLD OYO
YORUBA STATES
BENIN
Benin
Brass
Bonny
Old Calabar
IGBO

HAUSA STATES
Kano

KANEM-BORNU
Ngarzagamu
Lake Chad

BAGIRMI
Biddefi

WADAI
Wara

DARFUR
El Fasher

SUDAN

CHAD
Ain Galakka
Sherda
Bilma

FUNJ
Dongola
Suakin
Sennar
Blue Nile
Gondar
Axum
ETHIOPIA
AWSA
Awsa

Massawa
YEMEN
Aden
Saylac
Berbera

Harer
SOMALIA

CENTRAL AFRICAN REPUBLIC

NIGERIA
CAMEROON

Fernando Póo to Spain
Príncipe to Portugal
São Tomé to Portugal
Annobón to Spain

BOBANGI
Ubangi

CONGO BASIN
Congo
GABON
CONGO (RO)
CONGO (DRO)
MPUMBU

LOANGO
KAKONGO
TEKE
NGOYO
Loango
Malembo
to Brazil
Cabinda
CONGO

Kasai
KUBA
Lomami
Lualaba

NDONGO
Luanda
to Brazil
KASANJE
MBUNDU
LUNDA
LUBA

OROMO
ETHIOPIA
Shebelle
RIFT VALLEY

UGANDA
Lake Turkana
KENYA

Lake Victoria

RIFT VALLEY STATES
Ujiji
Tabora
TANZANIA
Lake Tanganyika
RIFT VALLEY

SULTANATE OF ZANZIBAR
Lamu
Malindi
Mombasa
Zanzibar
Kilwa Kisiwani
Indian traders

Mogadishu
Baraawe

INDIAN OCEAN

Portuguese traders

OVIMBUNDU
Benguela
to Brazil
ANGOLA

Ibo
MAKUA
Mozambique

Vohémar

Tananarive
Madagascar

Cuanza
Cuango

Okavango
NAMIBIA
Cuando
LOZI
Kafue
ZAMBIA
Zambezi
Luangwa

ZIMBABWE
ROZWI
Khami

BOTSWANA

Namib Desert

Tete
Sena
Quelimane
Sofala
Inhambane
Delagoa Bay

Fort Dauphin
to France

Kalahari Desert
SOUTH AFRICA
Limpopo
Vaal
Orange

CAPE COLONY
Cape Town
to Brazil

Africa in the late 18th century

- state important as a slave source
- other African state
- under Dutch control
- under Ottoman control
- under Portuguese control

→ Moroccan conquest, 1543–91
→ slave trade route
👤 slave depot
🌴 oasis
— trade route
— approximate border of state or composite state, late 18th century (where known)

0   800 km
0   600 mi

B   C   D   E   F   G   H   I

2

3

4

5

6

7

the east, Islam and Christianity came into direct conflict, mainly because of the survival of the ancient Christian kingdom of Ethiopia. Adal, an alliance of Islamic states in neighboring Somalia, attempted to conquer Ethiopia in 1527 under the leadership of Ahmed Gran, an *imam*, who declared the campaign a *jihad* (holy war). Fighting lasted until 1543, when a small Portuguese force came to Ethiopia's aid. The invasion was repelled, and Gran was killed in battle.

RISE & FALL OF SLAVERY

In the early 1500s only about 2,000 slaves were annually exported out of Africa, but by 1680 this figure had risen to 10,000. At the peak of the trade, in the second half of the 18th century, as many as 100,000 men, women, and children were shipped to the Americas in a single year. By this time, British shipping and commercial interests controlled the slave trade into the Caribbean (slaves for Brazil were supplied by the Portuguese from Angola). Ships voyaged to west Africa from Bristol, Liverpool, and London to exchange firearms, textiles, liquor, and other goods for slaves before sailing on to the Caribbean. Here the slaves were sold for rum and molasses for the return journey, or shipped on to North America, where they were exchanged for cargoes of tobacco, timber, and other raw materials. The entire round trip became known as the "Triangular Trade." The second stage, in which the human cargo from Africa was shipped across the Atlantic, was simply called the "Middle Passage."

The transatlantic slave trade, carried out in conditions of the utmost inhumanity, inflicted appalling human misery. It caused enormous social disruption in the worst exploited areas of west and central Africa. Europeans did not take part in slave raids themselves but bought them from African traders. A kingdom could become wealthy through slavery but could only meet the demand for ever more slaves by constant attacks on its neighbors. Sometimes rulers even sold some of their own people, such as criminals, into slavery.

Some people, such as the Quakers, were always opposed to slavery. During the 18th-century, opinion against it spread further

THE TRIANGULAR SLAVE TRADE

→ British trade in the North Atlantic, 18th century

iron commodity traded

NORTH ATLANTIC OCEAN

Liverpool
Bristol

tobacco, timber, fish, furs

New York
Boston

NORTH AMERICA

molasses, rum, sugar

mahogany,

Charleston

fruit, mahogany, molasses, rum, sugar

slaves, mahogany, molasses

iron, firearms, rum

firearms, textiles and manufactured goods

Kingston

AFRICA

Fort James

slaves, gold, pepper

Lagos
Brass

SOUTH AMERICA

SOUTH ATLANTIC OCEAN

Right Conditions on the Middle Passage were appalling. The slaves were chained and crammed in their hundreds below decks with barely enough room for them to lie down. Food and water were in short supply, and sanitation non-existent; many slaves died of disease before reaching the Americas. Most who survived could expect only brutal treatment and a short life on the plantations. This picture of captives on board a slaver was painted by an officer of a British anti-slavery patrol that intercepted the ship in 1840.

THE ROYAL BRONZES OF BENIN

The forest societies around the Niger delta developed the technique of bronze casting between the late 12th and 14th centuries. The raw materials were bars of copper alloy imported from the interior. When the Portuguese came to the area in the 1480s, they brought brass bracelets as trade goods, which were melted down and recast. One of the most prolific centers of bronze casting was the court of Benin. Unique to Benin are highly crafted decorative plaques, which are thought to be imitations of illustrations in Portuguese books. They were fixed to the pillars of ceremonial buildings: a 17th-century Dutch traveler to the kingdom of Benin described the king's palace as having "wooden pillars encased in copper, where their victories are depicted."

Above *Benin plaque of a Portuguese soldier.*

with the development of libertarian ideals, but abolitionists faced enormous resistance from commercial interests. Participation in the slave trade was outlawed by Britain in 1807 and the United States in 1808. However, slave-owning was allowed in British colonies until 1833, French colonies until 1848, and in the United States until 1865. The Portuguese did not ban the slave trade in their colonies until the 1880s.

In 1787 British philanthropists bought an area of land on the west coast of Africa to found a settlement for freed and runaway slaves, which became the colony of Sierra Leone. In 1816 Liberia was founded in an region to the south as a colony for former slaves from the southern United States.

THE FIRST COLONY

The largest concentration of Europeans in Africa, numbering some 15,000 by 1800, was at Cape Colony, in south Africa, founded in 1652 by the Dutch East India Company as a stopping point for its ships on the long voyage to the East Indies. It had a Mediterranean climate and good land, and soon grew into a thriving colony. As well as Dutch settlers, it attracted large numbers of French Huguenots. In 1814 it was ceded permanently to Britain by the Dutch.

TIMETABLE

1529
Songhai empire dominates west Africa

1531–32
The Portuguese build fortresses at Sena and Tete on the Zambezi River

1543
Portuguese help the Ethiopians defeat a Muslim invasion by Ahmed Gran of Adal

1570
Idris III Aloma establishes Kanem-Bornu as the greatest power between the Nile and the Niger

1575
The Portuguese settlement of Angola begins at Luanda

1591
A Moroccan army overthrows the empire of Songhai

1633
Uprising by empire of Mwenemutapa against the Portuguese is suppressed

1652
Cape Town is founded by Dutchman Jan van Riebeeck

1698
The sultan of Oman establishes a sultanate at Zanzibar to dominate east African coastal trade

1713
British slave trade to Spanish America begins

1724
Dahomey grows in power as a partner of European slave traders

1780
Transatlantic slave trade at its peak

1787
British settle 400 freed slaves in Sierra Leone

1795
Great Britain seizes Cape Town from the Netherlands

1808
The United States bans further shipments of slaves from Africa

1816
The American Colonization Society begins the "Liberia Project" to provide a home for freed slaves

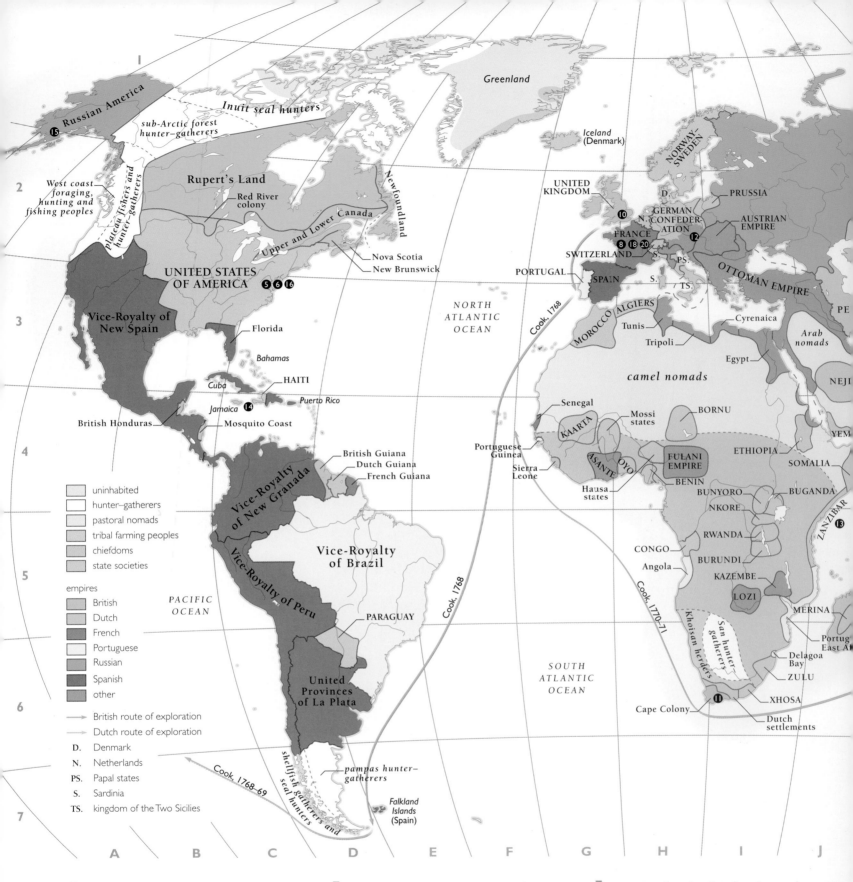

Greenland

Russian America

15

Inuit seal hunters

sub-Arctic forest hunter–gatherers

Iceland (Denmark)

NORWAY-SWEDEN

UNITED KINGDOM

10

D.

GERMAN N. CONFEDER-ATION

PRUSSIA

AUSTRIAN EMPIRE

12

Rupert's Land

Red River colony

Newfoundland

West coast foraging, hunting and fishing peoples

plateau fishers and hunter–gatherers

Upper and Lower Canada

FRANCE

8 **18** **20**

SWITZERLAND

S.

PS.

S.

TS.

OTTOMAN EMPIRE

PE

Nova Scotia

New Brunswick

PORTUGAL

SPAIN

UNITED STATES OF AMERICA

5 **6** **16**

NORTH ATLANTIC OCEAN

Cook, 1768

MOROCCO ALGIERS

Tunis

Tripoli

Cyrenaica

Arab nomads

Vice-Royalty of New Spain

Florida

Egypt

YEM

Bahamas

Cuba

HAITI

camel nomads

Senegal

Mossi states

BORNU

NEJI

Puerto Rico

Jamaica

14

KAARTA

Portuguese Guinea

Sierra Leone

Hausa states

ASANTE OYO

FULANI EMPIRE

BENIN

ETHIOPIA

SOMALIA

British Honduras

Mosquito Coast

British Guiana

Dutch Guiana

French Guiana

BUNYORO

NKORE

BUGANDA

ZANZIBAR

13

uninhabited

hunter–gatherers

pastoral nomads

tribal farming peoples

chiefdoms

state societies

Vice-Royalty of New Granada

CONGO

RWANDA

BURUNDI

Angola

KAZEMBE

Vice-Royalty of Brazil

Vice-Royalty of Peru

PACIFIC OCEAN

LOZI

MERINA

empires

British

Dutch

French

Portuguese

Russian

Spanish

other

Cook, 1768

Cook, 1770–71

Khoisan herders

San hunter gatherers

Portug East A

PARAGUAY

SOUTH ATLANTIC OCEAN

Delagoa Bay

ZULU

→ British route of exploration

→ Dutch route of exploration

D.   Denmark

N.   Netherlands

PS. Papal states

S.   Sardinia

TS. kingdom of the Two Sicilies

United Provinces of La Plata

Cape Colony

11

XHOSA

Dutch settlements

Cook, 1768–69

shellfish gatherers and seal hunters

pampas hunter–gatherers

Falkland Islands (Spain)

A   B   C   D   E   F   G   H   I   J

1 1557 The Portuguese establish a trading base at Macau, China

2 1596 The first Dutch trading expedition reaches the East Indies

3 1603 The Tokugawa shogunate is established in Japan with its capital at Edo (Tokyo)

4 1615 The Manchus begin the conquest of the ailing Ming empire

5 1620 The Pilgrims land at Cape Cod, Massachusetts

6 1626 The Dutch found the colony of New Amsterdam (New York)

7 1632 Shah Jahan begins the Mughal conquest of the Deccan (central India)

8 1638 Birth of Louis XIV of France; he succeeds to the throne in 1643, at the age 5

9 1638 The Japanese close their ports to foreign traders

10 1649 King Charles I of England is found guilty of high treason and executed

11 1652 Dutch settlers found a colony at the Cape of Good Hope, South Africa

12 1683 An army led by John Sobieski, king of Poland, defeats the Ottomans outside Vienna

13 1698 The Omanis drive the Portuguese from Mombasa and set up the Zanzibar sultanate

14 1713 Britain takes over control of the African slave trade to the Caribbean from the Spanish

15 1784 Russian fur traders found a settlement in Alaska

THE WORLD BY 1815

BY 1815 THE EUROPEAN AGE OF DISCOVERY WAS
COMING TO AN END. EXPLORATION OF THE PACIFIC HAD
ADDED AUSTRALIA AND ANTARCTICA TO THE KNOWN
WORLD. HOWEVER, WHILE EUROPEAN COLONIZATION
HAD HAD GREAT IMPACT IN SOME PLACES, MUCH OF THE
WORLD WAS STILL UNAWARE OF OR UNAFFECTED BY
EUROPE. CHINA, THE WORLD'S LARGEST EMPIRE, HAD
DISTANCED ITSELF FROM CONTACT WITH THE WEST.

In 1492, the year that Columbus landed in the New World,
Europe had occupied a fairly inconsequential position on the world
stage. China was far advanced in technological skills, and it was
reaching heights of prosperity and stability under the Ming. Asia's
Islamic empires controlled international trade. Europe was unable
to match the military and naval strength of the Ottoman empire.
Over the next three hundred years, the European pursuit of wealth
and territory had established colonies in every continent of the
world. Their empire-building had had enormous impact on indigenous populations: in the Americas, thousands had been killed
by war and disease, or displaced from their traditional
lands. Millions of Africans had been enslaved and
shipped across the Atlantic to provide labor
on European plantations.

However, in 1815, European power
was by no means global. Colonial
settlement in Australia and
Africa was limited to small
coastal areas; their vast
interiors remained unex-
plored. Through its con-
trol of trade in east Africa,
the sultanate of Oman had
greater territorial influence
in Africa than the combined

Map labels

RUSSIAN EMPIRE

Central Asian khanates

MANCHU EMPIRE

Ainu hunter–gatherers

AFGHANISTAN

KOREA   JAPAN

Indian princely states

NEPAL   BHUTAN

India

BURMA

Taiwan

OMAN

LAOS

ARAKAN

ANNAM

Goa

SIAM

Philippine Islands

CAMBODIA

COCHIN CHINA

KANDY   Ceylon

ACEH   Malay states

Celebes

Borneo

Dutch East Indies

New Guinea

Papuan farmers

Solomon Islands

Sumatra

Melanesians

Tasman, 1642–43

Java

Timor

Cook, 1770

New Hebrides

Fiji Islands

Tasman, 1642–43

Mauritius (Britain)

Cook, 1770

INDIAN OCEAN

Australian Aboriginal hunter–gatherers

New South Wales

New Caledonia

Tasman, 1642–43

Van Diemen's Land

Cook, 1769–70

Polynesians

Bay of Islands

Cook, 1769

Maori chiefdoms

L   M   N   O   P

Timeline

⑯ 1776 The American colonies declare their independence from Britain

⑰ 1788 Britain founds a penal colony at Port Jackson (now Sydney), Australia

⑱ 1789 The French Revolution begins

⑲ 1796 The emperor Qianlong abdicates in China in order not to rule longer than his grandfather

⑳ 1815 Napoleon is defeated at Waterloo; the Congress of Vienna redraws the map of Europe

Right A 19th-century
European's impression
of a Tasmanian
Aborigine. Australia
was the last frontier of
European colonization.

presence of European traders. The Chinese empire, the most populous in the world, was greater in size than at any previous time in history and had extended its influence far into southeast Asia. Although the military strength of the Ottoman empire was in decline, it was still a major territorial power in the Middle East and southern Europe.

By 1815, however, Europeans controlled the sea routes that acted as arteries for trade between the continents. Western traders were no longer reliant on overland caravan routes and Islamic middlemen. Until the 19th century, European goods had little allure for Indian and Chinese merchants, so silver and gold from the New World was used to buy the spices, cottons, silks, and porcelain that were so highly valued in the west. To facilitate this trade, European traders—especially Portuguese, Dutch, and British—had established permanent bases in Asia. In time, in southeast Asia and India, native traders were forced out of business and the European trading companies became territorial powers in their own right. A new global economy had come into being, from which the nations of the west derived almost exclusive benefits.

EUROPE

Rivalry between the colonizing European nations was fierce, and by the end of the 18th century, dynastic and trade wars had come to replace the religious conflicts that had divided post-Reformation Europe. The

18th century saw a series of conflicts in Europe that spilled over into the colonies, especially North America. The French Revolution (1789) had plunged the continent into war, but Napoleon's defeat in 1815 saw a new balance of power emerging. The kingdom of Prussia was set to dominate European politics in the coming century. Russia, which had begun to modernize its feudal society in the early 18th century, continued to advance its borders in Asia and eastern Europe. Britain's naval strength and technical advances had made it the world's greatest manufacturing and trading power.

THE AMERICAS

The rising power in the Americas was the United States. Since winning its independence from Britain in 1783 it had doubled in size with the purchase of Louisiana from France (1803). The War of 1812, fought over British restrictions on U.S. shipping, had heightened national pride and identity. As European settlers in the United States spread into the interior, Native Americans were pushed farther west into unsettled territory. In Central and South America, growing demands for independence, inspired by the American revolution and by Napoleon's occupation of Spain, had seen revolts break out against Spanish rule in Mexico (1810), Paraguay (1811), and Venezuela (1810–12). Haiti was the only island in the Caribbean to have won its independence, from France, after a slave revolt (1804).

THE MIDDLE EAST

During the 18th century Ottoman power weakened in the Middle East and North Africa, with outlying states such as Tunis, Tripoli, Qatar, and Oman (which controlled trade with east Africa) declaring their independence. In Egypt, Mehmet Ali, an Albanian, succeeded in making himself viceroy in 1805. A dynamic, modernizing ruler, he helped to expel the fanatical Wahhabi sect from its control of the holy cities of Mecca and Medina, but became increasingly independent of the sultan. Despite signs of decline, however, the Ottoman empire was to survive for another century: it still controlled the Balkans from Greece to Romania, and Turkey, Syria, and Mesopotamia. Since the conquests of Nadir Shah's reign

Left Britain's early lead in the textile industry propelled it to a commanding position in the global economy. Mechanized production began to replace traditional hand-crafting and Britain sought a larger market overseas for its manufactured goods. Seen here is Arkwright's spinning frame (1769).

Above With the establishment of overseas empires, wars between European powers took on a global aspect. In 1798 Napoleon invaded Egypt to try to cut off Britain's sea route to India, fast becoming its most important colony. His plan failed when the French fleet was defeated by the British in 1798 and its army was beaten in 1801.

(1736–47) Persia had become a cultural backwater and would find itself squeezed between the territorial ambitions of Russia in central Asia and British power in India.

EAST & SOUTH ASIA

Under the Qing dynasty, China had made great territorial gains during the 18th century. The emperor Qianlong (r. 1736–96) had shunned the technical innovations of the west and successfully forced restrictions on foreign merchants, but his successors were unable to match his skills. Japan had deliberately closed its doors to European trade since the 17th century, and the mainland states of southeast Asia such as Burma and

Siam (Thailand) also resisted the incursions of the west. The Dutch had established a commercial empire in the spice islands of southeast Asia (the Dutch East Indies) in the 17th century, but by 1815 had lost their monopolies in the face of strong competition from British, French, American, and Chinese trade. The British had taken advantage of the decline of the Mughal empire in India to become the ruling power there.

THE SOUTH PACIFIC

Parts of the Australian and New Zealand coastlines were first charted in the 17th century by Dutch mariners from the East Indies, but no attempt was made to settle

there until late in the 18th century, after Captain Cook, on his first Pacific voyage (1769–71), had claimed both for the British crown. The British government decided to found a convict colony in Australia: the first shiploads arrived in 1788. The Aboriginal population, which had inhabited Australia for at least 40,000 years, probably numbered around 300,000. European contact had catastrophic consequences. As many as 20,000 Aborigines may have been killed in early conflicts with settlers; others died in epidemics. As white settlement expanded, those living along the coasts were dispossessed of their lands and driven into the interior, where fierce intertribal conflicts developed. Their culture was destroyed.

THE MODERN WORLD

The 19th and 20th centuries have seen unprecedented global change. In 1815, it would have taken several months for a message to travel from St. Petersburg to Washington or from London to Sydney, Australia. By 1900, the telegraph and radio had reduced this interval to minutes; today we have instant access via the internet to information anywhere on Earth. Improvements in communications began in the 19th century with the coming of steamships and locomotives. In the same period, European rule extended over much of the globe. In 1914 the British empire covered one-fifth of the world's land surface and ruled one-quarter of its people.

European and U.S. financial investment extended into Russia, China, and Japan, and throughout Latin America. The creation of a truly global economy, industrial labor markets, and cheap modes of travel gave rise to some of the largest migrations of people in world history. Between 1815 and 1914, in excess of 40 million people left Europe to settle in the United States, South America, Canada, South Africa, Australia, and New Zealand. Millions of Asians also migrated around the globe in search of work.

The 20th century has seen more conflict than any other in history. Two world wars, revolutions, independence wars, border conflicts, and civil wars have cost millions of lives. Millions more have been killed or injured by the oppressive actions of their own governments, for example in Stalinist Russia, Nazi Germany, by Communist regimes in East Asia, and military dictators in Africa and Latin America. In the second half of the century, the Cold War between the United States and the Soviet Union, in which both sides built up huge arsenals of nuclear weapons, dominated global affairs. This came to end in 1991, following the collapse of Communism and the break up of the Soviet Union.

Huge technological and medical advances saw standards of living rise for most people in North America, Western Europe, Australia, New Zealand, Japan, and the countries of the Pacific rim. But the gap between the rich and poor regions of the world grew ever wider as developing countries in Africa, Asia, and Latin America struggled with problems of debt, starvation, and environmental degradation. In the course of the 20th century the human population increased from about 1.5 billion to almost 6 billion. Industrial pollution, overcrowded cities, and increasing demands on natural resources raised environmental issues of urgent concern.

Left The business district of Hong Kong, 1998.

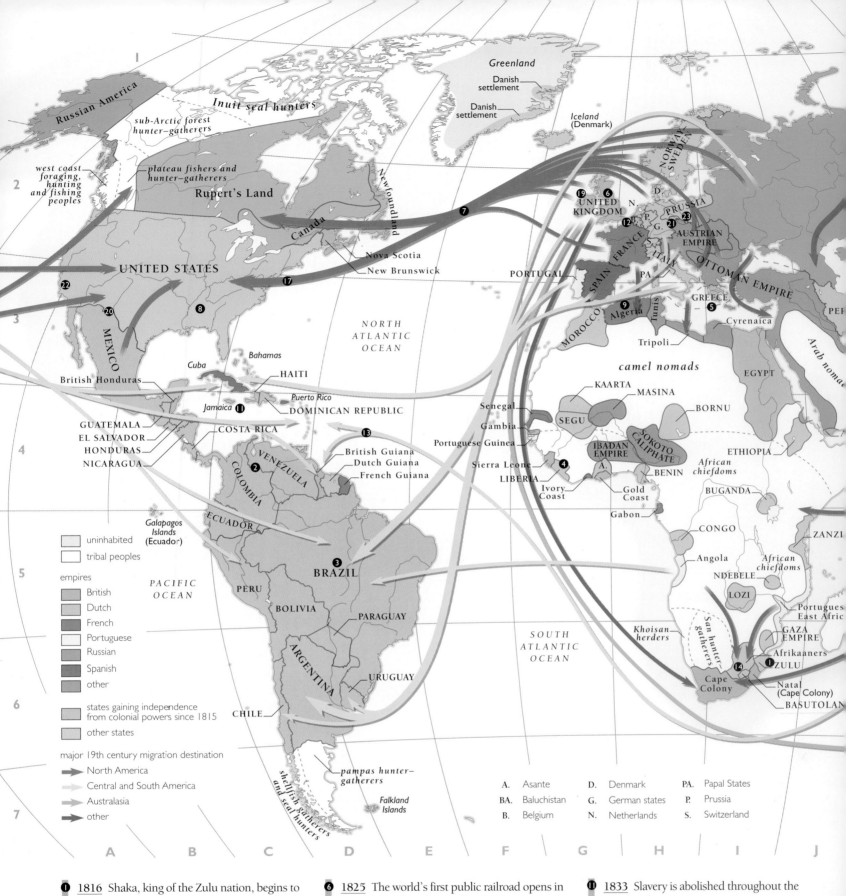

1 <u>1816</u> Shaka, king of the Zulu nation, begins to expand the Zulu empire in southern Africa

2 <u>1819</u> Simón Bolívar founds Republic of Gran Colombia (present-day Ecuador, Colombia, Venezuela, and Panama; disintegrates in 1830)

3 <u>1822</u> Brazil wins independence from Portugal

4 <u>1822</u> The colony of Liberia is founded for freed slaves from the United States

5 <u>1824–26</u> Greece wins independence from the Ottoman empire

6 <u>1825</u> The world's first public railroad opens in the industrial northeast of England

7 <u>1827</u> First steam-assisted crossing of the Atlantic (it took 29 days, most of it under sail)

8 <u>1830</u> Native Americans forced west on the "Trail of Tears"

9 <u>1830</u> France begins conquest of Algeria, not completed till 1847

10 <u>1830</u> Australian Aboriginals slaughtered by colonists on Van Diemen's Land

11 <u>1833</u> Slavery is abolished throughout the British colonies

12 <u>1830–33</u> Belgium becomes a sovereign state after fighting for freedom from Dutch rule

13 <u>1834</u> First Indian indentured laborers arrive in the Caribbean

14 <u>1835–37</u> Afrikaners begin the "Great Trek" from the Cape into the interior

15 <u>1839–42</u> First Opium War fought between Britain and China

THE WORLD BY 1850

THE EARLY 19TH CENTURY SAW RAPID INDUSTRIAL GROWTH IN THE WEST. EUROPE'S DOMINATION OF THE GLOBAL ECONOMY ENABLED IT TO EXPAND ITS COLONIAL EMPIRES: ONLY THE UNITED STATES AND JAPAN WERE UNAFFECTED. THE "SHRINKING" OF THE WORLD LED TO THE BIGGEST MIGRATIONS OF PEOPLE EVER RECORDED.

Enormous advances in transportation in the first half of the 19th century quickened the pace of communications around the globe. The first public railroad was inaugurated in Britain in 1825, and by the 1840s there was a regular steamship service across the Atlantic, with ships taking a little over 2 weeks to make the journey. As ocean travel became cheaper and quicker, more and more settlers began to make the journey from Europe to North America in search of better prospects. Many of the earliest immigrants were small farmers from Germany. One of the most tragic episodes was the arrival in Canada and the United States of thousands of victims of the famine that devastated Ireland (and large areas of eastern Europe) after the potato crop was destroyed by disease in 1845–47. Already starving and ill, very many of the immigrants did not survive the long Atlantic crossing in crowded, unsanitary ships.

The quickening pace of industrialization, coupled with changes in land use and farming practices, brought vast social upheaval to

Map labels

RUSSIAN EMPIRE

MANCHU EMPIRE

Ainu hunter-gatherers

KOREA

JAPAN

Central Asian khanates

AFGHANISTAN

KASHMIR

NEPAL

BHUTAN

BA.

Indian princely states

India

OMAN

Goa

BURMA

Macau (Portugal)

Hong Kong (Britain)

LAOS

ANNAM

Indian princely states

SIAM

Tenasserim

Ceylon

CAMBODIA

COCHIN CHINA

Philippine Islands

ACEH

Malay states

Celebes

Sumatra

Borneo

Singapore (Britain)

Dutch East Indies

New Guinea

Java

Timor

Papuan farmers

INDIAN OCEAN

Fiji Islands

New Hebrides

New Caledonia

Western Australia

New South Wales

South Australia

New Zealand

Van Diemen's Land

L M N O P

Below A contemporary cartoon shows King Frederick William IV of Prussia and his army commander shutting out liberal petitioners in 1849. Monarchs throughout Europe used force to suppress their subjects' growing calls for reform.

16 1840 Maoris cede sovereignty of New Zealand to Britain in Treaty of Waitangi

17 1840–50 First wave of mass immigration to the United States

18 1843–49 Britain annexes the provinces of Sind and the Punjab in India

19 1845–47 1 million perish in the Irish Potato Famine; a million more emigrate

20 1846–48 War between the United States and Mexico; much of the southwest is won

21 1848 Liberal and nationalist revolutions sweep across Europe

22 1849 California Gold Rush attracts settlers

23 1849 Frederick William IV of Prussia rejects offer of German imperial crown from Frankfurt National Assembly

24 1850 Taiping Rebellion begins in China against the Qing dynasty

25 1851 Discovery of gold in New South Wales boosts immigration to Australia

Europe in the early 19th century. Rural poverty and unemployment drew large numbers from the land to the factories. Great cities grew up around the new manufacturing centers, with overcrowded, squalid, and insanitary housing. Conditions of work were dangerous; wages low. Protesters were summarily dealt with; a revolt of weavers in Silesia, Germany, was brutally smashed by Prussian troops in 1844. Economic hardship forced growing numbers of people to seek a new life overseas, and the trickle of emigrants to North America became a flood. By the end of the century, most were from southern and eastern Europe. Immigrants from China and (later) Japan were drawn to the west coast by the lure of the Californian goldfields and construction of the transcontinental railroads.

EUROPEAN UNREST

Fear of political repression at home also led large numbers of people to flee Europe in the years before 1850. At the end of the Napoleonic wars, liberals and nationalists had hoped for the introduction of democratic systems of government, but the Congress of Vienna (1815) reinforced conservative rule by restoring monarchy throughout Europe. New crowns were created when Greece secured its independence from the moribund Ottoman empire (1824–26) and Belgium was proclaimed a sovereign state after rebelling against Dutch rule (1833).

European civil unrest peaked in 1848. A number of nationalist uprisings saw liberal administrations briefly installed in several countries, but within a year conservative forces had once again stamped their authority on Europe, with much bloodshed.

NEW NATIONS

As a result of the Napoleonic wars, Spain and Portugal lost their hold on their possessions in South America. The campaigns of Simón Bolívar (in the north) and José de San Martín (in the south) had seen most of the modern states of South America come into being. In Brazil, change came less violently, as the country proclaimed its independence in 1822 under the liberal emperor Pedro I, son of the king of Portugal. The United States was a

beneficiary of the collapse of Spain's American empire. In 1823, the Monroe Doctrine proclaimed the Americas a U.S. sphere of influence, warning off the European powers from interfering there.

Bolívar's vision of unity for the continent was never realized; tensions caused by debt and social inequality soon caused rifts within, and between, the new nations, many of which fell under the control of military dictators (*caudillos*). From the 1830s on, there was increasing immigration to South America from southern Europe. Over 3 million had settled in Brazil and 4.5 million (mostly Italians) in Argentina by the century's end.

THE RISE OF IMPERIALISM

Europe's colonial powers, Britain in particular, exploited their economic and technological advantage to extend their imperial interests throughout the world, especially Asia. In India, what had begun as a trading venture developed into full-fledged colonial rule ("Raj") as the British East India Company formed alliances with local rulers and introduced administrative and educational reforms in areas under their jurisdiction. To secure India's borders, the British began a series of invasions of Burma in 1824–25.

Insistent pressure by European traders in China to open up new markets prompted the Qing rulers to take renewed measures against foreigners. Yet this only made their crumbling empire prey to further incursions. Britain won control of Hong Kong in the First Opium War (1839–42) and forced five other "treaty ports" to be opened to foreign ships. By 1844, several more western nations had imposed humiliating "unequal treaties" on China, weakening the dynasty.

Above The California Gold Rush of 1848–49 attracted many new settlers to the American West. Later discoveries of gold in Australia and South Africa stimulated emigration there.

Below Burying victims of the Irish famine. The failure of the potato crop, the staple food of the poor, caused terrible starvation and resulted in mass emigration from Ireland.

Britain's establishment of a free port on the southeast Asian island of Singapore in 1819 allowed it to compete on equal terms with the Dutch for access to the region's rich resources. It soon became the leading commercial center of southeast Asia.

COLONIAL MIGRATION

By 1833 Britain had ended slavery in all its colonial possessions. As a result, new sources of labor were needed for sugar plantations in the Caribbean. This was met by importing indentured laborers from India: migrants were sent overseas for a fixed period for the price of their fare. They could rarely afford the ticket home at the end of the expiration of their contract, and worked for low wages in conditions little better than slavery. Later in the century, the system was extended to Fiji and east Africa.

Although Australia was originally founded as a penal settlement, by the 1840s large numbers of people were emigrating there from Britain's industrial cities. The flow rose sharply after the discovery of gold in New South Wales in 1851. The influx of settlers led to the decline of the Aboriginal population, already decimated by European diseases and the genocidal policies of the colonists, who considered the country *terra nullius*, or virgin land to be exploited at will. Tribes resisting European settlement were massacred or deported: "ethnic cleansing" of the Aboriginal population of Tasmania (then known as Van Diemen's Land) had brought about its almost total eradication by 1835. Land settlement schemes encouraged a steady flow of emigrants from Britain to New Zealand in the 1830s. The Treaty of Waitangi (1840), establishing British sovereignty over the islands, recognized native Maori land rights. However, its terms were ignored and violated by the white settlers from the outset, and there was sporadic warfare for the next 40 years.

CHANGES IN AFRICA

The French invasion of Algeria (1830) was a sign of growing European interest in the continent, but Islam remained the main influence north of the Equator, with powerful states like the Sokoto caliphate and Ibadan empire emerging south of the Sahara.

Despite international moves to ban it, the slave trade had not yet vanished from Africa. Arab traders were active all along the east coast, and the Portuguese were shipping slaves from Angola to the lucrative Brazilian market until late in the century.

In 1835, Dutch-origin settlers (Boers, or Afrikaners) left Cape Colony, under British rule since 1814, in protest at Britain's ban on slavery and journeyed northeast on the "Great Trek." As they moved inland, they met with fierce resistance from the Ndebele and Zulu nations but eventually succeeded in founding two republics, Transvaal and the Orange Free State.

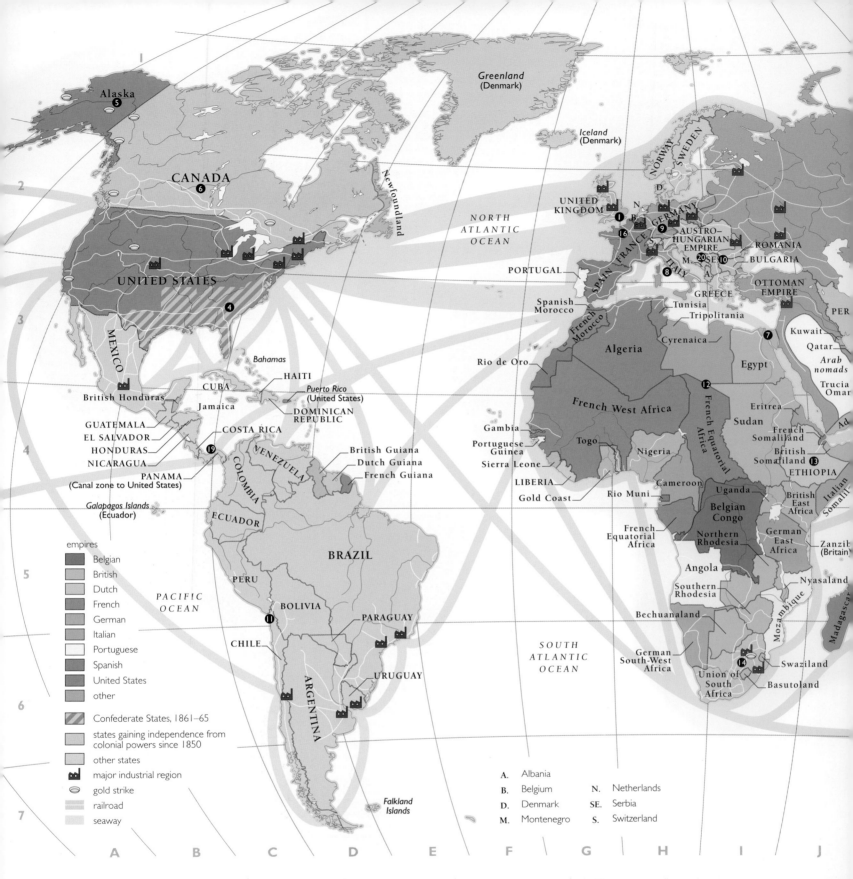

Alaska ⑤

Greenland (Denmark)

Iceland (Denmark)

NORWAY SWEDEN

CANADA ⑥

NORTH ATLANTIC OCEAN

UNITED KINGDOM ①

N
B
GERMANY ⑨
D
AUSTRO-HUNGARIAN EMPIRE
ROMANIA ⑬
FRANCE
S
A
M. ⑳ SE ⑩ BULGARIA
ITALY ⑧
SPAIN
PORTUGAL

GREECE
OTTOMAN EMPIRE

UNITED STATES

④

MEXICO

Spanish Morocco
French Morocco
Algeria
Tunisia
Tripolitania
Cyrenaica
Egypt
PER
⑦ Kuwait
Qatar
Arab nomads
Trucia Oman

Bahamas
HAITI
CUBA
Puerto Rico (United States)
DOMINICAN REPUBLIC
Jamaica

British Honduras
GUATEMALA
EL SALVADOR
HONDURAS
NICARAGUA
COSTA RICA
PANAMA (Canal zone to United States)
⑲

Rio de Oro
French West Africa
Gambia
Portuguese Guinea
Sierra Leone
LIBERIA
Gold Coast
Togo
Nigeria
Rio Muni
Cameroon

⑫
French Equatorial Africa
Sudan
Eritrea
French Somaliland
British Somaliland ⑬
ETHIOPIA
Italian Somali

VENEZUELA
British Guiana
Dutch Guiana
French Guiana

COLOMBIA
Galapagos Islands (Ecuador)
ECUADOR

BRAZIL

Uganda
Belgian Congo
Northern Rhodesia
German East Africa
Zanzibar (Britain)

PERU
⑪
BOLIVIA
PARAGUAY

French Equatorial Africa
Angola
Southern Rhodesia
Nyasaland
Mozambique
Madagascar

CHILE

PACIFIC OCEAN

SOUTH ATLANTIC OCEAN

Bechuanaland
German South-West Africa
⑭
Union of South Africa
Swaziland
Basutoland

URUGUAY
ARGENTINA

Falkland Islands

empires
Belgian
British
Dutch
French
German
Italian
Portuguese
Spanish
United States
other

Confederate States, 1861–65
states gaining independence from colonial powers since 1850
other states

major industrial region
gold strike
railroad
seaway

A. Albania
B. Belgium   N. Netherlands
D. Denmark   SE. Serbia
M. Montenegro   S. Switzerland

① 1851 The Great Exhibition, the world's first industrial exposition, is held in London

② 1853 U.S. Commodore Perry opens Japan to western trade

③ 1857–58 Indian Mutiny: Muslims and Hindu troops rebel against British rule

④ 1861–65 American civil war: Northern states fight to preserve the Union against the secessionist south

⑤ 1867 Russia sells Alaska to the United States

⑥ 1867 Canada becomes a self-governing Dominion of the British Empire

⑦ 1869 Suez canal opens, linking the Mediterranean to the Indian Ocean

⑧ 1870 Seizure of Rome completes Italian unification under Sardinia-Piedmont

⑨ 1871 Wilhelm I is proclaimed German emperor following the unification of Germany

⑩ 1878 Congress of Berlin; Bulgaria, Serbia and Romania freed from Ottoman rule

⑪ 1879–83 War of the Pacific: Chile gains territory from Bolivia and Peru

⑫ 1884–85 Berlin Conference divides up Africa between European powers

⑬ 1896 Ethiopia secures its independence by defeating the Italians at Adowa

⑭ 1899–1902 British overcome Afrikaner resistance in the Second Anglo–Boer War

⑮ 1900–01 Boxer uprising in China against foreign domination brings swift reprisals

THE WORLD BY 1914

BY THE END OF THE 19TH CENTURY, A HUGE EXPANSION OF INDUSTRY AND WORLD TRADE HAD TAKEN PLACE. KEEN ECONOMIC COMPETITION AMONG INDUSTRIALIZED NATIONS FUELED THEIR POLITICAL AND MILITARY RIVALRY. IMPERIALISM REACHED ITS ZENITH AS AFRICA CAME UNDER EUROPEAN DOMINATION. THE DANGEROUS GLOBAL RACE FOR PRESTIGE LED TO THE OUTBREAK OF WORLD WAR IN 1914.

Industrialization grew rapidly in the second half of the 19th century throughout most of Europe and the United States. The introduction of mechanized methods of production greatly improved the efficiency of heavy industries such as iron and steel making. The spread of railroad networks and steamship routes reduced the time and cost of obtaining raw materials and distributing manufactured goods. The development of new technologies, especially electrical power, the internal combustion engine, and the manufacturing of petroleum-based chemicals, meant that a second Industrial Revolution was underway by the start of the 20th century.

No less revolutionary was the shift that occurred in people's attitudes to the institutions that governed their lives. Factory workers began to demand better working conditions and an extension of the right to vote, leading to the rise of the trade union movement and socialist parties. Although reforms were won in most western countries, the majority of the world's populace would be without a political voice until well into the 20th century. Women began the long struggle to win political rights. Most male governments were

RUSSIAN EMPIRE

Sakhalin

MONGOLIA

Korea
(Japan)

CHINESE
REPUBLIC

AFGHANISTAN

⑰

⑮⑱

TIBET

② JAPAN

NEPAL
③ BHUTAN

Burma

Oman

India

Hong Kong
(Britain)

Goa

Macau
(Portugal)

SIAM

Ceylon

French
Indo-
China

Philippine
Islands

Palau
(Germany)

Malay states

Celebes

Borneo

New Guinea

Sumatra

German New
Guinea

Dutch East Indies

Java

Papua

Timor

Solomon
Islands
(Britain)

New Hebrides
(Britain/France)

INDIAN
OCEAN

AUSTRALIA

New
Caledonia
(France)

NEW
ZEALAND

Tasmania

L   L   M   N   O   P

⑯ 1904 Britain and France agree upon the Entente Cordiale, an informal alliance

⑰ 1904–05 Russo-Japanese war: Japan wins major sea and land victories

⑱ 1911 Revolution overthrows the Chinese Qing dynasty: republic set up in 1912

⑲ 1914 Panama canal opens, linking the Pacific and Atlantic Oceans

⑳ 1914 Assassination of archduke Franz Ferdinand in Sarajevo sparks World War I

Right The opening decades of the 20th century saw the rise of popular mass culture. This trend was strong in the United States, where ragtime music accompanied the birth of cinema.

reluctant to allow women to vote. The first country to do so was New Zealand in 1893, but elsewhere women faced a hard, sometimes violent struggle, and many were imprisoned for their political activism. The outbreak of war in 1914 brought a temporary halt to the suffragist movement.

WORLD TRADE

The boom in international trade in the second half of the 19th century was largely based on the systematic exploitation by the industrial nations of their colonies, often with long-term harmful results. Plantation farming of crops such as rubber, bananas, or coffee for export to the colonizing country disrupted traditional rural economies. India's thriving local handicraft industries were destroyed by the construction of the railroad network, which flooded the market with cheap imported manufactured goods.

The imperial powers built major new port facilities to handle their growing commerce. Long sea passages around Africa and South America became a thing of the past with the opening of the Suez (1869) and Panama (1914) canals. Advances in steam power and ship design meant that bulk cargoes could be carried faster; the world's first purpose-built oil tanker was launched in the 1880s. With the invention of refrigerated holds, cargoes of meat could be exported from Australia, New Zealand, and Argentina. The total tonnage of merchant shipping rose fourfold between 1850 and 1914.

To regulate global trade, the gold standard was created in the 1870s, enabling assets in different currencies to be converted into gold on demand. This system was promoted by the major gold strikes in California, Australia, South Africa, and Canada.

CONQUEST & WAR

Worldwide, technology helped imperial interests impose their will on native peoples. British rule in India, shaken by a mutiny of native troops in 1857, was reinforced by the coming of the railroads: soldiers could now be transported quickly around the country to quell disturbances. By 1870, telegraph and railroad networks spanned North America; the last pockets of native resistance had been overcome by 1890. Construction of the Trans-Siberian railroad,

begun in 1891, strengthened Russia's hold on the Muslim khanates of Central Asia and the Far East. In Africa, the deployment of rapid-fire Maxim guns and artillery helped impose European rule in the frantic race for colonies. Western military strength forced China and Japan to accept foreign trade.

Warfare became mechanized. Tactics and medical care lagged behind new, terrifyingly efficient means of killing, and battle fatalities soared in number. A Swiss humanitarian, Jean-Henri Dunant, was so horrified by the carnage he saw at the battle of Solferino (1859) that he founded the International Red Cross. More Americans died in the Civil War, the first conflict to employ mass-produced munitions and mobilization by

train, than in all the country's other wars. More than 300,000 Paraguayans died in the War of the Triple Alliance (1864–70), the bloodiest conflict in South America's history. These costly wars were a foretaste of the mass slaughter of the World War I trenches.

GERMAN AMBITIONS

Competition was fierce between Europe's industrializing states. One event above all sent shockwaves through the continent: the formation of the Second German Empire in 1871. The militaristic state of Prussia dominated the new Germany. The empire had abundant reserves of coal and iron ore, and built a dynamic economy around its heavy

took place, as Germany tried, without success, to outdo Britain in building more and better battleships and cruisers.

GREAT POWER RIVALRY

The climate of growing suspicion and fear gave rise to international crises, many of which were played out in Africa. In 1898, French and British forces confronted one another over the control of Sudan at Fashoda on the White Nile. German challenges to French rule in Morocco (1905 and 1911) also aroused widespread alarm.

The period was characterized by shifting political and military alliances. On the eve of World War I, Europe was divided into two major groups: the Central powers (Germany, Austria–Hungary, the Ottoman empire) and the Allies (Britain, France, Russia).

By far the most dangerous flashpoint for great power rivalry remained the Balkans— Serbia, Bulgaria, and Romania—which had long been the scene of hostility between Russia and Turkey. Control of the Balkans started to slip from the grasp of the ailing Ottoman empire after 1878, and by 1913 Russia and the Austro–Hungarian empire were making aggressive attempts to extend their influence there. The spark that finally ignited world war was the murder of the heir to the Austrian throne by a Serbian nationalist at Sarajevo in 1914.

industry. By 1914, it had far outstripped Britain in the production of iron and steel. Germany's most powerful magnate was the industrialist Alfred Krupp, who began by manufacturing railroad wheels and rails but then turned to armaments. Krupp's cannon and armor helped Prussia achieve military supremacy over its neighbors in 1864–71; at the outbreak of World War I, over 40 countries were equipped with his products.

Germany's ambition to expand within Europe and overseas brought it into conflict with the established powers. In particular, Germany longed to possess a strong fleet to match its victorious army, guard its new colonies, and challenge the superiority of the British navy. An expensive "Naval Race"

Above Industrial production in the Krupp works at Essen, Germany. The "Cannon King" Alfred Krupp amassed a vast fortune from exporting his armaments and transportation technology worldwide. Among all the major powers, industrial might went hand in hand with military expansion.

Right In June 1914, the heir to the Austro-Hungarian imperial crown, archduke Franz Ferdinand, was shot dead by an extremist in Sarajevo, Bosnia. Within weeks, the whole of Europe was at war.

RISE OF THE UNITED STATES

WITHIN 70 YEARS OF GAINING INDEPENDENCE, THE UNITED STATES
REACHED TO THE PACIFIC OCEAN. CANADA ALSO UNDERWENT RAPID
WESTWARD EXPANSION. THE VAST TERRITORIES BEYOND THE EASTERN
SEABOARD ALLOWED THESE COUNTRIES TO ABSORB MILLIONS OF EUROPEAN
IMMIGRANTS, WHO CAME IN SEARCH OF A BETTER LIFE. TO MAKE WAY FOR
WHITE SETTLEMENT, EXISTING POPULATIONS OF NATIVE AMERICANS WERE
DISPOSSESSED, DEPORTED, OR KILLED.

Left *Buffalo grazing on the Great Plains. Native Americans relied on the buffalo for food, shelter, and clothing, but the vast herds were brutally slaughtered by white settlers, who then plowed the prairies for farming.*

The territorial expansion of the United States began with the purchase of Florida from Spain in 1819. Texas joined the Union in 1845 after freeing itself from Mexico, and the rest of the southwest, including California, was won from Mexico in the war of 1846–48 or gained through the Gadsden Purchase (1853). The fixing of the border with Canada at the 49th Parallel in 1846 added Oregon Country, and Alaska was bought from Russia for over $7 million in 1867. That same year the Dominion of Canada came into being through the union of Nova Scotia, New Brunswick, Quebec, and Ontario. Manitoba and British Columbia also joined soon after, completing the coast-to-coast union of Canada.

THE NATIVE TRAGEDY

White Americans believed it was their "manifest destiny" to spread across the continent. To make way for the settlers, Native Americans were cleared from their lands. In 1830 the U.S. government passed the Indian Removal Act. This forced the Cherokee, Chickasaw, Creek, Choctaw, and Seminole nations to move out of the southeast to "Indian Territory" west of the Mississippi. Thousands died on the long journey, which became known as the "Trail of Tears."

As more homesteaders came to farm and set up ranches on the prairies, seminomadic peoples such as the Sioux and the mixed-race Métis of Manitoba, Canada, were displaced. The advent of railroads hastened the spread of settler culture. Even the "reservations"—land set aside exclusively for Indian use by government decree—were not respected. Parts of the Indian Territory were opened up to settlers as early as 1834. In 1874, the arrival of gold miners in the Black Hills reservation of the Sioux in Dakota was fiercely resisted, and the U.S. cavalry unit sent to protect the prospectors was wiped out by the Sioux and Cheyenne at the battle of Little Bighorn. The Sioux leaders Sitting Bull and Crazy Horse were hunted down

Map labels

St Lawrence Island
Nome
Alaska 1959
Fairbanks
Yukon
Anchorage
Dawson
Yukon Territory 1898
Kodiak Island
Whitehorse
Gulf of Alaska
Juneau
Sitka
British Columbia 1871
Prince Rupert
Queen Charlotte Island
COAST MTS
Vancouver Island
Vancou
Victor
Se
Olymp
Portla
Salem
Modoc W 1872
Sacramen
San Francisco

expansion of the United States

- United States territory in 1815
- territory ceded by Britain, 1818 and 1842
- Florida (purchased from Spain), 1819
- Texas (annexed 1845)
- Oregon Country (assigned by treaty), 1846
- territory ceded by Mexico, 1848
- Gadsden Purchase from Mexico, 1853
- Alaska (purchased from Russia), 1867

expansion of Canada

- Canadian provinces, 1867
- territory added 1870
- province added by 1873
- territory added 1880
- territory added 1949

1787 date of admission as a state to United States, or of achieving provincial status within Canada

- Native American reservation, 1875
- massacre of Native Americans
- Métis rebellion under Louis Riel
- goldfield
- railroad
- borders, 1949

0   900 km
0   600 mi

Victoria
Island

Baffin Island

Hudson Strait

Great Bear
Lake

LABRADOR
1809 to Newfoundland

orthwest Territories
organized into districts 1882–95

Yellowknife

Great
Slave Lake

60th Parallel

**NEWFOUNDLAND
1949**
St John's•

Newfoundland

Left *North America
was home to 400,000
Native Americans when
westward expansion of
settler culture began.*

Quebec
(Lower Canada)
1867

St Pierre &
Miquelon
to France

Lake
Athabasca

Anticosti
Island

*Cape Breton
Island*

Prince Edward
Island
1873

**Alberta
1905**

CANADA

**Manitoba
1870**

New
Brunswick
1867

Nova
Scotia
1867

**Saskatchewan
1905**

Edmonton

1885
1885
1885
1885

Saskatchewan

Saskatoon

Lake
Manitoba

Lake
Winnipeg

Ontario
(Upper Canada)
1867

Québec

1842
to US

St John

Halifax

**Maine
1820**

Montréal

Vermont
1791

Calgary

Regina

Winnipeg

1869–70

Fort
William

Timmins

Sudbury

Ottawa

St Lawrence

New Hampshire
1788

Medicine
Hat

49th Parallel

Missouri

1818 to United States

Duluth

L Superior

L Ontario

New
York
1788

Boston

Massachusetts, 1788

Rhode Island, 1790

ington
889

Montana
1889

Bismarck

**North
Dakota
1889**

Minnesota
1858

Wisconsin
1848

**Michigan
1837**

Toronto
(York)

Buffalo

L Erie

New York City

Connecticut, 1788

New Jersey, 1787

Helena

Minneapolis

Lake
Michigan

Detroit

Pennsylvania
1787

Philadelphia

Delaware, 1787

Butte

Little Bighorn
1876

**South Dakota
1889**

Milwaukee

Cleveland

Pittsburgh

Washington

Idaho
1890

Boise

Wyoming
1890

Wounded Knee
1890

**Iowa
1846**

Chicago

Des
Moines

**Ohio
1803**

West
Virginia
1863

Virginia
1788

Maryland
1788

Norfolk

egon
859

Snake

Nebraska
1867

Omaha

Lincoln

Missouri

Illinois
1818

Indiana
1816

Cincinnati

Kentucky
1792

Ohio

North Carolina
1789

Promontory
Point

Cheyenne

Salt Lake City

Denver

Kansas City

Topeka

Missouri
1821

St Louis

son City

Utah
1896

Sand Creek
1864

Kansas
1861

Jefferson
City

Nashville

Tennessee
1796

South
Carolina
1788

Charlotte

Nevada
1864

Colorado
1876

**UNITED
STATES**

Arkansas

Arkansas
1836

Memphis

Atlanta

Charleston

ifornia
1850

Santa Fe

Oklahoma
City

**Oklahoma
1907**

Little
Rock

Birmingham

Alabama
1819

Georgia
1788

Savannah

os Angeles

Arizona
1912

Albuquerque

New Mexico
1912

Jackson

Mississippi
1817

Jacksonville

San Diego

Phoenix

Dallas

Red

Louisiana
1812

Mobile

Tallahassee

Florida
1845

*Bahamas
to Britain*

Tucson

El Paso

**Texas
1845**

Brazos

New Orleans

Miami

Nassau

Rio Grande

Austin

San Antonio

Houston

MEXICO
1821 independent from Spain

Laredo

**GULF OF
MEXICO**

*ATLANTIC
OCEAN*

Havana

CUBA
1898 independent from Spain
1908–09 United States
occupation

CIFIC
CEAN

THE AMERICAN CIVIL WAR

Above A Union officer in the Civil War. The war broke out in 1861 after the southern states opposed to President Lincoln's stand against slavery left the Union and formed the Confederacy. In the end, the industrial strength and manpower of the Union triumphed over the rebel states.

Mason–Dixon line
borders, 1861
Confederate state, 1861,
slave state loyal to the Union
Union state, 1861
Confederate campaign
Union campaign
Confederate victory
Union victory
cotton growing area, 1860

and eventually forced to surrender. In New Mexico and Arizona, the Apache leader Geronimo waged a guerrilla war until 1886.

Despair at the destruction of their way of life led many Native Americans to join the Ghost Dance cult, which promised salvation from white rule. The most infamous act in the Native American tragedy occurred at Wounded Knee, South Dakota, when U.S. troops massacred over 200 Sioux dancers. That same year, 1890, the western frontier was officially declared to exist no more; the West was "won," but at high human cost.

THE CIVIL WAR

The authors of the American Constitution had envisioned the end of slavery in the United States, but were forced to bow to pressure from the "planter aristocracy" of the South. The growing commercial importance of cotton led to the development of large, labor-intensive plantations, and by the mid 19th century the African American slave population, who were deprived of all basic human rights, numbered around 4 million. Planters in the South began to fear that President Abraham Lincoln's moves to ban slavery in the new western territories would lead to its total abolition throughout the Union. The slavery question reopened the argument that had so perplexed the Framers of the Constitution, of how far federal government should be allowed to overrule individual states' rights.

In 1861, civil war broke out over the issue. The southern Confederacy won early victories, but the war began to turn in favor of the Union army of the north after the battles of Gettysburg and Vicksburg in 1863.

Efficient artillery and rapid-fire guns inflicted terrible slaughter on both sides. Field hospitals were ill-equipped to cope with the flood of casualties. The South, brought to its knees by starvation and a shortage of essential supplies, was forced to surrender in April 1865. Within five days of winning the contest to preserve the Union and free the slaves, Lincoln was assassinated.

The North emerged from the war with its industry and commerce strong, poised to begin an era of great economic expansion. In contrast, the rural economy of the South was ruined, and it took many decades to recover from the devastations of the war. In 1868 former male slaves won U.S. citizenship and, a year later, the right to vote, but African Americans were still persecuted, especially in the South. Many migrated to the cities of the north in search of work.

THE BOOM YEARS

A major factor in the economic expansion of North America was the railroad. It linked farms to commercial centers, allowed mineral deposits to be exploited, and speeded distribution of manufactured goods. The first transcontinental line was completed in 1869. The Canadian Pacific Railway (1885) had a vital role in unifying that country; British Colombia agreed to join the Dominion of Canada in 1871 on condition that it was built. As in the United States, Canada's westward expansion was stimulated by gold rushes.

Immigrants to the United States were attracted by the prospect of freedom from persecution, steady work, and free education. The first wave of immigrants came from Ireland, Britain, and Germany in the mid 19th century; later they were joined by people from Scandinavia, Italy, eastern Europe and east Asia. A great number traveled west to escape chronic overcrowding in the large industrial cities, but many more experienced squalor and poverty as they struggled to make a living. Conditions of work were hard, and labor disputes culminated in the Great Strike of 1877. By 1910, the United States had over 90 million inhabitants, fifty times more than in 1776, and was the world's foremost industrial power.

Global political power accompanied the economic rise of the United States, which in 1898 enforced the Monroe Doctrine by helping Cuba to liberate itself from Spain. In gaining control over Cuba, Puerto Rico, and the former Spanish territory of the Philippines, the United States joined the ranks of the modern imperial nations.

THE GREAT TYCOONS

In the economic boom of the late 19th and early 20th centuries, several U.S. entrepreneurs built up vast commercial empires. J. Pierpont Morgan made his fortune in railroad speculation, Andrew Carnegie in iron and steel, and John D. Rockefeller in oil. One of the most famous of the American magnates was the automobile manufacturer Henry Ford (below left). The son of an Irish immigrant farmer, Ford founded his own company to produce a cheap and reliable motor car for the mass market. Assembly-line production, in which each worker performed a limited task, increased output and kept costs low. Ford motivated his labor force by offering a high minimum wage of $5 per day. His Model T was a huge success, with 15 million sold worldwide.

Below *Henry Ford's Model T assembly line.*

EUROPE IN THE 19TH CENTURY

THE 19TH CENTURY SAW NATIONALISM EMERGING AS A POLITICAL FORCE IN EUROPE. UNIFIED NATIONS WERE CREATED, IN VERY DIFFERENT CIRCUM-STANCES, IN ITALY AND GERMANY. AS AUSTRIA DECLINED, GERMANY BECAME THE DOMINANT POWER IN CENTRAL EUROPE. RAPID INDUSTRIALIZATION INCREASED MILITARY POWER, AND IN THE LAST YEARS OF THE CENTURY A WEAPONS RACE DEVELOPED BETWEEN EUROPE'S MAJOR NATIONS.

In the early years of the 19th century, the ideas of the Romantic movement became influential throughout Europe. An intellectual and cultural movement, Romanticism rejected the rationalism of the 18th century and embraced revolutionary ideals. Emphasis was laid on individual self-expression, promoting the rise of nationalism and self-determination as political aims. Many of those who shared a common language and culture but were divided among a number of small states (for example, Germans and Italians) wanted to be united within a single, representative system of government, while other ethnic groups, such as Hungarians and Czechs in the Austrian empire or Serbs and Greeks in the Ottoman empire, longed to go their separate ways.

The victorious allies who met at the Congress of Vienna in 1814–15 to dispose of Napoleon's empire saw things differently.

Led by Austria's archconservative foreign minister, Klemens Metternich, Austria, Britain, Russia, and Prussia formed a pact, the "Holy Alliance," dedicated to the restoration of monarchy and suppression of radical ideas. Popular rule was to be avoided at all costs. The Holy Alliance intervened in Spain by sending French forces to quell a popular uprising in 1820–23, and Austrian troops helped the king of Naples crush a rebellion in 1821.

Elsewhere, national uprisings met with greater success: Greece won its war of independence against the declining Ottoman empire (1821–29), and Belgium broke away from the United Kingdom of the Netherlands in 1830–33. Constitutional monarchies were established in both countries with the support of the Great Powers. In France, Louis-Philippe (called the "Citizen King") gained power through a revolt in

1830, but he was no revolutionary. His support came from the new, prosperous middle class that was developing in France, as in many other European countries.

REVOLUTIONS OF 1848

The greatest challenge to Europe's conservative monarchies came in 1848, the "Year of Revolutions." In France, Louis-Philippe was removed from power by a popular uprising and Louis Napoleon, nephew of Napoleon Bonaparte, elected president (in 1852 he styled himself Emperor Napoleon III in emulation of his uncle). Revolutions broke out in Austria, Hungary, Croatia, and the Czech lands, threatening the Habsburg empire. After nearly 40 years in power, Metternich was driven from

Left The 19th century was a time of rapid industrial advance and technical innovation. London's Great Exhibition of 1851, held in the Crystal Palace, a specially built hall of iron and glass, was the first international trade exposition, bringing together 13,000 exhibitors from around the world. Crowds flocked to see the latest advances in manufacturing.

1815–1914

Left Otto von Bismarck, Prussia's "Iron Chancellor" and architect of the modern German empire.

Legend:
- borders, 1848
- Austrian empire, 1848
- Russian empire, 1848
- Ottoman empire, 1848
- France, 1848
- French territorial gains by 1860
- Prussia, 1848
- Prussian territorial gains by 1866
- other German states, 1866
- Prussian campaign
- route of Garibaldi, 1860
- Italy, 1861
- German empire, 1871
- nationalist revolt or uprising, 1848–49

0   400 km
0   300 mi

NORWAY in union with Sweden
Christiania
Göteborg
Stockholm
Vänern
Vättern
SWEDEN in union with Norway
Gotland

North Sea

DENMARK
Copenhagen

Baltic Sea

Königsberg
Schleswig
Holstein
Danzig
East Prussia
Pomerania
MECKLENBURG-SCHWERIN
Hamburg
Bremen
Stettin
PRUSSIA
HANOVER
Oldenburg
Brandenburg
Poznan
Warsaw
Hanover
Berlin
BRUNSWICK
Vistula

Amsterdam
NETHERLANDS
UNITED KINGDOM
London
Westphalia
Breslau
Silesia
POLAND
RUSSIAN EMPIRE
Dresden
Langensalza 1866
Brussels
BELGIUM
Luxembourg
Frankfurt
HESSE
1866
Prague
Königgrätz 1866
Krakow
Lvov (Lemberg)
Galicia and Lodomeria
Oder
Dniester
Amiens
1866 SAXONY
Moravia
Brünn (Brno)
SLOVAKIA
Sedan 1870
Champigny 1870
Gravelotte & Mars-la-Tour 1870
Paris 1870
Spicheren 1870
Metz 1870
Wissembourg & Wörth 1870
BADEN
BAVARIA
Nuremberg
Bohemia
AUSTRIAN EMPIRE
Vienna
Pressburg
Debrecen
Bukovina
Jassy
Mans 70
Orléans 1870
Tours
Alsace-Lorraine
WÜRTTEMBERG
Hohenzollern
Munich
Linz
Austria
Salzburg
Buda
Koloszvar
Hungary
Transylvania
Blaj
ROMANIA
FRANCE
Lyon
Savoy
SWITZERLAND
Tyrol
Salzburg
Styria
Carinthia
L Balaton
Temesvár
Danube
Venetia 1866 to Italy
Carniola
Agram
Slavonia
Sava
Bucharest
Milan
Lombardy
Venice
Croatia
Belgrade
Danube
Avignon
Piedmont to Sardinia
Parma
Modena
BOSNIA HERZEGOVINA
Toulouse
Genoa
YUGOSLAVIA
BULGARIA
ANDORRA
Tuscany
Florence
MONTENEGRO
ALBANIA
Talamone 1870 to Italy
PAPAL STATES
ITALY
OTTOMAN EMPIRE
Corsica
Rome
Volturno 1860
BENEVENTO
Naples
GREECE
Ionian Islands 1863 to Greece from Britain
SARDINIA
KINGDOM OF THE TWO SICILIES
Missolonghi 1826
Balearic Islands
Athens
Palermo
Milazzo 1860
Catalfimi 1860
Sicily
Cythera 1863 to Greece from Britain

Mediterranean Sea

Malta to Britain

Mediterranean Sea

FINLAND

185

office to find refuge abroad. Republics were established in Italy, and a parliament met in Frankfurt with the aim of uniting Germany. The revolutionaries were disorganized, however, and all the new administrations, aside from that in France, were soon overthrown by conservative-led armies.

ITALIAN UNIFICATION

The advance of nationalism, however, was not easily halted. It was to have its first success in Italy, a land of many small kingdoms that had been occupied for over 200 years by a succession of foreign powers. Attempts to create a single Italian nation after the collapse of Napoleon's empire had failed. But the campaign for unification (called the *Risorgimento*, or "resurrection") acquired new energy under the leadership of Victor Emmanuel II, king of Sardinia–Piedmont. With the support of his prime minister Camillo di Cavour, Victor Emmanuel transformed Piedmont, in northern Italy, into a modern industrial state and gave it a liberal constitution. In 1859 he turned to Napoleon III of France for help in freeing the rest of northern Italy from Austrian rule.

At the same time, a charismatic adventurer called Giuseppe Garibaldi, a veteran of revolts in Italy and South America, invaded Sicily in support of a republican uprising. At the head of a force of only 1,000 soldiers, who were known as "Red Shirts" from their distinctive uniform, Garibaldi won control

of much of southern Italy. The Piedmontese reformers feared Garibaldi's popularity and revolutionary aims, but he handed his conquests over to Victor Emmanuel, who was crowned king of Italy in 1861. Austria still had control of the area around Venice in the northeast of Italy, but gave it up in 1866 after the Italians sided with Prussia in the Seven Weeks War. Unification of the entire Italian peninsula was completed in 1870 with the handing over of the papal states, and Rome was made the national capital.

Above An advertiser's image of the new woman.

THE RISE OF GERMANY

In the first half of the 19th century Prussia acquired political and economic control of the German Confederation, the alliance of German-speaking states established at the Congress of Vienna. The short-lived, liberal Frankfurt National Assembly offered the German imperial crown to Prussia in 1849, but Frederick William IV was no friend of reform and refused it. Germany would be united on Prussia's own terms.

A CHANGING WORLD FOR WOMEN

The industrial age brought into being a new urbanized middle class that had money and time to spend on consumer articles and leisure activities such as tennis, bicycling, and golf. Men and women shared many of these pursuits, helping to break down the formal barriers that existed between the sexes. By the end of the century some colleges and professions had begun to open their doors to women. Only a tiny minority, however, was able to take advantage of these new freedoms. Divorce was rare, and married women had almost no legal or property rights of their own. In factories and mills, female employees— many of them young girls—labored long hours for extremely low wages.

Prussia had access to huge seams of coal and iron ore in the Ruhr and Upper Silesia, and rapid industrial development allowed it to build up its military strength. William I (r.1861–88) undertook major army reforms with the help of his prime minister, Otto von Bismarck. Violently opposed to liberal reform, Bismarck pursued Prussian dominance through "iron and blood." He seized the duchies of Schleswig and Holstein from Denmark in 1864, and in 1866 defeated Austria after a lightning invasion.

Prussia now controlled almost all northern Germany. The existence of this powerful neighbor caused tension with France, and in 1870 Bismarck maneuvered Napoleon III into declaring war, leading the states of southern Germany to unite with Prussia against the common enemy. The Prussian army invaded France from the Rhineland, decisively defeated the French army at the battle of Sedan, and besieged the capital. People had to eat the animals in the city's zoo, so desperate were conditions in Paris during the siege. Paris fell in January 1870, and William I was proclaimed emperor of a united Germany in the palace of Versailles. France was forced to give up two territories east of the Rhine: Alsace, and the vital iron ore region of Lorraine.

Bismarck combined social reform with repressive policing to quell internal dissent in the German empire. A brilliant diplomat, he secured peace in Europe by playing off Austria against Russia and France against Britain, and gave Germany a colonial empire in Africa and the Pacific.

PRELUDE TO WAR

Bismarck's careful work was undone by William II (r.1888–1918), who forced his resignation as chancellor. Pursuing aggressive policies against his neighbors, William antagonized Britain, by trying to match its naval strength, and Russia, by encouraging the expansion of Austria-Hungary in the Balkans. His use of "gunboat diplomacy" in Africa was a threat to Britain and France. In 1907 they formed the Triple Entente with Russia, balancing the Triple Alliance of Germany, Austria–Hungary, and Italy.

Industrial might and technical innovation had equipped Europe's military powers with fearsome weapons: machine guns, high explosive shells, battleships, and submarines. Armies could be moved easily and quickly by mechanized transportation; the Germans had a strategic plan to invade Russia and France by railroad. Most European countries had conscripted armies, creating huge reserves of trained soldiers. By 1914 both France and Germany could mobilize a million men in days. Aggressive patriotism, the dark face of nationalism, prevailed as the European powers edged closer to war.

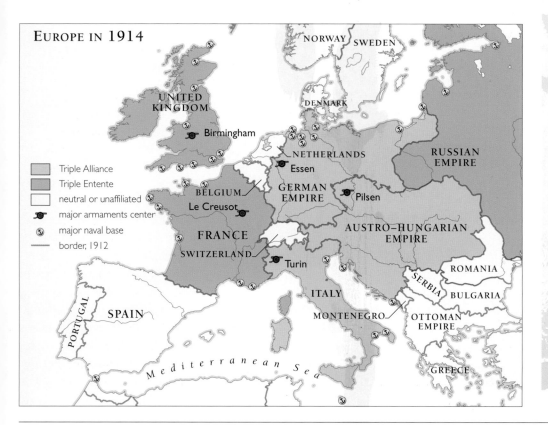

EUROPE IN 1914

Triple Alliance
Triple Entente
neutral or unaffiliated
major armaments center
major naval base
border, 1912

NORWAY SWEDEN

UNITED KINGDOM
Birmingham

DENMARK

NETHERLANDS
Essen

GERMAN EMPIRE
Pilsen

RUSSIAN EMPIRE

BELGIUM
Le Creusot

FRANCE
SWITZERLAND
Turin

AUSTRO–HUNGARIAN EMPIRE

ROMANIA

SERBIA
BULGARIA

MONTENEGRO

OTTOMAN EMPIRE

ITALY

PORTUGAL

SPAIN

Mediterranean Sea

GREECE

WORLD WAR I

In late 1914, more than 20 years of mounting tension in Europe finally exploded into war. The men who rushed to enlist in their countries' armies were in high spirits and confidently expected the fighting to be over by Christmas. But the war was to last for 4 years, devastating the continent, costing millions of lives, and changing the face of Europe forever.

Germany's ambition and insecurity—a product of its recent coming to nation-hood—lay at the root of World War I. After unification in 1871, the country had industrialized faster than any other; by 1914 it led the world in manufacturing. It had become a world power by building an overseas empire and maintaining a strong army and navy. Germany's central location in Europe, which was a great economic asset in peacetime, made it vulnerable to joint attack from Russia and France. Germany's generals devised the Schlieffen Plan to neutralize this threat: in case of war, a surprise attack on France would prevent it from taking any further part in the conflict, freeing troops to be sent east to fight Russia.

On July 28, 1914, four weeks after the heir to the Austrian–Hungarian throne had been killed by a Serbian nationalist (see page 179), the Central Powers of Austria and Germany declared war on Serbia. The European alliance system escalated the conflict. Russia came to the defense of Serbia, its ally, whereupon Germany at once attacked Russia and France. To outflank French defenses, the German army first invaded neutral Belgium. This brought Britain, which was pledged to defend Belgian neutrality, into the conflict. Japan, Britain's ally, also joined the war against Germany, and the Ottoman empire entered on the side of the Central Powers in October. Italy wavered before joining the Allies in April 1915.

WAR ON TWO FRONTS

The German invasion force raced swiftly through Belgium and into northern France toward Paris. The French army was quickly mobilized—Parisian taxicabs were used to take soldiers to the front—and halted the German advance 50 miles (80 km) short of the capital (the battle of Marne, September 1914). The strategy of the Schlieffen Plan had failed: France had not been neutralized, and the Germans now faced a long war on two fronts.

On the Western Front, extending from the coast of Belgium all the way to the border of neutral Switzerland, both sides dug defensive trenches lined by barbed wire.

All attempts to force the other side to retreat met with the same result. Before an assault the trenches of the opposing line were bombarded with shell fire. Defenders found shelter in underground bunkers; when the shells had ceased falling, they turned their machine guns against the attacking side's infantry as it advanced across No Man's Land, the wilderness between the two front lines. Even if trenches were captured, they could not be held, because heavy gunfire

Lake Onega

Lake Ladoga

L Peipus

Helsinki

Petrograd (St Petersburg)

RUSSIAN EMPIRE

Latvia 1917

Riga

L onia

nland

Western Dvina

Vitebsk

huania

Vilna

urian Lakes 4–15

Minsk

Belorussia

Brest-Litovsk 1916

Brusilov offensive 1916

1918 • Kiev

Dnieper

Lvov 1916

Przemysl 1915

Ukraine

Dniester 1918

USTRO-NGARIAN EMPIRE

1916

ROMANIA

Bucharest Danube

Varna

BULGARIA

Sofia

Edirne

Constantinople

Doiran 1917

918

Thessalonica

Gallipoli 1915–16

GREECE

Athens

B l a c k   S e a

GEORGIA

Tbilisi

AZERBAIJAN

Trabzon 1916

Erzurum 1916

OTTOMAN EMPIRE

T U R K E Y

Konya

Mosul

Aleppo

Euphrates

Tigris

S Y R I A

I R A Q

I R A N

Dodecanese Islands to Italy

Cyprus to Britain

Crete to Greece

Damascus 1918

Megiddo 1918

Jerusalem 1917

JORDAN

Baghdad 1917

Kut 1915–17

PERSIA

Port Said

Suez Canal

Cairo

Nile

Egypt

Aqaba 1917

Basra

Kuwait

S A U D I   A R A B I A

Bahrain

Qatar

Trucial Oman

Oman

Right Students in Berlin cheer the news of war in 1914. Throughout Europe men hurried to enlist, looking forward to a brief, glorious war. Optimism soon faded as armies fought each other to a standstill; 8 million soldiers did not return from the front.

	borders, 1914
	Allied powers and associates, June 1917
	Central powers, June 1917
	Allied or Central power capitulating before Nov 1918
	neutral state
	farthest advance of Central powers
	farthest advance of Russian forces
	Armistice line, Nov 11, 1918
→	Allied offensive
→	Central Powers offensive
	Russian territory lost at the Treaty of Brest-Litovsk

0   600 km
0   400 mi

ON HER THEIR LIVES DEPEND

WOMEN MUNITION WORKERS

Enrol at once

Left American women are urged to become munition workers to support the war effort in Europe.

turned the battlefield into a sea of deep mud, bogging down reinforcements.

Poor military strategy and massive firepower led to an appalling level of mortality. Over 300,000 French soldiers and nearly as many Germans were killed at the battle of Verdun (February–July 1916). Over 20,000 British and Commonwealth soldiers died on the first day of the battle of the Somme (July 1, 1916). New weapons such as poison gas (first used by the Germans in 1915) and tanks (introduced by the British the next year) failed to break the stalemate and added to the horrors of the trenches.

On the Eastern Front, the Russians suffered huge early losses to the Germans, but made equally heavy gains against Austria. Casualties were as high as they were in the west. Troops had to be moved huge distances along the front, which ran from the Baltic to the Black Sea. An Allied attempt to secure a sea route to Russia through the Dardenelles ended in failure at the unsuccessful Gallipoli landings (April 1915).

THE HOME FRONT

For the first time in the history of modern warfare, women played a major active role, both at the battlefront and behind the lines. Thousands volunteered for service as nurses and ambulance drivers. Others worked in munitions factories and other vital industries to keep the war economies of the combatant nations running. The war saw the first use of aerial bombing against civilian populations by airplanes and Zeppelin airships. Few people were killed in these raids, but they heralded the mass destruction of cities that would take place in World War II.

THE WAR AT SEA

To prevent munitions and other essential supplies reaching Britain from the United States and Canada, the Germans used submarines ("U-boats") to torpedo merchant ships. In May 1915 the liner *Lusitania* was sunk without warning, and 128 U.S. citizens were among the 1,200 lost. As popular feeling turned in favor of the Allies, it was only Germany's promise to halt unrestricted U-boat attacks that kept the U.S. government from declaring war. The British navy had blockaded German ports since the start of the war. The German fleet failed to break the blockade at the battle of Jutland, the only major naval battle of the war (May, 1916). Germany, desperately short of supplies, resumed its U-boat attacks, and the United States joined the war in April 1917. The boost to Allied morale was considerable, but U.S. troops did not reach the front line until spring 1918.

Above Senior generals on both sides have been accused of prolonging the war through inept leadership. Britain's General Haig (left) and France's General Joffre (center) confer with British prime minister David Lloyd George.

Below British troops "go over the top" to attack the Germans. For infantrymen, long periods of boredom in waterlogged, disease-ridden trenches were only broken by such terrifying charges into "No Man's Land."

POSTWAR EUROPE

— border, 1921
⧫ German gains, 1935–39
ITALY Axis power

type of government, 1939
- Communist
- fascist dictatorship
- royal or other dictatorship
- democracy

NORWAY
SWEDEN
FINLAND
DENMARK
ESTONIA
LATVIA
LITHUANIA
UNION OF SOVIET SOCIALIST REPUBLICS
IRELAND
UNITED KINGDOM
NETHERLANDS
GERMANY
East Prussia to Germany
POLAND
BELGIUM
LUXEMBOURG
CZECHOSLOVAKIA
SWITZERLAND
AUSTRIA
HUNGARY
FRANCE
ITALY
ROMANIA
YUGOSLAVIA
BULGARIA
ALBANIA
PORTUGAL
SPAIN
GREECE
TURKEY
Mediterranean Sea
Morocco to France
Algeria to France
Tunisia to France
Tripolitania to Italy
Cyrenaica to Italy

REVOLUTION & DEFEAT

In Russia, the hardships of war put an unbearable strain on the population. The army had suffered enormous casualties, the economy was in ruins, and there was widespread famine. Resentment of the country's incompetent government led to revolution in 1917, and the czar was overthrown (see page 204). The new Bolshevik government promptly surrendered to Germany at the treaty of Brest-Litovsk (December, 1917) and immediately withdrew from vast territories in Ukraine and southern Russia.

Germany was now free to concentrate its war energies in the west, against Britain, France, and the United States. In March 1918 it launched a massive offensive that broke through the Allied lines and threatened Paris. Once again, French defense at the Marne was vital in halting the advance. The Allies regrouped and counterattacked, employing their artillery and tanks to devastating effect. The Germans were driven back, and by September were in full retreat.

In the east, the Ottoman empire was collapsing under the weight of the renewed Allied assault, and the Austrian–Hungarian empire was beginning to disintegrate as nationalists demanded independence. The effects of the long blockade were starting to tell in Germany, with chronic food and fuel shortages. Riots and revolutions broke out, and sailors mutinied when their officers ordered them to engage in one last, suicidal battle with the British fleet. On November 11, 1918, William II abdicated and fled the country, and Germany signed an armistice with the Allies.

AFTER THE WAR

With hostilities at an end, Germany sued for peace on the basis of the "Fourteen Points" proposed by President Woodrow Wilson. The terms eventually imposed by the Allies in the Treaty of Versailles (1919) were much harsher than these. Germany's colonies were shared among the victors and territories ceded to Poland, Denmark, and France. It also had to disarm and pay reparations (compensation) for war damage.

With the break up of the Central Powers, new democratic nation-states were created in central Europe. But popular resentment against the terms of the Versailles settlement, together with rampant inflation and high unemployment, led to dictatorships taking hold in the 1920s and 1930s. In Germany, the Nazi Party under Adolf Hitler set about rebuilding the army and expanding Germany's borders. Neighboring territories were overrun, bringing the world to the brink of war once more.

TIMETABLE

July 28, 1914
Austria–Hungary declares war on Serbia

August, 1914
Germany declares war on Russia and France; Britain, France, and Russia on Germany and Austria–Hungary

August, 1914
Germans launch the Schlieffen Plan. The Russian invasion of Germany is smashed at Tannenberg

September, 1914
Failure of the Schlieffen Plan, as the French halt the German advance at the battle of the Marne

April, 1915
The Allies land troops at Gallipoli in a bid to seize Constantinople, but they are held down by Turkish fire

February–December, 1916
The French resist German offensives at Verdun

May, 1916
British and German fleets clash off Jutland, Denmark

July–November, 1916
A major British offensive on the Somme fails to break through German lines

March, 1917
Revolution in Russia forces the abdication of czar Nicholas II

April, 1917
United States declares war on Germany

November, 1917
The Bolsheviks seize power in Russia and make peace with Germany

November–December, 1917
The British use mass tank formations at the battle of Cambrai in France

March–July, 1918
The final German (Ludendorff) offensive is defeated

August, 1918
The Allies break through German lines

November 11, 1918
Kaiser William II abdicates and Germany signs an armistice

1919
The Treaty of Versailles shapes postwar Europe

THE SCRAMBLE FOR AFRICA

AS LATE AS 1870 EUROPEAN SETTLEMENT IN AFRICA HARDLY EXTENDED BEYOND THE COASTS, BUT WITHIN 30 YEARS ALMOST THE ENTIRE CONTINENT WAS UNDER COLONIAL RULE. THE GREAT ATTRACTION WAS AFRICA'S MINERAL WEALTH, ESPECIALLY COPPER, GOLD, AND DIAMONDS. THE BUILDING OF RAILROADS HELPED OPEN UP THE INTERIOR. IN THE SOUTH, CONFLICT BETWEEN BRITAIN'S IMPERIAL AMBITIONS AND DUTCH-ORIGIN SETTLERS RESULTED IN WAR.

Left A carved wooden model from Nigeria of a European missionary and his attendants.

In the 17th and 18th century Africa was, for European traders, primarily a source of slaves. After the abolition of the slave trade in the 19th century, the emphasis shifted to other commodities such as palm oil, timber, gum, gold, beeswax, ivory, and hides. Britain paid compensation to some west African states whose livelihood was threatened by the ban on slavery. The British government managed to persuade the sultan of Zanzibar to stop the shipment of African slaves to the Middle East and Asia in 1873, but Portugal did not end the slave trade from its territories until the 1880s: slaves were exported in great numbers from Madagascar and Angola to Brazil. Before abolition in 1865, many were illegally shipped from there to the United States.

The activities of Muslim traders (Arabs, Swahilis, Egyptians, and Sudanese) in central Africa stimulated the development of a number of commercial empires, who competed with each other with rifles for control of the trade in slaves and ivory. Africans and Europeans frequently clashed over trade and access to raw materials, but until effective drugs were found against tropical diseases, Europeans were reluctant to travel far into the interior. Before 1870, the only sizable European colonies in Africa were the French in Algeria and the Dutch and British in Cape Colony. The only Europeans to venture far inland were Christian missionaries and explorers. The Scot, David Livingstone, made many journeys in southern and central Africa between 1840–73. He was the first European to see the Victoria Falls and was later sent by the Royal Geographical Society on an expedition to try to find the sources of the Nile. But the chief motive for his travels was his desire to end the activities of Portuguese and African slave traders and found a missionary settlement.

MINERAL WEALTH

The discovery of diamonds at Kimberley, South Africa, in 1871 opened a new chapter in the history of European exploitation of Africa's resources. By now, drugs had been developed against malaria and yellow fever, so territorial expansion became a practical possibility. A "scramble for Africa" took place, with European colonizers rushing to stake out claims to vast areas of land and seize control of the continent's enormous untapped mineral wealth.

Amid growing rivalry and friction, representatives of the major European powers met in Berlin in 1884–85 to settle their competing claims. The French had pushed east across the Sahara from their territories in north and west Africa, while the British had recently secured control over independent Egypt and the Suez Canal, adding to their extensive interests in west and south Africa. The Germans, latecomers to imperial conquest, were eager to become a world

CECIL RHODES: EMPIRE BUILDER

Cecil Rhodes (1853–1902) was the most ambitious empire builder of the 19th century. An English-born entrepreneur, he made an early fortune from diamond and gold mining in South Africa before turning to politics. A man of enormous energy, he was also a visionary who dreamed of building a railroad to run from Cairo to the Cape. With this aim, he brought huge territories to the north of Transvaal under British rule in the 1880s; the area around the Zambezi river came to be named Rhodesia in his honor. He resigned as prime minister of the Cape in 1896 after a failed attempt to overthrow the Boer republic of Transvaal.

Right A cartoon shows Rhodes measuring out the distance between Cairo and the Cape.

Canary Islands

Cape Verde Islands

St Louis
Dakar
Senegal
Kaédi
Nior
Senegal
Kayes
Gambia
Fort James
Cacheo
Portuguese Guinea
French Guinea
Conakry
Freetown
Sierra Leone
Monrovia

Maurita

Rio de Oro

Mahdist state, 1881–98

territory controlled by
European powers

Belgian, 1914
British, 1881
British, 1914
French, 1881
French, 1914
German, 1914
Italian, 1914
Portuguese, 1881
Portuguese, 1914
Spanish, 1881
Spanish, 1914

→ exploration by David Livingstone, 1840–73

→ French expeditionary force, 1896–98

◆ diamonds
◇ gold
◈ copper
◆ coal

railroads by 1914
borders, 1914

0   1000 km
0   800 mi

OTTOMAN EMPIRE

TURKEY

SYRIA

IRAQ

Tangier
Algiers
Tunis
Sicily
Malta
Crete
Cyprus
Mediterranean Sea

Fez
French Morocco
dir

Laghouat
Tunisia
Tripoli
Benghazi
Derna
Tobruk
Alexandria
Cairo   Suez
Kuwait
Bahrain
Qatar

Algeria

In Salah

LIBYA
Fezzan

Egypt

SAUDI
ARABIA
Riyadh
Trucial
Oman   Muscat

Ghat   Murzuq

udenni

HOGGAR
MASSIF   SAHARA   DESERT

Red Sea

ARABIA

Medina

Oman

TIBESTI
MASSIF

Dongola
Suakin

Massawa
Sana
Yemen

Hadramaut

Socotra

Bilma

Agadez

FRENCH WEST AFRICA

Niger

Chad

Omdurman
1898   Khartoum

Eritrea
Adowa
1896

French
Somaliland
Djibouti
Aden
West Aden
Protectorate

British
Somaliland
SOMALIA

Upper Volta

Say   Sokoto

Kano

Lake
Chad

FRENCH
EQUATORIAL
AFRICA

Sudan

Blue Nile

Addis Ababa

ETHIOPIA

Shebelle

gu

Gold
Coast
Kumasi

Togoland
Dahomey

Nigeria

Lokoja
Lagos
Porto Novo

Ubangi
Shari

CENTRAL
AFRICAN
REPUBLIC

Fashoda

White Nile

Lake
Turkana

Italian Somaliland

Accra
Takoradi

Douala
Cameroon

Congo

Uganda

British East
Africa

Mogadishu

Fernando Póo
Spanish Guinea
Príncipe

São Tomé

Libreville

Ubangi

Kisuma
Entebbe
KENYA
Nairobi

Annobón

Gabon
to French
Equatorial Africa
Middle Congo
Brazzaville

Leopoldville

Belgian Congo
(Congo Free State)

CONGO
(DRO)

Ujiji

German
East Africa

Lake
Victoria

Mombasa

Tanga
Pemba
Zanzibar

Seychelles

INDIAN
OCEAN

Cabinda
to Angola

Cuango

Kasai

Lake
Tanganyika

TANZANIA

Dar es
Salaam

Kitopi
Kilwa Kisiwani

Luanda

Benguela

Angola

Cuanza

Cuando

Okavango

Northern
Rhodesia

ZAMBIA

Lusaka

Lukanga

Zambezi
Tete

Lake
Malawi

Nyasaland

Mozambique

Comoros
Islands

Madagascar

Cuando

Livingstone

Southern
Rhodesia

ZIMBABWE

Salisbury

Mozambique

Quelimane

Tananarive

Mauritius

Okavango
Delta

Bulawayo

Beira

Réunion

German
South-West
Africa

Bechuanaland

BOTSWANA

Walvis Bay
to Union
of South Africa

Windhoek

NAMIBIA

Limpopo

Fort Dauphin

Lüderitz

Johannesburg

Lourenço Marques

Swaziland
Rourke's Drift
1879

Kimberley

Orange

Vaal

Durban
Basutoland

UNION OF
SOUTH AFRICA

Cape Town

Cape of
Good Hope

Port
Elizabeth

power. Leopold II, king of the Belgians, claimed an enormous area of central Africa (the Congo Free State) as his personal possession and amassed a vast fortune from its ivory, rubber plantations, and copper.

Europeans believed themselves racially superior to Africans and assumed they had the right to impose their rule throughout the continent. African resistance was often fierce and courageous but was unable to make a lasting defense against European machine guns and rifles. In 1879 the Zulu king Cetshwayo disobeyed British demands to disband his huge army, estimated at between 40,000 and 60,000 soldiers, and fought a six-month war before being forced to submit. A religious leader, Al-Mahdi ("the divinely guided one"), created an Islamic state in the Sudan, then a dependency of Egypt, itself a British puppet state. He died in 1885, soon after defeating a British army at Khartoum, but his empire lasted until 1898. It was ended by a British-Egyptian army at the battle of Omdurman, in which 11,000 Mahdist soldiers were slaughtered. The most successful resistance to European imperialism came in Ethiopia, when an Italian invasion army was defeated and routed at the battle of Adowa in 1896. By 1914, however, virtually the whole continent was under European imperial control.

IMPERIALISM IN ACTION

For Africa's peoples, European rule had enormous and far-reaching consequences. The continent was carved up into colonies whose frontiers took no account of existing tribal boundaries: they often cut across natural linguistic areas or networks of trade, and colonial governments frequently ruled by exploiting rivalries between different tribes and ethnic groups. Christianity, European languages, and European systems of law and administration were imposed without regard for traditional cultures. Objects such as funeral masks, coronation regalia, or gold and bronze sculptures were looted and dispatched to western museums or private collectors.

SOUTH AFRICA'S ANGLO-BOER WARS

In the 1830s, a group of Afrikaner (Dutch-origin) settlers, dissatisfied with British rule, left Cape Colony and journeyed northeast into uncharted country to found the republics of Transvaal and the Orange Free State (the "Great Trek"). They were known as Boers ("farmers"). The discovery of gold in the Transvaal brought a huge influx of British settlers to the region in the 1880s, and tensions rose high. The Boers refused to give these settlers political rights, and a bitter war broke out in 1899. The Boers used guerrilla tactics in defense of their homelands. The British burned their farms and interned women and children in camps, forcing the Boers to surrender in 1902.

Far right *Three generations of Boers prepare to resist the British.*

Left *The opening up of Africa caught the world's imagination, largely due to the exploits of journalist and explorer Henry Morton Stanley. He first made the headlines in 1871 when the New York Herald sent him to find David Livingstone, who had not been heard of for five years. Stanley later helped create a private empire in the Congo for the Belgian king Leopold II and traced the course of the river Congo. This children's board game represents his final expedition in 1887–88, when he set out to rescue the Egyptian governor of Sudan from Mahdist rebels.*

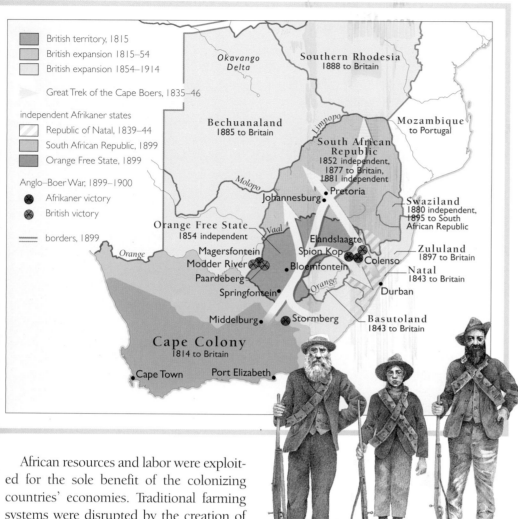

Map legend:
- British territory, 1815
- British expansion 1815–54
- British expansion 1854–1914
- Great Trek of the Cape Boers, 1835–46

independent Afrikaner states
- Republic of Natal, 1839–44
- South African Republic, 1899
- Orange Free State, 1899

Anglo–Boer War, 1899–1900
- ⊗ Afrikaner victory
- ⊗ British victory
- borders, 1899

Map labels:
Okavango Delta
Southern Rhodesia 1888 to Britain
Bechuanaland 1885 to Britain
Limpopo
Mozambique to Portugal
South African Republic 1852 independent, 1877 to Britain, 1881 independent
Molopo
Johannesburg • Pretoria
Swaziland 1880 independent, 1895 to South African Republic
Orange Free State 1854 independent
Vaal
Elandslaagte
Spion Kop
Colenso
Zululand 1897 to Britain
Magersfontein
Modder River
Paardeberg
Bloemfontein
Orange
Natal 1843 to Britain
Springfontein
Durban
Orange
Middelburg • Stormberg
Basutoland 1843 to Britain
Cape Colony 1814 to Britain
Cape Town   Port Elizabeth

African resources and labor were exploited for the sole benefit of the colonizing countries' economies. Traditional farming systems were disrupted by the creation of labor-intensive plantations to grow rubber, sugar, cocoa, tea, and coffee for the European market. The confiscation of land and introduction of money taxes meant that thousands of African men had to leave their communities and travel long distances to find work as migrant laborers in mines and industrial cities.

The treatment of Africans by the colonial powers varied considerably. Leopold II's regime in the Congo was so brutal that half the population was worked or starved to death within 15 years. In 1908, international outrage forced the Belgian government to take over the colony from their king. Other colonizing powers introduced elementary education and medical services, often run by missionaries. In Britain's colonies, a system of "indirect" rule (a very limited form of self-rule) was allowed. However, imperial rule generally left deep, often insuperable, problems for Africa's new states when they achieved their independence in the decades after World War II (see page 219), particularly in the form of bitter ethnic divisions and chronically weak economies.

A WHITE STATE IN AFRICA

In 1910 the Boer republics (see box) were united with Cape Colony and Natal to form the self-governing Union of South Africa within the British empire. To accommodate minority white rule, African peoples were deprived of their lands. A large Asian community also existed, originally imported as indentured laborers to work on sugar plantations in Natal in the 1860s. The Indian nationalist leader Mohandas Gandhi (see page 210) was one of the original founders of the African National Congress (ANC), created in 1912 in order to fight discrimination. In 1948, the official racist policy of *apartheid* forced South Africa's black and colored citizens to live in townships and barren homelands, banned interracial marriage, and reserved the best land, jobs, and education for whites. Black majority rule was finally achieved in 1994, when Nelson Mandela was elected as first president.

TIMETABLE

1816
Shaka creates the Zulu nation in southeast Africa and begins a period of Zulu expansion (the *mfecane*)

1830
The French conquest of Algeria begins

1835–36
Afrikaners begin the "Great Trek" out of Cape Colony

1858
John Speke is the first European to reach Lake Victoria, which he identifies as the source of the Nile

1871
Stanley tells the world he has met Livingstone at Ujiji on Lake Tanganyika (Tanzania)

1874
In west Africa, the British defeat the Asante empire and found the colony of the Gold Coast

1879
The Zulu war ends in Britain's conquest of the Zulu kingdom

1881–1900
The French rapidly expand their territories in west Africa

1882
Britain establishes a protectorate over Egypt

1884–85
The Berlin conference agrees on the European carve-up of Africa

1885
British general Charles Gordon is killed when Mahdist forces take Khartoum

1898
War almost breaks out between Britain and France after their forces meet at Fashoda on the White Nile

1899–1902
The Anglo–Boer War: Britain conquers Transvaal and Orange Free State

1910
The Union of South Africa is formed as a Dominion of the British Empire

1914–18
German colonies in Africa are captured by the Allies during World War I

THE RISE OF JAPAN IN ASIA

THE BALANCE OF POWER IN THE FAR EAST CHANGED RADICALLY DURING THE LATE 19TH AND EARLY 20TH CENTURIES. CHINA ENTERED A PERIOD OF LONG DECLINE UNDER THE QING DYNASTY, WHILE JAPAN EMERGED FROM TWO CENTURIES OF ISOLATION TO BECOME THE FOREMOST INDUSTRIAL POWER IN ASIA. TO SUPPORT ITS RAPID MODERNIZATION, IT BUILT A MILITARY EMPIRE ON THE ASIAN MAINLAND AND WENT TO WAR WITH CHINA AND RUSSIA. JAPAN'S CONTINUED EXPANSION IN THE PACIFIC THREATENED U.S. INTERESTS AND OPENED UP A NEW THEATER OF CONFLICT IN WORLD WAR II.

During the 19th century the weak Qing dynasty of China maintained an isolationalist policy toward the west but could not prevent European traders from increasing their commercial interests. Britain, whose main import to China was opium grown in India, gained the island of Hong Kong as a trading colony and the opening of five "treaty ports" to foreign trade as the result of fighting two "Opium Wars" (1839–42; 1856–60). China also lost its dominance in Central and Southeast Asia: Russia seized territories in Siberia; Britain took control of Burma (Myanmar); France of Indochina.

Far from the Qing court, official corruption and crippling taxes caused severe hardship. Local uprisings were frequent. Most serious was the Taiping rebellion (1850–64), which threatened the survival of the Qing and was put down with heavy loss of life. Measures to build an industrial base and reform the army achieved too little, too late. Dissent made itself felt in violent feeling against foreigners. In 1900–01, "Boxer" rebels (so called because they belonged to the secret society of the "League of Righteous Harmonious Fists") attacked foreign embassies and trade legations and murdered Chinese Christians. The west sent troops to put down the uprising; many ringleaders were publicly beheaded. China was made to pay huge sums in compensation, foreign troops and gunboats were stationed there, and the economy was put in the hands of western bankers.

As Qing authority disintegrated, the nationalist *Kuomintang* ("Revolutionary Alliance") seized power in 1911, forcing the child-emperor Pu Yi, last of the Qing dynasty, to abdicate. A republic was founded, and Tibet and Mongolia threw off Chinese rule. But the Kuomintang leader Sun Yixian

(Sun Yat-sen) was soon ousted. Total anarchy followed as China fell under the sway of local warlords. In 1917, the Kuomintang regained control of southern China, but in 1927 a civil war broke out between them and the Chinese Communist party. The situation worsened when Japan occupied Manchuria in 1931.

JAPANESE EXPANSION

Since the expulsion of Portuguese traders and missionaries in the 17th century, Japan had had limited contact with the outside world, shunning all foreign influences and technological advances. The arrival of a fleet of U.S. warships in 1853–54 persuaded the shogun, Japan's military ruler, to change his mind, and two ports were opened to foreign trade. Treaties with other western powers soon followed, but the introduction of outside influences undermined the power

Below A Japanese print shows the arrival of US Commodore Matthew Perry's fleet of "black ships" in Edo (Tokyo) Bay in 1853. He returned the next year with a squadron of warships and 4,000 marines, forcing Japan to end its isolation.

1815–1945

Amur
1858 annexed by Russia

1860 annexed by Russia

Sakhalin
1875 to Russia,
1905 southern
half to Japan

Above Boxer rebels
attack a foreigner in
Beijing: an illustration
in a contemporary
European magazine.

Chita
Nerchinsk
Aigun
Khabarovsk

Manzhouli

**Manzhougou
(Manchuria)**
1931 under Japanese occupation

*Inner
Mongolian
Plateau*

Harbin

*Lake
Khanka*

Suifenhe

Changchun
Hur chun
Vladivostok

*Sea of
Japan*

Hokkaido
Sapporo
Hakodate

MONGOLIA
1912 independent

Gobi Desert

Mukden
(Shenyang)
Niuzhuang
Liaoyang
Dandong

*Chosen
(Korea)*
1910 to Japan

Honshu
Tokyo
Yokohama

Qinhuangdao
Yalu River
Pyongyang

Nagoya

Beijing
Tianjin
Dalian
Seoul

Kyoto
Kobe
Osaka
JAPAN

QILIAN MTS
Ganzhou
Pingluo

*Ordos
Desert*

Yulin

Lushun
(Port Arthur)
1898 to Russia,
1905 to Japan

Chefoo
Longkou

Yellow
Sea

Tangjin

Pusan

Shimonoseki

Shikoku

*Lake
Qinghai*

Yan'an
Hegang

Jinan

Weihaiwei
1898–1930
to Britain

Tsushima
Straits

QIN MTS
Hezhou
Gangu

Yellow

Lianyungang

Qingdao
1898 to Germany,
1914 to Japan

Nagasaki

Kagoshima

Kyushu

*NORTH
PACIFIC
OCEAN*

Zhengzhou
Kaifeng

*Yellow
Sea*

Yanguan
Xi'an

Han

CHINA

DABA MTS

Nanjing
Zhenjiang
Shanghai

Wanxian
Yichang

Wuhu
Suzhou

Hankou
Wuchang
Hangzhou

Ningbo
(Mingzhou)

*East
China
Sea*

Lancang (Mekong)

Chongqing
Shasi

Yeuyang

Jiujiang

*Lake
Pengli*

Wenzhou

Jinsha Yangze
Yalong

Mianning
Luzhou

Nanchang
Tanzhou

*Lake
Dongting*

Santuao

Ryukyu Islands
1879 to Japan

Fuzhou

Tan-shui

Kunming

Xiamen
(Amoy)

Taiwan
1895 to Japan

Tengyueh

Lashio
dalay

Mengzi

Sanshui
Wuzhou
Nanning

Guangzhou
(Canton)

Shantou
(Swatow)

Tainan

Manhao
Simao

Longzhou
Pakhoi

Macau
to Portugal

Kowloon
Hong Kong
1841 to Britain

Irrawaddy
Salween

BURMA
to Britain

MYANMAR

Hanoi
Haiphong

Zhanjiang
1898 to France

Xi

Qiongzhou

Hainan

Luzon

Rangoon

FRENCH
INDO-CHINA

LAOS

Mekong

SIAM

THAILAND

*South
China
Sea*

Manila

VIETNAM

CAMBODIA

Legend

⬭ Qing empire, mid-19th century
⬭ Japan, mid-19th century
▨ Japanese gains by 1931
▨ Japanese gains by 1937
▨ Japanese gains by 1941
▨ China under Nationalist control, 1941
▨ China under warlord control, 1941
▨ Chinese Communist headquarters after 1935
● port open to foreign trade under the
   Treaty of Nanjing, 1842
⌖ treaty port opened from 1858
⊗ Sino-Japanese War, 1894–95
⊗ Russo-Japanese War, 1904–05
▨ Boxer uprising, 1900–01
— railroad
═ borders, 1941

0 ————— 1000 km
0 ————— 800 mi

of the shogunate. For centuries the emperor had been a remote, divine figurehead, while the shogun exercised absolute power, but a brief civil war in 1868 brought a return to full imperial rule (the Meiji Restoration). Japan began to modernize rapidly, using western machinery and technical expertise; the first railroad was opened in 1872, and a modern army and navy were developed.

Japan, which had limited resources for expansion, set out to acquire an overseas empire. It gained the Kuril and Ryukyu islands and then, in 1894, went to war with China in support of a Korean bid for independence. Japan's warships destroyed the Chinese navy at the battle of the Yellow Sea, and the island of Taiwan was won. In 1904, conflict with Russia over influence in Korea and Manchuria, the rich industrial northeastern province of China, exploded into war. After the Japanese sank Russia's Pacific fleet in a surprise attack on Port Arthur, Russia sent its aging Baltic fleet halfway around the world to the Pacific, but the Japanese

navy destroyed it at the battle of Tsushima Straits in May 1905. Victories on land confirmed Japan's superiority, and five years later it took over the direct rule of Korea.

Japan sided with the Allies during World War I, and was rewarded with former German possessions in China and the Pacific. But its territorial ambitions were not yet satisfied. In 1931, it took advantage of China's civil war to occupy Manchuria, setting up a puppet state there with Pu Yi at its head. This action was widely condemned, and as a result Japan left the League of Nations; in 1936 it allied itself to the fascist dictatorships of Italy and Germany (see page 200). In 1937, Japan began a full-scale war against China. The Kuomintang and Chinese Communist Party made an uneasy alliance, but their forces were powerless to prevent Japan from overrunning most of northern China. Bombing and indiscriminate slaughter were used to subdue the Chinese populace; in one atrocity, 200,000 citizens of Nanjing were massacred.

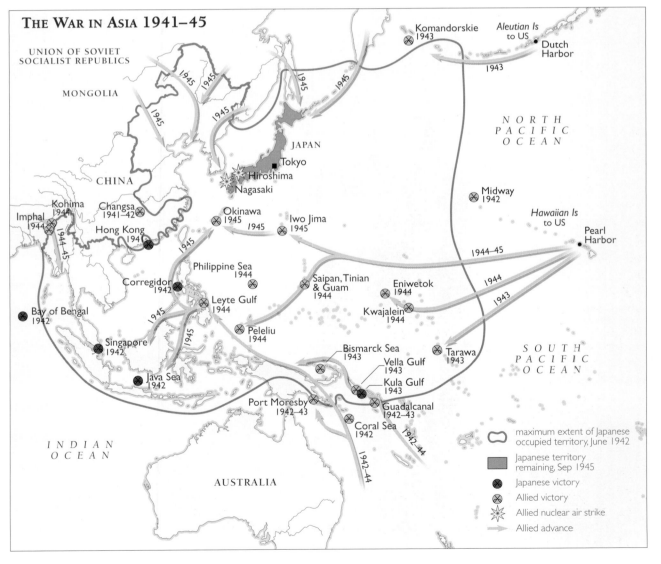

THE WAR IN ASIA 1941–45

Above U.S. forces on the Japanese island of Iwo Jima in February 1945. The battle to take Iwo Jima was one of the fiercest of the war in the Pacific; 25,000 Japanese defended it to the death, causing 26,000 American casualties. Military experts predicted that more than 1 million U.S. soldiers would die in an invasion of the Japanese home islands. Accordingly, President Harry Truman assented to the use of the world's first atomic weapons against Japan.

HIROSHIMA, 1945

On August 6, 1945, a U.S. aircraft dropped the world's first nuclear weapon —a uranium-based bomb nicknamed "Little Boy"—on the industrial city of Hiroshima, which lies in the south of the main Japanese island of Honshu. The intense heat of the blast, which was equivalent to 13,000 tons of TNT, destroyed the city and killed 80,000 of its inhabitants in an instant. In some places, all that remained of people were their shadows, seared against walls and sidewalks by the flash of the explosion. Within a year 150,000 had died and, for decades after, radiation sickness and leukemia claimed the lives of thousands more victims.

When he realized the destructive power of the atomic bomb, its designer, J. Robert Oppenheimer, quoted an ancient Indian sacred text: "I am become Death, the destroyer of worlds."

Right *A scorched watch records the exact time of the Hiroshima explosion.*

THE PACIFIC WAR

Japan needed raw materials such as rubber and oil to continue the war against China. After 1939, it saw an opportunity to obtain them by invading Southeast Asia while the French, Dutch, and British colonial powers were preoccupied with the war in Europe. To forestall U.S. intervention, its airplanes attacked the naval dockyard at Pearl Harbor, Hawaii in December 1941.

By mid 1942, Japanese troops occupied French Indochina, the Dutch East Indies, the Philippines, Malaya, and Burma. Many atrocities were committed against civilians and Allied prisoners of war (surrender was considered a disgrace by the Japanese). The turning point came with Japan's failure to seize Port Moresby on New Guinea and its defeat at the battle of Midway (June 1942). American forces began slowly to retake the Pacific islands. The Japanese resisted fiercely, using suicide pilots (*kamikazes*) and piloted bombs to crash on Allied warships. The use of atomic weapons against Japan hastened the end of the war, and emperor Hirohito surrendered unconditionally on September 7, 1945.

WORLD WAR II IN EUROPE

THE IMMEDIATE CAUSE OF WORLD WAR II WAS THE GERMAN INVASION
OF POLAND IN SEPTEMBER 1939, BUT THE ROOTS OF THE CONFLICT LAY
IN THE POST-WORLD WAR I SETTLEMENT OF EUROPE AND ECONOMIC
DEPRESSION, WHICH NOURISHED THE RISE OF FASCISM. AFTER SIX YEARS
OF INTENSE FIGHTING, EUROPE WAS LEFT DEVASTATED IN 1945.

The peace treaties at the end of World War I failed to create a lasting political settlement in Europe. The League of Nations was set up to resolve any disputes that might arise, but had little political weight as the United States refused to join. The Wall Street Crash of 1929 led to the withdrawal of U.S. loans and created a worldwide economic depression. These conditions sowed the seeds of instability in Europe and helped to spread the popularity of rightwing extremist movements like the fascists in Italy, led by Benito Mussolini, who promised a return to civil order and full employment.

The National Socialist German Workers' (Nazi) party founded by Adolf Hitler shared similar goals. The payment of large sums of money to the Allies for war damages, which helped to produce soaring inflation, was a cause of deep popular grievance, exploited by the Nazis. As soon as he became chancellor of Germany in 1933, Hitler assumed dictatorial powers. Nazi propaganda was spread by mass political rallies that glorified the role of the *führer* (leader) and reinforced by brutal secret police tactics targeted at minority groups such as Jews. Determined that Germany would never again be defeated in war, Hitler rearmed, and in 1935 he reoccupied the Rhineland.

In 1936 Hitler and Mussolini made a mutual pact, known as the Rome–Berlin Axis. The same year, civil war broke out in Spain when an alliance of the right, led by General Franco, attempted to overthrow an elected republican government. In the three years' conflict that followed, Soviet Russia (see pages 204–207) aided the republicans, while the Axis powers helped Franco secure victory.

THE ROAD TO WAR

At the center of Hitler's program was the foundation of a "Third Reich" (empire) of German-speaking peoples. In 1938 he united Austria with Germany, in defiance of the treaty of Versailles, and then took over the Sudetenland, the German-speaking part of Czechoslovakia. Now he showed he wanted nothing less than the conquest of eastern Europe as *Lebensraum* ("living space") for German settlers. He seized the rest of Czechoslovakia and turned to Poland, having first made sure of Soviet Russia's cooperation by promising it a share of the spoils.

Up until now, Britain and France had tried to appease Hitler by giving in to his demands, but the invasion of Poland led to war in September 1939. The German army took less than four weeks to defeat Poland. The following spring, it occupied Denmark

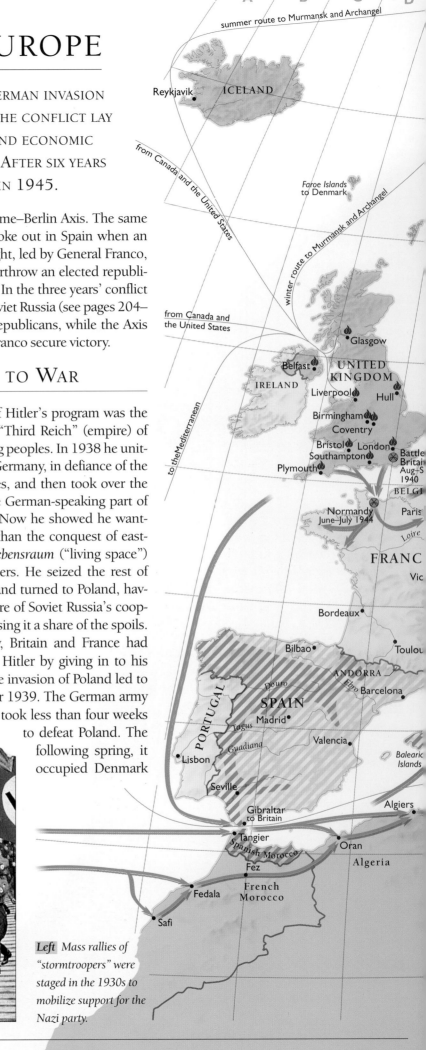

Left Mass rallies of "stormtroopers" were staged in the 1930s to mobilize support for the Nazi party.

THE FINAL SOLUTION

*A*ccording to Nazi racial theories, Jews, Slavs, Gypsies and others were inferior peoples. Jews especially were unfairly blamed for all Germany's troubles; persecution began with boycotts of Jewish businesses, beatings by Nazi stormtroopers, and attacks on synagogues. Later, Jews were expelled from most professions, deprived of German citizenship, and forbidden to marry non-Jews. Many were driven to emigrate. When Germany's armies overran neighboring states, Jews were forced to wear a distinctive badge, made to live in segregated ghettos, or murdered in mass shootings.

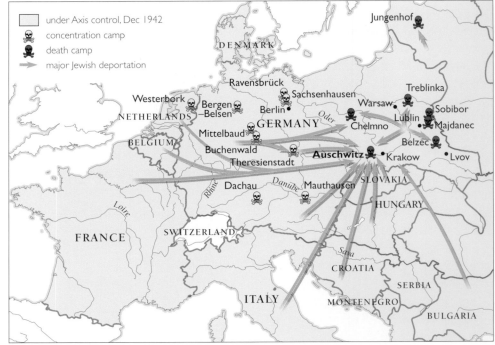

In 1941, the Nazis formulated a plan for the "final solution of the Jewish question." So began the Holocaust, the systematic extermination of Jews throughout Europe. Whole communities were rounded up and transported to concentration camps in the east, such as Auschwitz and Treblinka. Here thousands

Left *A grandmother and children in Auschwitz.*

were killed daily in gas chambers and crematoria. Able-bodied men and women were put to work as slave labor in camp factories until they died of exhaustion and malnutrition. By the end of the war, over six million Jews out of a total of eight million living in countries occupied by the Nazis had been murdered—the most barbarous genocide in recorded history.

and Norway and then swept on through the Netherlands and Belgium to invade France, which surrendered six weeks later. German troops occupied the north of the country, while a French collaborationist government based at Vichy ran the south.

Britain was now the only opponent left in Europe against Nazi Germany. Hitler planned to invade, but was thwarted by the defeat of the German air force in the Battle of Britain (August–September 1940). Britain concentrated its war efforts on fighting Germany's ally Italy in North Africa, on protecting vital Atlantic shipping lanes against U-boats, and on building bomber planes to strike at German industries and cities. Hitler intensified bombing raids against British cities, but his main ambition was to extend Germany's frontiers in eastern Europe.

"Operation Barbarossa," the invasion of the Soviet Union, began in June 1941. After early successes, the coming of winter halted the German advance outside Moscow. The following spring, Nazi forces launched new offensives to take the valuable oilfields of the Caucasus, but by now the German supply lines were dangerously overstretched.

THE TIDE TURNS

*I*n December 1941, the Allied cause gained a powerful boost when the United States entered the war after the Japanese attack on Pearl Harbor (see page 199). By the end of 1942, the Allies had greater reserves of military equipment, munitions, and manpower than the Axis powers. The British defeated the Italians and Germans in North Africa at El Alamein (October 1942) and, with the United States, invaded Sicily and the Italian mainland in 1943. But the decisive theater of the war was the Russian front. Leningrad was besieged, and one-third of its inhabitants died of cold or starvation. Yet, in spite of such appalling losses, the Soviets were able to draw on massive reserves, as Joseph

Stalin, the Soviet leader, ordered its heavy industries to relocate east of the Ural mountains when the Germans invaded. During the battle of Stalingrad (September 1942–February 1943) as many as 100,000 German soldiers were killed and 90,000 taken prisoner in savage house-to-house fighting. The Soviet Red Army gradually forced the exhausted, poorly supplied German army to retreat. In July 1943, at Kursk, south of Moscow, the greatest clash of armor ever seen resulted in the complete destruction of a huge German tank force by Russian tanks and planes. Russian armies were now able to begin the advance across eastern Europe all the way to Berlin.

Germany's main ally, Italy, collapsed and fierce fighting left most of the peninsula in Allied hands by mid-1944; Mussolini (soon to be hanged by partisans) controlled only a puppet state in the north. On June 6, 1944 ("D-Day"), an Allied invasion force landed in Normandy, on the north coast of France and began slowly to advance toward the Rhine. Paris was liberated at the end of August. U.S. and British bombers pounded German cities to rubble. In one mass raid, the city of Dresden was razed to the ground and 60,000 of its citizens were killed. When the Red Army entered Berlin in April 1945, Hitler committed suicide. On May 7, Germany surrendered.

Among the 60 million who died between 1939–45 were 20 million Russians, 6 million Poles, and 6 million Germans. Millions of Slavs and others were deported to provide slave labor in German factories. At the end of the war, Europe swarmed with refugees trying to return east or west. The Allies, horrified by the evidence of the Jewish extermination camps, executed the Nazi leaders after finding them guilty of war crimes at Nuremberg. Germany itself was split up into four occupation zones under Soviet, U.S., British, and French administration.

Above A Soviet poster celebrates the defenders of Moscow. Like Napoleon before him, Hitler was defeated by a harsh winter and the resilience of the Russian people.

Left Aerial bombing caused enormous destruction and killed millions of civilians. In July–August 1943, Allied planes attacked the German port of Hamburg. Their bombs started a firestorm, in which up to 42,000 people perished.

TIMETABLE

1933
Adolf Hitler is elected Chancellor of Germany

1936–39
Nationalists overthrow the elected Republican government in the Spanish Civil War

1938
Munich Agreement: Britain accepts Germany's takeover of the Sudetenland

September 1939
Germany invades Poland. Britain and France declare war on Germany

April–June 1940
Germany conquers Denmark, Norway, the Low Countries, and France. Italy joins the war on the German side

August–September 1940
The battle of Britain is fought in the air over southern England

1940–43
German U-boats attack British convoys in the battle of the Atlantic

June 1941
Germany invades the Soviet Union

July 1941
The Soviet Union and Britain sign a pact of mutual assistance

December 1941
Germany declares war on the U.S.

August 1942
U.S. bombing raids begin over Europe

October–November 1942
Italy and Germany are defeated in North Africa

July 1943
Soviets defeat German offensive in a massive tank battle at Kursk

September 1943
Italy surrenders to the Allies and declares war on Germany (October)

June 1944
D-Day: Allied forces land in Normandy

December 1944–January 1945
Final desperate German offensive fails in the battle of the Bulge (Belgium)

April–May 1945
Berlin falls to the Red Army, Germany surrenders

RUSSIA IN THE 20TH CENTURY

REVOLUTION IN RUSSIA ENDED CZARIST RULE IN 1917 AND BROUGHT THE WORLD'S FIRST COMMUNIST REGIME, THE SOVIET UNION, INTO BEING. CENTRALIZED PLANNING FAILED TO SOLVE RUSSIA'S PROBLEMS AND IMPOSED GREAT HARDSHIP ON ITS PEOPLE. THE SOVIET UNION HELPED TO DEFEAT NAZISM IN WORLD WAR II, BUT AFTERWARD USED ITS MILITARY STRENGTH TO TAKE CONTROL OF EASTERN EUROPE. RISING NATIONALIST FEELING BROUGHT ITS DOWNFALL IN 1991.

At the end of the 19th century, the Russian empire extended from the Baltic Sea to the Pacific, from the Arctic to the Black Sea, and contained around a hundred different nationalities. Within this vast domain, the majority of people were poor and uneducated, communications inadequate, and huge natural resources largely unexploited. The czars believed they had a God-given right to rule and refused to answer calls for political reform and change. Russians were denied representative government and terrorized by the secret police.

THE END OF THE CZARS

In 1904–05, Russia was defeated by Japan (see page 198). The news caused unrest at home, which grew still greater after a peaceful demonstration was fired upon by troops in St. Petersburg. Czar Nicholas II (r. 1895–1917) was forced to legalize political parties and set up an elected national assembly (the *duma*), but did not give up real power. The military disasters of World War I were

Left This 1929 Soviet propaganda photograph shows peasants voting to set up a collective farm. In reality, the policy of collectivization was bitterly opposed and Stalin took savage reprisals against the peasantry—some 14.5 million were executed or starved to death.

therefore attributed directly to the czar, and he was forced to abdicate in March 1917. A liberal provisional government was set up by the *duma* but its decision to continue the war was very unpopular. Growing unrest among peasant farmers, mass desertions in the army, and the establishment of *soviets* (councils of workers, soldiers, and sailors) undermined its authority. In October 1917, a second revolution ousted the provisional government and put the Bolshevik ("majority") party in charge. The Bolsheviks were

Left *Soviet Russia industrialized rapidly under Stalin, and grim apartment buildings like these were built to house factory workers.*

Above *Lenin was an inspired speech maker and revolutionary who led the 1917 October Revolution that brought the Bolsheviks to power and later became the first leader of the Soviet Union. On his death, his body was embalmed and placed in a mausoleum on Red Square, Moscow.*

New Siberian Islands
Wrangel Island
Nordvik
Novyy Port
Dubinka
Norilsk
Igarka
Tiksi
Ambarchik
Kolymskaya
Anadyr

UNION OF SOVIET
SOCIALIST REPUBLICS
from 1923

Ob
Yenisey
Maklakovo
Tomsk
Krasnoyarsk
Stalinsk
Lena
Magadan

Sea of Okhotsk
Petropavlovsk

Lake Baykal
Cheremkhovo
Irkutsk
Ulan Ude
Chita
Magdagachi
Nikolaevsk
1925 to Russia
Aleksandrovsk
Komsomolsk
Sovetskaya Gavan
Khabarovsk
Sakhalin

Kuril Islands

NORTH PACIFIC OCEAN

MONGOLIA

Harbin

Gobi Desert
CHINA

Mukden (Shenyang)
Vladivostok
Sea of Japan

Japanese, 1918–22

Lushun (Port Arthur)
Japanese, 1918–22
Korea to Japan
JAPAN
Yellow Sea

- Russian territory lost, 1916–21
- principal town where Bolsheviks seized power, Nov–Dec 1917
- area controlled by Bolsheviks, Aug 1918
- advance of anti-Bolshevik armies, 1918–20
- area controlled by Bolsheviks, Oct 1919
- Union of Soviet Socialist Republics, 1939
- border, 1939
- main area of collectivization
- area under *gulag* administration
- new town founded 1925–38
- railroad

0   800 km
0   500 mi

led by Vladimir Ilych Lenin (1870–1924), who promptly ended the war with Germany (see page 191). The czar and his family were secretly executed in 1918.

The Bolshevik "Red Army" now fought a bloody civil war against the "White" (anti-Bolshevik) forces, consisting of aristocrats, liberals, peasants, and national minorities opposed to their regime, with some support from outside powers such as Britain. By 1921 the Red Army had gained control of the whole country, but the Bolsheviks

were forced to concede independence to Poland, Finland, and the Baltic states (Latvia, Lithuania and Estonia). In 1923, Russia was renamed the Union of Soviet Socialist Republics (USSR); at the same time, the Bolshevik party was renamed the Communist party. During the civil war the Bolsheviks had requisitioned food for the army and cities from peasant farmers, causing widespread revolts and a famine that killed 5 million people in the Volga region. To rectify this, Lenin adopted the "new economic policy," which allowed limited free trade and private agriculture.

THE STALINIST ERA

Lenin died in 1924 and was succeeded by Joseph Stalin, a ruthless Bolshevik who had played a leading role in the revolution. His first step was to "collectivize" farming. Peasant farmers were forced to give up their land, which was merged into large state-run farms. Those who resisted were deported to *gulags* (forced labor camps) in Siberia.

A series of "Five-Year Plans" was set up to boost industrial output. Production of coal, iron and steel, and armaments all rose, but still fell short of impossible targets. Stalin looked for scapegoats. In 1934 he began

purges to eradicate "subversives"—anyone who was felt to be a potential threat. Public show trials of supposed enemies of the state were held, on falsified charges. Thousands of officials were secretly tortured and killed, or sent to labor camps. People were encouraged to denounce their neighbors. Millions died during the "Great Terror," from which Stalin emerged with absolute power.

The rise of Nazism alarmed Stalin, who signed a non-aggression pact with Hitler in 1939. while building up the Soviet Union's armaments. The German invasion in 1941 took the Red Army by surprise. The Russian people endured terrible losses and hardship, but its huge supply of human labor and military–industrial capacity enabled it to halt and then push back the Germans.

ART, DISSENT, & THE SOVIET STATE

In the early years after the Russian Revolution, experimental writing and avant-garde art, architecture, and music were welcomed as representing the progressive spirit of Communism. Stalin, however, saw things differently. He had convetional taste in art and literature, and modernism and experimentation were condemned as "anti-Soviet." Instead, artists were told to celebrate the Soviet Union's heroic achievements and goals in an approved style known as "Socialist Realism." Those who refused to do so were punished; their works were suppressed and many died in forced labor camps. Persecution and censorship continued into the Brezhnev era. Dissident writers circulated their works secretly in the form of typed "samizdat" that passed from person to person.

Left Anna Akhmatova's poems were banned by Stalin.

By 1942, it was turning out more and better tanks and planes than Germany. The Soviets played a crucial role, at heavy cost, in World War II (see pages 200–204), a conflict they called "the Great Patriotic War."

SOVIET POWER POLITICS

After the defeat of Germany in 1945, the Red Army occupied the countries of eastern Europe it had freed from Nazi rule, including the eastern half of Germany itself. Communist governments were imposed in one after another, to form a power bloc of Soviet-dominated states. As relations with the west worsened, an "Iron Curtain" separated Communist from capitalist Europe (see page 218). In 1949 the Soviet Union successfully tested the atom bomb to became the world's second nuclear power.

Stalin died in 1953, regretted by few. The new Soviet head Nikita Khrushchev relaxed his repressive measures and released many political prisoners. Great efforts were made to increase agricultural yields and produce more consumer goods. But poor harvests continued and living standards remained low. The Soviets dominated the eastern bloc (Warsaw Pact) countries and used extreme measures to suppress revolts in East Germany (1953) and Hungary (1956). Khrushchev began a "space race" with the United States, launching the first artificial satellite (*Sputnik*) in 1957. The arms race with the United States also intensified, and the effort

to build a stockpile of weapons put severe strain on the Soviet economy and threatened world peace. In 1962, the Cuban missile crisis came close to triggering world war (see page 218). Khrushchev was forced to back down, and was replaced as leader by Leonid Brezhnev.

The Brezhnev era (1964–82) was marked by a gradual, slight easing in relations with the west, though the build-up of nuclear arms continued unabated. Khrushchev had allowed greater freedom of expression to writers and other artists but now there was a return to the earlier stifling of dissent. In 1968 Czechoslovakia attempted to liberalize, but was crushed by Warsaw Pact tanks, and the Soviet army became bogged down in a long war in Afghanistan from 1979–89.

FALL OF COMMUNISM

Mikhail Gorbachev, who became leader in 1985, reduced nuclear arms spending and started reforms to liberalize political and economic life in the Soviet Union. As the new freedoms brought old grievances to the surface, nationalist demands for independence grew in the Baltic, Caucasus, and Central Asian republics. In 1991, hardline Communists staged a coup to try to halt the reform program. They failed, and the Soviet Union broke up. All the newly independent states faced severe difficulties as they made the switch to a free-market economy, and many were divided by ethnic violence.

BREAK UP OF THE SOVIET UNION

Warsaw Pact member

former Soviet republic becoming independent in 1991

border, 1991

☆ uprising against communist state

✳ nationalist uprising

GERMANY 1953 / 1980–84 / ESTONIA / LATVIA / 1968 / POLAND / LITHUANIA / HUNGARY / 1953 / BELARUS / CZECHOSLOVAKIA / 1956 / 1956 UKRAINE / ROMANIA / MOLDOVA / BULGARIA / Black Sea / Mediterranean Sea / GEORGIA / ARMENIA / AZERBAIJAN / Caspian Sea / TURKMENISTAN / UZBEKISTAN / KAZAKHSTAN / KYRGYZSTAN / TAJIKISTAN / RUSSIA

ASIA SINCE 1945

ASIA SAW DRAMATIC CHANGES AFTER WORLD WAR II AS NATIONALIST MOVEMENTS LED TO THE INDEPENDENCE OF FORMER EUROPEAN COLONIES. SOME OF THEM BECAME COMMUNIST, ALARMING THE UNITED STATES, WHICH INTERVENED BUT FAILED TO STOP COMMUNISM IN CHINA, NORTH KOREA, VIETNAM, CAMBODIA, AND LAOS. JAPAN RECOVERED FROM THE WAR TO BECOME ASIA'S ECONOMIC POWERHOUSE, STIMULATING RAPID GROWTH ACROSS MOST OF THE REGION.

When Europe's colonial powers tried to resume control in Asia at the end of World War II they found that strong nationalist movements had developed during Japanese occupation, and were forced to withdraw, often after lengthy independence wars. The two superpowers, the Soviet Union and the United States, started to compete for regional influence. The United States was anxious to limit the spread of Communism. The "domino theory" argued that if one country turned Communist, its neighbors would follow; it lay behind U.S. intervention in civil wars in Korea (1950–53) and Vietnam (1965–75), and its support for corrupt regimes such as that of Ferdinand Marcos (1966–89) in the Philippines. In 1955 the Philippines and Thailand formed, with the United States, Britain, and France, the Southeast Asia Treaty Organization (SEATO), a counterpart to NATO, to defend the region against Communism. Other Asian nations joined the nonalignment movement, which tried to avoid siding with either superpower.

RISE OF A NEW CHINA

After Japan's surrender in 1945, the civil war began again in China (see pages 196–199). When the Communists took Manchuria, the United States withdrew support for the nationalist Kuomintang. In 1949 the last nationalist strongholds fell and Communist Party chairman Mao Zedong proclaimed the People's Republic of China. The nationalists established a state on Taiwan. Under U.S. protection, it occupied China's seat in the UN until the 1970s.

Mao reasserted Chinese power, invading Tibet in 1950 and intervening in the Korean War (1950–53) on the side of Communist

North Korea. Though Mao accepted Soviet aid at first, he refused to become a satellite state. Relations with the Soviets collapsed after 1960, and China urgently developed its own atomic bomb (1964). Mao's greatest problem was how to relieve China's poverty. He drew up a Soviet-style plan to modernize industry and increase agricultural productivity by setting up collective farms. The experiment failed: incompetent planning combined with bad weather to cause terrible famine, which killed millions.

In 1966, Mao launched the "Cultural Revolution" to bring about change, recruiting cadres of young people (Red Guards) to denounce "enemies of socialism" in education, industry, and even the Communist Party itself. Foreign influences and classical culture were attacked, and educated Chinese were humiliated, tortured, sent to labor

Left Mao Zedong glorified himself as the "Great Helmsman" and was idolized by Chinese Communists for over 30 years. His personality cult allowed no criticism until after his death in 1976.

KAZAKHSTAN

Lake Balkhash

Shihezi
Urumqi

KYRGYZSTAN

Yarkand

1962

AKSAI CHIN

1962

Xizang
(Tibet)

1950–59 ☼

Brahmaputra

Kathmandu
NEP.

INDIA

Bay of
Bengal

Communism in China
- area of Communist soviet, 1927
- Long March of Chinese Communists, 1934–35
- area of Communist headquarters after 1935
- Communist occupation by 1946
- Communist gains, 1946–48
- Communist gains, 1948–49
- Communist gains, 1949–50
- annexation of Tibet, 1950
- annexation of Aksai Chin region, 1962

Communism in Korea and Indochina
- Communist North Korea, 1948
- temporary gain by North Korea, 1950
- Communist North Vietnam, 1954
- other areas of Communist control within Indochina, 1954
- Communist gains in Indochina by 1976

1946 date country changed to Communism
- Chinese troop movements, with date
- Ho Chi Minh trail
- ☼ uprising
- borders, 1976
- .... disputed border

0   1200 km
0   800 mi

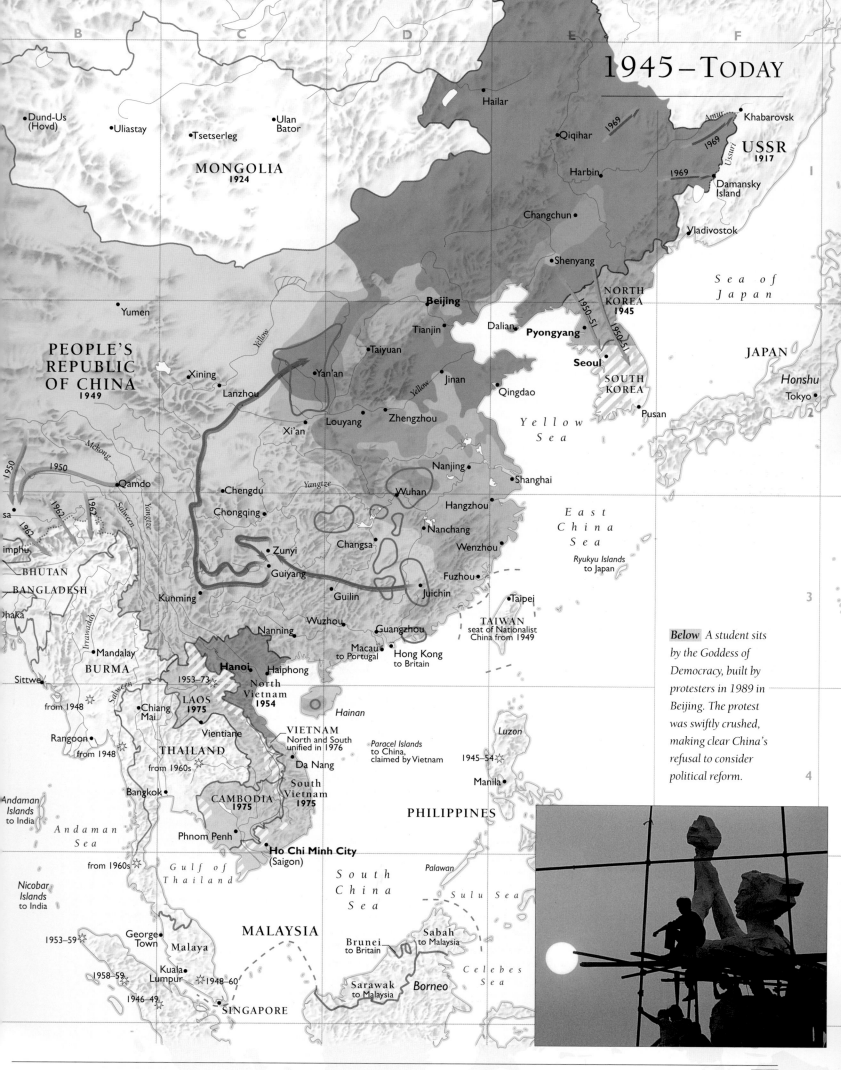

B   C   D   E   F

Dund-Us (Hovd)
Uliastay
Tsetserleg
Ulan Bator

MONGOLIA
1924

Hailar

1969

Amur   Khabarovsk

Qiqihar

1969

USSR
1917

Harbin   1969

Damansky
Island

Changchun

Vladivostok

Shenyang

Sea of
Japan

Yumen

PEOPLE'S
REPUBLIC
OF CHINA
1949

Xining

Lanzhou

Yellow

Yan'an

Beijing

Tianjin

Dalian

NORTH
KOREA
1945

Pyongyang

1950–51

Seoul

SOUTH
KOREA

JAPAN

Taiyuan

Yellow

Jinan

Qingdao

Pusan

Honshu

Tokyo

1950

1950

Mekong

Qamdo

Chengdu

Yangtze

Xi'an

Louyang

Zhengzhou

Nanjing

Yellow
Sea

1962   1962

Salween

Yangtze

1962

imphu

Chongqing

Wuhan

Shanghai

Hangzhou

East
China
Sea

BHUTAN

BANGLADESH

Dhaka

Zunyi

Changsa

Nanchang

Wenzhou

Ryukyu Islands
to Japan

Guiyang

Guilin

Juichin

Fuzhou

Kunming

Wuzhou

Guangzhou

Taipei

TAIWAN
seat of Nationalist
China from 1949

Irrawaddy

Mandalay

BURMA

Nanning

Macau
to Portugal

Hong Kong
to Britain

Sittwe

Salween

1953–73

Hanoi   Haiphong

North
Vietnam
1954

from 1948

Chiang
Mai

LAOS
1975

Vientiane

Hainan

VIETNAM
North and South
unified in 1976

Luzon

Rangoon

from 1948

THAILAND

from 1960s

Da Nang

Paracel Islands
to China,
claimed by Vietnam

1945–54

Bangkok

CAMBODIA
1975

South
Vietnam
1975

Manila

Andaman
Islands
to India

Andaman
Sea

Phnom Penh

PHILIPPINES

from 1960s

Gulf of
Thailand

Ho Chi Minh City
(Saigon)

Palawan

South
China
Sea

Nicobar
Islands
to India

1953–59

George
Town   Malaya

MALAYSIA

Brunei
to Britain

Sabah
to Malaysia

Sulu   Sea

Celebes
Sea

1958–59

Kuala
Lumpur

1948–60

Sarawak
to Malaysia

Borneo

1946–49

SINGAPORE

Below A student sits by the Goddess of Democracy, built by protesters in 1989 in Beijing. The protest was swiftly crushed, making clear China's refusal to consider political reform.

Left As Saigon, the capital of South Vietnam, fell to North Vietnam in 1975, remaining American personnel and their South Vietnamese associates were evacuated by the U.S. military. The long, bitter war left millions of Vietnamese homeless and the devastated country even poorer than it had been as a French colony. Unified Vietnam began rebuilding with the help of the Soviet Union, but refugees—"boat people"—attempted to escape by sea to Hong Kong in the late 1980s, causing deep friction in the British colony's relations with China.

separate states. North Korea invaded South Korea in 1950 but was pushed back to a treaty line by a U.S.-led United Nations' force. North Korea's Communist ruler Kim Il Sung (1948–94), who encouraged a personality cult, pushed through a program of massive industrialization. The government remained totalitarian after his death. Its failure to bring about economic reform led to severe food shortages in the late 1990s.

Anti-Communist South Korea was a one-party state under military rule until 1987, when its first free elections were held. It underwent political reform to transform itself into one of the fastest growing economies of the Pacific rim, but was badly affected by the slowdown of the late 1990s.

INDONESIA & VIETNAM

The Dutch East Indies became independent as Indonesia in 1949 after a long war against the Netherlands. It later seized control of western New Guinea (1963) and of East Timor (1975). Suharto, military dictator from 1967, resigned in 1998 after mass protests against his rule.

One of the longest wars of the 20th century was fought against the French in Indochina. Nationalist resistance was led by the Communist Vietminh movement under Ho Chi Minh, and by 1954 the French were forced to withdraw, leaving Vietnam divided between the Communist north and a weak republic in the south, backed by the United States. The north used guerrilla warfare against the south. From the 1960s, the

camps, or executed. Confusion and chaos followed, and by 1968 Mao had to call in the army to restore order.

After Mao's death in 1976, his successor, Deng Xiaoping, moved slowly toward free-market reform, inviting foreign investment. The coastal cities were given wide economic freedoms and headed China's transformation. Living standards began to rise, but unemployment, official corruption, and inequalities of income caused unrest to grow. In 1989 hundreds of students were killed when the authorities used tanks to clear a pro-democracy protest in Beijing's Tienanmen Square. The British colony of Hong Kong, with its thriving capitalist economy, was returned to China in 1997.

JAPAN & KOREA

Japan was so devastated at the conclusion of World War II that it was unable to feed its people. The United States saw Japan as a buttress against Communism and helped to reconstruct its economy. In return for aid, Japan was forbidden to rearm and its

emperor became a constitutional monarch. Shielded from the chaos on the Asian mainland, Japan recovered fast. By 1970 it dominated electronics technology and was the world's second largest economy.

In 1945, Korea was divided into Soviet and American spheres, which became two

FOUNDERS OF MODERN INDIA

India's path to independence from British rule began with civil disobedience in the 1920s, organized by the Congress Party of Mohandas K. Gandhi and Jawaharlal Nehru. Gandhi, known as Mahatma ("great soul"), developed a policy of nonviolent resistance to oppression while working in South Africa, where all nonwhites were treated as second-class citizens. On returning to India, he galvanized the ineffectual Congress Party and won the support of educated Indians such as the Nehrus, a family of

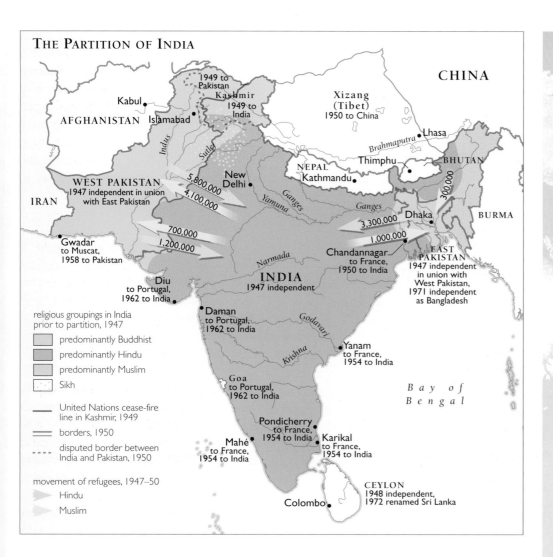

THE PARTITION OF INDIA

CHINA

Kabul

AFGHANISTAN Islamabad

1949 to Pakistan

Kashmir 1949 to India

Xizang (Tibet) 1950 to China

Lhasa

Brahmaputra

IRAN

WEST PAKISTAN 1947 independent in union with East Pakistan

Indus

Sutlej

NEPAL
Kathmandu

Thimphu BHUTAN

New Delhi

5,800,000

4,100,000

Yamuna

Ganges

Ganges

Dhaka BURMA

300,000

3,300,000

Gwadar to Muscat, 1958 to Pakistan

700,000

1,200,000

Narmada

INDIA 1947 independent

Chandannagar to France, 1950 to India

1,000,000

EAST PAKISTAN 1947 independent in union with West Pakistan, 1971 independent as Bangladesh

Diu to Portugal, 1962 to India

Daman to Portugal, 1962 to India

Godavari

religious groupings in India prior to partition, 1947

predominantly Buddhist

predominantly Hindu

predominantly Muslim

Sikh

Krishna

Yanam to France, 1954 to India

Goa to Portugal, 1962 to India

Bay of Bengal

United Nations cease-fire line in Kashmir, 1949

borders, 1950

disputed border between India and Pakistan, 1950

Pondicherry to France, 1954 to India

Mahé to France, 1954 to India

Karikal to France, 1954 to India

movement of refugees, 1947–50

Hindu

Muslim

CEYLON 1948 independent, 1972 renamed Sri Lanka

Colombo

U.S. poured equipment and troops into the conflict, but could not defeat North Vietnam, which unified the country in 1975.

The war destabilized neighboring Cambodia. From 1975–79 it was ruled by the dictator Pol Pot, leader of the Khmer Rouge. Millions of people were executed or worked to death in labor camps simply for speaking English or French, or even for wearing glasses, held to be a symbol of western technology. Vietnam and the Soviet Union drove out the Khmer Rouge, which was backed by China, who then invaded Vietnam. Only Thailand remained stable in this period.

INDEPENDENT INDIA

By the 1930s the British had realized that India would become ungovernable if it was not given self-rule. Because Indian Muslims demanded their own state, India was partitioned into two states, India and Pakistan, in 1947. In the resulting chaos, 12 million people became refugees. India and Pakistan went to war in 1948 and 1965 over Kashmir, which remains contested. Indian prime minister Indira Gandhi (Nehru's daughter) was assassinated in 1984, as was her son Rajiv in 1991, but India remains the largest democracy in the world. Pakistan has had several periods under military rule. In 1971 the eastern half of the country broke away to become the state of Bangladesh.

lawyers. While Congress supporters went on mass boycotts and strikes, Gandhi and other Congress leaders served time in jail. To secure cooperation in World War II, the British promised early independence.

A deeply religious Hindu, Gandhi responded to ethnic violence with fasting, which often shamed the factions into a truce. He was murdered by a Hindu extremist during the riots of 1947. Nehru became India's first prime minister.

Left *Nehru (left) and Gandhi in 1946, a year before India won its independence.*

TIMETABLE

1945
Japan's surrender ends World War II

1946
The Philippines become independent of the United States

1947
India and Pakistan become independent

1949
Communists win the civil war and found the People's Republic of China

1950
North Korea invades South Korea starting the Korean war (ends 1953). China conquers Tibet

1952
United States' occupation of Japan ends

1954
France is defeated at Dien Bien Phu and withdraws from Vietnam

1958–60
Mao's "Great Leap Forward" attempts to modernize China; it fails

1965
U.S. ground troops are sent to Vietnam

1968
Japan becomes the world's second largest economy

1971
Bangladesh becomes independent following Pakistani civil war

1973
American troops are withdrawn from Vietnam

1975
Saigon, the South Vietnam capital, falls and Vietnam is unified. Khmer Rouge come to power in Cambodia

1978
Deng Xiaoping begins reform of the Chinese economy

1988
Military coup in Myanmar (Burma)

1989
Pro-democracy demonstrators massacred in Tienanmen Square, Beijing

1997
Britain returns Hong Kong, its last significant colony, to Chinese rule

THE MIDDLE EAST SINCE 1948

THE MIDDLE EAST HAS BEEN A BYWORD FOR STRIFE IN THE LATE 20TH CENTURY. ARAB NATIONALISM, BORN OF OPPOSITION TO OTTOMAN RULE AND, AFTER 1918, BRITISH AND FRENCH COLONIALISM, WAS GIVEN FRESH IMPETUS BY THE FOUNDATION OF ISRAEL IN 1948, WHICH CREATED MANY THOUSANDS OF PALESTINIAN REFUGEES. THE CONTROL OF OIL WEALTH, AND DEBATE ABOUT THE ROLE OF ISLAM IN MODERN ARAB SOCIETY, ADD TO REGIONAL TENSIONS.

Mediterranean Sea

France and to a greater extent Britain were given protectorate rule over the Middle Eastern territories of the former Ottoman empire after World War I. Although most Middle Eastern countries had nominal independence by 1945, Britain still tried to control the region's valuable assets, but withdrew when Iran nationalized its oil industry (1951) and Egypt the Suez Canal (1956). The superpowers at once moved in fill to the resulting power vacuum. The United States forged close ties to conservative, oil-rich monarchies in Iran and Saudi Arabia, the Soviet Union to Arab socialist dictatorships in Syria and Iraq.

Arab nationalist discontent with western influences grew, helping to bring about an Islamic revival. Among many Arab Muslims this was expressed by a renewed sense of cultural unity, though Islamic tradition was

Above *European Jewish refugees arrive at a resettlement center near Haifa in 1945. Israel was founded as a homeland for survivors of the Nazi Holocaust.*

Below *Sacred to Jews, Muslims, and Christians, Jerusalem remains at the heart of the bitter territorial dispute between Palestinians and Israelis.*

often at odds with the programs of modern governments. Since 1948, opposition to Israel has united Arabs, but deep rivalries exist: between Sunni and Shiite Muslims; rich and poor; progressive and conservative states; Arabs and ethnic minorities.

THE FOUNDING OF ISRAEL

Jewish emigration to Palestine began in the 1900s when the first Zionists, European Jewish settler-activists seeking the Promised Land of the Bible, began to arrive there. They were resented by the local Arabs, who had lived there for centuries. As the trickle of Jewish immigrants became a flood in the 1920s, Britain, which now controlled Palestine, advocated separate Jewish and Arab states, but this was rejected by the Arabs. After 1945, the conflict in Palestine became so fierce that Britain handed it over to the United Nations to administer. The state of Israel was created in May 1948 on the wave of international sympathy for the Jews after the Holocaust (see page 202). Expecting an easy victory, Egypt, Jordan, Syria, and Iraq invaded, but their defeat led to the displacement of a million Palestinians. Some fled abroad, others to Gaza and the West Bank of the Jordan, which included Jerusalem.

Israel overcame further Arab invasions in 1967 and 1973 and took over Jerusalem, the Golan Heights, and the Sinai peninsula. The newly formed Palestine Liberation Organization (PLO) began a terrorist campaign against Israeli occupation, and Arab oil exporters struck back at the west's support for Israel by raising oil prices in 1973.

The huge influx of Palestinian refugees destabilized Jordan and Lebanon. The PLO, expelled by Jordan in 1970, moved to Lebanon, using it as a base for raids on Israel. This helped to bring about civil war in 1975

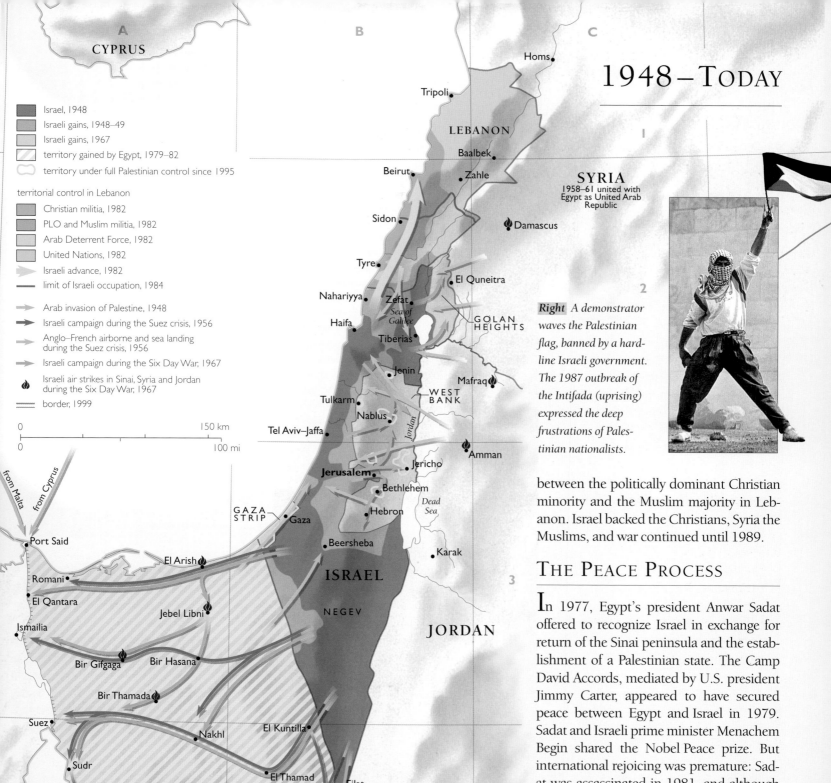

Legend

- Israel, 1948
- Israeli gains, 1948–49
- Israeli gains, 1967
- territory gained by Egypt, 1979–82
- territory under full Palestinian control since 1995

territorial control in Lebanon

- Christian militia, 1982
- PLO and Muslim militia, 1982
- Arab Deterrent Force, 1982
- United Nations, 1982
- Israeli advance, 1982
- limit of Israeli occupation, 1984

- Arab invasion of Palestine, 1948
- Israeli campaign during the Suez crisis, 1956
- Anglo–French airborne and sea landing during the Suez crisis, 1956
- Israeli campaign during the Six Day War, 1967
- Israeli air strikes in Sinai, Syria and Jordan during the Six Day War, 1967
- border, 1999

0   150 km
0   100 mi

CYPRUS

LEBANON

Homs
Tripoli
Baalbek
Beirut
Zahle
Sidon

SYRIA
1958–61 united with Egypt as United Arab Republic

Damascus

Tyre
El Quneitra
Nahariyya
Zefat
GOLAN HEIGHTS
Haifa
Sea of Galilee
Tiberias
Jenin
Mafraq
WEST BANK
Tulkarm
Nablus
Jordan
Tel Aviv–Jaffa
Amman
Jerusalem
Jericho
Bethlehem
Dead Sea
Hebron
GAZA STRIP
Gaza
Beersheba
Karak
ISRAEL
NEGEV
JORDAN

from Cyprus
from Malta

Port Said
El Arish
Romani
El Qantara
Jebel Libni
Ismailia
Bir Gifgaga
Bir Hasana
Bir Thamada
Suez
Nakhl
El Kuntilla
Sudr
El Thamad
Eilat
Aqaba
SINAI
occupied by United Nations peacekeeping force, 1956–67
Abu Zenima

SAUDI ARABIA

EGYPT
1958–61 united with Syria as United Arab Republic

Gulf of Suez
Gulf of Aqaba

Dahab
Mt Sinai
El Tur
Sharm el Sheikh

Right A demonstrator waves the Palestinian flag, banned by a hard-line Israeli government. The 1987 outbreak of the Intifada (uprising) expressed the deep frustrations of Palestinian nationalists.

between the politically dominant Christian minority and the Muslim majority in Lebanon. Israel backed the Christians, Syria the Muslims, and war continued until 1989.

THE PEACE PROCESS

In 1977, Egypt's president Anwar Sadat offered to recognize Israel in exchange for return of the Sinai peninsula and the establishment of a Palestinian state. The Camp David Accords, mediated by U.S. president Jimmy Carter, appeared to have secured peace between Egypt and Israel in 1979. Sadat and Israeli prime minister Menachem Begin shared the Nobel Peace prize. But international rejoicing was premature: Sadat was assassinated in 1981, and although Israel returned the Sinai, it took no steps to permit Palestinian autonomy. Jewish settlers continued to move into the occupied West Bank, and the Israeli army moved in to protect them from angry, dispossessed Palestinians. Israel also invaded Lebanon to clear out the PLO and its Syrian supporters. Israel was widely condemned for this.

In 1987, Palestinian frustration burst out in the *Intifada* (uprising). Bombs in Jerusalem and Tel Aviv killed Israeli civilians; almost daily, crowds of young Palestinians threw rocks at Israeli soldiers, who panicked and opened fire. Israel imposed military curfews, detention, and expulsions.

213

The PLO chairman Yasser Arafat—now in exile in Tunisia—renounced terrorism in 1988 and emerged as the leader of the Palestinian cause, but the government of Yitzhak Shamir, Begin's successor, refused to negotiate with the PLO and declared its opposition to a Palestinian state. Arafat's public sympathy with Iraq in the Gulf War of 1990–91 cost him the financial support of his patrons in the Arab world, significantly weakening the PLO's position.

Secret negotiations between Israel and the PLO yielded a new agreement in 1993. In return for Palestinian self-rule, to start in Gaza and Jericho, the PLO recognized the state of Israel. But the details had not been fully ironed out, and Israel delayed relinquishing control, citing concern over the PLO's ability to maintain security.

Extremists held prime minister Yitzhak Rabin, who signed the 1993 accords, to be a traitor and he was assassinated. At the same time, Arafat and the PLO lost credibility with Palestinians. Many thought that the negotiations were one-sided and that Arafat was chiefly interested in improving his own position. His new Palestinian administration was accused of corruption, cronyism, and incompetence. In this atmosphere of distrust, Israel continued to encourage Jewish settlement of the West Bank.

WAR IN THE GULF

In 1979, an Islamic revolution overthrew the unpopular U.S.-backed government of Iran. The country's new leaders backed a militant form of Shiite Islam, opening a rift

with its Sunni neighbor Iraq, which has a significant Shiite minority. The Iraqi leader Saddam Hussein invaded Iran in 1980, citing the need to protect its access from the Euphrates to the Persian Gulf. The United States, Soviet Union, and oil-rich, conservative Gulf states were all nervous about the Iranian revolution continuing and tacitly backed Iraq. Syria (and, secretly, Israel) backed Iran. The fighting dragged on until 1988 and ended in stalemate. There was massive bombing of cities on both sides, and more than 2 million people were killed.

Iraq was bankrupted by the war, but when Kuwait demanded repayment of outstanding debts in 1990, Saddam invaded the tiny state. To stop him from taking over Kuwait's oil supplies, a U.S.-led coalition of western and Arab states, using Saudi Arabia as its base, attacked and defeated Saddam. Punishing sanctions imposed on Iraq's oil exports impoverished the country. Saddam crushed several domestic uprisings, notably by the Kurds, whom he attacked with poison gas, and continued to provoke diplomatic crises as he blocked UN inspection of Iraqi nuclear plants, suspected of being used to construct nuclear weapons.

THE IRANIAN REVOLUTION

Iran's postwar ruler, the Shah, alienated many of his subjects and their religious leaders with pro-western modernizing programs. Popular discontent built up, leading to demonstrations in the 1970s. In 1979 the government collapsed and the Shah fled to the United States. Iran came under the control of a radical Islamic cleric, the Ayatollah Khomeini, at the head of a Revolutionary Council. Strict Islamic laws were introduced controlling women's dress and banning popular music and other western influences.

When the United States refused to extradite the Shah, the U.S. Embassy in Tehran was attacked and 52 employees held hostage for over a year. In 1989 the Ayatollah issued a death sentence against Salman Rushdie, a British writer whose work had offended Muslims. Khomeini's death the same year led to mass mourning, but Iran's new leaders have proved more conciliatory to other countries.

Below Armed, veiled Iranian women marching in front of the U.S. Embassy in Tehran, 1979.

Left U.S. troops drive through the wasteland of Kuwait in 1991. In the background are oil wells set on fire by retreating Iraqi forces at the end of the Gulf War. The Iraqi leader Saddam Hussein enjoyed covert support from the United States and many Arab states during his war with Iran, and he was surprised when a coalition led by the United States and Saudi Arabia quickly took up arms to liberate Kuwait from Iraqi occupation.

THE GULF WARS

Lake Van
Lake Urmia
Caspian Sea

TURKEY
Tabriz
Qazvin
Tehran
• Zakhu
KURDISTAN
Mosul
Arbil
Qom
southern limit, 1991
Sulamaniyah
Kirkuk
Hamadan
Euphrates
Baiji
Kifri
Qasr-e-Shirin
Kerman
IRAN
SYRIA
Bahr al Tharthar
Tigris
Khorramabad
Isfahan
• Ilam
IRAQ
Baghdad
Dezful
northern limit, 1996
Al Kut
Masjed Soleyman
An Najaf
northern limit, 1992
Ramhormoz
Khorramshahr
Bandar Khomeyni
Basra
Abadan
Al Faw
Kharg Island
Bushire
Kuwait
KUWAIT

Iran–Iraq war, 1980–88
🔥 Iran–Iraq war air strike, 1980–88
▨ territory captured by Iraq, Sep–Dec 1980
▨ territory captured by Iran, Oct 1984

Gulf War, 1991
➡ Coalition offensive in Gulf War, Feb 1991
── UN-imposed Iraqi "no-fly" zone
── border, 1997

Shiite population within Iraq
area claimed by Kurds as national homeland

SAUDI ARABIA
Persian Gulf

TIMETABLE

1948
Israel founded, Arab countries invade and lose, Palestinians flee

1956
Egypt nationalizes the Suez canal. Britain, France, and Israel invade

1964
The Palestine Liberation Organization (PLO) is founded in Jerusalem

1967
Six-Day War. Israel controls the Sinai, West Bank, and Golan Heights. More Palestinians flee to Jordan and Lebanon

1970
The PLO is expelled from Jordan

1973
Israel defeats Egypt and Syria in the Yom Kippur War

1974
A summit of Arab countries accepts the leadership of Arafat and the PLO

1975–89
Civil war in Lebanon, involving both Syria and Israel

1978
The Camp David Agreement. Israel withdraws from the Sinai peninsula

1979
Iranian revolution. The Shah is deposed; Ayatollah Khomeini takes power

1981
Egyptian president Sadat is assassinated

1980–88
War between Iraq and Iran

1982
Israel invades Lebanon to stamp out PLO

1987
Beginning of Palestinian *intifada* (uprising) to protest the delay of self-rule

1988
Arafat and the PLO renounce terrorism

1990–91
Iraq occupies Kuwait but is defeated by a United States-led coalition

1993
The Oslo Declaration: Israel and the PLO agree to found a Palestinian state

1995
Israeli prime minister Rabin is shot dead by a Jewish student

Greenland
(Denmark)

Svalbard
(Norway)

Alaska
(United States)

ICELAND

FINLAND

NORWAY
SWEDEN

CANADA

NORTH
ATLANTIC
OCEAN

UNITED
KINGDOM

IRELAND

D

N.
B.
WG.
L.
S.
C.
AU

POLAND
EG
21
10

HUNGARY
ROMANIA

UNITED STATES

PORTUGAL

FRANCE

ITALY

YU.

BULGARIA

Bermuda
(Britain)

Azores
(Portugal)

SPAIN

MALTA

GREECE

TURKEY

MEXICO

BAHAMAS

HAITI

CUBA

Puerto Rico
(United States)

Canary Islands
(Spain)

Gibraltar
(Britain)

MOROCCO

TUNISIA

CYPRUS

SYRIA
IRAQ

LE.
20

ISRAEL

KUWAIT

ALGERIA

LIBYA

EGYPT

JORDAN
BAHRAIN
QATAR

British Honduras
(Britain)

JAMAICA

DR.

GUATEMALA
EL SALVADOR
HONDURAS
NICARAGUA
COSTA RICA
PANAMA
(Canal Zone to United States)

GRENADA

BARBADOS

TRINIDAD & TOBAGO
GUYANA
SURINAME
French Guiana
(France)

VENEZUELA

COLOMBIA

ECUADOR

Western Sahara
(Spain)

CAPE
VERDE

MAURITANIA

SENEGAL
GAMBIA
GUINEA BISSAU
GUINEA
SIERRA LEONE
LIBERIA

MALI

IVORY
COAST

GHANA

NIGER
UPPER
VOLTA
BENIN
NIGERIA
TOGO

CHAD

French
Somaliland
(France)

SUDAN

CAMEROON

CAR.

SÃO TOMÉ &
PRÍNCIPE

EQUATORIAL
GUINEA

GABON

CONGO

ZAIRE

UGANDA
RWANDA
BURUNDI

SAUDI
ARABIA

Y.

ETHIOPIA

SOMAL

KENYA

TANZANIA

Seyche
(Brita

BRAZIL

PERU

PACIFIC
OCEAN

SOUTH
ATLANTIC
OCEAN

ANGOLA

ZAMBIA

MALAWI

COMO

BOLIVIA

PARAGUAY

RHODESIA

BOTSWANA

MOZAMBIQUE

MADAG

CHILE

URUGUAY

ARGENTINA

South West Africa
(South Africa)

SOUTH
AFRICA

SWAZILAND

LESOTHO

NATO member

Communist state

Warsaw Pact member

other state

dependency

states gaining independence since 1914

military or authoritarian regime in Latin America

Interstate conflict since 1945

Civil War since 1945

Nationalist conflict since 1945

Falkland
Islands
(Britain)

A.	Albania		
AU.	Austria	LE.	Lebanon
B.	Belgium	L.	Luxembourg
CAR.	Central African Republic	N.	Netherlands
C.	Czechoslovakia	S.	Switzerland
D.	Denmark	U.	United Arab Emirates
DR.	Dominican Republic	Y.	Yemen Arab Republic
EG.	East Germany	YD.	People's Democratic Republic of Yemen
WG.	West Germany	YU.	Yugos avia

1 1945 The United Nations is founded

2 1947 Independent states of India and Pakistan are founded amid widespread violence

3 1948–49 Berlin airlift breaks Soviet blockade

4 1949 The People's Republic of China is declared after Communists win civil war

5 1949 Soviet Union tests its first atomic bomb

6 1949 Germany divided into Federal Republic (West) and Democratic Republic (East)

7 1950 Korean War begins as Communist troops invade the south; UN forces resist

8 1954 Algerian war of independence starts

9 1954 The French leave Indochina after losing battle of Dien Bien Phu to the nationalists

10 1956 Soviet tanks crush Hungarian revolt

11 1956 Egypt nationalizes the Suez Canal; Anglo-French invasion fails

12 1959 Fidel Castro seizes power in Cuba

13 1960 15 new states are created in Africa as the French decolonize

14 1961 The Berlin Wall is built

15 1962 Cuban missile crisis

16 1963 (August 28) More than 200,000 people join civil rights march in Washington

17 1963 (November 23) U.S. president John F. Kennedy is assassinated in Dallas, Texas

18 1965 U.S. sends soldiers to South Vietnam

THE WORLD BY 1975

IN 1945, THE UNITED NATIONS WAS FOUNDED, REFLECTING INTERNATIONAL DETERMINATION NEVER TO LET ANOTHER WORLD WAR OCCUR. BUT AN ARMS RACE BEGAN WITH THE DEVELOPMENT OF THE COLD WAR, AS THE WORLD'S TWO SUPERPOWERS COMPETED TO BRING OTHER STATES INTO THEIR SPHERE OF INFLUENCE. BY 1975, NEARLY ALL THE FORMER COLONIES OF AFRICA, THE CARIBBEAN, AND ASIA WERE INDEPENDENT.

In 1945, the United States, the only nation in possession of nuclear weapons, stood unchallenged as the world's only superpower. Having led the alliance to restore democracy in Europe and Asia, its prestige was high. Its economic strength helped war-damaged countries rebuild their shattered industries. A great deal of assistance (nearly $13 billion from 1948–52) was given through the Marshall Plan, which was set up with the long-term strategic aim of buttressing Europe against Communism, but aid was also offered to the countries of eastern Europe, which Stalin rejected. Within 20 years the Japanese and German economies had become the world's strongest, second only to the United States. The Soviet Union had suffered greater war losses than any other country, and was determined to create a buffer zone against future invasion from the west. It used its military strength to impose one-party Communist rule across eastern Europe. Stalin tolerated no dissent, and closed the borders with the west to prevent emigration (the "Iron Curtain").

The United Nations (UN) was founded in 1945 to promote international cooperation and maintain peace. Its membership

Map labels

UNION OF SOVIET SOCIALIST REPUBLICS

Sakhalin

MONGOLIA

NORTH KOREA

AFGHANISTAN

PEOPLE'S REPUBLIC OF CHINA

SOUTH KOREA

JAPAN

PAKISTAN

NEPAL

BHUTAN

BANGLADESH

OMAN

BURMA

INDIA

Macau (Portugal)

TAIWAN

Hong Kong (Britain)

LAOS

THAILAND

VIETNAM

PHILIPPINES

CAMBODIA

SRI LANKA

MALDIVES

Brunei (Britain)

Palau Islands (United States)

MALAYSIA

Celebes

SINGAPORE

Sumatra

Borneo

New Guinea

MAURITIUS

Réunion (France)

INDIAN OCEAN

INDONESIA

Java

PAPUA NEW GUINEA

AUSTRALIA

NEW ZEALAND

Tasmania

L   M   N   O   P

19 1967 Biafran civil war begins in Nigeria

20 1967 Israel defeats Arab nations in Six-Day War

21 1968 "Prague Spring" reforms in Czecho-slovakia are crushed by Warsaw Pact forces

22 1973 United States-backed coup overthrows elected Marxist government in Chile

23 1975 Helsinki conference on Security and Cooperation confirms human rights

24 1975 Portugal gives up its African colonies

Right In the 1960s, a peace movement arose in western democracies, calling for nuclear disarmament and protesting against U.S. intervention in Vietnam. Many young people were attracted to this cause.

217

had risen from 52 to nearly 150 countries by 1975. Despite its good intentions, the UN could not prevent the Cold War developing between the world's superpowers.

THE COLD WAR

At the end of the war, Germany was divided into four zones of occupation under separate Soviet, U.S., French, and British control, a pattern that was repeated in the capital, Berlin. In 1948 the Soviets tried to force the other occupying forces out of West Berlin by blockading their sectors. Only a huge airlift of supplies from the west saved West Berlin from starvation. In 1949, Germany was divided into two separate countries.

In 1949, also, the Soviet Union developed its own atomic bomb to challenge the United States. To build up its own sphere of influence, it began to give financial and military backing to the new states and independence movements that were created as former colonies shook off their imperial past. United States' foreign and domestic policy was aimed at resisting Soviet domination. It stationed large forces in Germany, and in 1949 joined with Canada and 10 western European countries (becoming 14 later) to form a defensive alliance, the North Atlantic Treaty Organization (NATO). After West Germany joined NATO in 1955, the Soviet Union set up the Warsaw Pact military bloc with its eastern European allies.

Fear of Communism caused the United States to sponsor coups against democratically elected left-wing governments in Guatemala (1954) and Chile (1973). In the Bay of Pigs invasion (1961), it failed to overthrow the Communist government of Fidel Castro in Cuba, its close neighbor. Massive intervention by the United States in Vietnam (1965–73) did not prevent the victory of Communism there (see page 211).

The superpowers stockpiled more and more nuclear weapons. By the 1960s, each had enough to annihilate the other ("mutual assured destruction," or MAD). A space race also developed after the Soviet Union launched the first space satellite in 1957. In 1969 the United States succeeded in landing the first astronaut on the moon.

The Cold War came closest to turning hot in 1962 after the Soviet Union installed ballistic missiles on Cuba. A U.S. naval blockade forced the Soviets to back down.

This incident frightened both sides enough to begin the process of "détente" with the aim of reducing international tension. Strategic Arms Limitation Talks (SALT) began in 1969. At the Helsinki Conference (1975), the Soviet Union promised to respect human rights in return for western recognition of postwar boundaries in eastern Europe.

NEW STATES

Europe's colonial powers had increasing difficulty in running their overseas empires. Lack of funds and the strength of the nationalist movement persuaded Britain to give

up its imperial role in India, and in 1947 two independent states, India and Pakistan, were created, though with heavy cost of life. In 1956 a joint British–French–Israeli invasion failed to prevent Egypt from nationalizing the Suez Canal and won international condemnation. It was now clear to most people in Britain that its colonial days were past; 34 colonies in Africa, the Caribbean, and the Pacific islands became independent between 1957 and 1975.

This transition was, with some exceptions, mainly peaceful, but other transfers of power were not. The Dutch reoccupation of it southeast Asian colonies after the war

was strongly resisted by Indonesian nationalists, who won independence in 1949. A terrible civil war broke out in the Congo after Belgium withdrew in 1960. France became caught up in a bitter 8-year struggle against a popular liberation movement before pulling out of Algeria, its oldest African colony, in 1962. Long independence wars were fought in Portugal's African colonies. A coup in 1974 brought a change of government in Portugal. It at once gave up all its colonies, but civil war broke out in Angola, in which the Marxist government, opposed by U.S.- and South African-backed rebels, called in Cuban military assistance.

Colonialism left a legacy of poverty and underinvestment. Many African states also had to struggle with problems of huge ethnic diversity: Zaire (the Belgian Congo) had 150 ethnic groups speaking more than 50 languages. An attempt by the Ibo people of eastern Nigeria to set up a state of their own (Biafra) resulted in bitter civil war (1967–70). Strong leadership was needed to hold many newly independent countries together, and one-party rule was often the result.

In 1955, at Bandung in Indonesia, the Nonaligned Movement was founded by 29 nations, including India, China, and Yugoslavia, with the aim of resisting superpower

Right A civil rights march in Danville, Virginia. Under the leadership of Martin Luther King Jr., African Americans demanded equality in education, voting, and jobs.

Left At the end of World War II, Berlin lay deep within the Soviet-occupied zone of Germany, but was jointly run by all the Allied powers. As more and more refugees fled Communism by crossing from the Soviet to the western sectors, the East German government built the Berlin Wall to keep their citizens in. Many were killed trying to escape; this deadly "No Man's Land" in the heart of the city was sown with mines, patrolled by guard dogs, and raked by machine guns.

domination and ending colonialism; many newly independent states joined, raising its membership to around 100 by the 1970s. Another power center emerged in the early 1970s around the Arab oil-producing nations. A sharp rise in oil prices to punish the west for supporting Israel caused an economic crisis, which increased the debt burden of the developing nations.

POPULAR MOVEMENTS

Despite the UN's Universal Declaration of Human Rights of 1948, people around the world still struggled for freedom. In the 1950s and 1960s the civil rights movement in the United States, led by Martin Luther King Jr., used nonviolent tactics to end race discrimination against African Americans. King's assassination in 1968 shocked the world almost as much as president John F. Kennedy's had five years earlier. The protest movement against the U.S. role in Vietnam marked a shift to the left in U.S. politics.

Popular revolts in Hungary (1956) and Czechoslovakia (1968) against Soviet domination were put down by Warsaw Pact tanks. The slaughter of Israeli athletes by Palestinian gunmen at the Munich Olympic Games of 1972 was part of a growing trend toward international terrorism.

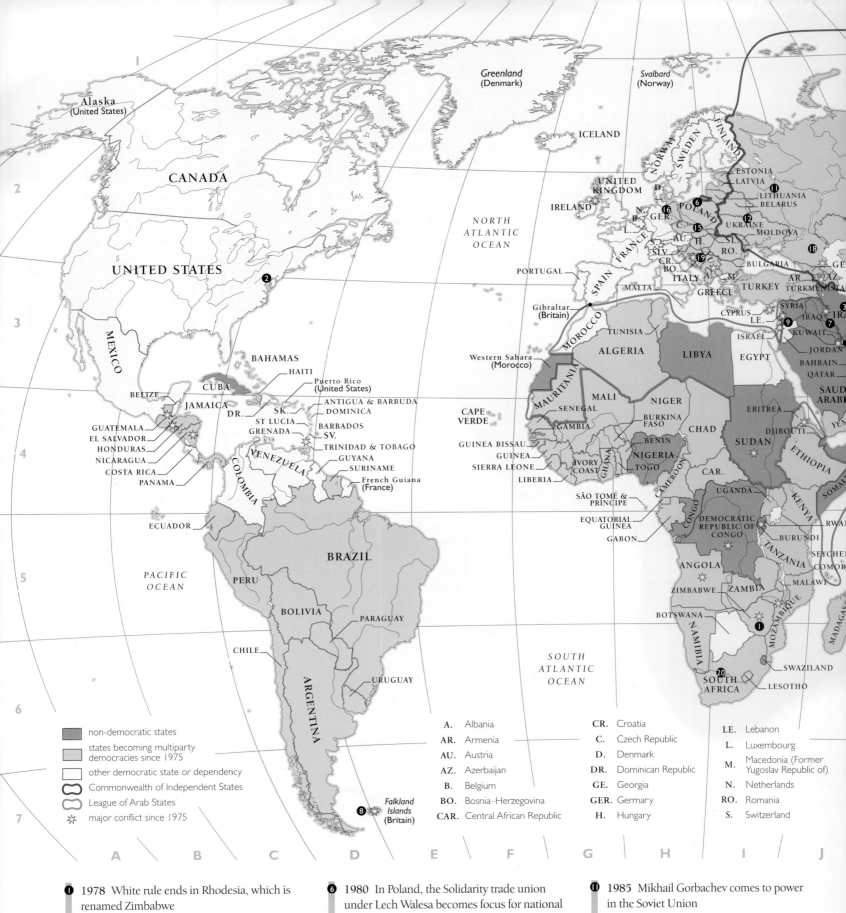

Greenland
(Denmark)

Svalbard
(Norway)

Alaska
(United States)

ICELAND

CANADA

NORWAY
SWEDEN
FINLAND

UNITED
KINGDOM

ESTONIA
LATVIA

IRELAND

POLAND

LITHUANIA
BELARUS

NORTH
ATLANTIC
OCEAN

UKRAINE

MOLDOVA

UNITED STATES

GER.

FRANCE

AU.
H.
SL.
RO.

BULGARIA

PORTUGAL

ITALY

TURKEY

TURKMENISTAN

SPAIN

GREECE

MEXICO

Gibraltar
(Britain)

MOROCCO

TUNISIA

CYPRUS
LE.
ISRAEL

SYRIA
IRAQ

MALTA

JORDAN

KUWAIT

BAHAMAS

Western Sahara
(Morocco)

ALGERIA

LIBYA

EGYPT

BAHRAIN
QATAR

HAITI

CUBA

BELIZE
JAMAICA

Puerto Rico
(United States)

SAUDI
ARABIA

DR.

SK.

ANTIGUA & BARBUDA
DOMINICA

MAURITANIA

MALI

NIGER

CHAD

ERITREA

GUATEMALA
EL SALVADOR
HONDURAS
NICARAGUA
COSTA RICA
PANAMA

ST LUCIA
GRENADA

BARBADOS
SV.

SENEGAL
GAMBIA

BURKINA
FASO

DJIBOUTI

TRINIDAD & TOBAGO

CAPE
VERDE

SUDAN

YEM

VENEZUELA

GUYANA

GUINEA BISSAU

BENIN

ETHIOPIA

COLOMBIA

SURINAME

GUINEA

NIGERIA

French Guiana
(France)

SIERRA LEONE

IVORY
COAST

TOGO
GHANA

CAR.

SOMAL

LIBERIA

ECUADOR

SÃO TOMÉ &
PRÍNCIPE

CAMEROON

UGANDA

KENYA

EQUATORIAL
GUINEA

CONGO

DEMOCRATIC
REPUBLIC OF
CONGO

RWA

GABON

BURUNDI

BRAZIL

SEYCHE

PERU

PACIFIC
OCEAN

TANZANIA

COMOR

ANGOLA

MALAWI

BOLIVIA

PARAGUAY

ZIMBABWE

ZAMBIA

MOZAMBIQUE

MADAGAS

BOTSWANA

CHILE

NAMIBIA

SOUTH
ATLANTIC
OCEAN

SWAZILAND

ARGENTINA

URUGUAY

SOUTH
AFRICA

LESOTHO

Falkland
Islands
(Britain)

Legend

- non-democratic states
- states becoming multiparty democracies since 1975
- other democratic state or dependency
- Commonwealth of Independent States
- League of Arab States
- ✳ major conflict since 1975

A.	Albania	CR.	Croatia
AR.	Armenia	C.	Czech Republic
AU.	Austria	D.	Denmark
AZ.	Azerbaijan	DR.	Dominican Republic
B.	Belgium	GE.	Georgia
BO.	Bosnia–Herzegovina	GER.	Germany
CAR.	Central African Republic	H.	Hungary

LE.	Lebanon
L.	Luxembourg
M.	Macedonia (Former Yugoslav Republic of)
N.	Netherlands
RO.	Romania
S.	Switzerland

① 1978 White rule ends in Rhodesia, which is renamed Zimbabwe

② 1978 Camp David Peace Accords lead to peace treaty between Israel and Egypt (1979)

③ 1979 Islamic Revolution in Iran topples the Shah; Ayatollah Khomeini becomes president of a theocratic state

④ 1979 Soviet troops invade Afghanistan

⑤ 1979 Vietnamese invasion of Cambodia; Khmer Rouge regime of Pol Pot ousted

⑥ 1980 In Poland, the Solidarity trade union under Lech Walesa becomes focus for national protests against Communism

⑦ 1980 Iran–Iraq war begins

⑧ 1982 Falklands War between Britain and Argentina

⑨ 1982 Israeli troops intervene in the civil war in Lebanon; massacre of Palestinian refugees

⑩ 1984 Chemical factory at Bhopal, India, explodes, killing 2,000 people

⑪ 1985 Mikhail Gorbachev comes to power in the Soviet Union

⑫ 1986 Nuclear catastrophe at Chernobyl spreads radiation over western Europe

⑬ 1986 Corrupt Marcos regime in the Philippines overthrown by "people power"

⑭ 1989 Student protest for democratic reform in China is crushed in Tienanmen Square, Beijing

⑮ 1989 Popular revolutions overthrow the Communist regimes of eastern Europe

THE WORLD TODAY

Dramatic changes altered world politics and economics in the last 25 years of the 20th century. European Communism collapsed as the Soviet Union broke up, ending the Cold War. Rich nations experienced cycles of "boom and bust" while poor nations became poorer. The drive for economic growth continued in spite of growing concern about environmental issues.

In 1975 nobody expected significant changes in the world order that had existed since 1945. The superpowers kept their stockpiles of nuclear and conventional weapons, though détente was underway, improving relations between them (and with China).

However, the Soviet Union was in steep decline. Its government was conservative and unimaginative, its industry and agriculture inefficient. Its rich natural resources were in remote areas and remained underdeveloped. Heavy spending on defense (twice as much as most other industrialized nations) and on trying to match the technological advances of the west prevented any improvement in standards of living. Strict censorship and suppression of political opinion continued in eastern Europe as well as the Soviet Union itself. International relations were set back when the Soviets invaded Afghanistan in 1979 and became locked into a long, bitter war with Muslim guerrilla fighters.

The reformer Mikhail Gorbachev came to power in 1985 after the death of two old guard leaders. He started negotiations at once with the United States to limit nuclear weapons, liberalized political and economic life, and undertook to withdraw the Red Army from Afghanistan by 1989. Popular support for these moves (in spite of the steep inflation that ensued) was so powerful that Gorbachev was unable

Map labels

RUSSIAN FEDERATION

Sakhalin

AZAKHSTAN
UZBEKISTAN
KYRGYZSTAN
TAJIKISTAN
AFGHANISTAN
PAKISTAN
OMAN
NEPAL
BANGLADESH
INDIA
MALDIVES
SRI LANKA

MONGOLIA
NORTH KOREA
PEOPLE'S REPUBLIC OF CHINA ⑭
BHUTAN
MYANMAR
THAILAND
LAOS
VIETNAM
CAMBODIA
SOUTH KOREA
JAPAN
TAIWAN
PHILIPPINES ⑬
⑤

④
⑩

BRUNEI
MALAYSIA
SINGAPORE
Sumatra
INDONESIA
Java
②
Borneo
Celebes
New Guinea
PAPUA NEW GUINEA
SOLOMON ISLANDS
Timor

AURITIUS

INDIAN OCEAN

VANUATU

New Caledonia (France)

AUSTRALIA

NEW ZEALAND
Tasmania

L   M   N   O   P

Legend

SK.	Saint Kitts–Nevis
SV.	Saint Vincent & the Grenadines
SL.	Slovakia
SLV.	Slovenia
U.	United Arab Emirates
YU.	Yugoslavia

Timeline

⑯ 1990 Germany reunified after 40 years

⑰ 1990–91 Gulf War; international force led by the United States drives Iraq from Kuwait

⑱ 1991 The Soviet Union breaks up following a failed military coup

⑲ 1992 Civil war in Bosnia–Herzegovina follows break up of former Yugoslavia

⑳ 1994 First multiracial elections in South Africa

㉑ 1998 "Tiger economies" of SE Asia in crisis

Right South African civil rights campaigner Nelson Mandela was released in 1990 after 24 years in prison. In 1994 Mandela was elected president of South Africa's first black majority government.

to control it. In late 1989 the Communist regimes of eastern Europe were toppled, one after the other, by popular revolutions. After months of demonstrations, East Germany opened its borders and the Berlin Wall was torn down. A year later the two Germanies were reunited after 40 years. Nationalist protests in the Soviet Union fed growing demands from the nonRussian republics for independence, and in 1991 it fell apart, to be replaced by a loose Commonwealth of Independent States (CIS).

THE NEW WORLD ORDER

When the Soviet Union collapsed, its former empire was destabilized. Many of the new independent states were divided by ethnic tensions or had border disputes with their neighbors. Moldova, Tajikistan, Kyrgyzstan, Azerbaijan, and Georgia all suffered civil wars or terrorism in the 1990s. There was savage fighting in 1994–96 when the Muslim people of Chechnya tried to break away from the Russian Federation.

In eastern Europe, the end of strong one-party rule caused the break-up of Czechoslovakia and Yugoslavia. In Czechoslovakia this happened peacefully, but the disintegration of Yugoslavia brought the worst bloodshed in Europe since World War II. The new republic of Bosnia–Herzegovina was ravaged from 1992–95 by civil war between its majority Muslim population, Serbs who wanted to be part of a "Greater Serbia," and Croats who wanted to join Croatia. Atrocities were committed on all sides; however, the Serbs were guilty of genocide by carrying out a policy of "ethnic cleansing." This involved the forcible removal, internment, or massacre of all non-Serbs. The United Nations sent troops but could not stop the slaughter.

The Soviet collapse ended the Cold War between the two world superpowers and both sides proceeded to disarm. The cessation of Soviet support for Ethiopia allowed Eritrean rebels to win their long war for independence in 1993. The economy of Cuba, the Soviet Union's ally in the Americas, was crippled when Russian aid dried up. The United States withdrew support for the white racist regime in South Africa, which it had backed as a defense against Communism, and in 1994 the first black majority government was elected.

THE RISE OF TERRORISM

The increasing availability of sophisticated weapons on the world market allowed small extremist groups to use campaigns of terror to publicize their agendas. Terrorist groups in many countries, including Israel, Spain, Northern Ireland, Italy, France, Germany, Peru, Egypt, and Japan, opposed the established regimes of their own governments. Attacks did not always end even after peace agreements were established.

International terrorism was sponsored by Muslim extremists, backed at different times by Libya and Iran. In 1986 the United States bombed Libyan leader Qaddafi's headquarters in Tripoli in retaliation for his alleged complicity in terrorist activities against U.S. personnel in Europe. Libya sheltered the alleged organizers of the bombing of a flight in 1988. The fear of terrorism increased after Islamic militants planted a bomb inside New York's World Trade Center in 1993— the first terrorist attack within the United States. When another bomb exploded in a federal building in Oklahoma City, suspicion fell first on Muslims, but the culprits were found to be two antifederal protestors. In 1998 the disaffected Saudi Arabian billionaire Osama bin Laden, who was exiled in Afghanistan, declared "total war on the United States and all its citizens" to force it to end its support for the repressive Saudi monarchy. He was believed to be responsible for two bomb attacks in Kenya and Tanzania that killed mostly African civilians.

Left *The continent of Antarctica is the last great wilderness on Earth. An international treaty preserves its status as a place for free and nonmilitary scientific investigation. However, a number of countries also have national territorial claims. This has raised fears that Antarctica may be explored for oil and mineral resources as supplies run out elsewhere in the world.*

Below right *A branch of the highly successful U.S. fast-food chain McDonald's in Beijing, China. In the 1980s, China undertook liberal economic reforms; it presented a huge potential market for foreign investors by the late 1990s.*

THE WORLD AT RISK

In the 1980s, ecologists began to warn that economic growth was seriously damaging the environment. Industrial pollution, marine oil spillages, and the spread of urbanization had wiped out many animal and plant species. Unregulated industry and military activity in the Soviet Union and eastern Europe had caused major ecological disasters: nuclear testing had spread radiation over parts of Kazakhstan, while huge irrigation schemes for growing cotton had dried up the Aral Sea, turning it into a desert.

In many cities, air pollution from auto exhausts and the burning of fossil fuels for electricity and industry was reaching unacceptable levels. The clearing and burning of rainforests added to atmospheric pollution and resulted in soil erosion and landslides. Increased carbon emissions were found to be a major cause of global warming and climate change. Fears mounted that sea levels would rise as the polar ice caps melted, causing widespread flooding.

The Earth Summit in Brazil (1992) was the largest conference yet held to discuss environmental issues. But it proved difficult to agree on international targets for change. Many developing countries felt the richer nations were unwilling to pay a fair proportion of the costs of putting things right.

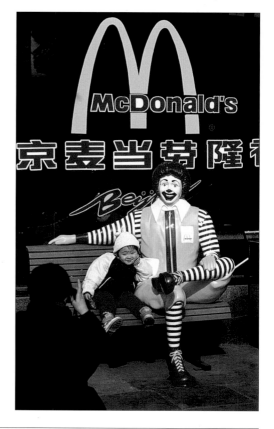

ECONOMIC CHANGES

In the industrialized nations of the west, the economic crisis caused by the raising of oil prices caused unemployment and stagnation. Growth returned in the 1980s but wavered in the 1990s, and unemployment remained endemic. Developing countries entered a spiral of debt and high inflation as they took out larger foreign loans, which rising interests rates made it impossible to repay. Many loans were later rescheduled or cancelled in return for moves toward multi-party elections, but much of Africa and Latin America remained desperately poor. Sub-Saharan Africa saw a series of terrible famines from the late 1970s, made worse by civil wars in Somalia and Sudan.

In the former Soviet Union, the transition from planned economies to a free-market system proved extremely difficult. In Russia, a few people grew wealthy as a thriving "black market" emerged, but the government was bankrupt by the late 1990s. State salaries were left unpaid for months and standards of living plummeted amid continuing political uncertainty.

Japan's meteoric rise to global economic dominance in the postwar period stimulated huge growth in other Pacific Rim countries. South Korea, Taiwan, Malaysia, Thailand, and Singapore had all become major industrial nations by the 1990s. In 1997–98 the collapse of these "tiger economies" sent unemployment spiraling. Even Japan felt the effects of the economic recession.

GLOSSARY

Abbasid The ARAB dynasty of CALIPHS who ruled most of the world of ISLAM from 750–1258.

abolitionist A campaigner against slavery or the international slave trade.

Aborigines The earliest inhabitants of Australia, so called by Europeans because they had been there *ab origine*, "from the beginning."

absolutism A political system in which unrestricted power is exercised by a single ruler. It was practiced by many European monarchs in the 17th and 18th centuries. *See also* DIVINE RIGHT.

African National Congress (ANC) The black nationalist party of South Africa, banned under APARTHEID. It became the ruling party in 1994 when its leader, Nelson Mandela, was elected president.

Afrikaner White Afrikaans-speaking descendants of the BOERS of South Africa, who retain a distinct culture based on their language and Dutch Reformed religion.

Albigensians A HERETICAL sect in southwest France in the 12th and 13th centuries. Also known as Cathars, they held that the universe is ruled by two powers, one good, one evil. A papal CRUSADE was launched against them, supported by the French king and the northern nobles.

Allied Powers Great Britain, France, the United States, and the Soviet Union—the principal members of the alliance that defeated the AXIS POWERS in World War II.

Amerindian One of any of the peoples who were in the Americas before the arrival of Europeans; a Native American.

Anatolia The large peninsula of Turkey, also known as Asia Minor, that lies between the Black Sea and the Mediterranean. It was an early center of farming and iron-working.

ancien régime Meaning "old regime," the political and social system of France before the outbreak of the FRENCH REVOLUTION in 1789. More generally, it describes the ABSOLUTIST monarchies of 18th-century Europe.

Anglo-Saxons The Germanic peoples (Angles, Saxons, and Jutes) who migrated to Britain from Germany and Denmark around 450. The period of English history before the NORMAN conquest in 1066 is commonly called Anglo-Saxon.

anthropologist A person who studies the origins, physical characteristics, social organization, and customs of humans.

apartheid Meaning "apartness," the official policy of racism in South Africa. The series of laws passed from 1948 segregated nonwhites (defined as mixed-race or coloreds; Asians; and blacks) from whites and denied them economic

and political equality. It was abolished in 1993.

appeasement The policy of giving in to another state's demands in order to prevent war.

Arabs The nomadic tribes of the Arabian peninsula who conquered the Middle East and North Africa after converting to ISLAM in the 7th century.

archeologist A person who finds out how people used to live by uncovering and examining the material remains (dwelling sites, burials, ARTIFACTS, monuments, etc.) of past societies.

Arianism A HERESY propounded by Arius, an Alexandrian priest of the 4th century, who held that Christ was not fully divine.

aristocracy A hereditary, privileged class of society; a noble elite.

arms race Competition between two or more states to build up a larger arsenal of weapons. It refers especially to the stockpiling of nuclear weapons by the United States and Soviet Union in the COLD WAR.

artifact Any object made by humans.

Aryans Nomadic pastoralists from Central Asia who migrated into the Indian subcontinent around 1500 BC.

Assyrians A powerful people of the Middle East named for the city of Ashur in northern MESOPOTAMIA (northern Iraq). The greatest period of Assyrian power lasted from about 1000–600 BC.

astronomical calendar The method of measuring the seasons, months, and days by accurate observations of the Moon, Sun, and planets.

autocrat A ruler who has unlimited authority. See ABSOLUTISM.

Axis Powers Refers to the Berlin–Rome Axis agreement of cooperation between FASCIST Germany and Italy (October 1936); Japan joined a month later. The Axis (which became a Tripartite Pact in 1940) later included all those countries that supported Germany in World War II.

Aztec An AMERINDIAN empire that controlled Mexico and parts of central America before the Spanish conquest of 1519.

Babylonians The people of the city of Babylon in southern MESOPOTAMIA. The first Babylonian empire, which arose around 1800 BC, was destroyed by the HITTITES in 1600 BC. After Assyria declined in 600 BC, Babylonia briefly enjoyed power once again.

Bantu The largest family of African languages, spoken in much of east, central, and southern Africa.

baptism The rite of admittance into the CHRISTIAN church by symbolic cleansing with water.

baroque style The art, architecture,

and music of Europe in the 17th and 18th centuries. In architecture, it is marked by extravagant, flamboyant decoration and a dramatic sense of movement and contrast, and is found in ROMAN CATHOLIC churches in contrast to the severe interiors favored by PROTESTANTISM. See also COUNTER REFORMATION.

Bastille A medieval fortress in Paris that was used as a prison in the 18th century. It was stormed by a mob in July 1789, beginning the FRENCH REVOLUTION.

Biafra A republic set up in eastern Nigeria from 1967–70, causing a civil war in which a million people died.

bishop A senior clergyman who has authority over priests and laymen.

Black Death The common name for the epidemic of bubonic plague that swept through Asia and Europe in the 14th century.

Boers White South African farmers (mostly of Dutch origin). They established an independent state in the mid 19th century, which was annexed by Britain after the Anglo-Boer war (1899–1902).

Bolsheviks The radical wing of the Russian Social Democratic Party, which broke away to form a separate party in 1910. They seized power in Russia during the October Revolution (1917) and set up a COMMUNIST state.

Bronze Age The period of Asian and European prehistory, lasting from about 4000 BC–1200 BC, when most tools and weapons were made of bronze. Bronze is an alloy of copper with arsenic and tin. It is harder than copper alone and provides a sharper cutting edge.

Buddhism A major Asian religion founded by the Indian mystic Siddhartha Gautama ("the Buddha") in the 5th century BC, which spread from India to Southeast Asia, Tibet, China, and Japan. It teaches that a moral life can free the individual from suffering.

Bulgars A TURKIC people from Central Asia who migrated into Europe in the 4th century AD. One branch eventually settled in the eastern Balkans in the 7th century and gave their name to modern Bulgaria.

Byzantine empire The name given to the eastern Roman empire from 610 until its fall to the OTTOMANS in 1453. It is derived from Byzantium, the Greek port that was the site of the empire's capital, Constantinople.

caliph The title used by the political and spiritual leaders of ISLAM after the death of Muhammad in 632.

Calvinism A PROTESTANT doctrine founded by the French theologian John Calvin (1509–64) during the REFORMATION. It stresses the doctrine of predestination—that from eternity God predestines the salvation of a chosen elect.

capitalism An economic system in which the means of production are privately owned, and in which the market is run to maximize profit for owners and investors.

Carthaginians The inhabitants of Carthage, a major port and trading city in North Africa founded by the PHOENICIANS in 814 BC.

cathedral A church that is the official seat of a BISHOP, from the Latin word *cathedra* (chair).

chiefdom A HIERARCHICAL SOCIETY ruled by a leader or CLAN-based elite.

chivalry An ideal code of behavior defining the duties of KNIGHTS in MEDIEVAL Europe. They were required to fight bravely in battle, show courtesy to women, and protect the Christian church.

Christianity The religion founded by Jesus Christ in the 1st century AD, which regards the Bible as sacred scripture. In the Middle Ages it was divided into two main churches, the ROMAN CATHOLIC and the ORTHODOX.

citizen In ancient Greece, a land-owning member of a CITY-STATE. Citizenship was inherited; outsiders, women, and slaves were excluded. Roman citizenship was more inclusive, and could be granted to conquered peoples and ex-slaves.

city-state An independent city that controlled a surrounding territory, large or small.

civil rights The rights other than political rights extended to a citizen, such as the right to move about freely and other forms of personal liberty.

civilization An advanced form of human society, with complex social structures and cultural achievements such as writing, mathematics, technology, and monumental architecture.

clan A group of people related by common ancestry or marriage.

Code Napoleon The law code compiled during the reign of the emperor Napoleon. It forms the basis of modern French law.

Cold War The long ideological conflict between the United States and its allies and the Soviet Union and its allies. It began when occupied Germany was divided into Allied and Soviet spheres in 1945 and lasted until the collapse of the Soviet Union in 1991. The buildup of political tension between the two SUPERPOWERS led to a nuclear ARMS RACE.

collectivization In state-run economies, the merging of small farms or factories to make large agricultural and industrial cooperatives under centralized control.

colonialization The occupation of foreign territory by a state for settlement and economic exploitation.

colony A group of people who found a

new community in a distant territory but retain ties with their parent state.

Communism A political system in which the ideal is communal living and common ownership of property, eliminating poverty and inequality. The theory was developed by Karl Marx and Frederich Engels in the 19th century in reaction to the social problems of the INDUSTRIAL REVOLUTION. In practice it led to totalitarian regimes in which a single party controlled all aspects of political, economic, and cultural life, as in the Soviet Union.

concentration camp A large prison camp. The most notorious camps were built by the NAZIS for Jews, Communists, gypsies, and other "undesirables."

Confederation of Independent States (CIS) The loose political association of the former Soviet republics after the collapse of the Soviet Union in 1991.

Confucianism The social and moral philosophy based on the teaching of the Chinese scholar Confucius (c. 551–479 BC), which emphasizes ethical values and respect for elders. It remains at the heart of Chinese society and CULTURE.

Congress of Vienna An international conference held in Vienna in 1814–15 to restore the balance of power in Europe after the defeat of Napoleon.

conquistadors The name given to the Spanish conquerors of the NEW WORLD, especially in Mexico and Peru.

Constitution of the United States The document embodying the fundamental principles upon which the law and federal system of government of the United States are based. It was drawn up at a convention of 55 delegates (the Constitutional Convention) who met at Philadelphia in 1787, and was ratified by the required number of states (nine) on June 21, 1788.

Consul A title (originally used in ancient Rome) adopted by Napoleon from 1799, when he became head of the French government, until 1804 when he made himself emperor.

containment The policy of the United States during the COLD WAR, aimed at preventing the spread of COMMUNISM around the world.

Cossacks From the Turkic word *kazak*, meaning "adventurer" or "free man," peasants who fled from serfdom in Poland, Lithuania, and Russia to settle north of the Black Sea, where they enjoyed semi-independence. In the 17th and 18th centuries they came increasingly under Russian rule and revolted several times. They provided the elite cavalry regiments of the Russian army from the 18th to early 20th centuries.

Counter Reformation A movement of the ROMAN CATHOLIC church to halt the spread of the REFORMATION among PROTESTANTS in Europe and redefine the teachings of the church. To foster a new spirit of religious revival, orders such as the JESUITS were founded and new churches built in ornate BAROQUE STYLE. Missionaries were sent to win converts in Asia and the NEW WORLD.

coup d'etat "Seizure of the state": a military takeover or other rebellion that overthrows a government.

crime against humanity A type of WAR CRIME in which a civilian population is subjected to extreme political, racial, or religious persecution. An example is GENOCIDE.

Crusades A series of military expeditions (usually counted as eight) made by CHRISTIAN armies from Europe against the MUSLIMS of Palestine and Egypt from the 11th to 13th centuries. Crusades also took place against the Muslims in Spain.

Cultural Revolution A period of chaos (1966–76) in China when Mao Zedong authorized the persecution of moderates in the Communist Party and all Chinese society in order to consolidate his power.

culture The shared ideas, beliefs, values, and knowledge of a particular society; the material goods (ARTIFACTS) that are produced by that society.

cuneiform The "wedge-shaped" writing used in MESOPOTAMIA from the 3rd to the late 1st millennium BC.

czar The title of the ruler of Russia, derived from the ancient Roman imperial title of *caesar*. It was adopted by Ivan IV, grand prince of Moscow, in 1547 and used by his successors until the monarchy was abolished in 1917.

Dark Ages The name commonly given to the period of European history that followed the ending of the Roman empire (476), when there was a decline in all forms of culture. It lasted until about 1000.

democracy In ancient Greece, the direct government of a CITY-STATE by the CITIZEN body.

depression A severe or prolonged decline in economic activity that brings high unemployment.

détente The relaxing of tension between states, used in a phase of the COLD WAR (1969–79) when the SUPERPOWERS sought ways to avoid escalating conflict.

divine right The idea that monarchs are granted their power by God, so that disobedience to the king may be regarded as disobedience to the will of God. It was central to ABSOLUTISM.

domestication The adaptation of wild plants or animals through selective breeding to make them useful for humans.

duchy Part of a kingdom that was entrusted to a duke by a king to be ruled on his behalf. In MEDIEVAL Europe, many dukes ruled their duchies as independent states.

Dutch Republic Known also as the United Provinces of the Netherlands, it consisted of the seven northern PROTESTANT provinces of the Netherlands that became independent of Spain (1558–1609). It became a major trading empire in the 17th century.

dynasty A ruling family or other group that holds power for several generations.

East India Company A company set up for the purpose of trading with east Asia. The Netherlands, England, and France all had national East India companies in the 16th and 17th centuries. They had their own armies for protection against European rivals and local resistance.

Edict of Nantes A proclamation of tolerance issued to French HUGUENOTS by Henry IV in 1598, ending the religious wars in France. It was revoked by Louis XIV in 1685, after which most Huguenots fled abroad.

Enlightenment An intellectual movement of 18th-century Europe that emphasized science and reason over religion and superstition.

Estates-General The French national assembly from the 14th to the late 18th centuries. It was organized on class lines: clergy (First Estate), nobility (Second Estate), and property-owning commoners (Third Estate). No assemblies were summoned between 1614 and 1789.

ethnic cleansing A political euphemism for GENOCIDE, practiced by the Serbian government against non-Serbian minorities in the 1990s.

Etruscans A people of north-central Italy, of unknown origin, who developed a distinctive culture in the 8th century BC. They were conquered by the Romans in the 4th century BC.

excommunication Exclusion from membership of the church, and especially from receiving the sacraments. The POPES used it as a way of bringing uncooperative monarchs into line.

fascism A political system that glorifies the state and its leader, seeks military expansion, and is fiercely anti-Communist. The ideology was first developed by the Italian prewar dictator Benito Mussolini.

Fertile Crescent A region of good soil stretching in an arc from modern Israel through Lebanon, Syria, southern ANATOLIA, and Iraq to the Persian Gulf. It was here that settled farming began 10,000 years ago.

feudalism The system of social and political organization that pertained in most of MEDIEVAL Europe, based on the relationship between a lord (emperor, king, or nobleman) and his VASSALS. Land and offices were given to vassals in return for an oath of loyalty and promise to fight for him at any time.

fief The estate or office granted by a lord to a VASSAL.

"Final Solution" Hitler's plan to eliminate by GENOCIDE the entire Jewish population of Europe during World War II.

Five-Year Plan A list of goals for agricultural and industrial production in a Communist state-run economy.

Forbidden City The residence of the Chinese emperor in Beijing.

fossil The remains of any animal or plant that have been preserved in sedimentary mud or rock.

fossil fuels Fuels such as coal, oil, peat, and natural gas, which are formed in the Earth from animal or plant remains. They give off carbon gases when burned.

Fourteen Points The peace plan proposed after World War I by President Woodrow Wilson.

Franks A Germanic people who settled in the Low Countries east of the Rhine. From the 6th to the 9th century their empire was the greatest power in western Europe.

free-market economy An economy in which private individuals and companies enter into transactions with very little interference or supervision by the government. *See also* CAPITALISM.

French and Indian War A war fought in North America between France and Britain (1754–63), which resulted in France conceding all its territories in North America to Britain.

French Revolution The movement that saw the end of the ANCIEN RÉGIME in 1789 and convulsed France until 1799, when Napoleon overthrew the Revolutionary government.

Gaza Strip A small area on the Mediterranean coast between Israel and Egypt, occupied by Israel in the Six-Day War of 1967. It became one of the first self-governing Palestinian territories in 1994.

genocide The deliberate mass killing of an entire racial or cultural group.

global warming The increase in the average temperature of the Earth, which is widely believed to be caused by the GREENHOUSE EFFECT.

glyphs Picture symbols used by the Maya, Aztecs, and other peoples of MESOAMERICA as a form of writing.

gold standard A system for keeping national currencies and international exchange rates stable by basing the value of currency on the price of gold.

Gothic A style of architecture that was widely used in western European churches, cathedrals, and palaces from about 1150 to 1500. Its chief feature was the use of tall, narrow columns and pointed arches to support high, vaulted ceilings.

greenhouse effect Gases such as carbon dioxide and methane in the atmosphere absorb solar heat thrown back from the Earth and prevent it from escaping into space. This keeps the Earth warm enough to support living things, but it is believed that the levels of these gases are rising as a result of the excess burning of FOSSIL FUELS, causing GLOBAL WARMING.

guerrilla warfare "Little war": a strategy of limited fast attacks rather than pitched battles, which allows a small, irregular force to fight a much bigger or better-equipped enemy.

guillotine A device for beheading people that became notorious in the FRENCH REVOLUTION, consisting of a weighted blade set between two upright posts.

gulag The former Soviet penal system of labor camps for political dissidents.

Habsburgs A German dynasty who became counts of Austria in 1273, which they ruled without interruption, as archdukes and emperors, until 1918. In 1452 they acquired the title of Holy Roman emperor and retained it until the empire's dissolution in 1806. At the peak of Habsburg power in the 16th century, Charles V ruled the HOLY ROMAN EMPIRE, Spain, southern Italy, Burgundy, the Netherlands, Mexico, and Peru.

hacienda A large estate in the Spanish empire.

Han The ruling dynasty of China from 206 BC–AD 220. It is also the name of the ethnic majority of Chinese people.

Hellenistic period The period of Greek and Middle Eastern history from the death of Alexander the Great in 323 BC to the Roman conquest of Egypt in 30 BC, marked by an increase in Greek cultural influence abroad.

heresy Any religious belief that did not conform to the teachings of the church.

hierarchical society A society in which some people enjoy higher rank and therefore more privileges than others.

hieroglyphic A system of writing that uses pictures to symbolize words. Hieroglyphics were used in ancient Egypt, Mexico, and other places.

Hinduism The dominant religion and CULTURE of India since ancient times. A complex system of beliefs and customs, it includes the worship of many gods (POLYTHEISM) and a belief in reincarnation (rebirth).

Hittites A people, probably from southeast Europe, who migrated into ANATOLIA about 2000 BC. They established an empire that extended into Syria and lasted until c.1200 BC.

Holocaust The systematic GENOCIDE of European Jews by the NAZIS during World War II.

Holy Roman empire The empire founded by the German king Otto I in 962, based on his claim to be the legitimate successor of the western Roman emperors and the guardian of western CHRISTIANITY. It controlled most of central Europe and northern Italy in the Middle Ages but slowly declined to become a loose confederation of semi-independent states. It was finally abolished by Napoleon in 1806.

hominid Any of the Hominidae family of primates (apes) to which modern humans and their immediate ancestors and related forms belong. They are distinguished by their ability to walk upright on two feet.

Homo erectus Meaning "upright man," the species name for a human ancestor that lived from 1.9 million years ago to 400,000 years ago.

Homo habilis "Handy man," the scientific name for a species of human ancestor that lived 2.4–1.9 million years ago. It was the first hominid that could make tools.

Homo sapiens Meaning "wise man," the species name for modern humans, who came into existence 400,000 years ago.

Huguenot A French PROTESTANT of the 16th and 17th centuries.

humanism An intellectual movement of the RENAISSANCE that emphasized humanity's free will, superiority to nature, and relationship to God. It is summed up in the saying "Man (humanity) is the measure of all things." The leading proponent of humanism was the Dutch scholar Erasmus.

human rights The most fundamental rights, to which every person is entitled. They include the right to be free from execution, torture, and unfair imprisonment.

Huns A group of nomadic TURKIC peoples who migrated from Central Asia to eastern Europe around 370. Legendary for their violence, they disappeared from history after the death of their leader, Attila, in 453.

hunter–gatherers People who follow a way of life based on hunting wild animals, fishing, and gathering wild food plants.

Hyksos A people from the Middle East who invaded northern Egypt from 1640–1532 BC and established a capital at Avaris in the Delta.

Ice Age A period of global cooling that lasted from one million years ago to 10,000 years ago. Ice covered large areas of land and sea levels were considerably lower.

icon A holy picture that is used as a focus for prayer and devotion, especially in the ORTHODOX church.

imperialism The process by which one country forces its rule on another.

Inca An AMERINDIAN group that controlled an empire in the Andes and on the west coast of South America in the 15th century. It was conquered by Spain in 1535.

indulgence In ROMAN CATHOLICISM, the remission, or cancellation, of part or all of the eternal punishment due for sins that have been pardoned by an act of penance. The practice of selling indulgences without exacting penance was one of the church abuses that led to the REFORMATION.

Industrial Revolution The development of modern industry and factory production, with accompanying economic and social changes, that began in Britain in the 18th century and spread to the rest of Europe and North America.

inflation A sustained rise in prices that results from an increase in the volume of money and credit relative to the availability of goods.

Inquisition An organization of the ROMAN CATHOLIC church charged with identifying and punishing HERESY. It was most active in Spain.

intifada "Uprising": The Palestinian protest against Israeli occupation and the long delay in implementing the 1979 peace agreement.

Iron Age The period of prehistory following the BRONZE AGE when iron became widely used for making weapons and tools. Iron SMELTING began between 1400 and 1200 BC in ANATOLIA and spread from there into the Middle East, Europe, Asia, and Africa. Iron was not introduced into the Americas until the arrival of Europeans.

Iron Curtain A term describing the ideological division between Communist eastern Europe and democratic western Europe, first used by British politician Winston Churchill in 1947.

irrigation The watering of crops by artificial means. In the ancient world, canals were built to carry water from rivers or wells to the fields.

Islam The religion founded by the Prophet Muhammad in Arabia around AD 610. The ARAB conquests helped to spread it rapidly through the Middle East and North Africa. Islam means "submission to God's will."

Jacobins A radical political group that engaged in terrorist activities during the FRENCH REVOLUTION.

Janissary A member of a corps of slave-soldiers in the OTTOMAN empire, made up of Christian youths from the Balkan provinces. They converted to Islam on being drafted into the Ottoman service. The Janissaries gradually became an elite hereditary class with great political influence.

Jesuit A member of the Society of Jesus, a ROMAN CATHOLIC order founded by Ignatius Loyola in 1534. It was principally involved in missionary and education work.

Jin A dynasty founded by the Jürchen, invaders who conquered the northern half of the SUNG empire in China. They ruled from 1127– 1234 until conquered by the MONGOLS.

Judaism The religion and cultural practices of the Jews, which center on the belief in one god (MONOTHEISM).

khanate In Central Asia, the area under the authority of a khan, a local chieftain or leader.

knight A mounted soldier in the service of a lord. According to the code of CHIVALRY, knights were inducted into their rank after service as a page and squire.

Koran The holy book of ISLAM, which records the teachings of Muhammad.

Kuomintang The Chinese Nationalist Party. After losing the civil war to the Communists, it set up a government on Taiwan in 1949.

Kushans Nomads from Central Asia who invaded Afghanistan and India in the 1st century AD. They founded a large empire that fell around 380.

Latin The language spoken by the Romans. Modern Italian, French, Spanish, Portuguese, and Romanian are descended from it.

libertarian A believer in freedom of expression and thought.

Louisiana Purchase An area of 828,000 square miles (2,144,520 sq km) lying between the Mississippi river and the Rocky Mountains, which was purchased for less than 3 cents an acre from France in 1803, doubling the size of the United States.

Lutheranism The branch of PROTESTANTISM that follows the principles of the German theologian Martin Luther (1483–1546).

Macedon A powerful kingdom of northern Greece. Its king Alexander the Great conquered the PERSIAN empire from 334–326 BC.

Mamluke A dynasty of slave-soldiers, similar to the JANISSARIES, that ruled Egypt from 1250 to 1811.

Manchu A people from Manchuria in northeast Asia who invaded and conquered China in 1644, founding the QING dynasty, which ruled until 1911.

Mandate of Heaven A doctrine used by all Chinese rulers until 1911 to justify their power. It stated that rulers were appointed by the gods.

Marathas A Hindu people of west central India (the present state of Maharashtra) who created a warrior state in the 17th and 18th centuries.

Marshall Plan A massive five-year aid package provided by the United States to help the war-damaged countries of western Europe rebuild their economies after World War II.

Marxism The political system derived from the writings of Karl Marx, who interpreted politics as a struggle between economic classes (see also COMMUNISM).

Mauryan A powerful dynasty that ruled most of India from 381-185 BC.

Medes A NOMADIC people from Central

Asia who settled in northern Iran during the 9th century BC. Their kingdom of Media was conquered by the PERSIANS in 550 BC.

medieval From the Latin for "middle age," the term used for the period of European history between the collapse of Rome (AD 476) and the discovery of the New World (1492), lying between the ancient and modern ages.

megalithic Describes any structure built of large stones. The term is used particularly of the NEOLITHIC tombs and stone circles of western Europe such as Stonehenge in England. Many pre-Columbian structures in America are megalithic.

Meiji Restoration The ending of rule by the SHOGUNS and the return of the Japanese emperor in 1868, which marks the beginning of modern Japan.

Mesoamerica The area of Mexico, Guatemala, Honduras, Belize, and El Salvador that was occupied by the Olmec, Maya, and Aztec civilizations in pre-Columbian times.

Mesopotamia Meaning in Greek "the land between the rivers," it is the name given by historians to the dry but fertile region between the Tigris and Euphrates rivers in modern Iraq where the world's first cities developed about 4000 BC.

Ming The ruling dynasty of China from 1368 to 1644. It was overthrown by the MANCHUS.

minority A group within a larger society that is seen as separate from the rest of that society on grounds of ethnicity, language, or religion.

monarchy A form of government in which power is held by one hereditary ruler such as a king or emperor.

monastery The residence of a religious community, especially of monks.

Mongols Nomad peoples of Central Asia who established one of the world's largest territorial empires in the 13th century.

monotheism Belief in only one god.

mosque A place of worship in ISLAM. It usually has one or more towers (minarets) and may be decorated with patterns and texts from the KORAN.

Mughals (also spelled Moguls) A Muslim dynasty that ruled a large part of India from the 16th to the 18th centuries. They were noted for their administrative efficiency and for their high level of cultural activity, especially in painting, textiles, and architecture.

Muslim A believer in ISLAM.

Mutual Assured Destruction (MAD) The argument in favor of stockpiling nuclear weapons in the COLD WAR, on grounds that neither side would be willing to start a war that could only end in their mutual destruction.

mythology A collection of ancient stories about gods and superhuman heroes that were made up to explain the origins

of the world, its natural phenomena, and the social customs of a particular CULTURE.

nationalism The idea that a group linked by territory, ethnicity, culture, or language should have its own state.

nation-state A state in which the inhabitants all belong to one nation or ethnic/linguistic group. In fact, though many states claim to be nation-states, almost all include MINORITIES.

Nazi A member of the National Socialist Workers Party, which seized power in Germany in the 1930s.

Neanderthals An extinct form of early humans who lived in Europe during the ICE AGE. They made flint tools and buried their dead.

Neolithic Meaning "new stone age," it describes the period of Asian and European prehistory between c.9000 and 2000 BC when crops and animals were domesticated and early farming societies developed.

neutral state One that pursues a policy of not joining military alliances.

New World The name given to the Americas by European explorers in the 16th century to distinguish them from the Old World of Europe, Asia, and Africa.

Ninety-five Theses An account of the failings of the ROMAN CATHOLIC church drawn up by Martin Luther in 1517. He nailed them to the door of the church in Wittenberg, an event that is held to mark the beginning of the REFORMATION.

nirvana In HINDUISM and BUDDHISM, the highest state that a soul can achieve, free of suffering and desire.

nomads People who move from one place to another in search of food or water as the seasons change.

Non-Aligned Movement A group of nations (mostly from the THIRD WORLD) that formed an association to avoid taking sides in the COLD WAR.

Normans People from Normandy in France, which is named for the Norsemen ("Northmen," or VIKINGS) who settled there in the 10th century.

North Atlantic Treaty Organization (NATO) A mutual defense association formed after World War II by the United States, Canada, and most of non-Communist Europe to protect one another from attack by a hostile Soviet Union. *See also* WARSAW PACT.

Nubia A region on the river Nile in Africa, roughly equivalent to modern Sudan, which was the site of an early CIVILIZATION that had close links to ancient Egypt.

Olmecs Corn farmers living on the Gulf coast of southeast Mexico who developed the first CIVILIZATION of the Americas (1200–400 BC).

Organization of Petroleum Exporting Countries (OPEC) A group founded in 1960 to give oil exporters more control

of the oil market. The members include all of the Middle East oil exporters plus Indonesia, Nigeria, and Venezuela.

Orthodox The form of CHRISTIANITY practiced in the eastern Roman empire. Its forms of worship and belief were later adopted by the SLAVS and Russians. It was (and still is) led by the PATRIARCH of Constantinople.

Ostrogoths "Eastern Goths," a Germanic people who conquered Italy in 489–93.

Ottoman A TURKIC dynasty, originating in Anatolia around 1280, that conquered the BYZANTINE empire in 1453. At its height the Ottoman empire covered parts of North Africa, the Middle East and southeastern Europe. It survived until 1923.

pagan In MEDIEVAL Europe, anyone who was not a believing Christian.

Paleoindian A name used by archeologists to describe the first humans to settle in the Americas, the ancestors of the Native Americans.

papacy The office of POPE.

papyrus A species of reed that was used in ancient Egypt to make paper.

Parliament The legislative assembly of Great Britain, consisting of the sovereign, the House of Lords, and the House of Commons. The English parliament formed the center of opposition to the king in the English Civil War (1642–51).

Parthians A nomadic people from Central Asia who ruled Iran and Iraq from about 238 BC to AD 226.

pastoralism Farming based on grazing domestic animals rather than growing crops. Because grazing animals need to be moved to fresh pastures, pastoral people are NOMADS or seminomads.

patriarch In the ORTHODOX church, a BISHOP who has authority over other bishops. There were five senior patriarchs in the early church: in Jerusalem, Antioch, Alexandria, Constantinople, and Rome.

patricians Members of the ARISTOCRACY of Roman society, descended from the original SENATE.

peon A peasant laborer in Spain's American colonies.

Persians The ancient Iranians, an Indo-European people related to the MEDES. The empire created by the Persian king Cyrus II (c.559–53 BC) dominated the Middle East until it fell to Alexander the Great in 330 BC.

pharaoh The title given to the kings of Egypt. It comes from an Egyptian word meaning "great palace."

Phoenicians The people of the narrow coastal plain of Lebanon and Syria, who established a trading empire in the Mediterranean from about 1000–500 BC. They were important in developing the alphabet from which later Middle Eastern and European alphabets are descended.

pictograph A symbol or picture that stands for a word or group of words. HIEROGLYPHIC writing used a form of pictograph. Chinese writing is based entirely on pictographs.

plantation farming A method of farming in which an entire large estate is devoted to farming one profitable crop, such as cotton, tea, or tobacco.

plebeians The name given to the ordinary working people of Roman society, who were not slaves.

PLO (Palestine Liberation Organization) Founded in 1964 as a terrorist organization, now the majority party of the Palestinian people and the elected ruling party in Palestinian-controlled territory (GAZA and the West Bank except Jerusalem).

polytheism Belief in several gods.

pope The title of the BISHOP of Rome, head of the ROMAN CATHOLIC church.

prime minister From the 18th century, the senior minister of the British government.

privateer A pirate licensed by the government of one state to attack the ships of rival states.

Protestantism A religious movement that broke away from the the ROMAN CATHOLIC church in the 16th century REFORMATION. Its name is derived from the "Protestation" issued by a number of German princes in1529 against Charles V's refusal to allow the princes of the HOLY ROMAN EMPIRE to decide the religion of their own states. *See also* CALVINISM, LUTHERANISM.

province A subdivision of an empire, from the Latin word *provincia*. Any area conquered by the Romans was ruled as a province under a Roman governor. In the PERSIAN empire, provinces were known as satrapies and their governors as satraps.

Ptolemaic The dynasty founded by the Greek general Ptolemy that ruled Egypt from 305 BC–30 BC. Its last ruler was the famous Cleopatra VII.

puppet state A state that retains its own identity but is under the political control of another.

Puritans English PROTESTANTS of the 16th and 17th century who were followers of CALVINISM.

pyramid A building with a square base and four sloping triangular sides. Enormous stone pyramids were used as royal tombs in ancient Egypt.

Qing The official name of the MANCHU dynasty that ruled China from 1644 to 1911.

quipu A device, made of knots of colored strings, used by the Incas for keeping records of supplies and taxes.

Raj The British empire in India, 1858–1947.

recession A period of reduced economic activity, usually lasting less than a year.

Reformation The demand for reform of perceived abuses within the ROMAN CATHOLIC church that created a religious and political divide in western Europe during the 16th century, resulting in PROTESTANTISM.

refugee A person who is forced to leave his or her country by war, or for political or economic reasons.

Renaissance A cultural movement (literally meaning "rebirth") that began in Italy in the 14th century and had spread throughout Europe by the 16th century. A revival of interest in classical learning gave rise to a flowering in art, architecture, literature, philosophy, and science. *See also* HUMANISM.

reparations Payments made by the loser of a war to the winner to compensate for the costs of that war. Damaging reparations were imposed on Germany after World War I.

republic A form of government in which elected representatives of the people have supreme power. The chief of state is not a hereditary monarch but an elected officer, usually a president (as in the United States). The Republic was the name the Romans referred to their state as.

revolution A sudden and usually violent change of regime.

Roman Catholicism The branch of Christianity that recognizes the supreme authority of the pope. It was the only church in western Europe until the REFORMATION.

Romanov The ruling dynasty of the Russian empire from 1613 to 1917.

Romanticism An artistic and intellectual movement of the late 18th to mid 19th centuries in Europe. It emphasized the beauty of nature and the value of emotion over reason.

Rus VIKINGS who settled in eastern Europe (Russia) in the 9th century.

Safavid The ruling dynasty of Persia (Iran) from 1502 to 1736.

samurai The hereditary warrior class of medieval Japan.

Scythians A fierce NOMAD people who dominated the plains of Central Asia from about 700–300 BC. The western Scythians, living north of the Black Sea, traded with the Greeks.

Sea Peoples Invaders of Egypt in the 13th and 12th centuries BC, probably from the northern Aegean.

Seleucid The dynasty founded by the Greek general Seleucos that ruled the Middle East from 312 BC–64 BC.

Seljuk A TURKIC dynasty from Central Asia that conquered most of the Middle East between 1037 and 1080.

Senate The ruling assembly of ancient Rome; originally the king's council. Under the REPUBLIC its members were appointed for life and advised officials such as the consuls.

serf A hereditary class of peasant farmer.

serfdom A medieval institution in which peasant farmers were owned by their landlords and bound for life to the soil. It survived in parts of Europe until the 19th century.

Seven Years War A major European conflict (1756–63) in which France, Austria, Sweden, and Russia were aligned against Britain, Prussia, and Hanover. Much of the fighting took place in Europe's colonial empires: the North American phase of the war is known as the FRENCH AND INDIAN WAR. France lost most of its overseas empire to Britain. Prussia emerged with the major gains in Europe.

Shang The first historical dynasty of ancient China. It ruled from about 1766–1122 BC.

Shia A Muslim minority, "the party of Ali," which broke with SUNNI Islam after a civil war in the 7th century. It is the form of Islam followed in Iran.

Shinto The POLYTHEISTIC ancient religion of Japan, still practiced today.

shogun The title of "commander in chief" held by the hereditary military dictators who ruled Japan from 1192 until the MEIJI RESTORATION of 1868. The emperor was relegated to a position of purely theoretical supremacy.

Silk Route An overland trade route across Asia linking China to Europe.

Slavs The largest ethnic and linguistic group of eastern Europe, including Poles, Russians, Belorussians, Ukrainians, Czechs, Slovaks, Slovenians, Croats, and Serbs.

smelting Extracting metal from mineral ores by heating them to very high temperatures.

soviet The Russian word for council. Under the Communist system, soviets were elected at all levels of government in the Soviet Union.

space race Competition between the United States and Soviet Union to be the first to develop a program for exploring space.

Sputnik The world's first space satellite, launched by the Soviet Union in 1957, beginning the SPACE RACE.

stela A large stone slab decorated with symbols or inscriptions.

Strategic Arms Limitation Talks (SALT) Negotiations to limit nuclear arms, held between the United States and Soviet Union from 1969–79, as part of DÉTENTE.

sub-Saharan Africa The part of Africa south of the Sahara desert, which acts as a barrier dividing it from the coastal regions of North Africa.

sultan The ruler of a Muslim country, from the Arabic word meaning "rule."

Sumerians The people of Sumer, southern MESOPOTAMIA, who developed the world's first civilization from c.3400–2000 BC.

Sung The dynasty that ruled China from 960 to 1279. It was overthrown by the MONGOLS.

Sunni The larger, orthodox branch of ISLAM that acknowledges the first four CALIPHS as Muhammad's successors. *See also* SHIA.

superpower The United States or Soviet Union, the world's two largest countries during the COLD WAR era and the first to have nuclear weapons.

Tang The ruling dynasty of China from 618 to 907.

Taoism (also called Daoism) A Chinese religious and philosophical system that, along with CONFUCIANISM, has shaped Chinese thought for 2,000 years, though many of the truths it stresses, such as individual freedom and spontaneity, are at variance with Confucianism.

Tatars (also spelled Tartars) A nomadic Turkic people of the south Russian steppes who were conquered by the Mongols in the 13th century and absorbed into the khanate of the Golden Horde, which dominated Russia until the late 15th century. As a result, the Mongols were frequently known as Tatars or Tartars.

terrorism The use of indiscriminate violence to achieve a political goal.

Teutonic Knights A German CRUSADING order founded in 1190 to convert the PAGAN peoples around the Baltic Sea.

Third World The poorer countries of the world in relation to the first (western) and second (COMMUNIST) worlds.

tiger economy One of the fast-growing economies of Asia that developed in the 1970s and 1980s, but were in DEPRESSION at the end of the 1990s.

Treaty of Tordesillas The agreement between Spain and Portugal in 1494 to divide the NEW WORLD.

Treaty of Versailles The treaty that ended World War I. The terms it imposed on Germany helped bring about the rise of the NAZIS, leading to World War II.

treaty port In 19th-century Asia, a port forced to open to western imperial powers who wanted to trade with the host country.

tribe A large social group comprising numerous families or CLANS united by ancestry, CULTURE, and territory.

tribune One of 10 representatives elected by the PLEBEIANS of ancient Rome to serve their interests.

tribute A payment, usually made in gold and silver but sometimes in people, by a conquered kingdom to the victor.

Trojan War A legendary war fought between the Greeks and the Trojans (the people of the city of Troy, on the coast of ANATOLIA).

Turkic Peoples belonging to a major linguistic group of Central Asia.

tyrant In ancient Greece, a ruler who seized power unlawfully. Tyrants were not necessarily oppressive rulers—this association came later.

Umayyad An ARAB dynasty that ruled the ISLAMIC world from 661 to 750. It was overthrown by the ABBASIDS.

United Nations An international organization, founded in 1945 to promote cooperation and peace.

universal suffrage The right of every citizen to vote in political elections.

vassal A person under the protection of a FEUDAL lord; a state that is subordinate or dependent to another.

Vietcong South Vietnamese GUERRILLA forces who fought the U.S.-backed South Vietnamese Army.

Vikings Scandinavian pirates who raided western Europe and Russia between the 9th and 11th centuries.

Visigoth "Western Goths," a Germanic people, related to the OSTROGOTHS, who invaded the Roman empire in 376. They founded a kingdom in southwest France and Spain (418–62), which was destroyed in the ARAB conquest of 711.

war crimes Acts that violate the accepted international rules of war. They include starting a war of aggression, mistreating civilians, and CRIMES AGAINST HUMANITY.

warlord An independent military leader who controls limited territory.

Warsaw Pact A Soviet-led military alliance of Eastern Europe, formed in 1955 to counter NATO.

yurt A large circular tent, made of skins, used by the MONGOL nomads of Central Asia.

Zealots Members of a Jewish sect who fought against Roman rule in Palestine around the time of Christ and were defeated at Masada.

Zhou The second and longest-ruling dynasty of China, which held power from 1122 BC–256 BC.

ziggurat In MESOPOTAMIA, a temple of rectangular tiers (large at the base, small at the top), linked by outside staircases and topped by a shrine.

Zionism Jewish nationalism, which sought to reclaim the Holy Land of the Jewish Bible. It began in late-19th-century Europe and caused a wave of immigration to Palestine.

Zoroastrianism A religion founded by Zoroaster (also known as Zarathustra), a Persian prophet of the 6th century BC, involving belief in a universal conflict between good and evil. It is still practiced by a few isolated communities in Iran, and also by the Parsis of western India, especially around Mumbai (Bombay).

FURTHER READING

Bahn, Paul G. (ed). *The Story of Archaeology*. New York: Weidenfeld and Nicolson, 1996.

Barber, Malcom C. *The Two Cities: Medieval Europe 1050–1320*. New York: Routledge, 1993.

Barraclough, Geoffrey (ed.) *The Times Atlas of World History*. 4th edition, New York: Hammond, 1993.

Blanning, T.C.W. *The Oxford Illustrated History of Modern Europe*. New York: Oxford University Press, 1998.

Blunden, Caroline and Elvin, Mark. *Cultural Atlas of China*. New York: Facts on File, 1998.

Briggs, Asa, and Clavin, Patricia. *Modern Europe 1789–1989*. Reading, MA: Addison-Wesley, 1996.

Brown, Dee. *The American West*. New York: Scribner, 1994.

Buckley Ebrey, Patricia. *The Cambridge Illustrated History of China*. Cambridge, MA: Cambridge University Press, 1996.

Burell, Roy, and Connolly, Peter. *Oxford First Ancient History*. New York: Oxford University Press, 1997

de Blois, Lukas, and van der Spek, R. *An Introduction to the Ancient World*. New York: Routledge, 1997.

Coe, Michael. *The Maya*. 5th ed., New York: Thames and Hudson, 1993.

Collcutt, Martin, Jansen, Marieus and Kumakura, Isao. *Cultural Atlas of Japan*. New York: Facts on File, 1988.

Conolly, Peter. *The Ancient Greece of Odysseus*. New York: Oxford University Press, 1999.

Conolly, Peter. *The Holy Land*. New York: Oxford University Press, 1999.

Cunliffe, Barry (ed.) *Prehistoric Europe: An Illustrated History*. New York: Oxford University Press, 1997.

Daniel, C. (ed.). *Chronicle of America*. 2nd ed. New York: DK Publishing, 1995.

Drinkwater, J.F., Drummond, Andrew, Freeman, Charles. *World of the Romans*. New York: Oxford University Press, 1993.

Dukes, Paul. *A History of Russia c.882–1996*.

Durham, NC: Duke University Press, 1998.

Fagan, Brian M., and Scarre, Christopher. *Ancient Civilizations*. Reading, MA: Addison-Wesley, 1996.

Freeman, Charles. *The Legacy of Ancient Egypt*. New York: Facts on File, 1997.

Freeze, Gregory (ed). *Russia: A History*. New York: Oxford University Press, 1997.

Hanawalt, Barbara A. *The Middle Ages: An Illustrated History*. New York: Oxford University Press, 1998.

Harris, Roberta. *The World of the Bible*. New York: Thames and Hudson, 1995.

Haywood, John et al. *Atlas of World History*. New York: M.E. Sharpe, 1997.

Haywood, John. *Historical Atlas of the Vikings*. New York: Penguin, 1995.

Hearder, Harry. *Europe in the 19th Century*. Reading, MA: Addison-Wesley, 1988.

Homberger, E. *Historical Atlas of North America*. New York: Penguin, 1995.

Hornblower, Simon and Spawforth, Anthony. *The Oxford Companion to Classical Civilization*. New York: Oxford University Press, 1998.

Hosking, Geoffrey. *Russia: People and Empire 1552–1917*. New York: Fontana, 1998.

Howard, Michael E. and Louis, William R. *The Oxford History of the Twentieth Century*. New York: Oxford University Press, 1998.

Iriye, Akira. *Japan and the Wider World*. Reading, MA: Addison-Wesley, 1997.

Johnson, Gordon *Cultural Atlas of India*. New York: Facts on File, 1995.

Kulke, Hermann and Rothermund, Dietmar. *A History of India*. New York: Routledge, 1997.

Lewis, Bernard *The Middle East*. New York: Weidenfeld and Nicolson, 1995.

McCarthy, Justin. *The Ottoman Turks: An Introductory History to 1923*. New York, Longman, 1997.

Matthew, Donald. *Atlas of Medieval Europe*. New York: Facts on File, 1983.

Middleton, Richard. *Colonial America: A History 1585–1776*. Malden, MA: Blackwell Publishers, 1996.

Milner, O'Connor, and Sandweiss. *The Oxford History of the American West*. New York: Oxford University Press, 1995.

Moseley, Michael. *The Incas and their Ancestors*. New York: Thames and Hudson, 1993.

Murray, Jocelyn (ed.) *Cultural Atlas of Africa*. New York: Facts on File, 1998.

The Oxford Atlas of Exploration. New York: Oxford University Press, 1997.

Riasanovsky, Nicholas V. *A History of Russia*. 5th ed. New York: Oxford University Press, 1993.

Roaf, Michael. *Cultural Atlas of Mesopotamia and the Ancient Near East*. New York: Facts on File, 1990.

Roberts, J.M. *A Concise History of the World*. New York: Oxford University Press, 1976.

Roberts, John. *Penguin History of Europe*. New York: Penguin, 1996.

Robinson, Francis (ed). *The Cambridge Illustrated History of the Islamic World*. Cambridge, MA: Cambridge University Press, 1998.

Sawyer, Peter. *The Oxford Illustrated History of the Vikings*. New York: Oxford University Press, 1997.

Schoeter, Daniel J. *Israel: An Illustrated History*. New York: Oxford University Press, 1999.

Thomas, Hugh. *The Slave Trade: The Story of the African Slave Trade 1440–1870*. New York: Simon and Shuster, 1997.

Tindall, George B., and Shi, David E. *America: A Narrative History*. New York: W.W. Norton and Co., 1996.

Weinberg, G.L. *A World at Arms: A Global History of World War II*. Cambridge, MA: Cambridge University Press, 1994.

INDEX

ACKNOWLEDGMENTS

1 Erich Lessing/AKG; 2–3 Michael Holford; 8 Erich Lessing/AKG; 12 Natural History Museum, London; 14–15 Hutchison Library; 15 AKG; 16–17 & 17 Erich Lessing/AKG; 19 WFA/Anthropology Museum, Veracruz University, Jalapa; 20–21 Robert McLeod/RHPL; 21 RHPL; 22 Erich Lessing/AKG; 23 B. Norman/Ancient Art & Architecture Collection Ltd; 24 & 25 Erich Lessing/AKG; 26–27 WFA; 27 Copyright British Museum; 28 WFA; 29 Copyright British Museum; 30t & 30b Erich Lessing/AKG; 31 The Stock Market; 32 Erich Lessing/AKG; 33 The Stock Market; 35 Hanny Paul/Gamma/FSP; 36 John Haywood; 36–37, 37t, 37b, 38t & 38b Erich Lessing/AKG; 40 John Haywood; 40–41 Erich Lessing/AKG; 42 John Haywood; 44 & 47 Erich Lessing/AKG; 48–49 Powerstock/Zefa Photo Library; 49 WFA/Private Collection; 50 & 51 Erich Lessing/AKG; 53 RHPL; 54 P. Koch/RHPL; 56 Adam Woolfitt/RHPL; 57 Ashmolean Museum, Oxford; 60 Tiziana & Gianni Baldizzone/Corbis; 61 RHPL; 62 Sonia Halliday & Laura Lushingron; 65 Bodleian Library; 66–67 WFA; 67 & 68 Erich Lessing/AKG; 70t Mick Sharp Photography; 70b & 71 Erich Lessing/AKG; 72 Copyright British Museum; 74t Board of Trinity College, Dublin; 74b Erich Lessing/AKG; 75 Adam Woolfitt/RHPL; 76 British Library; 78t Erich Lessing/AKG; 78b British Library; 79 Erich Lessing/AKG; 80, 82 & 82–3 RHPL; 84t Erich Lessing/AKG; 84b John Haywood; 86 Giraudon; 87, 88 & 90t Erich Lessing/AKG; 90b WFA/National Palace Museum, Taipei; 92 Vanessa S. Boeye/Hutchison Library; 93 National Palace Museum, Taipei/RHPL; 94 WFA/Gulistan Imperial Library, Teheran; 94–95 Sonia Halliday; 96 Tokyo National Museum; 97 WFA; 98t WFA/Boston Museum of Fine Arts; 98b WFA/L.J. Anderson Collection; 100 RHPL; 102 Robert Aberman; 103 WFA/Victoria & Albert Museum; 104–105 Robert Frerck/Odyssey/Chicago/RHPL; 106 Erich Lessing/AKG; 106–107 WFA/British Museum, London; 107 WFA/Museum fur Volkerkunde, Basel; 108 N.J. Saunders/Barbara Heller; 110–111 N.J. Saunders; 110 WFA/Dallas Museum of Art, U.S.A.; 111 Loren McIntyre; 113 Bodleian Library; 114–115 Gavin Hellier/RHPL; 116 ETA/Prado Madrid; 119 Bibliothèque Nationale; 120–121 Erich Lessing/AKG; 122 N.J. Saunders/Barbara Heller; 123 & 124 AKG; 125 Thomas Hoepker/MP; 126 ETA/British Museum; 128–129 Dennis Stock/MP; 129 HG; 130 & 132 AKG; 132–133 HG; 134 MEPL; 136t & 136b AKG; 138 Erich Lessing/AKG; 140t & 140b AKG; 142 ETA/Ironbridge Gorge Museum; 144–145 & 145 Erich Lessing/AKG; 146 ETA/Musée de Versailles; 148t AKG; 148b ETA/Decorative Arts Library, Paris; 148–149, 150 & 152 AKG; 152–153 Michael Holford; 153 ETA/Historical Museum, Moscow; 154 Michael Holford; 156 Davic Jacobs/RHPL; 157 Michael Holford; 159 Images Colour Library; 160t MEPL; 160b Jeremy Homer/Hutchison Library; 160–161 WFA/Courtesy Christie's; 161 MEPL; 162 Bruno Barbey/MP; 164–165 ETA/National Maritime Museum; 165 AKG; 167 ETA/Queen Victoria Museum; 168 & 168–169 AKG; 170 Gamma/FSP; 173 Thomann/Bildarchiv Preussischer Kulturbesitz; 174 HG; 174–175 ETA; 177 Culver Pictures; 178–179 Ullstein; 179 ETA/Decorative Arts Library, Paris; 180 Stan Osolinski/Oxford Scientific Films; 181 Archiv für Kunst und Geschichte; 183 inset Popperfoto; 183 From the Collections of the Henry Ford Museum & Greenfield Village; 184t HG; 184b ETA/Victoria & Albert Museum; 186t ETA/Cavalry Museum, Pinerolo; 186b ETA; 189t Harlingue-Violet; 189b ETA; 190t & 190b Imperial War Museum; 192 HG; 194 J.L. Charmer; 196 ETA/British Museum; 197 MEPL; 198–199 Popperfoto; 199 Associated Press/Topham Picturepoint; 200 HG; 202 Wiener Library; 202–203 Imperial War Museum; 203 John Erikson; 204 Arkady Shishkin; 205 Peter Marlow/MP; 206t Burt Glinn/MP; 206b Mikhail Nappelbaum; 208 ETA/William Sewell; 209 Fallander/Sipa Press/Rex Features; 210t Francolon/FSP; 210b & 212t HG; 212b Richard T. Nowitz/Corbis; 213 Topham Picturepoint; 214 HG; 214–215 Bruno Barbey/MP; 217 ETA/Library of Congress; 218–219 Gamma/FSP; 219 Danny Lyons/MP; 221 G. Mendel/MP; 222–223 Colin Monteath/Gamma/FSP; 223 Anderson/Gamma/Liaison/FSP

Timetable backgrounds (7) 25, 29, 33. 37, 41, 45, 49, 53, 57 & 61 Babylonian plan of the world (detail): Michael Holford; (6) 71, 75, 79, 83, 87, 91, 95, 99, 103, 107 & 111 The Peutinger Table, a medieval copy of a late Roman map (detail): Österreichische Nationalbibliothek; (6) 125, 129, 133, 137, 141, 145, 149, 153, 157, 161 & 165 A map of the world by Gerhard Mercator, 1587 (detail): MEPL; (6) 183, 187, 191, 195, 199, 203, 207, 211 & 215 Computer-generated map: Terra Forma™ Copyright © 1995–1997 Andromeda Interactive Ltd.

Abbreviations

AKG	Archiv für Kunst und Geschichte
ETA	E.T. Archive
FSP	Frank Spooner Pictures
HG	Hulton Getty
MP	Magnum Photos
MEPL	Mary Evans Picture Library
RHPL	Robert Harding Picture Library
WFA	Werner Forman Archive

Artists

John Fuller; Charles Raymond, Roger Stewart, Andrew Wheatcroft

Every effort has been made to trace copyright holders of the pictures used in this book.
Anyone having claims to ownership not identified above is invited to contact Andromeda Oxford Limited.